"There are tears in my eyes as I finish this book. It is wrong to say I enjoyed it. I loved it! John Gruberg has captured the very soul of a teaching pro. It is my story too. Gruberg's imagination and deep understanding of tennis makes for a true celebration of the game's inner workings, and of life. I just wish I could express the emotion I'm feeling right now. Wow, I am really stunned!"
                                        ... Roger Kahn, *USPTA*

* * *

"I really enjoyed this book. I can relate to it. Great tale!"
                    ... Peter Smith, *Men's Tennis Coach,* USC

"Fantastic ... this is a lot of what I experienced back in the day, and a lot of what I am experiencing right now!"   ... Chris Magyary
                    Teaching Professional and Former Touring Pro

* * *

"I've read lots of sports books, biographies, and novels ... but I have not found a great tennis novel. Until now!"   ... Gary Glassman
              Stony Brook University, *Women's & Men's Tennis Coach*

The Author

John Gruberg considers himself a small-time writer/inventor/tennis pro type of a guy. He has been mentioned on the *Tonight Show* and in *Playboy Magazine*, the *San Francisco Chronicle* and *Encyclopedia Brown's Book of Wacky Sports*. Gruberg is a former junior coach for Aruba in the Netherlands Antilles. Originally from Berkeley, he was a longtime teaching pro at Fresno's Roeding Park. He lives in Monterey and Fresno with his wife, Meijing and his dog, Ulysses.

John Gruberg's credits include:

Net Results
Inside Tennis
Valley Tennis
Florida Tennis
The Fresno Bee
Colorado Tennis
The Center Line
Crosscourt News
Addvantage Magazine
Monterey County Herald
San Mateo County Times
The Fresno Sporting News
KVPR Valley Public Radio
International Tennis Weekly

* * *

— for any kid who likes to hang out at the playground
or on a sports field or court of any kind
my heart goes out to each of you
and to any adult who in times past
was one of those kids
JG

Inventor Press

Is This A True Story?

Much of this book is autobiographical, and much of it is fictitious. Those who know the author personally will have an easier time noting these sometimes subtle differences. And so, this is a memoir that has been derailed; and not just by the facts, but by a sport that pulled the author off the tracks of his life when he was a teenager and never let him back on board.

Actual people and events match the historical record as closely as possible (although occasional liberties are taken with regard to precise dates.)

Cover Artwork by Brian Riedel

Published by Inventor Press
In Collaboration With
Tennis Brothers & Sisters
A USTA Service Organization

First Edition November 2016
LCCN 201-691-3738
ISBN 978-0-9976-5780-7

John Gruberg — Tennis Hobo

www.TennisHobo.com

Printed in the United States of America

Tennis Hobo

by John Gruberg

Inventor Press Monterey California

A Derailed Memoir

Contents

Contents

Times have changed —

"It's not enough to practice. These days you've got to practice faster than the next guy." ... Steve Docherty
Champion of the Pacific Northwest

Chapter Zero

Familiar Flatlands

Tennis, like the sun, leached into my restlessness, even on a rainy day. It came dressed in the perfect backhand of an old school chum. We talked about girls and played ping pong in his basement; then sometimes I'd get lucky and Spiegel would drag me off to a rundown court in Richmond or El Cerrito where he would beat the tennis pulp right out of me. If it was a weekend, we might take the long hike up to Tilden Regional Park to play there. At the time, Spiegel was taking lessons from Tom Stow, the guy who had coached world champion Don Budge, and occasionally I'd get to tag along as a punching bag. But for the most part, my tennis took place on the rear wall of my father's little office building on University Avenue. There, on the blacktop of the parking lot, I tried to emulate Spiegel's perfect backhand. Nothing else was back there but a warehouse with boarded-up windows, so the noise of the tennis ball didn't seem to bother anybody, except my dad, who dressed in his white smock, would stick his head out the back door now and then.

"So, your tennis shenanigans are more important than your schoolwork?" That's what he wanted to say, but he never said a word. He just stood there with various looks of puzzled exasperation.

My father was Theodore Dubitski, M.D., a bespectacled Berkeley doctor whose patients included the actor Robert Culp and Mario Savio, leader of the Free Speech movement. "He's just a regular family man," my dad would tell my mom at the dinner table every time Mario was in the news, or if my dad had dropped by on a house call. My father always wanted me to be a doctor, too, and if possible, a great Russian novelist on the side. He certainly expected me to become more than just a tennis gigolo, as he would come to call it (and there was always a nervous edge to his voice.)

Soon, the interplay of mind and medicine caught the interest of Dr. Theodore Dubitski, and he became a psychiatrist, partly in an attempt to figure out his three children, especially me. But he offered too long a leash, and I ended up with a headful of tennis balls and a pen at the end of an overdeveloped right arm.

Now I was practically middle-aged and still hanging around Berkeley. I had a little pad way down on 2nd Street next to a railroad crossing. I drove over those tracks every day. Or, I might be on foot in the neighborhood and negotiate the long thin rails with carefully placed steps.

The freighter came only occasionally during daylight, but in the middle of the night its far away horn moaned along the flats of the bay; then came the clanking crescendo of rolling metal and I knew it was three in the morning and I was being awakened so at least something could whisper a loving good night to me. Then that forlorn moan would sound again, this time faint, and I would go back to sleep satisfied.

Sometimes after the freighter woke me I would think about my old pal Spiegel; I hadn't seen him in years. I heard he became a successful corporate attorney in Southern California and that he played tennis with an occasional senator or congressman (no doubt displaying his perfect Tom Stow backhand.) Of course, I always knew Spiegel would be successful — he was so smart. He was the only guy I ever met who got psyched up for final exams the way a football player might get pumped up for a home coming game. He couldn't wait for the day of those damn tests! (And he did a great job of passing on his keen intelligence — for a couple of decades later, Spiegel's son would create Snapchat, a company Facebook would offer to buy for three billion dollars!)

Three billion dollars would have been a difficult figure for me to fathom back in those days, even though I was well into my thirties and supposedly an adult. Hell, the most I ever had in my bank account was about seven hundred dollars. Besides, the only time I ever heard a number in the billions was when Carl Sagan was on TV; and he was talking about stars, not dollars. Anyway, my TV wasn't working half the time, probably something to do with the antenna.

I was definitely in a rut, stuck in those all too familiar Berkeley flatlands. And my playing days were pretty much over; not that they ever amounted to anything. Come to think of it, I hadn't amounted to much of anything either. I was just a small time tennis teacher. And sometimes I did feel like a gigolo. I probably should have listened to my father. I should have become a doctor, or at least a lawyer or a dentist. I was thirty-seven years old and teaching tennis to housewives. It was at a little club in Lafayette, out near Walnut Creek. At least it was sunny there. Anyway, that's where I'd be headed in the morning after the freighter rocked me back to sleep.

Chapter One

The Feel Of An Overhead

It was a cloudless day with blue sky and a sun the color of a new tennis ball. The warm weather made me feel good all over, kind of tingly, as I strolled towards the pro shop. Of course, it was always nice out here in Lafayette where the tennis club was. In the flats of Berkeley where I had come in from, it was dismal before I left and the sun in the overcast sky looked like the most worn-out ball in my teaching basket.

But here in Lafayette all the neighborhoods were sunny! I entered the pro shop confidently and got my shopping cart from a storage area in the back. I liked the solid feel of the cart as I rolled it away from the shop; it was weighted down with a couple hundred tennis balls. At the bottom of the cart were pale old balls that had lost their bounce, but near the top the balls were alive and well; and some were brand new yellow, just like that feel-good sun above.

"Dubitski! Hey, Stefan, wait a minute," the girl at the front desk came running after me. "There's a message for you." She was slightly out of breath as she handed me the note.

Apparently, Evonne Lutzborg had called to confirm her ten o'clock lesson. (Hardly an emergency, but the greater message was that the girl was reliable.) Evonne was my newest tennis student. She was single, nice looking, intelligent. Also athletic, which was like icing on the cake; or maybe that was the cake and the other was the icing. The distinction could be difficult at times.

Evonne was a brunette, though all of her sisters and others she knew of Swedish descent were blond. "So I always felt a little odd," she confessed one day after her lesson. And yet, the fact is, Evonne was downright attractive. She wasn't what you would call a knockout, but she was cute in an outdoorsy sort of way, as are lots of women in Lafayette, Orinda, and Walnut Creek, a sunny triangle inland of the Berkeley hills on the east side of San Francisco Bay.

Evonne was originally from Kingsburg, a sleepy farm town south of Fresno in the San Joaquin Valley, but she went to school at San Francisco State and she stuck around. After battling what she said seemed like every guy in a suit for ten years, she emerged as a high-powered mover and shaker in the west coast financial sector. But all that was behind her now; she had achieved independence. It came time to relax and play a little. She would do some of the things she had never, even as a kid, had time for. And tennis was one of those things, even though Evonne knew absolutely nothing about it.

The bubbly Evonne decided to join a tennis club, our tennis club, after seeing a few minutes of the US Open on TV. And it was a real pleasure to see her at the club. Indeed, this happy lady had an air of innocence about her that was refreshing to see in an adult, and I wondered if this was a trait she always had, or if it was somewhat of a rebirth to youth upon having pulled out of the rat race.

From my perspective, Evonne's tennis naiveté made her perfectly coachable and easy to mold. Tuned up by aerobics, she had a streamlined body with a feminine edge that managed to stay soft in all the right places. She also had better than average hand-eye coordination. So, even though Evonne had only been taking lessons a few weeks, my assistant pro and I felt she was ready for the club championships. Besides, the tournament was going to start tomorrow and one of the 3.0 ladies needed a partner. Anyway, since that was a novice division, I figured she'd be alright.

"But I don't really know how to play." Evonne seemed amused but also a little concerned.

"There's nothing to it," I assured her. "Todd and I will show you everything. Besides, that's what a tournament is for, to learn how to play."

She looked a little unsure of herself. "Really?" she asked. "I mean, I thought you were supposed to already know how to play before you get in a tournament."

"Not always," Todd put in, "sometimes the fastest way to learn is to play a tournament."

A few years younger than I, Todd was a youthful thirty-three-year-old who was still playing small pro events with the hopes of breaking into the big time. Not only was he a great assistant pro, but he could hold up his side of a doubles court. He was also a good friend. Optimistic and generous, he was the kind of guy who always did more than was expected, one of those rare individuals who gave without asking for anything in return. Todd would lend a hand if he thought a hand was needed, even to a complete stranger. He was also capable of amusing philosophical comments that I often did not understand at first; but then later, I could be driving home from the club, waiting at a red light, for instance, when suddenly I might chuckle and cruise through the intersection with a smile on my face as if it were Todd himself who had turned the light green.

Although it wasn't part of his official duties, Todd was more than happy to help me on the teaching court with Evonne. Usually, he just walked right out there without my asking. And today he would really be an asset; we would team up on that cheerful beginner and give her a crash course in doubles. We would also teach her how to serve. After all, she was about to play in her first tournament.

I could see Evonne was concerned about playing with the other ladies, about not letting her partner down. Her head was cocked with curiosity as we discussed the matter. Then she offered an enthusiastic smile. "Well, OK, if you really think I should play," she told me, "you're the pro."

So I rolled my shopping cart of balls to a spot near the baseline and we began this now all-important lesson with the serve. It would not be a fancy serve, just a mechanical racket lift, followed by a stiff ball toss (kind of like John McEnroe's serve without the frills.)

In a few minutes, Evonne was getting the hang of a rudimentary service motion. It wasn't much, but it allowed her to tap a ball over the net and into the appropriate service box. And she seemed pleased with herself ... until she looked over to a nearby court where Gaylord Hitchcock, one of our better men, was practicing his serve.

"Is my serve going to look like that one day?" she asked with some doubt.

"Heck no," I said, "it's going to be a lot prettier than that, don't you worry. We'll take our time with it and make it perfect."

"That guy's serve looks fine to me. I'd be happy to settle for it."

I began to wonder if Evonne might be interested in more than just Mr. Hitchcock's serve; after all, he was a rather distinguished looking gentleman. Come to think of it, Hitchcock had been practicing his serve on the same court last week as I gave Evonne her tennis lesson. Maybe she had noticed him then, too. And then it struck me that Hitchcock usually practiced in more privacy, on one of the courts at the far end, and not on one so close to my teaching court. Ah yes, that was probably it, it was he who had noticed her.

"I would be happy to introduce you to Hitch after your lesson," I said, "maybe he'd like to hit some balls with you."

"Oh no, that's not what I meant ..... I just like his serve, that's all. Not that I'm much of a judge, by any means," she admitted almost shyly.

"Anyway, I'm not good enough to play with him."

"Well, maybe next time. Play with the ladies tomorrow, we'll see how you feel after that."

Hitchcock had gathered up his practice balls and was now leaving the court. As he went out the gate, his head turned for a quick look in our direction, and Evonne immediately shifted her gaze.

We got right to reviewing Evonne's groundstrokes, and soon most of the session was over. So I told her about the doubles alleys and not to aim for them, except occasionally. Then I put Todd on my side of the court and we showed her how to hit between us, at the "T" where the lines of the service boxes intersect. As a rule of thumb, this would be a safe place for her to hit the ball in doubles.

"OK, you're all set," I said. Todd winked at me.

"Hey, but what about when I'm near the net?" Evonne asked, "I don't know how to hit those."

"She means volleys," Todd said.

"Just stay away from the net." I was firm. "Those other ladies only think they know how to volley, believe me. Just stay back near the baseline, even when your partner is serving, you'll do fine. If the other guys come to the net, aim for the T like I showed you, or lob over them. You can do that, can't you?"

"I can try. But what about scoring? I don't even know how to keep score," Evonne complained good-naturedly.

"Just let the other ladies keep score."

"But I should know something about it, don't you think? I saw tennis on TV and it's a little confusing."

She had me there, besides, she seemed so cute and innocent, just like a little school kid. "OK, three more minutes, just on scoring," I told her.

So Todd and I played a mock game. After each point Todd called out the score and I had Evonne repeat it. "Don't try to make any sense of it, it's pretty weird," my assistant warned her, "just say what I say."

Todd's voice bellowed like an opera tenor in short pants as he called out the score and awaited the happy echo of Evonne's reply.

"Fifteen" … "Thirty" … "Forty-love." All was going smoothly. Deuce, Ad-in, Ad-out. Todd sang out and Evonne mimicked perfectly. I could tell she was slightly unsure at times, but at least she was getting familiar with the scoring, certainly familiar enough to tag along in the tournament tomorrow and let the other ladies lead the way.

Soon, our enthusiastic protégé was strolling between us as we escorted her to the lot out front where her BMW was parked in the warm sunshine. Her arms and legs were richly tanned and she looked like she had been a tennis player all her life. She looked good standing next to the car in her sporty Nike outfit. Todd opened the door for her and she slid down into the driver's seat.

"OK," I said, "see you tomorrow, nine o'clock sharp, for the tournament."

Todd and I watched as her handsome car swung out of the lot.

"Hey man," I said, as the car disappeared around the corner, "I think Hitchcock has his eye on Evonne."

"You think so?" Todd turned to me with a grin.

"Yeah man, he's been working his serve on court three last couple of weeks, and right about the time Evonne has her lesson."

"Now that you mention it, maybe so. Can't say that I blame the guy. He's probably over his wife by now. What's it been, about five years since she? … … Died." (I hated that word too, so I understood Todd's delay in using it.)

"Some people never get over something like that." I said. "But at least Hitch has his work."

"What's he do, anyway? I heard he's some sort of international consultant."

"Yeah, he's an engineer, specializes in uranium production. But he doesn't like to talk about it. He goes to a lot of really weird places, and then when he gets back home he seems kind of depressed. So he has a drink and comes to the club."

"Maybe we should put Evonne and Hitch in the mixed doubles tomorrow." Todd winked at me. "He could just play easy, teach her the ropes."

"They'd have to be in the novice group, and everybody would complain about Hitchcock being too good, especially old Schumley."

"Htich could play left-handed."

"Wouldn't work, you don't know Schumley, he'd still raise hell, probably go right to the club manager."

We both decided we had better things to think about than old Schumley, so we put aside our matchmaking ideas and called it a day. I had to hurry off to the University for an appointment at the enrollment office. I was about to begin work toward a master's degree, something I had been contemplating for several years. It wouldn't be the medical degree my father had long since given up on, but surely it would add stability, if only psychological, to the up and down life of a tennis teacher.

The freighter rocked me thoroughly that night. It had announced itself some time earlier, sending vibrations into my mattress from far away. Then came the great rattling and clanking as it swept by, diminishing gradually, until now in the distance its moan was a faint plea. I longed for it to come back, to talk to me again and hold me, and then I drifted back to sleep.

The morning felt sad and gray in the Berkeley flatlands as I bounced over the railroad tracks in my front yard. But soon enough I had driven over the hill, through it actually, in the Caldecott Tunnel, and when I came out the other side, the sun shone with a Saturday magic. Orinda, Lafayette, Walnut Creek — how I envied the weather of those inland towns! In fact, there were several club members, who like me, also came in from Berkeley — Hitchcock, Smitty, and Mrs. Cho among them.

The warm air was thick with the smell of freshly mowed grass when I arrived. A flock of small birds darted and swooped through the grounds without seeming to notice the yellow tennis balls (fuzz nugs, as we called them) that streaked back and forth in their midst. The new yellow fuzz nugs contrasted nicely with the forest-green courts and the dark green windscreens that hung from the fences. As if empowered by a mind of its own, a fuzz nug suddenly cruised over the fence and sat on the lawn like a big yellow toadstool. Yes, the club championships were officially underway, on all twelve courts. Todd had got the matches going. The 3.0 ladies doubles was being played in round-robin format out back, while nearer the clubhouse the 4.5 men were playing singles.

I walked down the tree-lined path to the more distant courts to see how Evonne was faring with the ladies. As I passed the first string of courts I couldn't help thinking of them as playpens, giant playpens for giant oversized babies. Thinking of the courts as playpens made my job go more smoothly; it kept everything in perspective, especially the part about the members being oversized babies. No matter how irate a member could be, I always kept my cool if I just imagined the person standing in front of me was wearing diapers instead of tennis shorts.

When I arrived behind the last playpen, I could see Evonne through the green of the windscreen. She really didn't look too bad for such a raw beginner. Her little poke of a serve was working just fine, and she managed to get more than half her groundstrokes back over the net. She got to almost all the fuzz nugs, running buoyantly here and there.

Actually, it was the other ladies who looked under par. With Evonne springing around so energetically, they looked more subdued than usual. Evonne saw me behind the court when she came over to pick up a ball.

"This is really fun," she said in a hushed tone through the fence. Then she skipped back to the baseline to return serve. I noticed that after each point she said the score to herself, a look of concentration on her face. Sometimes she repeated the score several times in a row as if in an effort to get herself pumped up.

"How's she doing?" Todd asked when I got back to the tournament desk. I would have suggested he go over and take a look, but she seemed to be doing OK and I didn't want to make her nervous.

"Not too bad," I said, "all things considered."

A couple of hours later, having finished their round-robin, the 3.0 ladies walked back to the clubhouse together with Evonne bouncing happily among them. We posted their scores, and then Evonne hung around. She seemed pleased with her results, after all, she and her partner hadn't finished last. It was close, but they actually beat one of the teams.

"Thanks a lot, you guys, it was really fun," she beamed.

"That's what we're here for — fun," Todd announced. He gazed at her with a pleased expression as she fumbled with her purse and car keys, getting ready to go. I could tell he didn't want her to leave.

"OK, then, I'll see you two later," Evonne said, and she began to walk away.

"Wait," Todd put in, "we need you to come back, for the men's singles final. It's going to be a good match, you wouldn't want to miss it. Three o'clock sharp." Evonne turned midstride and called back, "OK, I'll be here."

Todd called out to her again, "Yeah, we need you to call the match, to be the umpire." Evonne waved but I could see she really hadn't heard what Todd said. I turned immediately to Todd.

"You think Evonne should call the final?!"

"It's going to be Hitchcock against McGraph, it'll be perfect. She'll get a chance to meet Hitch. And he'll have occasion to walk up to the chair and help her with the score now and then, or a questionable line call. It'll be perfect!"

I chuckled at the thought. What would it be like to have Evonne call the men's final?

"Maybe we shouldn't do it," I said, "I'm not worried about Hitchcock, but what about McGraph? He might not be so patient. And sometimes the crowd gets into it, too. Things can get pretty scary sitting high up in that chair. It may be too much for her." I thought about the quietly sophisticated lady who lay camouflaged deep within Evonne's superbly cheerful disposition. As a successful business woman, she had conquered the odds before. No doubt, she had handled things a lot more tricky than tennis players.

"Oh come on," Todd urged, "it will be great for everybody. You'll see."

The matter was settled almost immediately, partly because Todd reminded me that if anything did go wrong, neither of us was going to be around much longer, anyway. After all, I had decided to go back to school, so it was my last month at the club; and Todd was going on tour. But more importantly, it was our last chance to do something meaningful for the club — we would introduce Evonne to the membership, and to Hitch.

"It's not like she's a klutz," Todd said, "what's she going to do, fall out of the umpire chair? Really, there's nothing to worry about."

And yet, there was so much to gain! We would give the crowd something special. The club people would get to know Evonne, their bubbly new member, and she would get to know them. "Just think how much Evonne will know about tennis when it's over!" Todd said.

Yes, and in a few minutes it would be underway. Todd and I could just relax in the bar, maybe even go home and let nature take its course. It would be a blessing to wrap up early while Evonne umpired the final. She already knew how to score; we had taught her that yesterday. And, she had reviewed it all morning, poking the ball around with the 3.0 ladies. Now she was more of an expert, although it did take some prodding for Todd to convince her of that when she returned at three o'clock. She thought she was just going to watch. But we had other plans for her.

Wearing an airy summer dress and a matching bonnet, Evonne looked very lady-like as we ushered her down to the stadium court (or, the court in the hole, as we liked to call it.) There were about fifty people in the hole already, poised to watch the final. Hitchcock and McGraph were almost finished warming up, so we helped Evonne climb up the ladder to the umpire chair. She seemed kind of quiet, a little nervous way up there as we gave her final instructions. "Remember, don't let them give you a bad time. You're the boss," I said, "if a player gives you a bad time, tell him you'll throw him out. And if the crowd gets too loud, tell them to pipe down." "Yeah," Todd put in, "say it like this: 'quiet please, ladies and gentlemen,' that always works." I handed Evonne the microphone and we eased our way out of the crowd, offering the usual pleasantries and the occasional handshake.

It was true, most club players could care less about watching other people play, especially people who weren't related to them and were in a different division. But Todd and I learned — if you offer good snacks, raffle off a racket, and hand out trophies, there's no telling how many members might show up to watch a club final. Besides, being players at heart, we felt it was important for lesser players to watch the better players occasionally. After all, wasn't that what the whole thing was about — to aspire to be better, to move ever upward, and to appreciate what there is at the top pulling everything up.

Todd and I used to talk a lot about that and about how some tournament directors were blowing it. One guy in particular used to irk the hell out of us, so we never played his tournament anymore. He was one of those guys who gave cash prizes based on the numbers of entries in a division. In which case, the hacker winning the 3.0's would get a bigger paycheck than the Open winner, since there were so few Open players and so many in the 3.0. That really didn't make any sense, unless the object was to inspire the good players to become worse players.

Last year at that jerk's tournament, Todd and I won the Open doubles, and the dork didn't even give us a T-shirt. He just handed us each a check for $12 dollars and treated us to the spectacle of a 3.0 men's team doing cartwheels on the grass, energized by the $50 they each received for losing in the finals.

"Hey!" Todd shouted at the guy when we were about a mile away in my car, "if you're going to have a bunch of divisions, make sure the top division gets a better prize than the bottom division. That's what it's all about!"

"Damn right," I said.

"The lesser players are supposed to support the better players!" Todd shouted. He was really ticked. "At Wimbledon who gets more money, the players on the court, or the players in the stands!"

"Yeah," I said, "the worse players, whether they know it or not, are actually bankrolling the better players. That's just the way it is."

Anyway, that was our philosophy at the club, to inspire the lesser players to be like the better players, and that's why we had the hole, to make the better players feel really special. We treated them as if they were the main event, even if there were fewer of them. And that meant today we would showcase the men's 4.5 singles. (We did have a man who was a 5.5, and there were a couple of 5.0's, but they never messed around with club tournaments. We also had a 5.0 woman, but most of them were 3.0's and 3.5's — no women had signed up for singles, anyway.) So, by putting the 4.5 men in the hole, we were rewarding the better players with better stuff — stuff like more spectators, nicer trophies, and an expert umpire. And if she wasn't an expert, at least she was downright attractive (certainly a lot nicer to look at than old Schumley was last year.)

We were at the parking lot now, about to leave the club when we heard a muffled gasp from the crowd down in the hole. It was followed by murmuring. Then our trusting protégé's voice came through the PA system: "Ladies and gentlemen, quiet please," and magically, the noise went away. "Thank you." Evonne paused briefly. Then she announced, more boldly now, "Correction. Mr. Hitchcock will serve. The score is deuce."

"I told you everything would be cool," Todd said.

With a sense of pride and renewed confidence, my faithful assistant and I hopped into my old Dodge Dart and puttered away from the club. We ended up at a small tavern along the highway, a place where we were known only to the bartender and could enjoy the anonymity and the easy sound of country music. Johnny Cash, Merle Haggard, Willie Nelson; we were one of them now (in spite of our short pants.) With a pitcher of beer between us, we sat ankle-deep in peanut shells and talked about old times. We cut right to the best stuff, episodes that seemed even better and more aglow than they had on the last occasion.

We also talked about the present, after all, we'd put in a long weekend running the club championships. We had done our best to please a great many people — McGraph, Hitchcock, old Schumley — so many others and countless women. Evonne, too. Yes! I looked Todd firmly in the eye for a long moment.

He nodded pensively with a subtle smile. Then he held up his mug. "Here's to the good we did for everybody."

"Right on." I extended my mug into his with a CLUNK, and it felt solid and satisfying, not unlike the clean feel of an overhead smash.

Indeed, we had done a lot of good for everybody. I got all the details from the club manager when I went back to work on Monday. It seems, Hitchcock played the first set nervously when he saw who was sitting so ladylike in the umpire chair. Eventually though he relaxed, after all, she kept calling him over for advice every time confusion set in. (Apparently, we had forgotten to tell Evonne about side-changes, foot faults, let serves, and tiebreakers.) So, there was plenty of opportunity to chat with the pretty umpire, something McGraph seemed uninterested in, preferring just to jog in place and swing his racket so as not to get cold. Meanwhile, Hitchcock began to look forward to his occasional stroll to the chair; and after each visit he resumed play with more confidence, until at last, he had come back from a deficit and won his first club championship.

A pleasant buzz ran through the crowd in the hole when they discovered Evonne was so new to the game. Now they could forgive her officiating blunders and all those unnecessary delays. They marched her up to the bar in the clubhouse. Hitchcock announced drinks for everybody, and then somebody got the music going. A party ensued with Hitchcock and Evonne dancing until nightfall with a handful of other couples. Even old Schumley hung out, a small trophy sitting near his drink at the bar.

The word spread quickly about our expert umpire and our new club champion. Evonne and Hitchcock had become club celebrities. They began to date, and suddenly, they were inseparable. She was his goddess of victory, he was her tennis hero. They were really getting serious, too. At the end of the month, on my last day at the club, they invited me and Todd to their engagement party. They said we were both going to be their best man. I wasn't exactly sure how it was going to work, but that night when we arrived at Hitchcock's place in the Berkeley hills, everybody from the club was there. It turned out it was also a good-by party for us; after all, I was headed to school fulltime and Todd was going on tour.

And now in those posh hills, things got more than a little wild as the evening progressed, largely because Hitchcock was such a beer aficionado. As a work related perk, he had acquired beer steins from all over Europe, even from the Middle East and Africa. He claimed he had at least one from every continent. "Tankards," he called them, big ornate mugs with exotic handles, many with hinged lids. There were more than one hundred of them, and now at the party, even the ladies were guzzling their wine out of them. Several tipsy 3.0's came over to hug me and Todd and wish us good luck in our lives and our careers and any marriages we might embark on.

"I guess we're everybody's best man," Todd slurred as the women fluttered off to congratulate Hitchcock. Then Evonne cornered us.

"Hey, you guys."

We all just looked at each other for a couple of long seconds, and then our arms raised simultaneously and three big tankards collided with a CLUNK. It felt solid, every bit as satisfying as a clean overhead from up near the net.

Chapter Two

Hitch-Hiking Pros

Not much had been going on. True, I was back in school now, so I was on the court less and in the library more. It was nice to venture out of the flatlands and up into the rolling green terrain of the Cal campus. I sure enjoyed seeing those coeds as I walked between my classes. And I have to admit, it was nice to feel the weight of some books under my arm. Sometimes I'd leave my car where it had been parked all night near the railroad tracks in front of my little pad on 2nd Street, and I'd hike up to campus just to get some exercise. Regardless, in the evening when I got back down to the flats, I was in the doldrums. By the time I hit the sack, it didn't feel like much had changed inside those four walls.

And yet, in the middle of the night that midnight freighter would come like a reliable lover. She was always there in the dark to moan a little and tell me things. We talked about my old pal Spiegel and his perfect Tom Stow backhand. Or was it really a Don Budge backhand? We wondered about that. We thought about Todd, Evonne and Hitch, and the club I had just left. But mostly we contemplated my misspent youth, which I was actually still misspending, at least my dad would have probably figured that was the case. My mother would have been more tolerant; she was always more relaxed, even about her own demise. Not that the cancer ever gave her a fighting chance. But she never complained. I remember one evening near the end. After doing the dinner dishes she sat down on the couch, which seemed odd to me at the time. I was already there staring at a TV that wasn't allowed to be turned on during the week. I was in the ninth grade now and thinking about ways to skimp on my homework. My mother just looked at me sadly and said that she felt tired. That was the closest thing to a complaint I ever heard. She rested for a moment; then she went upstairs to get my little brother to bed. My sister was already up there studying to keep up her A average.

My midnight lover moaned as she made her way along the dark edges of the bay, and we discussed these things, mostly stuff from the past. The future was too big to think about. I was back in school, true, but I wasn't even sure that would amount to anything. I was stuck in a mire of uncertainty, so from that standpoint my life in those all too familiar flatlands felt pretty much as it always did.

Occasionally to break the monotony in the evening, I'd walk over and have a beer at Spenger's Fish Grotto, which was only a few blocks away near the foot of University Avenue. Frank Spenger had been a patient of my dad's, and we ate there a lot when we were kids. I especially liked the old-time sailing vessels they had on display, all that intricate rigging in big glass cases. Even now, I am drawn to the detailed workmanship of those little ships. The problem is, some of the same waiters still work at Spenger's and they recognize me. They always ask how my dad is doing; and then I have to fake it because I haven't seen him in years, either. I was thinking I might head over anyway, have a beer, maybe a cup of coffee, I wasn't sure. Then the phone rang; its discordant plea nagged at the silence in my meager 2nd Street apartment.

It was Todd. I hadn't heard from him in months, not since he split to go play the tournaments. I had seen Evonne and Hitchcock a time or two after their party, but I rarely even drove out to the old club anymore, though as pro emeritus, I was an honorary member. I was too busy studying, trying to get my Masters degree in Psychology. Also, I was coaching the local junior college team on the side. Or maybe I was in school on the side, it being difficult at times to know if one is on the side of something or actually on top of it and on the side of something else.

At any rate, out of the blue Todd called me up. I had wondered how he was doing and often found myself scanning tennis results in the newspaper in search of his name.

"Dude. It's me." The voice on the other end of the line was so familiar. What the? "Hey, Todd, son of a bitch! How the hell are ya? I saw where you went a couple of rounds in Miami. Where are you calling from? You're home, in Berkeley? Well, then get your butt over here!"

It was good to see Todd. Not only was he an old friend and doubles partner, but he was the best assistant pro I ever had. His face was more suntanned than before, and the hair on his arms now had a golden tinge.

"You know, Evonne and Hitch asked about you."

He smiled, nodding slowly, introspectively. "That was a good one," he said.

I told him about the psych courses I was taking and the team I was coaching, and he told me about the tournaments he had played. But as we kicked back at my place in the flats of Berkeley, I could see he wasn't eager to reveal all the gory details; I had to pry them out of him. It seems Todd only did really well in a tourney in Florida where he got to the quarters. All things considered, though, he didn't do too badly, making expenses most of the time. But now he was no longer interested in playing the circuit, even though it was a necessary step on the trail to stardom. The trail was too steep, and too long, and time was running out for Todd. Now he would play renegade tournaments, small independent events with decent money, events that nobody talked about, especially not the guys winning them. Todd wasn't after the big time anymore; he would travel, have fun, and grab the money where he could. A world ranking, especially a low one, was of no use to him.

He had brought over a six-pack of Heineken, but because I had a Psychology final in the morning, I only drank two and let him have the rest; but then Todd began to feel bad about having more than his share of the beer. He tried to convince me that if I had just one more Heineken I would do better on my exam since most of the course was on the unconscious workings of the mind.

"If you want to do any good at all, you've got to get unconscious," Todd told me, at least half seriously. "It's just like tennis, you don't want to over-concentrate."

We talked about athletic performance and Zen, stuff like effortless effort and less is more. "If less is more then more has to be less at least some of the time," Todd said as he put another beer in front of me. "This is one of those times."

I resisted, but I wasn't strong enough to say no when he asked me to play a renegade tournament in Montana with him. "It begins next week, when you get a break from the University, so what do you say? We've got a real shot at the doubles, the two top guys are just playing singles. I know, I just spoke to the tournament director, a guy named Charley Finger."

It was true, I would have some time to kill before the summer session started.

"How's the money?" I asked.

"Great! Eighteen hundred for the winning doubles team and three grand for the singles. The money starts in the first round, plus, get this, there's hospitality for the whole week, even if we get bumped. Charley Finger owns some sort of hotel, that's where we stay. Not bad, eh?"

"That depends on what we spend to get there. Getting to Montana could get expensive." Driving out there in my old Dodge Dart was out of the question. It was somewhat of a classic, and although that old slant six had been to every major tennis center in California at least once, it had acquired an uncanny consumption for oil and water, and now also brake fluid. Anything could go wrong. I always made sure it was equipped with flares, jumper cables, and a can of that whipped cream tire inflater goop. And I always carried an AAA card, just in case.

As we sat at the little kitchen table in my funky flatland pad, I contemplated the fact that Todd didn't even have a car. I guess there was no need. His grandfather had taken him in as a kid (when his folks went berserk after an ugly divorce) and now Todd still lived with the old man, partially out of habit and partially just to keep an eye on him; and so there was always a set of wheels he could borrow. But not for extended trips. I figured we had no choice but to fly to Montana.

"We'll have to get to the semis at least to pay for our plane fare," I said. "And, unlike you, I've got to get back to the Bay Area, I can't just hang out in Doublefault, Montana giving tennis lessons at the local park in exchange for a place to crash."

"We're taking the train," Todd said matter-of-factly.

"We'll need a sleeper and it'll still be expensive."

"Expensive hell, we're goin' for free, and it'll be on a sleeper alright."

"Now I suppose you're going to tell me Charley Finger owns Amtrak."

"Dude," Todd spoke uncomfortably close to my face, like a bar fly trying to make a point. "Dude, we're going to go down to the yard and hop a freighter. I've done it before, remember? That way, anything we make will just be spare change."

Instinctively, I gazed toward my bedroom and thought about the freighter that would be getting intimate with me in the wee hours of the night — how gigantic it was when I saw it up close in daylight! The floor of those boxcars was up high, almost out of reach, and everything swept by rather quickly, even though at first glance those big old cars just seemed to clank and creep along.

"I thought you said hopping a freight is dangerous," I told Todd, "and that you'd never do it again."

"Naw, that's not what I said. I said it's dangerous if you don't know what you're doing, and that I'd never do it again, alone. It's too powerful an experience not to share with somebody."

I told him I didn't think I had enough hobo blood in me for such a powerful experience. Todd backed away as if I had given off a very peculiar odor. He stared at me with disapproval. And I began to wonder what other people would think. Would I be known as the guy who wisely decided not to fall off a freight train at seventy miles an hour, or would I be forever branded as the all-time pussy of the modern world? Judging by his contorted face, Todd was obviously leaning toward that last thought.

"You know how to find out about all the connections?" I asked meekly, as I pictured the two of us in the middle of nowhere, standing on the track bed alongside an abandoned railroad shack.

"Nothing to it, just leave it all to me." His what-are-you-a-wimp look morphed into a solid right-on-dude gaze, and I began to feel boldy adventurous. The wind of the speeding train swept back my hair and whistled past my ears. I imagined sitting on the edge of an open box car with my legs dangling out.

And sitting with a slightly more formal posture in the Psych Building the next morning, I aced my final exam, which just goes to show, less *is* more, more or less.

A couple of days later we set out for Portland on the advice of a tramp Todd had met in the Oakland freight yard. Portland would put us at the right latitude to ride the rails straight across to Montana. But the tramp had advised that we hitchhike to Portland, since the Oakland yard workers didn't take near as kindly to freeloaders as the guys up in

Oregon. So now, on an overcast day by the Bay, we were perched on the side of a freeway onramp with our thumbs up and our big tennis bags on the ground.

"Why don't you turn your bag around," Todd suggested, "so the word Nike shows. I think it'll be easier to get a ride that way, people like Nike." (Todd had a big black Wilson bag with worn-out letters.)

So I turned my tour bag around, and then we put our tennis rackets in a big pile so people could see we were highly cultured individuals. "There, that's bound to work," Todd said, "some hacker will probably think we're John McEnroe and Bjorn Borg."

"Get real. What would McEnroe be doing hitchhiking? He doesn't even live around here. And Borg lives even further away, or hadn't you heard? And they're not even playing that much these days."

"So maybe they came out to California to surf or play music or something. I hear McEnroe plays in a band."

"Well then what would he be doing by the freeway next to a pile of tennis rackets?"

"We could put the rackets back in our bags."

"That's not the point."

"Anyway, it would be just our luck to get in a hippie van and have the driver throw us out when he discovers I don't have a Swedish accent and you don't know a damn thing about music."

"You got that right."

"So you admit it, I could be Borg? And you could be McEnroe?"

"That's not what I said. I said I couldn't be McEnroe, I don't know a damn thing about music. And I'm not even lefthanded!"

"Well, no wonder the cars aren't stopping," Todd quipped as strangers continued to go by our pile of tennis rackets at fifty miles an hour.

"You know what we need," I suggested, "is a big sign that says we're not killers."

"Yeah, that'd work great. Let's go get some cardboard."

"Where are you going to get some cardboard?"

"I don't know, somewhere. I'll look around."

"Yeah, you go look around and when a car stops for me I'll just tell them Bjorn Borg is out looking for cardboard but he'll be back real soon."

A few minutes later Todd came back with a big piece of weathered cardboard. One side had uneven writing on it about being homeless and needing work, but the other side wasn't too messed up. Todd used a marking pen he had in his bag, and now at the edge of the onramp he held his sign high — TENNIS PRO, LIMO BROKEN. A couple of cars swerved, but still, nobody stopped.

"You know what we really need is a chick," Todd whined as what seemed like the millionth car whizzed by. He put down the big sign. "Cars always stop for chicks."

"Yeah, especially if there are no guys around. A single, good-looking chick always gets a ride."

"Hey, what about Evonne?" Todd said. "I bet she could get a ride easy. And she owes us a favor."

"She's definitely the type cars would come to a screeching halt for. Too bad she's engaged."

"I was just thinking Hitch might loan her to us until somebody stopped, then you and I could jump out of the bushes and get in the car. That'd be cool," Todd said, but I could tell his enthusiasm was waning. He was dejected about the fact that we had already wasted two hours.

Our conversation became sluggish, and the pauses between replies grew lengthy, as did the intervals between cars going up the onramp. Then suddenly, Todd had a stroke of brilliance — we decided to try a *less is more* technique. So we stood with our backs to the traffic and our thumbs in our pockets.

"This is going to work," Todd said, "I can feel it." And then, sure enough, a vehicle came to a stop alongside our pile of tennis rackets. It was a police car.

"Well, what do we have here?" the cop said, "a couple of longhairs with tennis rackets?" The big man in the uniform was walking toward us.

It was in instances like this that I learned to let Todd do the talking. It was like when the opponent loses a crucial exchange in the third set and says, "The serve was a let, I tried to return the ball to you but you kept playing it. Didn't you hear me? I called a let." In those situations, I never know what to say, or rather, I have too many things to say, all of which render me speechless. On the other hand, Todd responds immediately. Although he too doesn't know exactly what to say, he at least says something. He acts without knowing. Todd doesn't let the inner workings of his mind confuse his actions; he isn't one to over-concentrate or get self-conscious. In short, he doesn't choke, so he's a good partner to have in a pinch.

"How are ya doin' officer?" Todd greeted the cop cheerfully, just like the guy was showing up f or a tennis clinic. I tried to imagine the big cop was wearing diapers instead of his gun belt, and that relaxed me a bit, but it had no bearing on the face of the officer who looked like he had swallowed something distasteful. I could see he was chewing gum, but that apparently wasn't enough to get rid of the sour taste in his mouth.

"What brings you out here today, officer?" Todd was in fine form.

"Let me see some ID," the cop said, and he began to write on a clipboard while Todd and I stood with our arms extended, drivers licenses in hand. When he was ready, the officer took our ID's and made some more notes on his clipboard.

"Don't you know you're not supposed to hitchhike from the middle of the onramp?" The cop handed us back our licenses.

"Are we in the middle of the onramp? I had no idea," Todd said, "I mean I know you're not supposed to hitch on the freeway but I thought the onramp was OK." Quickly, he shouldered both our tour bags and began walking toward the base of the onramp. I followed, juggling our pile of tennis rackets.

"Hold it right there," the officer said calmly, surprisingly calmly. And then he added, "where do you think you're going with all those tennis rackets?"

"Portland, and then Montana," Todd offered enthusiastically. "We've got a tournament to play."

"I suppose you're professionals?" The cop emphasized the word "professionals."

"Yeah," Todd replied, "we're hitchhiking pros."

The officer looked at his watch. "I think we better get you two boys down to the station."

At last we were in a car. A brand new, black and white police car with a cage divider behind the front seat staring us in the face. As I looked through it, I began to have visions of jail cells and prison violence. Suspended on the cop's side of the wire cage was a very sober looking 12 gauge shotgun.

Todd sat slumped; I had never seen him with a wrinkled forehead before. He leaned toward my side of the police car. "At least we're not handcuffed," he whispered, offering a shred of optimism.

As the patrol car cruised through the less picturesque parts of Oakland, the cop began to talk to us through the wire cage.

"Tell me more about this tournament in Montana," he said.

"It's just a small independent event with pretty good money," Todd said, after some hesitation.

"How much money?" the cop asked.

"Only nine thousand dollars," Todd replied. "If we play well we stand to win about three grand between us, and since we're more or less broke we thought we'd hitch out there."

The cop's voice came through the cage again. "My kid plays tennis. He's on the JV's at school."

"What grade is he in?" Todd asked politely.

"He's just a junior, next year he's hoping to be on varsity," the cop said, and right away I knew the kid was doomed — if he wasn't good enough to be on varsity as a junior then he was pretty sorry for his age and it was over; there would be no college tennis for the kid, and certainly no free world travel. Not that the kid couldn't enjoy the game for fun and all that.

"He must be pretty good," I volunteered nervously.

"Not bad, I guess," the cop said, as he pulled up to the curb in front of the Greyhound Bus Station.

"OK pros, we're at the station. Hop out and get your gear."

The officer got out of his idling patrol car; he stood on the sidewalk with us for a while. "I always liked that Bjorn Borg fellow," he said, "even if he is a longhair. My son likes him too. We've never seen him play for real, though, just a few times on TV. My boy's not very good at sports, you know, wants to work on computers. I thought tennis would be good for him."

Suddenly the radio in the patrol car became fuzzy with police talk, and the officer's face turned sour again. Quickly, he thumbed through his wallet. He pulled out a $100 bill and shoved it into the bottom of my shirt pocket. Then he got into the idling patrol car and picked up the handset of his radio. He said something at it and pulled away from the curb so fast I was expecting to hear a screech, but it was just the sticky sound of rubber making traction across the wide blacktop as the patrol car hung a U turn and sped down that sad Oakland street with its lights flashing.

We stood there watching until the cop was out of sight. Finally, Todd said, "I told you Borg would come through for us."

"Yeah, " I offered, somewhat dazed, "good old Borg. Maybe he'll show up at the tournament, too, and hit a few groundies for you."

"That's fine with me, so long as he lets me do the volleying, I like my volley."

"Come on," I urged, feeling suddenly resilient with the goodness of being alive. "Let's go to Portland!" So we shouldered our big bags and headed in to get our bus tickets.

Chapter Three

Reborn Socks

The acrid odor of perfume that had mixed unkindly with somebody's body chemistry hung unpleasantly in the stale air. The aroma seemed to be coming from the seat in front of us, where two elderly ladies sat in long coats. There being no other places available on the bus, we had no choice but to get used to the fragrance.

Olfactory conditions aside, the journey to Oregon was surprisingly comfortable and swift. Todd and I just Zenned out in our own minds for the most part, having used up much of our social banter on the freeway onramp in Oakland, though initially there were some wordless exchanges parlayed through facial acrobatics, primarily twisted noses and bulging eyeballs. Then we grew accustomed to the strange smell and even slept a little during the long night that rambled in and out of Sacramento, Redding, Yreka, Ashland, Medford, Eugene, Albany, Salem, and what seemed like every other town that lay in our path.

Finally, at eight in the morning, we de-bused into the wonderful fresh air of Portland. The first order of business was to hit some fuzz nugs around and find a place to crash for the night, so Todd called a tennis club he found in the Portland yellow pages. He stood at a wall of pay phones in the dreary bus terminal while I sat on a nearby bench guarding our gear. I could hear him talking.

"Oh, hello ... is this the East Moreland Racquet Club? ... You're the manager? ... Excellent ... my partner and I are pros from California, we just arrived in Portland. One of the players we met at Wimbledon mentioned the East Moreland Club, said it was a rather fine facility ... Yes, that's right, Wimbledon, his name escapes me, Canadian I think, a very gentlemanly type, though his game seemed to be a little rough around the edges, lost in the first round ... Yes, that's right, we're from the San Francisco area and we're headed to a tournament back East ... thought we might come by for a bit of a hit, if that's OK with you. We'd be happy to pay guest fees, or perhaps knock the ball around with some juniors, or even play a little social tennis, whatever you think."

I noticed that Todd avoided saying exactly where we were going and also that we were from Bezerkly, a wise precaution perhaps. However, anybody who really knew tennis would know that as bizarre a reputation as Berkeley had, when it came to high level tennis it was the premier site in Northern California. The Berkeley Tennis Club, in particular, would be forever marked by the deep footprints of Stow, Budge, Wills, Van der Meer, McManus, and Borowiak; as well as a dozen other players who had left a permanent imprint on the sport. Situated below the sprawling white elegance of the Claremont Hotel, the Berkeley club often looked like a training camp for touring pros, such were the number of name players who might be hanging around at any given time. Todd and I used to drive over there for some outrageous pickup games when things got slow at the club in Lafayette.

In the dismal gray of the Portland bus terminal, Todd hung up the phone. "Easy as pie," he said, "they're sending a car for us."

As ambassadors of tennis goodwill, we did the correct thing by playing doubles with a couple of eager hackers and getting ourselves invited for dinner and a place to stay for the night. Our host, a dentist with a topspin volley, had to go to the office for a while, but he would come back for us later. So we stayed at the club and played a set of singles to work the hack out of our games (those dinks and trick shots are fun for social tennis, but they play havoc with the instinct to put the ball away.) Then we played ping pong for twenty minutes before taking long steamy showers. A jacuzzi would have been nice, but apparently the East Moreland Club didn't have one. So, now we were hanging out in the locker room in our underwear and flip-flops, waiting for our bodies to cool down before putting on the rest of our clothes.

"Hey, Stretch, check this out." (Todd had come to call me "Stretch" some time ago, a statement honoring my proclivity for assuming yoga-like positions at all otherwise idle moments of the day.) He was standing in front of the vanity counter in the locker room, looking back at me in the mirror as I stretched my hamstring on one of the long wooden benches. He held up a brand-new pair of tennis socks he found hanging over the edge of the trash bin. They looked like they had just come out of the package, all fluffy and white with bright burgundy bands around the tops. The only thing missing on each sock was a considerable portion of the toe section, which had worn clean through, the result of shoes with holes in them.

"Whoever these socks belonged to is a good player," Todd said, obviously pleased. "Look, he wore out his shoes at the toe before he went through the ball of the foot. The guy is probably fast as hell."

"Either that or he's an oaf and he wore them out from excessive toe drag while serving," I suggested.

"In that case he would've only worn through the rear shoe, and the rear sock would be the only one wrecked."

"Yeah well, he could've worn through the other shoe while stretching wide to the backhand, some guys do that, you know."

"No, I think he's a good player and fast as a cat. The only thing I can't figure out is if he's rich or poor. He can't afford new shoes, but he's willing to burn a pair of socks for each match, and that adds up. Either way, he must be crazy, and that's even more proof he's a good player."

I told Todd I agreed with him now that I had thought it out. The guy was after performance, and he was obviously a lot more nimble in his well worn shoes. Plus, he was bucks up or he would have surely put on old socks for such a thrashing. Of course, maybe he didn't have any old socks left by now, and this being an important match he had to spring for the new socks, in which case he might not be so well-to-do. To be certain, though, he was a good player.

We cooled down in the locker room enough to finish getting dressed, and now we were waiting for our host in the lobby of the club, with our big solemn-looking tour bags ready to go by the door.

"Just a minute," Todd said, looking suddenly enlightened. He ran back into the locker room and came out with the abandoned socks. "Watch this," he announced as he pulled a small clasp knife out of his pocket. He opened the blade and sliced each sock below the ankle, and then he threw the foot part away. He kept the burgundy topped sleeves and was now in the process of trying them on over the old gray saggers he was wearing. Then he put his tennis shoes back on. "Well," he said, "what do you think?"

There was no comparison. Todd appeared to be wearing expensive new socks, yet in reality, they had been resurrected from a trash bin. They were in fact, reborn socks, socks that had been born again and rather severely circumcised. They looked terrific with their thick white ribbing and bright burgundy bands.

"You could've fooled me," I said, authentically impressed. But then I had second thoughts and asked Todd if he was really going to wear someone else's socks.

"Dude, it's not like my feet are really in them. Besides, the guy is a good player and he obviously intended somebody to use them or he wouldn't have left them hanging over the edge of the garbage can. From now on," Todd said proudly, "these are my lucky socks. I'm going to wear them in Montana. For every match."

The dentist with the topspin volley walked into the lobby just then and hoisted my big Nike bag to his shoulder. "Come on, men, let's go, the wife's got something cooking."

As we walked out to his car, I could see he was enjoying carrying my tour bag — he felt as if he were going with us, going pro. And the fact that we were only going to Charley Finger's little tournament in Doublefault, Montana didn't seem to bother him. He opened the trunk of his Mercedes and put our gear in with great satisfaction and tidiness.

The dentist lived in the suburbs on a forested hillside, with his wife and two teenage daughters; and a full-grown golden retriever who remained outside, being too playful to introduce to important guests. The daughters, however, being less likely to jump on strangers, were allowed free reign of the house, where they terrorized their parents in subtle ways, and now Todd and me with their teasing glances, which wouldn't have been so bad, but with father nearby, eyeballing was severely restricted.

With our stomachs rumbling, my partner and I sat down with the family for dinner. The good china was on the table, and though all kinds of warm, savory aromas were coming from the kitchen, the only food in sight was a tossed green salad that lay on small plates at each setting.

"Tell us, gentlemen," the dentist said from the head of the table, "what's it like being a tennis pro?"

"In a lot of ways I suppose it's like being a dentist who wears shorts and doesn't have to go to the office," Todd said. And so we exchanged lighthearted banter with our eager host and his two giggly daughters. One was seventeen, the other a year or so younger, and they were both rather attractive young ladies. However, with dad present, small talk was easier if I pretended the girls were hard to look at, something my doubles partner didn't bother with as he sat by my side. In an effort to keep me apprised of the situation, he stroked my thigh with his hand from time to time, lest I forget about the two beauties sitting opposite us.

At last, having finished up in the kitchen, the dentist's very good looking wife joined us in the dining room, where she was seated formally, the back of her chair receiving the unnecessary but dexterous hand of her husband who probably hadn't made such a gesture since Thanksgiving. Then he sat down, and a famished Todd, taking that for a signal to get started, stabbed a forkful of lettuce and tomato and shoved it into his mouth. He chewed eagerly, hungrily, but then sensing that nobody else had begun to eat, his jaw slackened. He looked around sheepishly, feeling the weight of it all. And then he decided to undo his terrible breach of etiquette. With all eyes on him, he spat the half-chewed lettuce and tomato back onto his plate.

The girls went wild with laughter. I too was about to burst.

"Dear Lord," our host broke through the various chortles and giggles Todd had inspired in the girls. "Dear Lord, please bless this food quickly, for we have with us tonight two special and very hungry guests. Thank you, Lord." Then he announced, "OK, everybody, you can eat now."

"Oh, Harold, you don't have to be so formal," his lovely wife said in a delicate voice, "you know not everybody says grace before every meal. It's not always natural." She emphasized the word *natural*.

"On the contrary," Todd said, trying to redeem himself, "it's not natural to eat before the hostess. That's why I ..."

"Go ahead and eat your salad," the hostess cut in, saving Todd from elaborating on his good manners. "I'll bring in the rest of dinner." She got up and went into the kitchen.

Despite keen looks from their father that said BEHAVE YOURSELVES, the girls continued to emit sporadic bursts of laughter. Indeed, having swallowed all of mine, I was about to implode. Then finally, the impulse subsided and I whispered to Todd. "Nice move with the salad, Borg."

"Not bad," he said, casually chewing his previously ejected morsels. Then in an audible voice, he added, "it's a good thing they don't start with soup around here."

The girls giggled, but soon they were looking at Todd with eyes that wanted to know secret things, things that weren't just funny. Things that a tennis pro with long, rock star hair would surely know. In the kitchen, their mother had begun to sing quietly; then she came in with platters of steamy food — baked chicken breasts, scalloped potatoes, and cauliflower sautéed with string beans and mushrooms.

Later, we all sat around the living room playing gin rummy, drinking cocoa and wine, and listening to Todd's jokes, which were sandwiched between card deals and questions the dentist asked about how to hit a backhand down-the-line, to which we discreetly tried to suggest that it would be a very good idea to first learn how to hit a standard backhand in the crosscourt direction; and that it might also be a good idea to learn how to volley properly.

We had become part of the family for the night, and found ourselves, eventually, in a lavish guest room with two double beds and a private bath. Exhausted, we flopped onto the beds with our clothes on and lay there.

There was a knock at the door. It was our lovely hostess, holding a laundry basket filled with clothes, mostly whites. "Boys," she asked, "do you have anything that needs washing?" We really didn't have much, having just begun our journey, but knowing only too well the value of clean clothes while on the road, we were more than happy to toss a few things on top of the pile. Then Todd's sleepy eyes lit up. He slipped off his fluffy new footless socks. "Here, better take these too," he offered.

"Oh," said the lady, somewhat shocked.

"Yeah," Todd explained, "they're my special foot warmers, sometimes my ankles get real cold when I'm playing, and I can't move right. Especially if they feature me for a night match."

"Well then, good night," the dentist's wife said. She glanced down at the scraggly gray socks that had fallen loosely around Todd's ankles. Then she shut the door to our room.

The next morning, the dentist went off to work wearing his tennis warmups. He was more, shall we say, inspired than usual. Todd and I waved from the driveway as he drove off with his two daughters (he would deposit them at school even though they appeared to be dressed for a night on the town.)

"I'll take you two to the airport when you're ready," the dentist's wife offered after we went back inside to finish our coffee.

Todd and I looked at each other. He knew damn well I would let him do the talking, but he got great satisfaction watching me sweat it out. The airport, right!

Finally, he told the lady, "That would be nice of you. Absolutely wonderful. We don't need to go for an hour or so." He put down his coffee mug and began to read the paper.

"Thanks for having us," I said to our hostess, "we really appreciate it. By the way, is the airport near the railroad yard by any chance?"

"The train yard?" she asked. "There are two of them, I think. One might be, I'm not sure. Why do you ask?"

Todd looked up from his paper. "Stretch here's got this thing about trains, he's got one that visits him every night, in fact it almost runs over him, and he misses it. Besides, when he was a kid, he used to get model trains for Christmas every year. So he likes to look at them, especially in the big freight yards."

Todd looked seriously at the lady. "Didn't your girls ever want electric trains for Christmas?"

"Can't say they did." She smiled sweetly. "The only things they ever wanted were electric boys, I don't even think they went through the Barbie stage. But trains, no we never had any. Though Harold did take us for a train trip once, across Canada. I loved it, but the girls, well you know how kids are when they're around their parents for too long." She sighed.

"I know what you mean," I said. "I always liked family vacations, it was just getting there that I hated."

"Yes, well, that's right," she said, "I guess for the girls that train trip was just one big getting there. It was some time before we all recovered from it."

"Everybody looks pretty normal now," Todd offered.

"Yes, thank you, we work at it."

Soon we were officially on the way to the airport in the Chevy Blazer the dentist's wife drove around town. In levis now, with her sandy brown hair pulled back in a ponytail, the lady looked surprisingly youthful, actually kind of foxy, as she sat high up behind the wheel of the big Blazer. Todd found a map of Portland in the glove compartment and directed her to the Southern Pacific freight yard.

"Excellent, just swing a left up ahead there," he said excitedly. "Yeah, Stretch here really loves those trains, can't play worth a lick unless he gets a good hit of railroad before a tournament. Perfect, we're just about there." Our hostess was more than happy to oblige; she seemed to be enjoying her part in our adventure.

The tracks were coming into view now. "You don't mind driving over a little loose gravel, do you?" Todd asked, "and a few railroad tracks? Your Blazer will probably thank you for it."

"Just tell me if I need to put it into four wheel drive," the lady said in a serious tone.

"Don't worry about that," I told her from the back seat, "if we need any help my partner will jump out and push us. He could use the exercise."

Todd pointed into the yard as the Blazer bounced over a double set of tracks. "Just drive out there where all those trains are," he said.

We passed alongside a string of reddish brown boxcars, and suddenly the Blazer didn't feel so big. "Are you sure we should go any further?" our driver asked, "this looks like a great spot right here to sightsee from, don't you think?"

Not wanting to worry her, we got out and the three of us walked into the vast yard. It was overwhelming. But Todd was eager, so we hiked way out into the dirt and gravel until we were surrounded by freight cars. About twenty yards dead ahead on parallel tracks were half a dozen complete trains. They all had big dark engines and mud-red caboose cabins attached far away at their tails. Hissing sounds were coming from nearby, where two very solemn-looking engines lay nose to nose pointing in opposite directions, their long strings of cars backing away from each other on separate tracks.

"I guess this is quite a sight," said the lady. It was obvious she wasn't entirely at ease, but now that she was out of her vehicle and standing on the gravel with us, she looked better than ever in her hip-hugging levis. Actually, they were more than hip-hugging, something Todd and I couldn't help but notice in spite of the distractions at hand.

Towering evergreens reached skyward at the edge of the yard. Beyond them in the distance, the ghosts of jagged peaks blended with the powdery horizon. But it was no time for idle gazing. Two trains were coughing and hissing right in front of us, making ready to pull out in opposite directions.

"I'll be back in a second," Todd announced, and he began jogging toward a workman in overalls he spotted at the rear of one of the monstrous engines. He talked to the guy for a while. The man pointed to a car in the middle of the long train. He reached out and shook Todd's hand, and then he climbed up onto the hissing engine.

"It's all set," Todd said, slightly out of breath after running back. "We better go get our gear."

Things happened quickly from that point. Our kind hostess was beginning to understand what was going on. Todd had her pull the Blazer alongside the middle of the long train next to an open green boxcar with the words Burlington Northern on it. Then we got out and pitched our tour bags up into the empty car. Todd climbed up first and the lady ran up and hugged me. She gave me a kiss on the cheek, and then I made the treacherous ascent to the high floorboards of the car.

A switchman in the yard was running toward us. There was something in his hand; as he approached I could see it was a hammer. Panting, he came to a stop below our boxcar and lifted the hammer. With one efficient blow he struck at a spike of wood he had in the other hand. "There," he said, after wedging the spike under the open door of the boxcar. "Now she won't jam shut on you. Have a nice trip, boys."

Below, on the track bed with the railroad switchman, the dentist's wife looked up at us. "Well for heavens sake," she said, "I can see you two really do have a thing for trains."

"I guess it was all those years my father used to get up early Christmas morning to set up the model railroad," I said, looking down at her. "Each year the layout got fancier. You know, I had plenty of cars just like this, but this is the first time I've ever been inside of one."

Our former hostess was beginning to look a little concerned. "Good luck in your tournament," she said.

"I guess we'll just cash in our plane tickets when we get to Montana," Todd said matter-of-factly, "save a little money, you know how that is."

She looked momentarily amused. "Yes, I know how that is."

I thought about Todd's scraggly socks and how kind the lady was to do our laundry and how lonely she looked standing there in her ponytail and her old faded jeans. I figured she probably hadn't worn those pants in quite a while. I wondered if my mother ever had a pair of jeans; I couldn't remember her wearing any.

We could hear great belches and hisses from up front where the engine was. Then the long train lurched forward with a groan. It crept slowly away from where the dentist's wife and the switchman stood alongside the track bed. Then it picked up speed and they shrunk ever smaller in the distance, waving one last time. From somewhere ahead, the horn sounded its forlorn plea. And now there was only the metallic sound of wheels and rails, and the rattling of the boxcar as the train gathered momentum. We scooted further and further from the wind of the open door, finding ourselves eventually at the forward end of the boxcar, where conveniently, a bale of hay had been placed in each corner.

Sitting on a bale with his feet up and his back against the wall, Todd looked rather comfy in his corner of the boxcar. "You know, it just doesn't get any better than this," he shouted through the clanking vibrations of the jiggling train.

"If this is as good as it gets," I yelled from my corner, "they'd make it into a beer commercial. Have you ever seen a beer commercial where two hobos are drinking cold ones in a boxcar?"

"Now that you mention it, no, but that's a great idea. I wonder why they haven't thought of it."

"I'll tell you why," I hollered, "because this represents the difference between as good as it gets and as good as it's gonna get."

"Yeah," Todd said, "this is definitely as good as it gets, I know what you mean."

You do? I wondered if he was toying with my head, or if he actually thought this was as good as it got.

Todd reached into his tour bag. He pulled out a couple cans of beer and tossed one over to me. But we both just sat there on our bales of hay, feeling the liquid weight of the brewski in our hands. Even Todd wasn't crazy enough to pop his open. It was no time to goof around; there were unseen variables and we needed our wits about us. After all, guys had met their fates on the freighters.

Chapter Four

Freightin' To Montana

As we flew across the wilds in our rattling Burlington Northern boxcar, we found ourselves daringly close to the rushing wind of the open door and the spectacular view it offered. White-water rivers and green forested mountains of the Pacific Northwest swept by like an unending mural. Once, the long train slowed down around a horseshoe bend and we could see both the engine and the caboose at the same time. But alas, there were other times when I cringed in my corner of the shaking car trying to forget I was in a thin metal box suspended on rails above the weathered timbers of a very tall mountain trestle.

"I'll feel a lot better when we get on solid ground again," I told my partner as the clanking vibrations of the wobbling train became suddenly more pronounced. I wasn't sure if we were crossing above a river gorge or just taking a shortcut between mountain peaks, and I wasn't about to find out. My mind sought out the earth below and the good things on it, the very flesh of life.

"Did you get a look at those faded old jeans the guy's wife was wearing?" I shouted.

"I'll give them more than a look," Todd quipped, "if she wants me to."

"I don't think she's that kind of woman," I said, suddenly realizing I couldn't be sure of that and the only reason I said so was because I liked her.

"You never know," Todd said.

At last, the loose clanking vibrations became muffled as the long train completed its crossing of the mountain trestle. I inched closer to the open door to inspect the scenery as it flickered by in frames like an old-time movie that had been colorized.

Snowcapped peaks reached up in the distance, while nearer, the forest was like a thick green carpet, except in places where mountainsides were pockmarked by clear-cutting for lumber. Gradually, the terrain became jagged as formations of granite began to appear. The rushing air smelled more arid. And then the freighter began to slow down, to a crawl, in fact. I moved gingerly to the big open door and stuck my neck out to see what was going on.

"Hey, bro," I called for Todd to come over. "Check this out." I pointed to the rocks ahead where some teenage boys stood on top of a cliff. They waved frantically at the train. The boy in front unzipped his pants and pulled something out larger than a can of tennis balls. He let it dangle loosely between his legs for a moment; then a huge yellow stream spilled from it. It was a flow that would have put a horse to shame.

"Can you believe that?" I said, truly amazed. The sun sparkled against the golden trail of liquid as it splashed down over the cliff face to the rocks below.

"The old bucket and hose trick," Todd said, chuckling. "We used to do it on freeway overpasses. Beer is the best thing to use, but if you can't afford it, a little yellow food coloring works OK too."

"The old bucket and hose trick?" I asked.

"Yeah, see that guy behind them, up above in the bushes?" Todd pointed.

"Okay, I guess so," I said, but actually, I could barely make out the bushes.

The glimmering stream of gold dissipated down against the jagged hillside as we crept by. Then the locomotive sounded its horn and the train sped up again. We waved from inside the boxcar and the boys waved back. I began to think about the lady again; I pictured her standing by the tracks in that sad Portland yard, waving at us, just standing there in the dust and gravel with her ponytail and her faded levis. She probably hadn't worn those pants in ten years, I figured.

"That was nice of the guy's wife to do our laundry," I said.

"Yeah," Todd got up excitedly, "she even fixed my lucky new socks, look at this." He went to the corner of the rattling car and got them out of his bag.

"See," he handed the socks to me. Now they really did look new; they had been hemmed at the bottom, whereas before they were uneven and frayed. Still footless, but fluffy and white with their burgundy tops, it was as if they were supposed to look like that right out of the package.

I felt a tinge of jealousy, not that I wanted his socks; but if only I had had something for the kind lady to repair, a hole in *my* clothes somewhere. But not in a smelly old sock, perhaps at the elbow of my sweater. Yes, then I would have had a really good reason to get in touch with her again, to thank her personally. And then I thought about her husband, the tennis-playing dentist to whom we owed it all — the food, the bed, the laughter; even the faded old jeans his wife was wearing — we owed it all to him.

"That was really nice of her to sew up your socks," I said.

Todd had begun to pace impatiently inside the boxcar, as if it were the lobby of a hotel and he were waiting for a taxi. He looked antsy. "We change trains at Lewiston, in a couple of hours," he said through the noise of the shaking car. "It'll be getting dark then. I think I better hit some balls."

So, to the clanketyclanking noise of the speeding train, and all the other incessant metallic rattlings, Todd added a new sound — the familiar thwap of a tennis ball being hit against a wooden backboard. He soon had a thumping groundstroke rhythm going against the wall toward the caboose.

I sucked myself into my corner just inches behind him, feeling much like I do in racketball, a sport where the primary object of the game is not to get hit by the ball from close range, or the opponent's racket from any range. But the fuzz nug rebounded true off the plywood interior of the boxcar, and Todd steered both it and his racket clear of my bale.

Clanketyclankety-thump, clanketyclankety-thonk — he was getting the topspin grooved now, hitting alternate forehands and backhands from an open stance, a great way to tune up for a variety of situations that appear suddenly in both singles and doubles.

Inspired by my partner's bout of training, I began to do exercises for my back and stomach, something I usually do before starting a stretching routine, although I'm generally not skating across the countryside in an oversized coffin. I'm usually in a carpeted hallway somewhere, on a picnic table or a bench, or if really lucky, on a workout mat in a gym. Sometimes a public restroom will have to do for a quick, private place to get the kinks out while on the road, in which case, the facility inside the lobby of a hotel is usually best, but in a pinch, a McDonalds or a Taco Bell is a lot better than nothing.

I really wanted to stretch out my spine by hanging from something. I imagined a bathroom stall, the kind with a rigid metal bar across the top of the door frame — how often had I hung from those handy structures! Of course, the top edges of those things can bite into the fingers, so I always wad up a couple of paper towels to make a pad for each hand. Then I pick up my feet carefully and just hang there resisting the temptation to do a pull-up, having learned the hard way that bathroom stalls aren't meant for acrobatic maneuvers once you're out of the 12's.

I noticed the thumping sound of the tennis ball had disappeared from inside the boxcar, leaving only the metallic rattlings of the train.

"Dude. I'm wiped," Todd said, and he handed me the fuzz nug. "You try it."

Why not? The freighter had begun to go around a curve, so I waited for the straightaway to resume before moving stealthily to get my racket.

It felt good to hit the ball again. Exercise demands exercise, and I had stiffened up considerably from not playing all day and so little the day before. As the ball struck my strings, welcome kneading sensations worked into my body — it was like a massage, especially for my right arm and the joints in my fingers. The ceiling was not quite high enough to accommodate leaping overheads, but there was no problem hitting serves and high volleys inside the speeding boxcar.

After a while I stopped for a breather. I moved to the wide open door and gazed out as the warm forested air of the Pacific Northwest swooped in with smells of earth and pine. My senses were acute, having just tamed the wall of a jiggling freighter; and as I squatted there admiring the sights, I felt completely in tune with the movement of the boxcar. Clankety-clank, clankety-clankety-clank — those metallic reverberations were more rhythmic than ever. Clanketyclanketyclank, clanketyclanketyclank — it was a mantra throughout my being, a musical presence that pulsed deep into my bones. Clanketyclanketyclank. And though we were sailing several feet above the track bed, I felt attached to the center of the earth, as if all those vibrations were originating way down there. I felt solid and grounded. And yet, another part of me was light and somewhere else in the universe, or perhaps just on another continent. I could have just won Wimbledon. Or at least the French. Such was my balance — light and heavy at the same time, powerful yet delicate. Maybe this is what they mean by being centered, I thought, but then I tried not to think about it for fear I would lose it.

The earthy air rushed in as the great out-of-doors reeled by. "Hey, Stretch!" Todd was sitting on his bale of hay, strumming his tennis racket like an acoustic guitar. He grinned with that slow, introspective nod of his. "You know, it doesn't get any better than this," he hollered from his corner of the shaking boxcar.

"I know what you mean," I shouted back, and I might have actually meant it.

Chapter Five

The Physics Professor

It is an easy thing to inadvertently wear out one's arm on the backboard or even just swinging at air in the living room (which can be deadly to the joints in no time) so I retreated to my corner of the boxcar and put my racket down while I was still a little hungry to hit the ball. Not that it isn't good to tune up, it's just that it's important to save the arm and more important yet to savor a hunger for the hit, to be a little anxious to set foot on the court again. You can be primed physically, but if you aren't there mentally, not eager, you might as well forget it. On the other hand, if you are off form or a little rusty, a sharp mental edge can get you where you need to go.

Most players overlook the importance of hitting on the wall altogether; they see it as a second rate warmup partner to help them get grooved when nobody else is around or no courts are available. And yet, a good tennis player needs a backboard just like a boxer needs a punching bag. Of course, there's no substitute for match play, but as far as training goes, there is no better tool, no more fierce opponent than a wall, provided you know what you're doing. Rhythm and repetition — that's what it's all about.

Of course when I started out on the back wall of my father's little office on University Avenue, I hardly knew what I was doing, but it still did me a lot of good. I had to develop careful aim to keep the ball away from the rear window. Even when I didn't hit it my dad might come out and give a look as if I had. But he always seemed bewildered; so I felt a little sorry for him. Come to think of it, he never did say anything about the big spidery crack I put in one corner of the glass.

With the train still rattling all around me, I imagined I was in Berkeley for a moment, stroking against the back of my favorite Safeway store. A big supermarket like that has enormous sections of hittable wall, so high you can even practice lobs. Sure, your strings get dirty when the ball bounces on the blacktop lot, but that's the tradeoff — a little dirt for a great wall. Besides, it can be fun sometimes to see that dark round spot in the middle of the string bed. Anyway, there's seldom any traffic back there behind those big concrete buildings, except for the occasional semi-truck that pulls in to make a delivery and run over you. Which conveniently, helps keep your footwork sharp.

A workout on the backboard will, however, take a greater toll on one's arm than an oncourt hit of similar duration, even if the backboard is on a speeding freight train. For this reason, I put my racket down somewhat prematurely, savoring the feel and ensuring that I would be hungry to pick it up the next day. But Todd's curiosity got the best of him — he wanted to do some experiments before quitting — he wanted to turn the shaking boxcar into a tennis laboratory.

The first thing he did was to see what it would be like to hit the now worn fuzz nug (which actually made it a bald eagle) into the forward wall of the boxcar, instead of the rear wall. A great discussion of theoretical physics ensued here in which Todd surmised that in that forward direction the ball would leave the racket at the same speed but hit the wall later since the wall was traveling away from the ball at the forward speed of the train; whereas when hitting toward the caboose, the rear wall would be moving toward the ball at the speed of the train, giving the impression that the ball was being hit harder since the interval between racket contact and wall contact would shorten. Contrarily, the in-flight return of the ball after striking the rear wall would appear slower since we were moving with the train, away from the returning ball (although obviously not fast enough since the ball always caught up with us.)

I, for one, was not able to notice any appreciable differences in ball speed as my partner hit forward first and then aft, although my mind appeared to be going sideways just thinking about it. I did notice, however, that Todd had a tendency to get down a whole lot lower while hitting from the rear of the car where the door was open, which seemed understandable enough. Naturally, he denied any such aberration in posture. Furthermore, he was certain he could discern a difference in ball speed when he shifted from one wall to the other. He shouted excitedly through the noise of the train. "Dude, we're traveling at 80 miles per hour, that's got to have some effect. Look. Now watch me hit the ball. Can't you see it gets to the wall quicker this direction but it comes back slower? Look. I'll do it again. Now for the other direction."

"You know what we really need is a radar gun," Todd hollered, "you should have borrowed the one from the club."

Yeah, I thought, I should have brought the radar gun. Right. If I had had that kind of inane insight, I wouldn't have come in the first place.

"Next time bring the radar gun."

Next time? "OK," I said, "next time I'll bring the radar gun, then we can measure everything, like how long it takes to get to Montana."

The rest of our workout was supplemented with good-natured though sometimes crude banter in order to minimize the monotony of the journey as the train crossed the shadowy forest lands of eastern Oregon and headed north. We did a variety of footwork patterns — sideskips, Aussie crossovers, duck walks, and lateral lunges — all within the confines of the jiggling boxcar. It was our intent to arrive at the tournament in better shape than we left in. We also did wind sprints, running toward the caboose, and then backpedaling carefully the other direction. I let Todd have the more air-conditioned side near the open door. Cool-down stretches followed, with a few dozen situps, pushups, and leglifts thrown in.

Then Todd's eyes lit up. "Hey, I got it," he said gleefully, "if we run in place slowly with real high strides, leaping up like gazelles, we should be able to get a treadmill effect from the moving train. When we're in the air, it'll move under us like a conveyor belt and we'll get a great workout."

I watched with intrigue as Todd ran in place doing gazelle leaps. It was pretty funny. "That's excellent training," I said, "you'll be great at leaping over the net. Just in case you lose."

"I'll tell you one thing," Todd said with surprising gravity, "I ain't freightin' it all the way to Montana just to lose. At least not before the semis."

He wiped the sweat from his brow and did a few more gazelle leaps. Then without warning, the little bearded physicist inside his cerebellum decided to take a sabbatical. "Ok, I'm ready to kick butt in Montana," he said, panting.

It was well over ninety degrees that afternoon as we sped through the timberland of southeast Washington and headed toward the Idaho panhandle. When we weren't by the door sucking in the breeze, we kicked back on our little straw couches. We leaned against the jiggling boxcar and let the train send its musical vibrations into our hot, weary bodies. It's a good thing the cans of beer in my partner's tour bag weren't cold, or I may have gone for one. I sipped at the warm water in my travel bottle, remembering that the Germans, who practically invented beer, prefer theirs at room temperature and not gulped from an icy mug, even on a hot day. So I imagined the water in my jug was wine. I had had both, hot wine and hot beer, and hot wine went down a lot better than hot beer, especially on a snowy night when you're lying around in front of a cozy fireplace with a babe who happens to be your mixed partner because at the last second you decided to go to an Aspen ski lodge instead of dealing with the ugliness of mixed doubles (which is not really tennis but primarily a matter of kill the girl and keep the ball away from the guy.)

"I think we're due in Lewiston pretty soon," Todd said, rudely cutting in on my tennis date in Aspen.

The romantic fires in my mind began to smolder, and then sure enough, the long train slowed down. There was the forlorn moan of the horn from up front as we passed a lumber mill on the outskirts of town. Small houses popped up in the weeds, their junk-filled yards protected by broken fences and tethered dogs who yelped and struggled to run after the train. Mowed green lawns and neat looking gardens began to appear, and then the neighborhoods grew more dense.

The sad horn pleaded again, and the freighter continued to slow down. Then came the railroad shacks and scattered freight cars of the Burlington Northern yard in Lewiston.

"This is where we transfer," Todd said as the train came to a gradual, creaking stop.

From high up in the boxcar, we looked out into the vast yard where parallel strings of freight cars were lined up, all with big solemn-looking engines or double engines. "We've got to find the right train," Todd said, and he leaped down to the gravel, landing in somewhat of a squat to absorb the shock.

I handed down our big tour bags, one at a time. Then I turned around and lowered myself down the weathered side of that old Burlington Northern boxcar. My fingers searched out less splintered sections of wood as my dangling feet scrambled for nonexistent toe-holds. Finally, I dropped to the ground.

"Let's boogie," Todd said, and we hoofed it full speed across the yard, from one set of tracks to another, searching in and around the various freight cars for a friendly face. Any face, but hopefully a friendly one like the switchman in Portland. Then we found it, the sooty face of a baby, attached to a small body in a worn-out tweed suit. The little hobo was sitting on the front end of a flatbed car just above the coupling. He was wearing a scruffy beret that matched his frayed suit, and he was traveling light — a brown paper bag was his only luggage. From up on his perch, the little man extended a bland, toothless smile.

Todd called up to him with a gracious reverence normally reserved for the Duchess of Kent. The hobo responded in a pleased manner and explained that the train he was on was going west to Spokane. What we wanted was the Sante Fe engine, three tracks over, going east to Omaha. It was a "hot-shot," which meant it was going straight through, with very few stops. And it usually pulled away at dusk. Except on Sundays. "You can never count on a Sunday," the little hobo said. "This ain't a Sunday, is it? I been settin' here a long while, thought she woulda started up by now. Not that I mind waitin'."

"It's a Tuesday," Todd reassured him, "she'll probably be pulling out any time now."

The little hobo glanced down at our big tour bags. "I see you boys are travelin' all loaded up, what kind of gear you haulin' there?"

Todd held up a couple of rackets. "We're tennis players, we got work to do in Montana with these."

"Well then, you're earnin' your grub, same as me, so you ain't no bums. You boys are tennis hobos, first I ever seen." He tipped his hat to us, exposing for a moment a shiny bald head.

"We're from Berkeley," Todd said. "By the way, thanks for the info, we'll just jump on that hot-shot, three tracks over you say?" The little baby-faced man just sat there in his frayed tweed suit, staring at the car in front of him, his toothless smile growing wide. He was obviously amused by the presence of a couple of greenhorn tennis hobos in the freight yard.

I looked at my watch. If the hobo was right, we had about an hour and a half to roust up some grub. We did have a loaf of sourdough with us, and a can of tuna, but those we were saving for an emergency. And this wasn't an emergency. Yet.

I knew Todd had to be at least as hungry as I was. Now that we were away from the noise of the jiggling train and in the relative quiet of the yard, our stomachs had struck up a conversation with each other. Like two people talking in a restaurant, the discussion was about food. "We better pick our spot on the train before we eat," Todd said, trying to shut them up, but our stomachs kept on sounding off, grumbling and growling like a couple of radios set between channels.

The only open door we found on the hot-shot was eight cars down from the engine, a brown Wasco boxcar with a pallet of two by fours inside. We figured that load of timber would help stabilize the car on the tracks, thus making it safer, unless of course, the train went down a hill and the pallet made a play for us. But that was unlikely since any grades the freighter negotiated tended to be gradual; at least that was my partner's opinion. "Don't sweat the small stuff," he said.

We were tempted to leave our heavy travel bags in the boxcar rather than drag them along on our hunt for a meal, but that would have been just plain stupid, and though our IQ's were dropping quickly, they hadn't quite reached just plain stupid. "Too bad we can't just leave our stuff here, that would be a lot easier," Todd said, giving dementia one last try.

Pleasantly, as we scouted beyond the railroad yard, toting the big bags gave us something to talk about. "Yeah," I told Todd, "it would have been great if we could have just left our stuff on the train."

"Look on the bright side," he said, "it's part of our workout, an extended workout."

"You mean an over-extended workout." I was glad I was carrying my bag and not his; each time I had to pick up Todd's bag I was struck by the fact that it seemed unnaturally heavy (of course, he was hauling those two beers, and his special new socks, and who knows what else.)

At a nearby crossroads, we found a dilapidated place that could have passed for a bait shop had it been anywhere near a river. Instead of worms, it appeared to serve gourmet meals. The sign on the shack said: FINE DINING. It was obviously the perfect place for a hobo wearing a tux, or a couple of tennis pros used to fancy banquets.

The menu had several Freight Yard Specials. "I'll have the Runaway Train Breakfast," Todd told the waitress. She looked confused as she scanned through the specials and the various combos.

"I don't think we have that one," she said nervously.

"I always have a Runaway Train Breakfast when I'm around these parts," Todd said with a frown, looking greatly disappointed.

"I think we do have it," the waitress put in quickly, "it just goes by a different name now, that's all."

"If it's not a Runaway Train Breakfast, it's not a Runaway Train Breakfast," Todd said sternly.

"I'll have the Engineer's Special," I said, not just to put the waitress out of her misery, but because I was damn hungry and I wasn't about to let Todd's shenanigans get in the way of my hotcakes.

"Ok, give me an Engineer's too," Todd said sadly.

"I'm sure the cook will be happy to make you a Runaway Train, if you really ..."

"NO," I cut in, "my partner was just kidding, he really prefers the Engineer's Special, that's his favorite. We'll have two. Please."

The lady finished pouring our coffee and left us to our rumbling stomachs. "Did you hear that?" Todd exclaimed after a particularly resonant plea from his abdomen, "sounded kind of like Chinese. I didn't even know I could speak Chinese. Just goes to show how smart you can be if you get hungry enough."

We talked about the merits of playing matches on an empty stomach, about going out there hungry, and a little angry like Pancho Gonzales used to. In the final analysis, as our food arrived, we decided that the empty stomach is good for struggle in general but that it's better to link it to a Zen approach, thereby deleting the anger — unless of course, one's life is in danger, in which case a sudden burst of rage might be just the stuff to turn things around.

Chapter Six

The Spaulding Toilet

Pleasantly satiated, we were soon awaiting the sounds of the engine from up front as we explored the nooks and crannies of our new ride, the brown Wasco with the pallet of two by fours at one end. The wood gave the place a gratifying sawmill odor.

We would be riding through the night, and that caused some uneasiness. I did have a small plastic tablecloth with me, which I used for doing exercises on the tennis court; I figured thin as it was, at least it was clean and something I was used to stretching out on. It would be my bed for the night, along with some clothes I could put under my hips and head for padding. But what about Todd? I pictured him sleeping on the dirty floorboards and I felt bad. If only I had brought two tablecloths. But check this out.

Todd reached into his tour bag and pulled out some nails and a hammer (a hammer, for crissake!) He began hammering a thick metal bracket onto the wood siding inside the boxcar as I sat dumfounded on my tablecloth. Then he attached a similar bracket to the other side of the car; and this is the clincher.

He put the hammer back in his bag, and this time he extracted a hammock (a goddamn hammock!) An old backyard hammock his grandfather had given him just for the trip, he explained, as he looped its cords around one of the brackets. In a moment he had the other end tied, and the big hammock was swaying freely across the chasm of the boxcar. "There!" He stood back with his hands on his hips and admired his bed.

A goddamn hammock, for crissake! suspended right in front of my head as I sat on my tablecloth staring in disbelief. My butt was already sore from the hardass floor.

Todd lay down on the hammock and stretched out his arms in the dusky light. He yawned sensuously. "Wake me up before noon, if you don't mind," he said, "I hate to oversleep and miss the sights." Then he shut his eyes and began snoring in slow, wheezy breaths.

"I'm going to nominate you for hobo of the year," I said from down below on the floor, still somewhat dazed.

"Wups," Todd got up suddenly, "I almost forgot." He was at the door of the boxcar now with his trusty hammer. He shut the big door and darkness closed in on us. "Dude, bring your Mag light over here, will you."

I held the beam of the little flashlight steady while my partner tapped an eight penny nail into the floor beneath the bottom of the door, thus fixing it in place slightly ajar and insuring that it wouldn't lock shut on us during the night (and also that no creature larger than a mouse would join us for midnight cocktails.)

On our separate "bunks" in the boxcar, we lay listening to the warm night, to the crickets and the mechanical sounds that gradually began to grind away at the silence of the freight yard. Then came hissings and rumblings from up front as the big double engines began to warm up.

There was a jolt, then the creak of cars stretching out. The boxcar jiggled as it moved slowly along the track. Clanketyclank. Clanketyclank. The sounds seemed amplified in the darkness. CLANKETYCLANK, CLANKETYCLANKETYCLANK.

I could barely make out that something was suspended across the car. "Hey, Hammer," I called out to the obscure shape. "That's what I'm going to call you from now on. Hammer."

"Hammer?" the shape replied sleepily. "Hammer? You really think so?"

"Yeah, man. It's either that or Hammock. Hammer's better, don't you think? I'd call you Nails, but there's an Aussie named Nails, so you've got to be Hammer. You don't mind, do you?"

"Whatever you think, Stretch,"

"Or, you could be THE Hammer. Would you like that better? What do you like better, Hammer, or THE Hammer?"

"Whatever you think, Stretch."

In the eerie darkness the rattling train picked up speed and played on my back like a snare drum. Clanketyclank, clanketyclank, clanketyclanketyclank. Soon I was rattled to sleep, a restless dream-spotted sleep where I was riding a different train, the midnight freighter that passed by my little Berkeley pad in the middle of the night; I felt I was in bed on 2nd Street and looking out from the boxcar at the same time. Then I had visions of Evonne in the hole at the old club, umpiring Hitch's match; but she was wearing a wedding dress and I was in the crowd, actually hovering over it on a buoyant king-sized bed. The spectators were all staring up at me. "I'm not a tennis gigolo," I shouted down at them, "I'm a tennis hobo." Next thing I knew I was being shaken. It was my partner, Todd. "Stretch, Dude. It's two in the morning, your turn for the hammock, Dude."

I vaguely remember waving him off, groaning at him. Then his voice again, this time fading. "OK, dude, if you're sleeping alright. OK then."

The train rattled into the darkness, through the Idaho panhandle and into west Montana, where a crescent moon illuminated vague suggestions of boulders and shrubs for any wild critter that may have been wandering through the timbered brush of the Bitterroot Mountains. Then in the morning, the sun came up over the Rockies and slipped through the narrow opening of the boxcar door, painting a wedge of light on the splintery floor. I had been lying on the lower bunk, as it were, awake but in a trance-like state from the various mesmerizing vibrations that had had their way with me all night. My partner, Todd, or rather, Hammer, lay sleeping in princely suspension with a smile on his face. He was probably dreaming he was king of the hobos.

Suddenly I got a tremendous urge to pee. I sat up stiffly to size up the situation. I wondered if I could shoot it clean through the narrow crack in the door; but there was a wind rushing by at 80 miles an hour out there, and that would have severe consequences even for a straight shot. Then in a move perhaps known to hundreds of tennis players spending the night in frigid mountain tents, automobiles, or other limited quarters, I reached into my tour bag and pulled out an empty can of Spaulding tennis balls I had actually brought along for just such an occasion. (I never did like Spauldings, anyway.)

Balancing precariously on feeble morning legs in the jiggling train, I held the clear plastic container as steady as possible. I could feel the warmth of the golden liquid as it worked its way up to about halfway across the word Spaulding. Like I said, I never did like Spauldings. They're too light and bouncy, and they actually seem a little smaller, traits which, come to think of it, I in fact love in a tennis ball. It's just that nobody uses Spauldings, especially not in tournaments, so none of us hit with them, and when we do they just go flying out. The only reason I had the balls in the first place was that a student gave them to me during a ball donation drive.

It was a tall 4-ball can, well suited to the job at hand, with room enough for two midnight specials, if required, and complete with attachable lid. Though I suppose it wasn't a "can" of tennis balls at all, as none of them are today, since cans are metal — everybody knows that. These things are made of clear plastic and they don't have the old-style sardine key attached to the bottom. Actually, they are "jars," and not cans, something I haven't quite gotten used to.

I'm just not used to opening up a jar of tennis balls, especially not for lunch, and though some people insist on calling them "tubes," they are more like jars than tubes. So, in trying to keep up with the latest tennis technology, my partner and I are weaning ourselves off the cans and into the jars. We find that, with spoon in hand, opening up a jar of tennis balls on the court is a good way to get rid of pre-match jitters. Plus, it gives you some round things to hit. After a while, though, I suppose the ritual will lose some of its charm.

The fuzz nugs we prefer come in jars that say Penn on them, or Wilson, and that's it; there is no other information on the jar suggesting that the nugs are longer lasting or good for practice or bigger, or any other such thing that will make them heavier and harder on the elbow. We just want them regular, good old regular Penns. Or Wilsons. That come in a jar. (You should have seen the old guy in the tennis shop, the sad look in his eyes when Todd asked him for a jar of tennis balls. "Never mind," Todd said, "we're not that hungry, anyway.")

Back on the freighter, the sun had just come up, allowing a beam of light through the crack in the boxcar door. I secured the round plastic lid above the odorous yellow elixir and put the half-filled Spaulding jar in the corner of the shaking car behind the pallet of two by fours, where it jiggled and sloshed with no apparent ill effects.

It is always best to store such rancid nectar in an upright position. Laying it on its side is not generally recommended because the plastic lid is only more or less leakproof, and this is a case of more being more and less actually being less (more or less all of the time.) Furthermore, when on its side, the jar has a tendency to roll. Consequently, it is advisable to keep the lethal concoction in vertical storage, and strap on the lid with duct tape, which I, unfortunately, did not have on the freight train.

My partner, Hammer, king of the hobos, was beginning to stir from his well-cushioned slumber on the luxurious hammock. With a yawn, he stretched out his limbs like a waking dog that has no special place to be. Then he sat up on the edge of his bunk. His arms connected overhead in the last sensual phase of a morning ritual.

"Dude," he called out through the noise of the moving train, "what time is it?" Then without waiting for an answer, he jumped up and announced, "Let's get this show on the road."

With his trusty hammer, Todd knelt at the crack of light on the floor and yanked out the nail from beneath the door. He opened the door wide, sliding it all the way across to the other side as if he were about to walk out into a courtyard. "A man's got to breathe," he exclaimed, and the fresh air rushed in like a cyclone. Outside, tall evergreens had given way to oak and sycamore as the mountainous terrain merged with the high plains east of the Continental Divide.

Now in broad daylight, the hammock looked natural in its surroundings, as if it had always been meant to be strung out across a boxcar. The thick ropy cords on either end vibrated with the jiggling train as the heavy canvas flapped noisily in the breeze. And I suppose we looked like we belonged there too, as we sat in jeans and T-shirts in front of the wide open door, watching the backyard of America go by.

"Dude," my partner just laughed when I offered him the half-filled Spaulding jar. "Stretch, dude, we're in the great out-of-doors, there's no need to be so delicate, we're not at a tennis club, you know." With that he put his back to the wind and leaned out the door. Holding onto the jiggling train with one hand, he guided his outflow with the other. I wondered what his chances were of falling off, and what my chances were of finding another doubles partner. I figured I could continue on to the tournament and hook up with Todd on the way home. He wouldn't be that hard to locate. I'd just gaze out to the horizon where buzzards would be circling in the sky, high above the desolate terrain like in a Western movie.

Hammer swung himself back into the boxcar just then, his long sunbleached hair completely disheveled from the noisy eighty mile an hour wind. "Gee, I hope there's nobody in the caboose," he shouted, "that's a mighty powerful breeze to be downstream from."

As the train took its course, speeding over miles upon miles of untamed countryside, fine particles of dust were stirred up from the track bed, and though black as soot, the stuff remained for the most part invisible until I noticed that Todd's face was three shades more tan than usual. I looked down at the film of grime across my forearms and the backs of my hands, and I wondered what *my* face looked like. "Hammer!" I practically yelled, "tell me, am I ... darker than usual? Do I look any different?"

"I don't know, I never really looked at you before."

"No, come on, really, I want to know, do I look any different?"

"Stretch, dude, let's put it this way, you're just as ugly as ever."

"No, come on, I mean really."

"Well, OK then, you're uglier than usual."

"Really?" I winced, and I could feel the stiffness on my cheeks.

"Come to think of it," Todd said, studying my face, "you're a lot uglier than usual. Or maybe I just never realized how ugly you were. I don't know. I'll tell you what, though, first thing when we hop off we'll find a mirror somewhere and you can figure it out for yourself while I'm washing up." Then he added, "I think I'll have me a jacuzzi, a nice long jacuzzi."

"Right on, bro," I said, "I think I'll have me a real good soak, too."

The pale rolling hills of the Montana wheat country had been sweeping by in pleasant monotony. Suddenly, the freighter let loose with its forlorn moan from up front. An industrial area on the outskirts of Billings came into view, and now the long train began to slow down as we rolled in past concrete loading docks and old brick warehouses where countless acres of grain were stored. Then came newer buildings, all metal structures where agricultural machinery was made beneath sprawling dome roofs. Fleets of big diesel semi-trucks lined vast expanses of blacktop.

The freighter continued to put on its brakes. Billings was to be our final stop. From here we would go by car to Charley Finger's tournament, about an hour and a half away.

Todd had begun to detach his hammock from the walls of the boxcar. In less than two minutes he had the whole thing rolled up inside his tour bag, alongside rackets, sweats, spare shoes, those two cans of beer, one hammer, and of course, his special new sock uppers. I was packed before he was, but then all I had to do was fold up my tablecloth bed and empty the Spaulding toilet.

I de-trained awkwardly again and caught up to Todd, who having leapt down, was hiking across the gravel of the yard in the direction of what appeared to be central Billings. Despite my heavy tour bag, it felt good to be on solid ground again. But without the boisterous rattlings of the train, the world seemed eerie, not so much because of the extreme quiet, but because of those very sounds — clanketyclanketyclank, clanketyclanketyclank. That rhythmical presence still filled my psyche. I guess two days and one night of railroad clatter doesn't flit away easily. As a matter of fact, it never disappears entirely, surfacing sometimes in my sleep; and then that midnight freighter rolls in from the flatlands and the two trains rattle and clank together as one endless freighter that rumbles on between my ears. But just as often those old boxcar sounds haunt me in broad daylight, beckoning faintly from afar like the call of the wild.

Chapter Seven

Pros And Ams

We got our bearings in Billings — we were at the rail yard, which was at Montana Avenue and 27th Street. The airport was up on the Rimrocks, a visible butte about a mile away. That was to be the rendezvous point for players who had just jetted in to Billings (like us) and needed a ride to the tournament. Charley Finger himself was going to be there with a car. We were to meet at the Hertz car rental at four o'clock, which meant we had plenty of time and didn't need to run, something Todd had actually suggested as a training exercise. But the idea that we should save our strength for an oncourt workout appealed to him too. Thank god. I was glad to find, now that we were nearing the battleground, that Todd was beginning to rely on more than just his impulse for excitement. But there was also a part of me that admired his free-spirited prematch disposition, for I knew it was a major part of his performance mentality — his go-for-it — his ability to act without hesitation, no second thoughts, to hit the big shots when needed, and to watch them fall without admiring them — to simply move on to the next shot, and then the next. Whereas I held back and was more calculating, and though I could play near flawless tennis, I couldn't do the damage Todd could. In singles he was capable of bigger wins, but in doubles we balanced each other and were a crack team, able to hang with the best of them. We beat a duo ranked seventeen in the world once.

The tournament drew nearer in our minds as we hiked through the quaint hubbub of old-town Billings. There was an instinctive bounce to our gait, the stride of confidence and anonymity that comes when two tennis hobos are on the road (headed to a tournament they might just as well have already won.) At first opportunity, the four of us — me, Hammer, and our two studly tour bags — swaggered into a convenience store, conveniently giving two hick employees something to gawk at as they handed us the key to the restroom. You'd think they'd never seen a couple of professional tennis players with soot blackened faces before.

We ducked into the bathroom and transferred the grime from our flesh into the perfectly white sink. Finally, after several rinses, the dark

streaks ran off the porcelain and down the drain. Then we filled up our
water bottles. On the way out the two guys gawked at us. "Maybe they
think we're funny," I confessed to Todd as we strolled out the store and
onto the sidewalk. "I mean, we did go in the bathroom together and
lock the door."

"Hell, women go in together all the time," he said, "just like we did,
to go weewee and fix their makeup."

"That's what I mean, they probably think we're funny."

"Well, how many chicks you seen with purses like this?" He gave his
big black Wilson bag a mid-stride lift.

"So, maybe they think we're funny women."

"Funny women. Or funny men. What's the difference what they
think?"

"That's it, they probably can't figure it out, they only know that we're
funny."

"Well, we are funny. Aren't we?"

"Not in California, we're not that funny. At least, I hope not."

"Stretch, dude, you're funny all the time, I just don't tell you. But as
far as I'm concerned those two were the odd ones, staring at us with their
bug eyes and their jaws hanging open. The girl was really weird. She
should have done something about all that fuzz on her cheeks."

"Was one of them a girl?" I asked, surprised. Maybe one of them
was a girl, I hadn't looked all that carefully. I just felt four bulging eyes
from across the counter.

"A girl, are you kidding? I thought you were going to make a play for
her, the skinny one with the missing tooth."

"Oh, that one." I recalled now the missing tooth. It might have been
a girl at that, an odd looking girl; or maybe it was just Todd the prankster,
trying to keep us loose as we macked up 27th Street. I played along. "Well
yeah, I would have gone for her alright, but you know the motto, no sex
before a tournament."

"That's old school and you know it," he countered. "The idea is not to
have marathon sex the night before. A little action can actually do some
good, get rid of anxieties."

"Or it might create anxieties if something goes wrong."

"Dude, what could go wrong? Just get it on and don't try to set any
records, that's all. A little sex won't hurt tennis performance, just don't
try to do it during changeovers. Unless the match is almost over, and
you've got a medical emergency which is really a prearranged date waiting

for you in the locker room. Remember when Blake Taylor came back to the court after that medical time-out when he was down in the third at El Paso? He came back all loose and sleepy looking, and he served and half-volleyed Brinkmeyer off the court like he was in a trance."

"Who could forget that, but I always thought it was pot or something that smoothed him out."

"No, man, Taylor faked a puke just for the umpire, and he had the chick waiting in the locker room and his partner guarding the door. Some stewardess he met the day before. She had a flight out so it was their only chance. He figured, why not. And it paid off. Not that it was supposed to be a crutch or anything to help him win. He had actually planned to beat Brinkmeyer in straights so he wouldn't have to rush back to the court in the middle of everything. That's just the way it turned out, one of the great experiments in loosey goosey tennis."

Such was our conversation as we strolled toward the table-like butte of the Rimrocks, which stood a short distance from town. Now that we were closer, I could see that its flat elevated surface had to be a great spot for an airport — the runway probably just shot right off the edge of the plateau, I figured. There had to be some advantage there, at least for taking off.

But as the incline before us grew steeper, it became obvious that getting up there wasn't going to be just a walk in the park. "Hey, man," Todd sighed, "I've got to stretch it out."

So we put our heavy bags down on the sidewalk and dillydallied around at the far edge of town. In no rush to go up the hill, we wiggled in and out of various exercise poses as the traffic went by, much in the carefree manner of two unabashed four-year-olds in the supermarket. Todd even stood on his head. At last we had no choice but to climb the Rimrocks.

Twenty minutes later and breathing deeply, we strode into the airport. "Look, over there, isn't that Fernando Vasquez?" I pointed to a pair of long legs in striped adidas sweats that were extended across a couple of chairs in the lobby near the Hertz car rental. The semi-reclined fellow was reading a newspaper, so it was impossible to tell who it was for sure, but it was definitely a tennis player; on the floor alongside his long legs were two travel bags, one with several racket handles sticking out. Then as we walked by I got a good glimpse. "It's Fernando, alright," I whispered. "I thought you said the big guns weren't playing this podunk tournament."

"I said they weren't playing doubles; and it's only Fernando and Brown, anyway. Just them and a couple of hot-shot college players."

Originally from Guatemala, but trained in Brazil, the debonair Fernando Vasquez had won the NCAA singles title ten years ago, but he never spent much time on the official circuit; he just went back to the good life in Guatemala, where he helped keep track of his family's business holdings. That is, until his father and older brother got disappeared. Now he was hanging out in the States, mostly in the South, where he had become as adept with a pool cue as he was with his tennis racket. Todd and I hadn't seen him since he won Colorado Springs, three years ago. He was obviously waiting for Charley Finger's car, too.

"Let's go see what Fernando's been up to," Todd said, "I haven't seen that sly dog in ages."

The tall, handsome Fernando wore his hair in a ponytail tucked under the collar of his warmup jacket. He told us he had a new business importing tennis equipment to Mexico with the help of his wife's uncle, a Mexican national who had an apartment on the Texas side of the Rio Grande. Fernando specialized in getting expensive rackets and warmups at good prices in the States, and the uncle specialized in bribing Mexican officials so the merchandise wouldn't get hung-up in customs. That aside, it was the same old Fernando. He and his wife were living in Baton Rouge, where he hung out mostly at the pool halls, but only because tennis players weren't a betting sort by nature and the independent tournaments with good prize money were getting more scarce all the time.

"You boys are waiting for Senor Charley Finger?" Fernando's Spanish accent added a touch of grace to an already suave demeanor. "He is late, no?"

I looked at my watch, the guy was forty-five minutes overdue. I viewed the fact that there were only three of us tennis players there in the lobby as both good news and bad news. I knew most of the other players wouldn't be arriving until tomorrow since that was the day before the tournament, but still, I had expected more guys to slide in by now.

Arriving two days early had its advantages, since it isn't always easy to get a good night's sleep in a strange room the night before a tournament. Todd and I preferred to arrive an extra night early, especially if the pad was paid for; that way we could have a practice run at trying to get a good night's sleep. Apparently Fernando was of the same school of thought. Of course, maybe the other players didn't get such good hospitality deals.

I turned to my partner. "Hammer, what do you think?"

"Charley Finger should have showed up by now. He's supposed to come again in the morning, but the hell with that, I don't like the idea of being stranded here for the night."

So Hammer went off to call the tournament director. In a few minutes he came back and announced that Charley Finger had telephoned earlier but the car rental clerk told him no tennis players had arrived. Now we were supposed to rent a car and the tournament would reimburse us. It would be an hour and a half drive.

"Do you know this Charley Finger?" Fernando asked Todd.

"I just met him a month ago, in Sarasota. He gave me his card, said he had an independent with good money, that he was only telling a few players, players whose games he liked, guys who could put on a good show. He said it was really more of an exhibition. We figure to at least break even. Why? What kind of a deal did he give you?"

"Not much." Fernando replied quietly, "just hospitality and one-way airplane. I have to win big to buy my wife new dining room table I promised her. If I don't make semis I hustle my stick in the bars, just so I can fly home."

"Charley Finger sent you a plane ticket?" Fernando nodded.

"Well then he can't be all bad."

"We will see," said the tall, soft-spoken Latin, and the three of us went up to the desk to arrange for a car rental.

The guy in charge was sitting behind the counter watching a small television set. He was in his early twenties and obviously too self-absorbed to be bothered with things like tennis players. He probably thought we were all at least partially gay, and he pretended not to notice our approach.

"I understand there was a call for us about an hour ago," Todd told the guy.

"Oh, you're the tennis players." The kid responded without getting up from his chair. "I thought you were rodeo men, some of them have big bags just like those." He leaned back with a smug expression. "But they don't have such long hair. I guess I shoulda known you weren't no rodeo men."

Todd smiled but there was a touch of disgust at the corners of his mouth; he knew the kid had shafted us. "I'm glad you mentioned that," he told the guy, "because we were just thinking we might use your head for a tennis ball, to see how long it will last, kind of like in a rodeo when the guy tries to stay on the bronco, if you know what I mean."

"What? Oh no, that's OK," the kid said, jumping up from his chair. "I guess I shoulda known you weren't rodeo boys, they're always spittin' tobacco juice on the sidewalk, and you fellas didn't spit none at all, as far as I can see. I shoulda known. I shoulda told you about the phone call. Sorry." We all just kept staring at him. Todd was a head taller than he was, and Fernando was taller yet.

"I tell ya what I'm gonna do," the kid said nervously, "I'm gonna give you our best car. And I won't charge you no extra for it. Matter of fact I'm gonna give it to you at thirty percent off. It's the only one with a radio that works when you get out of town. And the air-conditioning works good, if you need it."

The car was small, but we squeezed into it as best we could. Todd did the driving, and Fernando rode shotgun so he could stretch out his long legs, although he was perfectly willing to sit in the back where I ended up sideways with my legs across the seat and my warmup jacket bundled like a pillow between my head and the side window. The trunk was jammed to the max with all our gear.

An hour and a half later, when the rouge cheek of the falling sun was at the western horizon, we pulled into Rock Creek, Montana, a hick hamlet on the Big Horn River. There was a combination gas station/bait shop on one side of the street and a post office/grocery store on the other. The only other thing going on was Charley Finger's dude ranch, which was also a restaurant and bar, something that provided minimal but regular income for him when the dude ranch was between gigs, which was most of the time, the action being pretty much limited to a tennis event in the summer and a fishing derby in the fall.

Lured by color brochures and local legend, trout aficionados from all over the country arrived for a week every September to try their luck at landing a prized rainbow trout tagged with a $25,000 marker. While some less redeemable fish have been hooked over the years, that big swimming pot of gold has never been caught, although sightings have been occasionally reported. Then every once in a while after the derby is over, one of Charley Finger's bar flies will show up at the bait shop with the $25,000 trout dangling from a stringer, thus proving that the fish is, indeed, catchable, and that Charley Finger is running a legitimate contest. Naturally, a press release goes out making the bar fly into a local hero and fueling interest in the derby for the next few years.

And then there's the tennis tournament, which despite being limited to four blacktop courts, has become surprisingly popular. Not that anybody ever comes to Rock Creek to see it, but Charley Finger has no problem recruiting players. There's a singles draw that features guys like me, Fernando, and Hammer in a sixteen-man tournament; but more importantly, there's a Pro/Am doubles which pairs the likes of us with hackers from all over the country who pay big money to come to the dude ranch to doublefault in front of us in the daytime and sip beers alongside of us in the evenings. Todd and I refer to these guys as "ams," as in pro/am.

The am is a special breed of hacker, usually loaded and plagued with a unique form of tennis elbow that needs to rub up against the elbow of a top player in order to be cured. Typically though, the remedy is only temporary, and the am will need another fix after a while like some guys need a shot of cortisone. So they sign up again the next year at Charley Finger's or wherever else their money will get them in.

And yet, there's prize money for the ams too, both in the pro/am and in a separate round robin event just for them — a "hacker special." So a portion of the purse is set aside for the ams, and occasionally one of them makes out big, in which case a press release goes out making the hack into a hero when he gets home (despite the fact that he spent twice as much money playing the tournament as he won.)

And so, Charley Finger survives each year with the help of his largely invisible $25,000 trout and his stable of tennis studs who never made it to the big time but who loom like top tenners in dude ranch promotional literature, a trick that comes easy for Charley Finger, the former New York advertising man of the year whose doctors told him to chill out. Or die. So he changed his name from Charles Heffinger III to Charley Finger, and he came to Montana. Originally it was his idea to set up a Sportsmen's Church, but he settled on a nonprofit dude ranch that would supplement its income by soliciting for donations in various religious publications under the name of "American Spiritual Athletes Foundation." That name appeared now across the door to his office, in back of the bar.

He was training a new bartender when we arrived, a formidable female with a low-cut blouse, who would pour drinks in the upcoming week and free him for the various complex duties of a one-man tournament director. Charley was tall and slim; he was wearing a yellow buckskin jacket with fringed leather when he saw us.

"Boys, boys, good to see you, glad you made it. Ah, Fernando, how's my number one seed?"

Todd introduced me to Charley Finger and we all shook his hand; he apologized for not being able to pick us up at the airport. We spoke for a few minutes, carefully saving the subject of rental car reimbursement for later. Then Charley Finger gave us copies of the draw and keys to a couple of bungalows behind the courts. He shooed us away with the reminder that the restaurant would be open until ten if we were hungry. "Come back and have a drink," he called out, "Marcie, here, will fix you up."

We could see the courts had no lights, so Hammer and I changed as fast as we could; then we went out to hit a few in the failing dusk. Fernando was already out there practicing his serve. Judging from the way the ball bounded high into the back fence, the tall Latin's delivery was working well on the swift blacktop.

We took a court one over and tried to get a feel for the surface by hitting halfvolleys to each other from midcourt. The court was marred with cracks not bad enough to trip on but which would occasionally throw the ball off course. And yet, we worked our way back, slowly, hitting deeper stronger groundstrokes, until at last we were pounding the ball from behind the baseline. But the light was getting bad and we began to frame shots, so we eased up and hit high arching moonballs that our eyes could follow in darkness that was illuminated only by a string of bungalow porch lights. Volleys would be out of the question, so we practiced our serves as best we could, firing from the same side of the court so as not to hit each other. Then it got too black and we began to frame serves. But alas, we still had another day to get used to the courts.

Sparse as it was, our new pad was like a royal suite compared to the Wasco boxcar we had the night before (although the view through the open door of the boxcar was a lot better.) In one corner of the room was an old armchair. There were two sagging twin beds separated by an end table, and along the opposite wall was a low dresser with a mirror above it. A closet and a small bathroom completed the room. The general appearance was like that of a low-grade motel room, except there was no TV or phone, and the top drawer of the dresser didn't have a Bible in it. I sat down on one of the sagging little beds and looked out the window to where the tennis courts stood ghostlike in the darkness.

Without even glancing at it, we put our copy of the draw in the drawer where the Bible should have been. There was no need to get all riled up about it and lose sleep, when we could have it in the morning with breakfast and just get indigestion; although even that was unlikely for veteran tournament players like ourselves (unless Charley Finger had done something ridiculous, like put us up against each other in the first round with the winner to play Fernando in the next.)

We cleaned up, savoring long hot showers, and it felt damn good, even though it wasn't the hot tub we had hoped for. Hammer slipped on a new pair of tennis shoes he was trying to break in; he put his match pair on the porch of the bungalow to get some air, as I did. (We had strict rules about where sneakers could bed down.) Then we went outside below the overhang of the bungalow, where above us, a mass of insects swirled around a bare light bulb. The licorice scent of wild anise rose in the tepid air. The crickets were pulsing in full blast; through their ringing we could hear the gurgling flow of the Rock Creek branch of the Big Horn River. And now, the black sky was suddenly sparkling with stars. Not a bad place to be, I thought.

We headed into the restaurant, which was also the bar and varied in name according to what you wanted to feed more, your stomach or your brain; or maybe it was a matter of what you wanted to kill more, a decision that became real for us at a tournament in Mexico one year. (We won the doubles despite being looped a good deal of the time.)

Nestled in pines, the restaurant in Montana was a wide log building. Broad wooden stairs spanned the entire front side and led up to an equally wide porch. Once inside, the place was cabin-like and spacious. Its high open ceiling was supported by massive timbers, many of them adorned with antlers, snake skins, flintlock rifles, and bamboo fly rods. Trout the size of small tuna fish were mounted on the walls, along with antiquated farm implements and old wooden tennis rackets. A few of the rackets were real antiques with cumbersome bare wooden handles, but for the most part they were just classics like Dunlop Maxplys and Wilson Kramers. The centerpiece on the wall behind the bar was a stuffed moose head, on either side of which were huge oversized posters of John Newcombe and Rod Laver. Just below Newk and The Rocket, presiding in a row over countless bottles of booze, were real *cans* of tennis balls — white Wilson Championships ("blue-dots") in yellow and red metal cans with the sardine keys still attached to the bottoms. Alongside the cash register, and of equal height, was a long-limbed photograph of Margaret Court with a signature across one of her legs.

This airy room would be the players' lounge for the week. Its rustic ambiance offered all the comforts of home: television set, juke box, pay telephone, quarter-slot pool table, and plenty of round cocktail tables. At the bar, two of the tall stools had saddles on them.

A stone fireplace was set deep into the back wall with a worn leather couch facing its big charcoal-stained rocks. On the other side of the room against the windows, several restaurant-style booths looked out to the front deck, where a scattering of chairs sat above the feature tennis court. This seating combined with the bleacher effect of the wide stairs to create a stadium for the court. This was Charley Finger's court in the hole, and though it wasn't much of a hole, all things considered, it was fitting.

At that relatively late hour, Todd and I were the only ones in the restaurant, except for Marcie and the fat guy from the bait shop who was shaking dice with her at the bar. After pouring him another drink, she came over to our booth and handed us each a menu. Then she bent over the table and gave it an unnecessary but very thorough scrubbing, which might have been her habit when wearing such a revealing blouse. She stepped back from the table and the jiggling parts of her flesh came to rest. "Well, what'll it be?" she asked.

"Jello," Todd announced brightly. "I'm in the mood for jello, if you know what I mean. Any kind, so long as it wobbles and knows how to walk." He tapped at my foot with his. "And my partner wants some jello too, don't ya Stretch?"

Marcie blushed, and I could feel my cheeks heating up too. She was more modest than I had figured.

"Now come on, boys, seriously, what'll it be?"

Todd laughed. "Well, OK. What kind of vegetarian dishes do you have?"

"We don't have any vegetarian dishes on the menu," Marcie answered, standing up very straight, pencil in hand.

"I didn't figure there'd be any on the menu, that's why I asked you, kind of special like, thought maybe we could work something out with the cook, if you know what I mean."

Marcie giggled. "He don't speak no English, I just tell him what number and he makes it, that's all." I knew Todd wasn't a pure vegetarian by a long shot and that he was just having his fun with the tempting waitress. But he cut it short; he must have been hungry. "OK," he winked, "come back in a minute and we'll give you some numbers."

"Okiedokie." Marcie went back to the bar without even suggesting that we might have a drink in the meantime. I thought that was rather thoughtful of her; she probably assumed we were in training. But then again it could have been lack of thoughtfulness. I wasn't sure. Maybe she just wanted to get back to the bait shop guy, to shake some more dice. I wondered if she was looking forward to having the place crawling with pros and ams tomorrow. I wondered if she would be able to tell the difference; probably not on the court, I figured, but in the bar the size of their wallets would give her a clue as to which was which.

Chapter Eight

A Jar Of Penns

Although the clubhouse was ablaze with activity, the big stone fireplace was silent as we stretched on the floor of the hearth. We were waiting to be called out for our singles matches

"You didn't tell me we had to play with ams!" I complained good-naturedly to my partner. It was true, not wanting to dampen my enthusiasm, Todd had avoided telling me some details of the Rock Creek tournament. At least we don't have to hang out twiddling our thumbs in teaching clinics, I thought. But I wanted to be sure. "What else didn't you tell me?" I asked.

"Nothing, but we do have to play with ams. Twice. It's part of the hospitality deal."

"Twice! What do you mean, twice?"

"There's a constipation round, so if you tank up front you're still in and you have to play again, but then they switch partners for that part. Anyway, you can tank again and you'll be done. Or you can try for the money. There's a little dough for winning, not much for us, but the hack gets a pretty good chunk, even in the constipation round."

I made a face. "Two separate hackers?"

"If you want just one am, don't lose in the first round. If you bother winning the whole thing, you get about a hundred bucks, I think."

It wasn't that either of us was opposed to social tennis and didn't sometimes enjoy playing with those of less fortunate skill levels; but we had traveled a long way (the hard way) to earn some money, and the toll the extra court time would put on our bodies could be crucial. At thirty-seven, I was among the oldest of the sixteen pros entered at Rock Creek, and Hammer was no spring chicken. Yet by golly, there were a few spring chickens strutting around the place, extremely fit college players, who hopefully, still had a few things to learn.

The steady murmur of conversation filled the room. In his buckskin outfit, tournament director Charley Finger sat at one end of the bar, busily organizing things and fending off the worries of anxious hacks who huddled around him. Most of the better players were just relaxing or playing cards. There was the occasional sound of the cue ball breaking the rack, a noise that cracked like a pistol shot in the big log room.

"Just relax, Stretch, it's not as bad as you think," Todd explained calmly through all the hubbub. "The pro/hack's not regular matches, they're just pro sets, so it's not so bad. You play a couple of pro sets, that's all. Or, you can go all the way and win four pro sets for a hundred bucks."

I didn't mind the idea of an extra hundred, but I had come to Montana to win the main event doubles, which was worth about a grand for my share. Plus, I was entered in the singles and had a fair shot at going a round, which was worth three hundred bucks. Worrying about that extra hundred in the pro/am was out of the question. I would definitely tank, thus contaminating my game for the start of the tournament only and none for the last two days when I expected to be focusing very keenly on serious doubles play. Of course, it was likely the pro on the other side of the net would be tanking too, especially in the second match, in which case it would be a matter of who was tanking better; and that was an art in itself, particularly when partnered with a raving gung-ho hack who called all the close ones out and scrambled around the court like his shorts were on fire.

I had no illusions about getting past the quarters in singles, but you never knew, and it was worth about six hundred dollars (nothing for a train hopping pro to scoff at.) In addition to a mental letdown, the pro/am wasn't worth its risk to endurance, feel, or injury. It kicked off at four o'clock that afternoon, and I planned to bail out as early as possible, which meant that if I sensed my partner was easy to lose with I might dig in a little and actually try to win the first round just so I could keep him for the second more crucial match the next day, which I absolutely did not want to win. On the other hand, if I got paired up with a real competitive brute, I'd play the other pro a little too much and let him finish us off. If that didn't work I'd feed easy balls to the am and let him do the job; and if neither of those losing strategies worked, I'd just miss a few too many shots.

I avoided discussing these strategic ploys with Hammer as we waited for the battle front because I didn't want to hear him tell me not to sweat the small stuff. There was no telling what he would do in the pro/hack. He would probably play it by ear and just go with his flow, even if it meant winning and playing extra rounds; but then going with his flow was a big part of Todd's game — he tended to just follow his instincts. Whereas, like I said, I'm more calculating and plan ahead more, which invariably means I have to sweat the small stuff sometimes. I pick and choose my moments to Zen out. But, Hammer, he's already there.

It was almost noon. A court opened up and Charley Finger summoned me for my match. I felt the adrenaline pumping as I walked out to the court; I tried to ignore the temporary clumsiness those juices inflicted on my body, on my very gait. I imagined it as some sort of bionic medicine in my veins that would make me stronger, faster, more alert; even though at present there was only a jittery sensation. By my side was a gangly kid who was reportedly playing number one for the University of Nevada.

We were to be on the honor system, that is, there weren't going to be any umpires until the finals, unless of course, somebody blew up (or somebody blew somebody up) in which case one of the hacks would be called out to make the peace. The kid looked innocent enough; I doubted I would get in a row with him, but if so, I knew relying on a nonprofessional referee was risky. Hell, even a pro umpire could blow it for you.

The kid seemed kind of skinny, but his long limbs would be lethal. Neither of us said a word after the initial handshake, except to ask for lobs and clarify who would serve from what side. I knew the kid was hungry and that he wanted the money as much as I did, but what was worse, just the idea of winning would be important to him, the mere notion that he had beaten a pro. That alone would make him dig in. I tried to focus on looking at the ball and moving my feet, and not aiming too near the lines; and not trying to compete with the kid's power, which was phenomenal. Then at last, after one hundred and thirty-five panting minutes of scrambling and lunging on the hot blacktop, we were done.

I headed back to the clubhouse to stretch down away from the increasing ferocity of the Montana sun. The kid had pushed me to the limits, and now as the match replayed in my mind, one very satisfying shot lingered sweetly. And actually, it hadn't even counted! It was a let serve that I returned. It had been an audible let, just clipping the net cord, but the ball was still coming at me at a million miles an hour. So I swung away, anyway. And I hit a perfect winner right down the line! How many times had I done that — hit a great shot when it didn't count! In fact, I had hit the ball absolutely perfectly, far better than I could have done if it had been a good serve and I was trying to actually play the point. Damn, I thought, why can't I do that when it counts? But I knew why — in that fraction of a second when I had sensed the ball was a let, I relaxed and lost all self-consciousness. I went into automatic flow, like Hammer, and played with almost no realization of what I was doing. No wonder Hammer was so good! Damn, I told myself, you've got to play like that all the time, and not only when the opponent hits a ball just beyond the sideline, for instance, and you tee off on it for the best shot of the day.

Engrossed in self-examination, I trudged up the broad wooden clubhouse stairs and opened the door. Hammer was already there under the rafters, below a rattlesnake the size of a boa constrictor. A huge set of buck antlers was on the near wall, and yet, animals of a more threatening nature were all around us — skinny Neanderthals with funny looking clubs and white shorts. Some were just hanging out, as we were, after their matches; others were waiting to go on.

I had barely squeaked by the kid in straights (two tie-breakers.) Hammer, on the other hand, had just beaten a better player by the following scores: 0-6, 6-0, 6-0. After casually dropping the first set at love, his game had zoned and he bageled the guy, scarcely giving up a point. In the lounge now, all eyes were on him. "Yeah, that's my partner!" I felt like shouting, "Bagel Boy! Bro with the Flow! Dude of the Go-For-It! King of the Tennis Hobos!"

Todd looked cool as a cucumber as he sat in a lotus position on the bear skin rug in front of the big fireplace. "I hear you really Zenned out," I said, the perspiration from my match still dripping off my forehead. He just sat there with that slow introspective nod of his, the corners of his mouth turned up in satisfaction. I knew it wouldn't be wise to talk too much about his performance — it was Hammer's job to ride it, gently, not to be aware of it, but to maintain it. So I left him there with an old Jim Croce tune playing on the juke box, amidst the talk and the rifling of cards, and the occasional pistol shot of the cue ball.

I found Fernando sitting in the shade on the front deck. He was at one end, almost in the trees, quietly reading a book of South American poetry. The braided ponytail between his shoulder blades gave him a very Native American look.

We exchanged pleasantries. Apparently he had advanced uneventfully. "I hope tomorrow you win," he said softly with his delicate Spanish accent, "then we can play in semis."

I chuckled at the thought, the unlikelihood, but at the same time I savored the fact that he was pulling for me, that he, Fernando Vasquez, was being a friend. It felt good, very good, kind of like when it's your birthday but you've forgotten completely about it; and then from out of the blue someone gives you a birthday present, some little trinket perhaps, and suddenly you feel like a kid again for a few minutes. "For me to win is a long shot," I said, humbly tickled, "so don't get your hopes up. Though I'm sure that would be better for you."

"And better for you too," he added, "a lot better." How true, I thought, and a wave of that birthday feeling ran through my body again as I sensed the sincerity and the accuracy of his words. It was nice to have somebody in my corner I didn't realize was there. "Anyway, good luck to you, too," I said, and I left him to his poetry.

I walked down to the bungalow to shower up and wonder what kind of hack I would get in the pro/am. On the way, I wouldn't bother scouting my next singles opponent; I would rely on the gods for any possible victory in that match. But the doubles was another story. If either one of those guys was still playing, I'd take a look.

As it turned out, everything went as expected, except for the fact that my partner in the pro/am happened to be a good guy, a fairly accomplished older player who I really liked. He was a retired silver-haired stock broker from New Hampshire who had actually donated to Charley Finger's Spiritual Athletes Foundation; and then he was sent literature about the tennis tournament, which, as a fundraiser for that same organization, was also tax deductible.

So I found myself trying to win just so I wouldn't let down the agile old gentleman. And now it was the next day, and we were scheduled to play again, after my doubles with Todd. I had lost gracefully in the singles in the morning, going 2 and 2 on the feature court with a former Canadian Davis Cup player who now, like Fernando, was only interested in select renegade tournaments. Obviously outclassed, I had played loose, saving myself for the doubles, which was about to start at this very moment.

Charley Finger handed Todd the jar of tennis balls and we walked away from the bar with our opponents leading the way. (Usually tournament players receive fuzz nugs already out of the jar, but Todd had requested an unopened jar. Of course, in local events it's typical to be handed only two balls, so it was nice that Charley Finger didn't skimp in that regard.)

"What do you think?" Hammer said slyly. He tapped at the jar of nugs with his forefinger. "Shall we open them up kind of special like? It might be entertaining. Besides, you look kind of tight."

He was right; now that I was out of the singles, I felt the pressure of performing in the dubs, of trying to bring home the bacon (so I could at least get home in more style than I had left in.) Our jar opening ritual was just what I needed to loosen up. Besides, the two guys we were playing were already rubbing us the wrong way. The one built like a fullback had laughed at Todd when he saw him meditating in the clubhouse. He had his hat on backwards now as we followed them onto the court in the glaring afternoon, and I wondered if he was going to switch the brim around to protect his eyes once we began, or if he was going to insist on his statement of defiance despite the glare and the fact that he would be getting a lot of lobs from us. Of course, he was a pretty tough mutha of a player, having just beaten Stick Brown, the number two seed. Hammer had also won, and now those two would meet in the semis tomorrow, so this was just sort of a preview. (On the other side of the draw, Fernando had won and would meet the Canadian who cleaned me out.)

Hammer and I had already nicknamed the big guy "The Bulldozer." His partner was lithe and speedy looking, so we called him "The Cat." They walked directly to a bench on one side of the court, so we parked our gear on the other.

The sun wasn't horrible, but from the north side it could be aggravating for a righthander hitting several overheads in a row. It was Todd's idea to spin for serve from the get-go and choose the south side for ourselves; then we could try to break down the Bulldozer's overhead in the warmup with a series of eye-watering lobs. First, of course, we would have them help us open the jar of tennis balls.

We walked over to their bench where they sat with such arrogant grins you'd have thought they were talking about the girls they had nailed the night before. They could have cared less about the fact that we were standing in front of them. "Why don't we spin now," Hammer said, "and get it over with."

"That's fine with us," the Bulldozer grunted. He nodded at the Cat, who stood up and held out his racket. And this is the part where we were supposed to get psyched out, because there at the bottom of the Cat's racket head, woven across the lower end of the string bed, was a prophylactic in all its pale rubbery glory. I had never seen such a thing used as a vibration dampener before; however, like well trained CIA agents, Hammer and I didn't so much as flinch or give each other acknowledging glances, despite the fact that the rubber looked pretty hilarious there in the strings, all shriveled up with the tip sticking out at one end and the circular rim popped out at the other.

"Well, what are you waiting for," Hammer said to the Cat, "go ahead and spin."

So the Cat spun and the prophylactic twirled like a top in the sunlight above the blacktop, and Hammer said, "up." When the racket came to rest, the Cat picked it up carefully, keeping it level; he held the butt cap toward his partner on the bench. "It's down," the Bulldozer grunted triumphantly, "we'll take the serve." He stood up as the Cat showed us the butt of the racket and the misfortune of our choice.

"OK, we'll start over here," Todd said, claiming the favorable south side, which was only favorable because with less sun it would allow us to warmup serves and overheads more comfortably, and hopefully, throw a little glare into the eyes of the opponents.

Now it was time for our action. "OK, dudes," Todd announced, "care to help us open up this fine jar of tennis balls?" And fine they were, our favorites, good old regular Penns — plain unflavored, with no special claims to longevity and no extraneous symbols on the napping. We stood at the net on our side of the court. In one hand, Hammer held the jar of Penns, in the other was a big stainless steel soup spoon he kept in his bag for just such occasions.

"What the fuck are you talking about?" the Bulldozer said. He and the Cat approached from their side and we all stood up at the net.

"Just thought you might want to help us open this jar of tennis balls," Todd said cheerfully, "they're really good, excellent Penns." He offered the soup spoon to the Bulldozer.

"What the fuck!?" the Cat exclaimed. "Are you kidding?!"

"OK, suit yourselves," Hammer said sadly. He held the jar of Penns up to his ear; and I stepped close to listen, too, as he popped open the tab as slowly as possible. Suddenly there was the hiss of escaping gas, that minute rushing sound, and then all at once it was loud and over — the *thart* — as we called it, was normally short-lived. (The record thart to date was six seconds, as witnessed at San Diego's Morley Field on a jar of Extra Duty Wilsons.)

After the precious thart had vanished, Todd tilted the jar of Penns toward me and I took a close whiff of the exotic aroma, that factory blend of plastic, rubber, and felt which is like a French perfume to tennis players good enough to appreciate new fuzz nugs.

"Are you sure you wouldn't care for a sniff?" Todd extended the jar to the opponents, but they just stood there with smirks on their faces.

Next, and with a ceremonious flair of his hand, Hammer pulled the aluminum lid completely off the jar. He tossed it like a miniature frisbee, watching it sail over the fence the way a pro golfer might study a tee shot.

Meanwhile, the Bulldozer and the Cat were beginning to look a little feverish. "I haven't had a fresh tennis ball in a while," Todd explained, soup spoon in hand. "Care for one?" He dipped in with the spoon and scooped out the top ball, balancing it on the utensil like a big yellow dumpling. "Are you sure?" He gestured again, but still there was no response from our opponents, except that their eyes appeared wider and more glazed. So Hammer spooned the ball onto the strings of my racket and I rolled it around on the inside of the frame the way a connoisseur swirls fine port around the bottom of a wine glass. I moaned, drawing it up to my nose for another wonderful whiff of new fuzz nug.

I felt kind of heady. Todd dipped into the jar again, and again he pulled out a bright new Penn. "You're sure?" he asked, as if politely checking the appetite of a bashful dinner guest. But still there were no takers, so he put the ball in his pocket; and then he scooped out the last Penn. "OK," he announced, "only one left, better get it while you can."

"These guys are nuts!" the Cat proclaimed, a kind of half-grin beginning to form on his face. But the Bulldozer was wild-eyed. "Are we here to play tennis or what?!" he grunted ferociously at our side of the net.

"What do you think we opened this jar for?" Todd said in a soothing, priest-like manner.

"Just gimme a ball," the Bulldozer hollered, "or I'll take that can and shove it up your nose."

"It's not a can, it's a jar." Hammer held up the empty plastic container. "Have you ever seen a can that looks like this?"

"I don't care what it is, I'm going to shove it up your butt if you don't gimme a ball right now." I wondered what would be better, the nose or the butt; it was a difficult choice. Meanwhile, the Bulldozer was fuming, and yet, next to him, the Cat looked confused, unsure of himself, like a hungry alley cat looking at a vulture.

"Well why didn't you just say so?" Todd said, and he took one last intoxicating whiff around the seam of the fragrant new Penn. Then he dropped it over the net and we walked back to the baseline.

"OK," I said, "you picked out your man. I guess I get the little guy."

And so the warmup had begun, with me and the Cat exchanging groundstrokes on one side, feeling each other out tentatively, while the Bulldozer smashed balls at Todd.

"Stretch, dude," Todd called out from his corner of the backcourt, "this guy hits harder than I thought. But he's a little wild, let's just keep the ball in play and not try to hit through them too much. What's your guy like?'"

"He's quick as lightning," I called back, "and he hasn't missed a ball."

"Great," he said. "We need to get something out of these guys, just to get on track, if you know what I mean." I knew what he meant but I didn't see the situation that optimistically. I was hoping I could get the Cat to miss something in the warmup, just to build my confidence. Maybe he would dump a volley. So I hit a real short ball and sure enough, the Cat came up to the net. So did the Bulldozer, and he still had his hat on backwards despite the severity of the sun.

Hammer was already at it, throwing up lobs to the Bulldozer, even though he hadn't asked for any. The big man hit the first two kind of awkwardly, then he framed one. "Hey, that's enough lobs," he grunted, squinting and rubbing his eyes. "I'll tell ya when I want some overheads."

The Cat finally netted a halfvolley, and I felt better. "Give me a few overheads and I'll be ready," he said. Now it was his turn in the glare.

Despite a hat and his natural steadiness, even the Cat managed to mis-hit an overhead (and I was giving him very easy stuff.) "OK, that's enough," he said, straightening out his strings with his fingers. He fiddled with his "dampener" and then he walked back to the baseline.

Todd and I took our time with volleys, and especially with overheads, hitting them one after another in perfect rhythm, much to the frustration of our opponents. "Aren't you chumps ready yet?!" the Bulldozer bellowed. "OK, yeah, just one more lob," Todd said; so the Bulldozer threw up a sky ball that was headed for the back fence. Hammer backpedaled to the baseline in a slow relaxed manner, and then he leaped up, appearing to hang in the air for a moment as he popped a perfect scissors-kick overhead. The ball rifled dead center in the court between the two opponents, and then it thumped into the fence, making the chain link rattle. "OK, just a few serves and we'll be ready," he said.

As the first set proceeded, it got ever closer. We barely eked it out. And now we were leading 4-3 in the second, when the Bulldozer stepped up to the line to serve. He still hadn't turned his hat around, and yet he was nails, but just erratic enough to give us an edge. His partner, the Cat, was a sly player who crossed beautifully and at exactly the right times, but unfortunately, he wasn't quite sly enough for two seasoned tennis hobos from Berkeley. We were scrapping now, with both of us back at the baseline as the Bulldozer served. Even if the opponent's delivery wasn't very big, over the years we found that the both-back tactic was a great way to break serve; it destroyed the other team's rhythm and changed their reference points, often giving a volleyer too many choices for his own good. Now, with Todd in his corner of the backcourt as I received the Bulldozer's heavy first serve, I could get away with a more mediocre return, since it took a pretty decent shot to put the ball away when we were both deep. We defended well and threw up some awesome lobs, so with the sun as our ally, we made short work of the Bulldozer's serve to go up 5-3 in the second. Steam appeared to be coming out of the Bulldozer's ears as he huddled with the Cat on the other side of the court.

Now I would be serving for the match. I prepared for my delivery. Hammer was at the net, signaling behind his back, as he had been doing the entire match. (We always used signals, even though it could put a little pressure on the guy serving. We used a closed fist to stay and an open hand to go, and we signaled on all serves, first and second, unless we were a little shaky, in which case we might not signal on second serves during the first set, for instance; but we would still pretend we were signaling just to keep the pressure on and our fakes alive.)

So far, we hadn't crossed much in the deuce court when dealing with the Cat's returns. Though he lacked power, he was a cagey player who in a pinch could throw up the most perfect lob over the backhand of the net man. Not that we didn't slam a few down his throat now and then.

I was, in fact, serving to the Cat now. The score was deuce (as it often is when it's just 30-all.) I had been popping a big first ball down the middle at the Cat's backhand, and backing it up with a kicker to that same spot. The Cat stood poised, bent and swaying behind the baseline. He was ready to pounce. It was about time, I figured, to slice him wide to the forehand. After all, I was serving for the match and what was the point in just keeping up a well proven strategy when you could tamper with it and finish with more flair. I knew there was the risk I could wreck the rhythm of my bread-and-butter second serve and that I could be blowing the whole match, but I tried not to think about that. It was high time for my go-for-it to come out of the closet and end the match, and even if we did drop the set, it wasn't like it was the end of the world — there would always be a third set for me to resort back to more traditional methods. Or, I could keep playing by intuition and give my go-for-it a chance to really kick in.

I tried not to get too analytical as I went into the service motion, telling myself stuff like he who hesitates is lost and look at the doughnut, not at the hole. (I told you I pick my moments to Zen out.) I still wasn't certain I would go for the Cat's forehand corner, but as I went into the service toss, the ball faded to the right slightly as if it had an intelligence of its own; and then I knew, YES, it's slice time; just keep your arm loose, I thought, and pull through the motion as hard as you can.

And what a clean hit that was! With a dash of overspin on it and a touch of slice, the ball went straight for its target, curving to the very outside corner of the service box; and then it bounded into the side fence. The Cat trotted up immediately and inspected the mark on the court.

"Nope, just out," he said and he walked back to receive again.

From his position up at the net, Hammer turned to me with a flat hand, signifying that the ball was good. We both knew the ball was an ace. But it wasn't time to get sidetracked; that serve had felt so good I knew I could hit another one, if I got right to it.

But this time I would hit that same serve (a one o'clock slice) to the other corner — down the middle to the Cat's backhand. So I rotated my stance a few degrees in that direction, something I doubted the Cat would notice from where he stood at the baseline; but in either case, when he saw my toss go up again to the right he would think I was slicing another one to his forehand. To make sure he fell for it I tossed even further to the right this time (which, to be precise, would produce a two o'clock slice at contact.) Then I hit the ball as loose and as hard as I could.

It was a very satisfying hit, but with that bit of added sidespin, the ball didn't have quite as clean a thump against my strings as the first delivery, and yet, that extra bite on the ball was doing its job now as it hooked its flight from right to left toward the "T" (and into the very corner of the deuce box where I had been previously delivering kick serves.) The Cat moved swiftly and beautifully from his perch on the other side, but he overshot by about an inch and the ball crowded him as it curved into his body, forcing him to shove at it awkwardly with his backhand. Instead of a lob, he flipped us a floater, which Todd put away, popping it like it was a balloon on a string. Ad-in.

OK, great, now it was match point, and I would be serving at the Bulldozer. We'd see what that mutha was made of. Behind his back, Todd threw me a new signal, one he had been saving for just the right moment. Instead of a closed fist or an open hand, he now displayed the V of two extended fingers. This special signal meant that Todd was going to make a full cross but that I was to say NO loudly, like I was calling off his move and telling him to stay. I felt a tickle of delight in my stomach in anticipation of this great event.

"Let me see the signal again," I said, just for good measure, to make sure the opponents knew we were up to something. Todd obliged, putting the V behind his back again and wiggling his butt a little. He knew what was coming down.

"No!" I said sternly (telling Hammer yes, to go.) And then I got ready to bear down, to hit a heavy-ass extreme kick serve into the corner of the ad court, to what would hopefully be the Bulldozer's backhand. I tossed way back and to the left (kind of like Edberg) and hit the shit out of the ball. The Bulldozer saw it coming and decided not to try to run around it with his forehand, after all, the net guy wasn't going to cross, so all he had to do was chip a routine crosscourt with his backhand.

This time Hammer didn't fake or anything, he just stood there at the net looking kind of lackadaisical; until the Bulldozer had actually begun to swing at the ball, and then he streaked across the court and set up right on top of the net, clutching his racket with two hands like a lefthanded baseball batter waiting for a pitch (this would be no feeble one-handed backhand volley!) The ball came quickly and predictably into Todd's power zone. He hammered it downward with the strength of a lumberjack, and the Bulldozer shrieked. The Cat, nimble as ever in his forward position, made an admirable attempt at the ball, but it smashed his foot and bounced over the fence.

My partner offered his condolences. "Wups, sorry about that."

OK, so now we were in the semis. With the relief of winning, I felt a little bad for the opponents, for their loss, and even the Bulldozer became more human and not just another rodent with his hat on backwards.

After the handshake we all stood there at the net, our sweat dripping onto the hot blacktop. The Bulldozer turned his hat around and tugged at the brim. (Perhaps his forehead had gotten a little toasty, or maybe he wanted to see better now that the match was over.) By his side, the Cat hung his head and fiddled around with his rather flaccid dampener.

"I wouldn't use that thing if I were you," Todd told him, pointing to the flimsy rubber.

"Whad'ya mean you wouldn't use it? It works great, I get great feel," the Cat said with a grin. He, too, was relieved now that the match was over.

"I mean I wouldn't use it for anything else, at least not without first checking it for leaks, if you know what I mean."

"Oh yeah, right," the Cat said with a chuckle. The Bulldozer looked like he was about to crack a smile, but it never came. "OK, nice match, you guys. And you, stud," he gave Todd a thumbs up salute, "I'll see you in the morning."

Our opponents walked off the court. The Bulldozer held the gate open and the Cat walked through it with a noticeable limp.

Chapter Nine

The Hacker

In the classic sense, a hacker is just that, a player who hacks (chops) at the ball. Thus, his game is pretty much limited to underspin. (Underspin, backspin, slice — it's all the same thing when talking about groundstrokes.) With the upsurge of topspin in the modern era, however, some self-taught players have evolved styles composed of nothing but frying-pan grips and primitive overspin. Consequently, today's hacker is capable of anything — he might possess the ability to hit topspin, and yet have no clue whatsoever when it comes to generating slice shots.

In general then, a hacker is a player with any type of inadequate or deformed game (and thus, he is not a "player" at all, but rather, a hack.) The most common examples are individuals with poke backhands and parachute-drop second serves, in which case it goes without saying that they have no inkling about how to volley properly. A slightly more sophisticated hacker might have a fairly well-developed backhand, but still a poor second serve, in which case it wouldn't matter how well he could volley, he would still be a hack to any player who knows what it is to have a strong second serve.

Having a good second serve and nothing else would, understandably, be a major deficiency. However, such a player could sidestep hacker stigma, since the second serve is the most crucial and distinguishing feature of any tennis player's game, and if strong, that alone demands a good deal of respect.

Of course, what we are talking about is all relative. You might consider so and so a hacker, and yet your neighbor might consider the same guy a great player. For me and Hammer, over the years, it has become easier to label anybody with a deficient game a hack. When we are tournament bound, our judgment becomes even more severe and the name applies to most anybody who is not up to us. This simplifies matters and saves energy — them and us — two classifications. So and so is either a player or he is not.

And so, if you aren't one of us, you're a hack. That is, until you prove yourself otherwise, which is something not so different from the way hacks treat each other in their own cliques. In other words, all tennis players are wary of outsiders and assume them to be a waste of their time on the court. Until proven otherwise.

And though some strangers may talk a very good game, that's not what counts. It doesn't matter how good you say you are — you might as well just shut-up and let your racket do the talking. And that's probably why the better players tend to be more quiet.

So Hammer and I aren't unnecessarily cruel or overly critical, we're just top-notch tennis players with naturally high standards. Heck, we've even known some hacks who've evolved over the years into distinguished players. But generally, there is a stubbornness and an ignorance to the mentality of hackers, and they resist changing their games — they are hacks for life. And yet there are other individuals at similar levels of play who show signs of trying to learn tennis properly; and because we, in turn, sense the potential they have for developing nice games, Todd and I might refer to them as "players," even though to the untrained eye they may appear no more accomplished than the hacks they play with. So you see, our intent isn't to humiliate others, we just like to tell it like it is, and that goes double when we're in the middle of a tournament.

It was the night before the finals. Our doubles semifinals had been uneventful, not near as sobering as our match against the Bulldozer and the Cat; and yet, I was haunted by two unusual low volleys I had hit. Both were backhands, but they were hit low on the *forehand* side of my body from a more or less upright posture. Two others I had dumped from that same zone trying to dig them out with the forehand face of my racket. Using the backhand had clearly proven more efficient.

I sat at a cocktail table in the bar trying to prepare mentally for that same low volley, imagining over and over my racket head dropping down to the outside of my right foot with the backhand face of the racket toward the oncoming ball. Hammer was seated next to me, quietly thinking about anything from nuclear fusion to absolutely nothing at all.

Most of the players had already left Rock Creek, but all the hacks were still there, since their round-robin had one more round to go. As much as they had craved for the presence of the big time, with few of the pros around now the ams felt less overshadowed, and here in the bar they held their heads higher with a new-found air of importance.

In the dim light the place was jumping in a quiet tennis player sort of way. A group of ams was watching television and another was playing low stakes poker. Three guys were in line waiting to challenge at the pool game, where the silver-haired partner I had in the pro/am was holding the table. Over by the jukebox two hacks were slow dancing with their wives, or maybe their dates, I couldn't be sure.

Having beaten the Bulldozer that morning, Todd would be playing Fernando in tomorrow's final; and then afterward, he and I would square off against a couple of guys from New Zealand.

Marcie came over and poured another drink for the middle-aged am who sat with his wife at the table next to us. The guy picked up his drink and turned to me.

"Jimmy Connnors' mom goes to the same beautician as my wife here," he said, holding up his glass like I was supposed to join him in a toast. "His mom's his coach, you know, had his game completely developed by the time he was eight years old."

I wasn't sure what to say, and Todd was busy eyeballing Marcie's rear end as it slinked away from us.

With his drink still up in the air, the am continued. "Connors has the best return of serve in the world, ya know. Probably the best backhand, too. He's a real interesting guy, kind of private though."

The somewhat sloshed hack told me his name, and I introduced him to Hammer. "He knows Jimmy," I winked. "They're from the same town."

"Jimmy?" Todd asked.

"Yeah, you know, Connors."

"Connors? Oh yeah, Connors." Todd turned to the hack. "You're from Belleville? Well, then you must know Connors. Really well, I'm sure."

"Honey, remember that time you saw him in Macy's?" the am's wife blurted out, "around Christmas time, over by the kitchenware. Remember?"

"At first he didn't recognize you, remember? But then he asked you what he should get his mother for Christmas. Remember, honey? Imagine that, Jimmy Connors asking you what he should get his mom for Christmas."

"That's what friends are for," Todd said.

The hack looked a little pink in the face. "Yes, er, that's right," he said, finally putting down his drink. "I told him to get a nice set of steak knives for his mom, and by god, Connors picked out a set of steak knives right then and there. And he had them gift wrapped."

"Imagine that," the guy's wife said.

I knew where the guy was coming from. Sure he knew Connors, it's just that Connors didn't know him. Hell, I didn't even know Connors, though I had been introduced to him a time or two. That's the way it works — you know somebody if you know about them. And of course, you don't actually come out and say you know them, you just imply it, you talk about the person as if you know them. All that's necessary is a link. Maybe you know the guy's brother (a fairly solid link.) Or maybe so and so's coach has a house down the street from a friend of yours, and though your friend has never seen the player or so much as said hello to the coach, you feel as if you know them both, at least a little.

Now in his last night at the Rock Creek bar, the am's wife was spoiling it for him; he probably wished he hadn't brought her along. She was, in fact, messing with his link. She served as a reminder of how far removed his world was from that of a real tennis player. If she hadn't come along he could have just been one of the guys, one of the guys who came to Rock Creek on business and didn't bring distractions along. He could have hung with his partner and with the pros better. And he probably would have played better too. Maybe even made some money.

"Honey," the guy's wife said, "did you tell them about the time you saw Arthur Ashe at the airport, how skinny he looked in his regular clothes? Remember, it was right after we got married?"

"Got to be going," Todd said standing up; he stretched his arms overhead and yawned. "Got work to do in the morning."

"Oh yeah, that's right," the am slurred. "You beat that big fella today, didn't ya. Of course, you're not no small fry yourself, are ya?"

The guy leaned toward me as Todd walked away. "Did you ever notice how tennis favors the big men?" he said matter-of-factly.

The guy was fairly small. I knew exactly how he felt. Hell, I was taller than average, but still, when faced with a player like Hammer or Fernando on the other side of the net, there was an automatic sense of intimidation. "You're right," I told the guy, "but all sports favor big men."

"Well, Jimmy Connors isn't a big man," the guy's wife put in.

"He's an exception," the am contended.

"That's right," I said, "all other things being equal, the bigger player has the advantage. If the big man is well proportioned, and coordinated and fast, then he has the advantage. If you're a little guy, it doesn't matter how quick you are if the opposition can do it all the same and at two sizes bigger."

"Hear, hear," the hack cheered, "I'll drink to that." He held his glass out toward his wife.

But she wasn't so easily convinced. "Well what about that Bjorn Borg," she countered. "He's no giant, either."

"Look," I intervened, "if Borg were two sizes bigger and equally talented in other departments, then he'd be just that much better, wouldn't you agree?"

The guy's wife puckered her lips in semi-inebriated thought. "Well, maybe so. Now that you mention it, a lot of the women tennis players you see on television are fairly good-sized, too. And real strong looking, like that Martina what's-her-name."

"Martina Schwarzennegger," the am slurred.

"Yeah, like that Martina Schwarz. Zenegger. She's really strong."

I stood up with a laugh. (It was true that Martina Navratilova was in superb shape and probably more fit than any previous tennis lady.) "Absolutely," I said, "the stronger the better."

"I told you," the guy said to his wife, "the big men have it easier, a lot easier."

As I left, I could hear the little hack calling out across the room to me. "Yeah, in all sports it's better if you're big, why do you think there aren't any Japanese football players!"

Good point, I thought, and I walked out into the star-studded darkness. I could hear Hammer and Fernando talking below the deck.

They were sitting on the broad wooden stairs, casually leaning back on their elbows, their voices murmuring softly over the ringing crickets and the gurgling flow of the not too far away river. I sat down beside them and listened.

"A split will be OK with me," Fernando said quietly, "it will be money enough and we can play looser. I can read poetry all night and it won't matter."

"You're sure?" Todd said, "I mean, you're definitely favored. If you win you get the full three grand. If we split the pie you only get twenty-three hundred."

"Twenty-three hundred is enough for me to fly home. Also, I can buy a dining room table for my wife. Yes, I am sure, a split will do. I want to share the quiet hours of this special night with Borges and Neruda. I think Lorca will be there too. Besides, you are playing well, it is you who should perhaps reconsider. If the tennis gods are with you tomorrow, you will be three thousand richer just for the singles."

"Maybe I don't want to work that hard," Hammer said. "Anyway, I could lose and only get sixteen hundred. Besides, I'm getting some bread for the doubles, too. No, I'm absolutely sure, a split will do just fine."

"OK then, it is settled." Fernando's Spanish accent hung delicately in the air, and then it disappeared in the darkness. We all just sat there smelling the pines and listening to the crickets and the gurgling flow of the river.

Chapter Ten

Window To The World

Charley Finger turned to me during the early part of the singles final. "Too bad there aren't more people watching," he said, "this is a great match, it's as good as any you see on national TV. But then, I guess spectators aren't what makes tennis go round, if you know what I mean."

"You got that right," I said, "about the only time you see a filled grandstand is at Wimbledon or the US Open, or some other big one. The rest of the time you see more empty seats than people."

"If it weren't for the sponsors the whole circuit would dry up and blow away," Charley said matter-of-factly. "I mean it's not like baseball or football, where the crowd actually buys enough tickets to support the game. Hell, the big guys are dumping about 400,000 a week into the tour, and all they'd have to do is pull out and the whole thing would collapse. I doubt anybody'd be crazy enough to put that much dough into baseball just to be the official sponsor, though it'd be better than burying the money in tennis."

Charley told me his tournament suffered a similar fate this year. One of the major contributors to his Spiritual Athletes Foundation hadn't renewed, and he had been forced to put in a couple of grand from his own pocket.

"You could have trimmed the prize money a bit," I suggested.

"Oh, no, I couldn't do that, the players deserve to get what they're promised. I have a rule — always make the tournament at least as good as the year before, and always pay the players the full amount. Besides, I like having them here. If I go in the hole a little, I go in the hole; the tournament's worth it, it keeps me in touch with my roots, my tennis roots. You know, I used to be a renegade just like you guys, playing the little ones, scraping by from one win to the next. 'Hit and Run Charley' they used to call me. Then my shoulder started to act up and I got into money-making, real money-making in the Big Apple. I got out just before it killed me and I came here."

Charley Finger took another swallow of his iced tea. "The quiet in Montana is nice, and I get out into the real world two or three times a year. Just enough to let me know I made the right decision moving."

Now that the tournament was almost over Charley looked more relaxed, but also a little depressed. He was probably missing the players already.

"Todd and I've been enjoying the place," I said. "I can see how it grows on you."

"You haven't even been fishing yet, wait'l you go fishing. Then you'll see what Montana's all about. I'll tell you what, if you can stay another day, we'll do some trouting. Then you'll be hooked, you won't even want to go home."

"One more day, maybe," I said, "but that's it, I've got obligations back home. Hammer might stay on for a while though. He knows something about fishing too, his grandfather taught him."

Meanwhile, in the hole below us, the action resounded powerfully as Todd and Fernando pressed into the third set, each man playing loose, offensive points. A dozen ams were watching from the big wooden steps, and a few others were up on the deck with us. Marcie came out now and then from the restaurant to put her hands on her hips and say, "My, my, that's what I call a couple of real good-looking specimens." She still didn't understand much about tennis, but she could appreciate the intrinsic beauty of the sport — the tall lean bodies, the fluid movement of limbs, the yellow blur arching quickly back and forth over the net. And the rhythmic thumping sound that resounded into the forest. That the men could run and jump was enough for her; she viewed the action as if she were watching a ballet, and she was perhaps right on the money, for the tennis between Todd and Fernando was more like an art form than a battle. The fact that they had agreed to split the prize money had taken the pressure off and they were able to really perform. It was stream of consciousness tennis, uninhibited loose power combined with touch. Perfectly placed half-volleys were hit off overhead smashes, fence-ringing aces and bullet passing shots mixed freely with delicate lob-volleys and ground-sucking drop shots. Streaking gets, lunges and leaps — all without letup. One amazing shot after another.

At the side changes, Hammer and Fernando shared a common bench and high-fived each other before sitting down to chat and rest up for the next barrage of spectacular points.

"Man, this is great stuff," Charley said, "these guys are playing like they haven't got a care in the world. I don't think it matters to them if they win or lose."

"It doesn't," I said.

Charley was quiet for a moment. "I thought so," he said, smiling. "Montana has a way of bringing out the best in people. Don't think Hit and Run Charley didn't split a few in his day. Even did it in the semis once in a while."

Next thing I knew, there was clapping, and Todd and Fernando were shaking hands up at the net; it was the thumbs-up clasp of one dude to another. Then they walked up the broad steps to where we were sitting on the deck. Charley and I looked at one another, each hoping for some clue — neither of us knew for sure who had won, though it appeared to me that on the last point Hammer hit a passing shot down the line, but then again, it may have just missed.

Todd and Fernando hadn't cared who won, and that had rubbed off on us — we hadn't cared either. There wasn't the usual close attention to score, and since the players had opted for no umpire, we were at a loss and now faced the awkward possibility of being disrespectful to the winner (and to the loser, too, for that matter.)

"He was too good for me today," Hammer said with a sigh, and he high-fived Fernando again. (OK, so now we knew.) In awe, the ams were still clapping. Then a couple of their more inspired brethren walked out to that red-hot court to hit some balls, and the applause dwindled off.

Charley stood up to congratulate Fernando and shake his hand, and then he shook Hammer's, mentioning something about the spectacular tennis from both of them. "Stick around, boys. I'm putting the amateurs on for their last round, then I'll be back with your checks and we'll talk fishing." He looked at me and Todd. "And then you two can show us what real doubles is all about."

Hammer immediately dropped into a cool-down stretching routine, while Fernando took a seat next to me and stretched his long legs out. He began to read his book.

"I like to be with the poems when my endorphins are in circulation," he said softly, his handsome face dripping with sweat. "It is now that the words become alive. They sparkle like the dew on a morning leaf."

As if in agreement with Fernando, a jay called out from the forest just then. I sat there in the blue Montana air, feeling the poetry of it all — the smell of the pines and the wild anise, my partner stretching in the sunlight, Fernando's braided ponytail, the peppered sound of the ams warming up, the gurgling river. I noticed the sky had become purple at the far ridge. Just then a squirrel scampered across the deck; it climbed up to the top of the tennis fence, where it paused to assess the action below. Then it moved along the rail to the next court, probably amazed that the humans were still down there in that hard flat place, a place that was vacant for most of the year.

Yes, tennis was truly a window to the world. That's what an old timer used to tell me when I first started playing. And he was right. We often shared the backboard at the Berkeley Rose Garden (when I wasn't busy playing baseball and could manage to take the bus over there.) "Young fella," the old guy would say, pausing to catch his breath, "I think you're going to be a good one — you be sure to stick with tennis. But remember, tennis is more than a sport, it's a window to the world. It will take you places and show you things. Whether you win or lose, tennis can be your window to the world, if you let it."

At twelve years old, I was too young to appreciate what the old man was trying to tell me. But now I knew what he meant by a window to the world.

Tennis had truly been good to me, in spite of the fact that I hadn't always been good to it, in as much as I had spent so much of my life trying to conquer it instead of just making it my friend. Of course, there was something to be said for the drive to win, the compulsion to master the game. After all, as one's on-court stature improved, the view through one's tennis window improved as well, although there was nothing wrong with what I was seeing through my naive twelve-year-old eyes in those early days at the Berkeley Rose Garden when the old timer used to catch his breath and give me pointers on the backboard.

"Better just to stay in one spot and hit ten in a row," he used to tell me. "Better to hit ten forehands in a row, and then hit ten backhands. Then you can mix it up, but you shouldn't move more than a step in either direction, unless you're doing a footwork drill."

I kind of shined the old timer on, slamming the ball willy-nilly against the wall with my trusty Wilson Kramer. But then I heard he used to be a pro and had actually beat Jack Kramer once. Suddenly the name that was inscribed on the throat of my racket took on a new meaning, and from that moment on, I did exactly as the old man said (even when I couldn't get up there and was just pounding the back of my father's little office building on University Avenue.)

Hammer was also a public parker at heart, having pretty much grown up on the gray concrete courts at Recreation Park in Long Beach. Those were the good old days in Southern California, before the public tennis centers became pay-for-play operations. As soon as the money became involved, players stopped hanging out and you couldn't just drop by for a pickup game. It was true, improvements were made and the courts at Recreation Park were fancier now, but something had changed dramatically. No longer was the park a natural spawning ground, a place where up and coming players hung out, a place where kids and old timers were drawn to each other with rackets in hand.

Fittingly, those Recreation Park tennis courts had been renamed the Billie Jean King Tennis Center, since her game had been born there and on other public courts in the area. But would a player of that caliber emerge again? After all, it wasn't the same fertile spawning ground anymore, where wisdom of old mixed with the fire of youth, and each gave what was needed. The young had gotten wiser, and the competitive spirit of the older players had been rekindled as each sought approval from the other. But now, court rental fees had dampened everybody's enthusiasm, and the great bulk of players drifted away.

With a reservation system in place, the courts had lost their spur of the moment charm — one had to think about it first before going over there. Even if money wasn't the issue, a tennis date would have to be arranged in advance, because with hardly anybody hanging out, just dropping by would be pointless. In that respect the place had become like a private club.

Also like a private club was the highly organized teaching program at the courts, where one person was put in charge and if you weren't working for the man, you couldn't even step onto the court with a basket of balls and feed your partner a bunch of practice shots. Such was the fear that someone might promote himself as a private instructor.

In the old days in Long Beach, before the pay-for-play, there were more than a few name teaching pros who used to drop by Recreation Park to play and give lessons. It was a matter of survival of the fittest — the pros with the most ability and the most to give developed the greatest following of students. Darwin's natural selection was at work, allowing the best instructors to survive, which in turn, allowed some of the best players in the country to evolve. Sometimes a youngster would wander out to the courts at Recreation Park, and if it was the right kid, one of the pros would take him under his wing at no charge and make a player out of him. Or, it might be a college player looking out for a high schooler, or an old timer helping out a novice. Regardless, the natural give and take at the courts had been stifled, the ebb and flow had become stagnant and limited to the jurisdiction of those officially in charge. The worst of it was that very few kids were hanging out after school now, and the old timers didn't gather any more to play among themselves, not even on Sundays. It seemed unlikely that the Billie Jean King Tennis Center would ever produce another Billie Jean King, and that made me sad.

Of course, when you had a kid like Billie Jean, a phenomenal athlete who was as hungry as she was talented, she kind of produced herself once the love of the game was instilled. And coach Clyde Walker did a fantastic job of that for young Billie Jean. But then Walker died, much too early. I realized that this little known coach, Clyde Walker, was one of the great unsung heroes of tennis, and I felt even more sad.

Hammer, along with George Hardie and some other very decent players, had emerged from the Recreation Park courts before the place changed. That was when his parents were still together, before he had moved to Berkeley to live with his grandfather. Later, when he and I partnered up, we always dropped by that old Long Beach park if a tournament brought us to Southern California. We'd pay the guy at the pro shop, and then we'd walk out to the court and sit on the bench for a long time while Hammer told me about the old days, days when there were players like Al Bray and Jack Lynch hanging around, guys good enough to teach you a thing or two about the game no matter how good you were, or how old they were. Local legend had it that Pancho Gonzales even showed up on occasion to pound his big serve into the fences. And so, Todd and I would sit on the bench and talk about how the tennis was back then. Then we'd hit a few balls and get in the car. I don't think he liked the place anymore, but still, he had to see it every time we were in Southern California. He'd also take me to see the little house in Long Beach where he grew up. A few blocks away, it was a house that, as he put it, seemed to shrink every year. Then we'd go out to Belmont Shore and stroll up and down Second Street and look at the people, and his spirits would pick up. We'd have a great meal at one of the little restaurants, then we'd walk the strip some more, maybe play some pool at The Acapulco or one of the other college bars. Naturally, we'd look at the girls. "This town's damn near as nice as Berkeley," he'd say, and I'd agree. Then we'd find a modest room for the night and leave the next morning for San Diego or wherever our tournament was.

Suddenly I felt a wonderful sensation deep in my neck, strong fingers kneading my trapezius muscles. It was Hammer, his voice behind me now. "Stretch, dude, are you just going to sit there and day dream, or do you want to warmup? You haven't hit a ball all day and we've got the doubles finals coming up." I didn't want to leave that old Southern California beach town, nor did I want the massage to stop, but it did, and I came back to the woodsy reality of Rock Creek, Montana.

We went down to the end court, where a foursome of ams was coming off. We warmed up for about ten minutes. Then we played halfcourt (crosscourt points.) I knew Hammer didn't need the hits, but he knew I did, and though he was surely tired after his match with Fernando, he hit into my rhythm perfectly, time and again, giving me the satisfaction of connecting clean with a variety of shots that would finish the point in doubles. Then we went into the log clubhouse to wait out of the heat and feel the bearskin rug under our butts.

The big stone fireplace had a calming effect on me. Todd went into a meditation, but for me it was enough just to sit in front of the empty fireplace and imagine what it would be like in winter when it was crackling with flames.

Our opponents were outside, sitting on a shady part of the steps. Rumor had it they had more than a few ATP points, that this stop in Montana was just a temporary break from the tour for them. They were here for the cash, as we all were. But they hadn't even entered the singles, figuring to put it all into the doubles. The idea of splitting the prize money with them was out of the question, for two reasons. Number one, they obviously wanted the whole pie, and number two, we also wanted the whole pie. At least I did. The money I had made in singles was minimal, and my half of a doubles split wouldn't be much better. Hammer and I needed a win for me to walk away from the tournament with decent money, money that would get me a plane ticket home and some spare bills in my pocket. Hell, if we lost the final I'd probably have to take the Greyhound just to get back to California with enough dough in my wallet to feel freighting out to Montana had been worth it. The worst was overcome, at least, and I wouldn't have to hobo my way home (although memories of that boxcar ride were becoming more precious all the time, as were thoughts of the dentist's wife, her sandy brown ponytail and her old faded jeans.)

"I wonder if we shouldn't go through Portland on the way back home," I said to Todd, "I think our friends are hoping to put us up again."

"Possibly so, only thing is I may not be going back right away. Fernando wants me to go to Louisiana with him and play a tourney. You and I could play it, but you've got to get back to the University."

"Go for it," I told him, "play it if you want. I can get back on my own no problem." Then I added, "if we win the doubles."

"No problem," Todd assured me. "You just take care of your half of the court, and I'll take care of mine, except when I'm taking care of yours and you're taking care of mine. Right?"

"Right on, bro," I said, "let's do it." We got up off the bear skin rug and went over to the bar to tell Buckskin Charley we were ready. Because he always wore that fringed leather jacket, Todd and I had come to call him Buckskin Charley. He was surrounded by ams now since all the matches in the hacker special had finished and they were anxiously reporting their scores, tallying and double-checking each other's total points. (The pro/ am had finished the day before without much ado, although the hack who won it walked away with three hundred dollars, something he could bring home proudly even though he was still in the hole for the tournament. His pro partner got the predictable hundred bucks and hightailed it out of Montana as fast as he could.)

Finally, Buckskin Charley got out from under his pile of arms. He seemed relieved to see us.

"Ready to play, boys?"

"You got it," Todd said, "but how about letting us use one of those cans of Championship Wilsons?" He pointed to the white balls with the blue dots on them that stood concealed in real metal cans across the back of the bar. There was a row of them, about two dozen cans, below the huge moose head and the big posters of John Newcombe and Rod Laver.

Buckskin Charley reached for one of the yellow and red cans. "You want one of these?" He smiled as he handed the can to Todd. "They'll play sweet and fast, like lightning. It's OK with me, but the opponents have to agree. And it'll cost you."

"How much?" Todd asked.

"Fifty bucks a can." Hammer's eyebrows shot up.

"I could unload the whole lot of them for a thousand dollars right now," Charley said, "if I wanted to. But I don't. I'd just sell a can to you as a favor."

Todd looked at me. "What do you think, Stretch?"

It had been some time since I connected with a real Championship ball, one that wasn't weighted down with "Extra Duty Felt," and I longed to feel one zing off my strings again, especially on the serve when I really took a whack at it. The only thing that flew better than real Championships were bald eagles, but because they were so worn out, little pleasure was associated with them. (Of course, at the complete opposite end of the spectrum were god-awful Tretorns, the original indestructible rocks of tennis, otherwise known as elbow crushers or racket breakers, depending on what you valued more, your arm or the frame of your racket.)

As much as I wanted to use the type of ball all the pros used to play with, it would have been an extravagant purchase for a potential Greyhound rider. I left it entirely up to Hammer. "If you're buying," I said.

But he didn't want to spring for the whole can. Even though Todd had already earned decent bucks here at Rock Creek, he would remain on the road for a while, and out there in the wilds of tennis, on an uncharted itinerary, fifty dollars could go a long way, especially for a guy who liked the road better than he did home.

"Oh well, the other guys probably wouldn't go for it anyway," Todd said sadly, and he handed the can back to Charley. "I doubt they'd drop any coin for blue dots, even if it did make their puny serves a little bigger."

It was a relief to see Hammer's competitive side kick in, it gave me confidence. For as well as he performed when at peace, he played even better when slightly aggravated. "We're ready to get it on," he announced, "if those punks are."

I was confident as hell when we went outside with Buckskin Charley to talk to the opponents. They knew what was coming down and were primed for battle; they stood up immediately and walked down in front of us into the hole. As we warmed up, the dozen or so remaining ams began to gather on the stairs and on the deck. This is what they had been waiting for, the tournament finale, the end of which would signify the end of their tennis tour, leaving them with no more elbows to rub and no more reason to hide out from the ho-hum life at home.

True to his word, Todd had worn his lucky new socks for every match in the tournament; he washed them in the bathroom sink each night and hung them to dry. In the mornings they had been slightly damp, but that was of little concern since they functioned only as decorative sleeves and not padding for the feet. One at a time now, with his shoe up on a net post, Todd readjusted the burgundy topped sleeves over his old socks; he tucked them in neatly around his ankles before cinching up his shoelaces. Then he picked up two of his Pro Staffs; he tapped one into the strings of the other, and vice versa. Holding the taut resonating gut of each near an ear, he listened simultaneously to the pinging strings. He settled on one of the rackets, pinged it again and held it to his ear with a dreamy look as if the racket were singing to him. Yes, that would do just fine. He put the other back in his bag alongside the one with the frayed strings he had worn out against Fernando. Now Hammer was ready to get down to business, to show these foreign pros a thing or two, and to help me make a little spare change for the trip home.

Our opponents were doubles specialists, two smallish brothers from New Zealand who had been on the tour five years, never doing much in singles but inching forward steadily in the doubles. And now it felt as if they were inching forward on us, but in theory we were tied, being on serve in the first set, with them up 5-4. And yet I couldn't help but think of them as being ahead, after all, it was they who had the 5 and not us. Of course, how many times had I been the first to reach 5, that magical evil number, and still lost the set! I tried not to think about it. Just flow,

I told myself, watch the ball. Behind me, Hammer had stepped up to the line to serve, so in a matter of minutes the score would be officially tied at 5-all. There was no question about that. I sure was glad I wasn't serving. Shut up, you idiot, I told myself, don't think, just watch the ball. And be ready to move. Flow with the point!

With the net in front of me, I signaled behind my back to stay. I was momentarily entranced as Hammer's serve thumped down the middle for a fence-ringing ace. Yes! Now in the ad court, I signaled to stay again, faked the cross and tried to suck the guy into firing one down the alley to my forehand volley. But Hammer's first serve missed. I let instinct take over and signaled behind my back to go now on the second serve. Hammer confirmed; then there was the sound of the serve and a rush of wind past my ear while in front of me the opponent set up to return a backhand. I flinched toward the alley and hesitated, then darted the other direction to intercept the return which ricocheted conveniently off my strings and shot past the feet of the brother who was at midcourt. Now it was thirty-love and I was riding a wave of confidence.

Hammer missed another first serve, practically knocking the racket out of the opponent's hand in the process. But then the guy got off an amazing return, ripping a backhand between us, which Hammer actually snagged on his way up, only to have it smacked down our throats.

Thirty-fifteen. I was still riding the wave, but better yet, I was at one with the free-spirited nuances that connected the minds of all of us out there in the doubles. Setting up noticeably further from the net than usual, I signaled this time to stay. Then as Todd connected, I moved aggressively forward, directly toward the opponent, which caused him instinctively to throw a lob over me. I was already backpedaling and feeling the rhythm of the leap — BAM, the ball thumped into the middle of the court for a winner. Forty-fifteen.

The next point became a series of quick exchanges at the net — us, them, us, them, us, them; until I eased up a bit and landed one in front of the enemy's foot. Todd sensed the halfvolley coming. He rushed forward and swatted the rising ball before it was scarcely over the net. OK, now we were officially tied at five-all in the first set.

It was time for me and Hammer to break, which we did as we always do, by staying in the backcourt and scrapping. We threw up some great lobs, including a topspin forehand I hit for a clean winner and a skyscraper Hammer slashed into orbit on break point. It was the highest lob hit in Montana that afternoon and possibly North America, or for that matter, the world. First one of the opponents called it, "Mine," but then his brother called him off, "No, mine, I got it." And yet, having so much time to reconsider, when the ball lowered to an altitude of about four stories, he changed his mind. "Ok, yours, you got it, yours," he yelled, and he ran off to cower in the corner and watch sheepishly as the ball sped downward toward his brother's head. It just missed his visor, THWONK it hit the court and bounced back up to the height of a telephone pole, giving him ample time to setup beneath it and wonder when and where to hit the ball, which was not an easy decision with us running football receiver patterns on our half of the tennis court. "Yours, take it, you got it, mate," his brother sang out, just to erase any possible confusion; and the hitter froze mid-swing. He poked the ball upward as if he were tapping it over a volleyball net. "Choke city," Hammer chuckled, and he trotted forward and spiked the ball down at an angle across the court. Now we were up 6-5.

It seems that lob broke more than a serve; we won the next seven games in a row to finish the opponents off at love. "I usually like my bagels with cream cheese on them," Hammer announced brightly as we all drifted up to the net, "but when you're on a tennis court, sometimes I guess a plain bagel will have to do." Judging from the looks on their faces, the opponents were not in a mood to appreciate bagels just then. I doubt even a slice of lox would have cured their blues.

"When I say 'mine' you don't have to tell me 'yours,' just back off and don't say a word," the one who had the official honors of eating the lob said to his brother. "I know it's mine, I'm the one who called it. If you want it, you call it. It's that simple, mate, whoever wants it calls it. You're supposed to call it for yourself, not for the other guy, and especially not when he's trying to hit it." We all shook hands and they left the court, still talking about the tactics of how to call the ball. "I thought maybe you weren't sure," the one brother kept saying, "since I'm the one who called it first."

OK, so now we had won the tournament and I could buy a plane ticket home. I felt good, and it was more than just the money; it was the win, the sense of victory and dominance that lies beneath all athletic endeavor. I knew from my studies at the University that such feelings are deeply rooted in humans — that our modern belly laugh, for instance, is related to the abdominal grunting displayed in the victory stance of an ape. Perhaps I was simply an ape in the jungle, jumping up and down with pleasure, grunting and laughing as my would-be attackers slinked away. Or maybe I was just another Cro Magnon with a fancy club sitting on a rock by the river.

As I said, I felt pretty damn good, and the money didn't hurt either. Happily, I thought maybe I'd stick around for another day and go fishing with Fernando and Hammer and Buckskin Charley.

Chapter Eleven

Berkeley Blues

Charley had the luxury of hiking boots, and he kept up a good pace, but as we trailed behind him in our tennis shoes, the three of us had to crouch here and there to keep from slipping on the wet rocks. Hot as it was, I figured if I fell into the river it would be a refreshing dip, at least where the water was clear and slow. In runs where the water was white with rapids I was more careful about my footing, although even then I imagined I would survive a downstream bobbing in great style. But the hike back up the river would be awkward and slow, if not impossible in places where the sides of the gorge were narrow and wall-like.

Actually, I was more worried about the snakes. I had seen a huge rattlesnake mounted on the rafters back at Charley's place, so I knew they were here. I tried not to let it bother me. But then the trail cut into the brush above the river and I got a little nervous.

"I hope we see a rattler," Charley announced, "it usually means we'll have good fishing." I didn't know what I would prefer, great fishing and rattlesnakes, or just a calm day of horrible fishing. "If you see something that looks like a coiled rope, don't step on it," he said.

A mile further up the river, after several bends, we came to a wide fork that tumbled down from the opposite bank. Charley gave us last minute instructions. "Flip your fly out into the water and let the current take it," he said. "Don't try to make a fancy cast, just flick the end of your pole and that'll do it."

In a moment, Fernando, who was more experienced, had a fish on. The tip of his pole vibrated downward in an arc as he fought to keep the fish out of the fast water, lest it get the full weight of the river behind it and be gone for good. The fish broke the surface in one glistening leap, and then slowly, it zigzagged its way to shore, urged by the patient Fernando, who guided it around rocks that lay in the shallows near us.

Charley came over and studied the submerged fish. It was a large Rainbow, about twenty inches long. "Hey," he said, enthusiastically, "you just caught Moby. I figured he'd be in this stretch. Last time I hooked him, it was up behind that log." He pointed to a fallen tree that lay in the water about twenty yards upstream.

Charley got down on one knee; he put his elbows into the clear water and worked a small pliers near the jaw of the big fish. Now released, the fish looked stunned for a moment; there was the flashing color of it's flank, and then it vanished into the current.

Buckskin Charley told us he had another favorite fish, too, a giant Cutthroat with a hooked jaw. He hadn't seen it in a while. "Probably went downstream in the storm last winter," he said.

Anyway, Charley was right, there was nothing like trout fishing. Hammer and I even caught some.

Another mile up river, as we climbed gingerly over huge granite boulders, Rock Creek became a series of waterfalls and plunge pools. Mist from the swirling waters blew all around us like fine white rain, and that was an awesome relief from the hot Montana sun. But there were times when we stayed in the icy spray too long, hoping for a big fish, and then the sun's prickly rays became a blessing to our frozen faces. "Talk about negative ions," Todd said with his teeth chattering, "I think I'll go sit on a hot rock for a while and dry out."

"There's a good rock over there," I told him, "where that rattlesnake is sunbathing."

Hammer went off, swishing the tip of his pole at the brush as if he were shooing away flies.

We released the fish we caught even though regulations said we could keep them; we were in Buckskin Charley's favorite home water and he wanted to preserve it. Hidden from view and practically inaccessible, he hiked down into that white-water gorge every couple of weeks.

Of course, we lost a few fish too, such was the nature of the throbbing tug-of-war battle with a big trout on the line. The size of salmon, we hooked them on special flies Charley had tied himself, and that made catching them even more thrilling for him. But for Fernando, Hammer and me, it was enough just to be hiking along the roaring river, immersed in the blowing mist. With fishing poles in hand, we had become hunters of trophy trout, and that really Zenned us out. It was as if we were dealing with a match point situation at every step along the slippery rocks. We were calm, alert, poised. That is, until one of the big fish struck.

Because the turbulent water was so frothy, when a fish hit our fly we never saw it coming, and that's what made the sport thrilling — the element of surprise. Those strikes were such an adrenaline-pumping shock at times that one might have supposed the trout were ambushing us, and not the other way around. Sometimes they danced and splashed in great style far out on the surface, as we coaxed them in. Others dove deep into the blue, where they anchored stubbornly to the bottom and tested our patience.

Intermittently, the action slowed down and the sound of the rushing water seemed suddenly amplified; and then we moved on along the misty river. All around, the warm scent of pine rose from beds of damp pine needles that lay drying in the sun. The aroma took me back to the California Sierras, to a week at Tuolumne Camp, where we Dubitski's vacationed when we were all still a family and didn't even know it.

At last, lengthening shadows closed over the river, and everything felt suddenly quiet. Charley broke down his pole. "That was pretty good fishing," he said, "especially when you consider we didn't even see a snake." I wondered how much better it would have been if we had seen a snake. It couldn't have been much better, I figured. And even if it were a lot better, the fact that we hadn't seen any rattlers was a good deal, as far as I was concerned.

Darkness set in as we climbed up out of the gorge. We went the same way we came in, ducking under huge limbs, and squeezing through crevices in the tall rocks. Twice we made use of cables and ropes Charley had installed when he first came to Rock Creek. At the top at last, we came to the main trail — the once roaring sound of the river was barely audible in the distance below. Now the warm air was thick with the scent of wild anise, while overhead, a faint twinkling of evening stars grew brighter by the minute. Fernando requested a rest, probably just to enjoy the moment. So we took a breather and Charley made us swear never to tell anybody about that piece of water. "Don't worry," Hammer quipped, "the only people who are ever going to know about that place are the fish. And the rattlesnakes. Isn't that right, Stretch?" I had an instinct to give him a high-five, but there was a fishing pole in my right hand, and then I realized that was the only hand I ever used for that sort of thing. My left arm was so ineffective and uncoordinated compared to my right! I felt suddenly lopsided as the four of us marched the rest of the way to the trailhead.

Our poles had been bent in the mist on that sunbaked day, and our lines had been throbbing, as were our hearts, with the thrill of trout fishing in Montana with Buckskin Charley. Now at an altitude of thirty thousand feet, on my way home to California, it was easy to confuse the drone of the jet engines with the rushing waterfall sound of the river. I could still smell the cedars and tall pines, and the anise lying low in the brush. I was glad Todd had talked me into going to Montana. I was satiated with contentment, about everything — the Oakland cop, the club in Portland, the dentist's family, rattling boxcars, the tennis I had played, the money I had won. Pleasant memories of the hacks I had encountered lingered in my mind (some of them actually had very effective games, and though they were flawed, they had retained an enthusiasm for the game I wished I still had.)

I thought about the Bulldozer and the Cat and the look on their faces when we offered them servings from that jar of Penns. I wondered if the Cat was still limping; I figured he was still using his special dampener. I pictured Todd's lucky new socks and the lob he slashed into orbit to break the backs of the New Zealanders. I wondered how much further one of the Wilson blue-dots would have shot into space. Then I thought about Fernando, the debonair Fernando Vasquez, his poetry and his braided ponytail, a ponytail that was so different from the one that tucked back the sandy brown hair of the dentist's wife when she stood on that lonely track bed waving good-by to us in her faded levis. I thought about her for a while, then the airy drone of the plane's engines brought me back to the sound of white-water and the fishing. Hell, looking back, it would have been worth it to freight out to Montana just for that day of trout fishing with Buckskin Charley.

Todd's grandfather picked me up at the Oakland airport just before nightfall. I had called him as a favor to Todd; he said the old man would want to know first-hand all about the tournament and our adventure on the freighters. So I spared no detail as we cruised into the sad flats of Berkeley in the old man's well kept Chevy Malibu. He drove peacefully, punctuating much of what I told him with a chuckle and a slow nod of his head. And then I knew where Todd got his introspective grin, indeed, his very outlook on life. By the time we got to the railroad tracks in front of my apartment, the old man was so pleased you would have thought he'd been on the adventure with us. He particularly liked the part about me nicknaming his grandson Hammer.

"Hammer, eh? That's a good one," he chuckled, "I knew that hammock would come in handy." His head bobbed up and down thoughtfully as he reviewed the situation out loud. "Won the doubles and almost the singles. Made some money and now he's out playin' another one. Hammer, haw! That's a good one." The old man was happy as a clam.

We shook hands through the window of his car in the darkness, and I thanked him for the ride. Then that sweet old Malibu pulled away from the curb and purred down the street like a kitten on wheels.

In spite of the fact that I felt as if I had left a piece of my heart in Montana (and on the freighters on the way out there) it was good to be home again. I put my big tour bag down with a sense of finality, and then I went to my nightstand to see if there were any messages on the answering machine. My half-made bed beckoned, and I felt like crawling in right then I was so exhausted. But the answering machine was blinking frantically.

There were a dozen messages, some which I had expected, like the call from the neighborhood kids wondering when I'd be back and the guys on the JC team getting anxious about the upcoming season. A professor I had been trying to get in touch with had returned my call, and then I heard Evonne's bubbly voice coming out of the speaker, then a few rushed words from my brother; I hadn't heard from him in a while. Then came the knockout punch, a message I had to play twice to be sure I wasn't imagining things. It was Bonnie, the dentist's wife, calling from Portland to say she was going to be on an extended trip to San Francisco for her aunt's funeral and would it be possible for us to get together? She would be around for a couple of weeks taking care of family matters. Ponytail of my dreams! Faded jeans of my wildest fantasies! Would it be possible for us to get together? Gee, I don't know, I told my pillow, let me check my schedule. I slipped between the cool sheets, my head spinning with the nearness of sleep and the anticipation of things I wasn't sure I should be thinking about.

And when my midnight lover rolled in from the distant flatlands, she wasn't jealous at all. She moaned sweetly in the dark and invited me to my first ménage à trois.

After some time on the road, crawling at last into one's very own bed is magical and reassuring. It's like curling up beside the mother of one's soul. And that goes double for a lost soul, which is how I felt as I lay under the covers late the next morning wishing I were still out on the road with Todd and Fernando. Eventually, I got up and walked around in a fog in my dismal little apartment. And then I came to my senses and realized I couldn't have it both ways. No matter how much the gunslinger wilds of tennis beckoned, I had made a decision to lay low and build a future. A future that would be determined more by school than the number of notches carved on the handle of my tennis racket.

I tried to see the good things I was going to have, and indeed, the good things I had right then. I mean, after all, my life in Berkeley wasn't so bad, and soon it would be spiced up by a visit from a woman who looked like she belonged on the cover of Vogue magazine, give or take a few very tidy wrinkles. Hell, Bonnie was probably younger than I was. That was one of the deceptions about life in the fast lane of tennis — being around young people so much of the time it was easy to forget how old one really was. Now at thirty-seven, I had to be realistic; my body was slowly but surely losing its magic. Besides, there was less opportunity to make money each year, with the independent tournaments becoming fewer as more and more of them upgraded to be part of the official circuit. And those ATP events were suicide — they were stacked with dozens of primed, youthful all-stars trying to work their way up to the big time. It's just that it was so hard to get the fray of tennis out of my system, and now that I had been to Montana, my appetite had been whetted again.

Out of habit, I went over to the bookcase and turned on the stereo to a laid back FM station. Suddenly, there was the sound of "Desperado," the Eagles' song, its lonely truths filling the room.

D e s p e r a d o — Why don't you come to your senses — You've been out ridin' fences for so long now

D e s p e r a d o — Oh, you ain't gettin' no younger — Your prison is walkin' through this world all alone

D e s p e r a d o — You better let somebody love you — You better let somebody love you — Before it's too late

The words washed into the back of my mind, pleading at my lifestyle, haunting me with their sad rhythm as I walked aimlessly through the kitchen and out to the cool of the back porch. *D e s p e r a d o.* I watched the sun peek blandly through the gray Bay Area sky, and then I came to my senses. That's it, I told myself, it's just like that dim sun — everything loses its luster, life is one big compromise. That's what growing up is all about. You can't be chasing the tournaments forever. Anyway, the body breaks down. Sure, you can hone the game like a sharp knife, and it cuts great — but then you sharpen it too much and it breaks. There comes a time when it's best just to chill out and go for the long haul.

The sun broke through overhead, creating an opening of blue in the haze. Maybe we would get a nice day, after all! I began to feel better about things, about the team I was coaching, about school. Anyway, I told myself, it wasn't like I was hanging up my rackets for good, I'd play another tournament sometime if I felt like it.

D e s p e r a d o — *Why don't you come to your senses* (The song was still lecturing me!)

You better let somebody love you

You better let somebody love you — *Before it's too late*

I began to think about the dentist's wife. Maybe she was the one, the one in the song for me. I tried to think of her as Bonnie and not as the dentist's wife; it was better that way.

Suddenly there was the flat buzz of the doorbell, summoning me up front for what I hoped wouldn't be a couple of Jehovah's Witness ladies with leaflets about the devil in their hands. It was two boys from the neighborhood. Thank god! Grins widened on their young black faces, their white eyes lit up.

"Where you been?" the tall one said. "We wanted to play tennis on Sunday."

"Yeah, where were you?" his little friend chimed in.

These two nine-year-olds were part of a group of neighborhood kids I taught on Sundays just for the hell of it. It was kind of like our church (and the congregation was getting bigger all the time.) I hadn't forgotten about them, it's just that there was the possibility I'd be back, and taking off to Montana had been kind of a spur of the moment decision.

The tall kid was Sheldeen. When we first met, he was alone in the neighborhood park, shooting baskets. So I joined him. He told me his name was Sheldeen and that he was named after a friend of his father's from the army. Apparently the guy never made it back from Nam.

I asked if Sheldeen was the guy's first name, or his last name. He said he didn't know. "My dad never talked about it much. My mom just told me he was a big blond guy."

And that was the last we ever discussed it.

Anyway, Sheldeen was glad I was back, but I could see his spirit was dampened. "Yeah," he said, "we waited at the park on Sunday, but you weren't there." I felt like a heel; I should have told them I'd be gone.

"How many of you showed up?" I asked.

"Everybody."

"Well then, you had each other to play with. Right?" I said firmly.

The two boys looked at the ground. "You did practice with each other, didn't you?"

"Coach, we tried to, but then some men came and they took our court."

"Were they good players?" I asked.

Sheldeen laughed. "Heck no, they couldn't even hit three in a row."

"Yeah," his little friend said, "we're better than they are."

I told them I was gone on business. "But I'll be there this Sunday for sure. Eleven o'clock sharp. But only if you two run along and get your rackets right now and practice with each other." They looked at me with dreamy kid eyes.

"It's not a weekend, no adults will be around. Go ahead," I insisted, "if you want to play with me on Sunday." They trotted off giggling. "And get Mei Mei too," I hollered. "You like playing with her."

Mei Mei was a ten-year-old Chinese girl who wandered onto the court with her father one Sunday. The next week she was escorted by her fourteen-year-old brother. After that it was just Mei Mei and us. Just the kids and me, and that's the way I liked it — with no parents hanging around. It was better for both me and the kids; I taught better and they learned faster. We were able to relate to each other more naturally when there were no extraneous authority figures to distract them. I became more like them, and I suppose they became more like me.

Of course, there was a price one paid for such an independent teaching program. Like the fact that there was no money in it — it had to be free. In general, the more you charged for a lesson the more parents you'd have sticking their faces in it. I guess that's only natural, but still, it's a big pain in the ass. There's always someone who has to yap at their kid, next thing you know they're trying to tell you how to teach. So my junior program might have been free, but at least I kept the parents at a distance. (Not that those flatland parents would have been a problem at all. It wasn't like the lessons I taught up in the hills where the kids were hand held.)

Understandably, my little Sunday congregation cost me a few bucks here and there for balls and incidental equipment. Which was ok; usually I just pestered friends for their old rackets, and I shortened the handles for the real small frys.

Naturally, we had to settle for the worst, most unpopular court around, which happened to be at a small rundown park not far from where we all lived in the flats. But in a town like Berkeley, even lousy public facilities get their share of traffic, so more often than not, we'd have to wait our turn before streaming onto the court.

Sometimes we'd have to wait out a game of roller hockey first, even though there was a sign clearly forbidding skating on the court. It was an old beat-up sign that said, TENNIS SHOES ONLY, NO BICYCLES, NO SKATING. The sign looked kind of helpless hanging there on the fence; it always reminded me of those Neighborhood Watch signs you see on residential street corners, the metal ones that are all dented up. Sure, there are good, bold intentions behind those signs, but after a while they get all rusted and dinged up from rocks and BB guns and the neighborhoods actually look safer without them. I kind of liked the sign, anyway.

It was a hapless court, but we learned to love every crack in the blacktop and even its droopy old net. Sometimes I'd take a ratchet out of the trunk of my car and raise the net to as much as half a foot higher than it was supposed to be. I figured, for practice, the higher the better; and it didn't seem to phase the kids in the least.

The benefits of my free teaching program went far beyond the fact that there weren't any parents to deal with. For one thing, the kids weren't spoiled club brats — they picked up the balls eagerly, not as if it were some distasteful chore. Often there were other youngsters anxious to help too, kids who were shooting hoops or just hanging out with their skateboards on the nearby blacktop.

Another nice thing was that some of these youths were first-rate natural athletes, the kind of kids who could have been all-star Little Leaguers, for instance, if their folks could have afforded to sign them up for organized baseball. As a teaching pro that was my biggest frustration, to be at the club giving a lesson to a promising junior; but then outside on the sidewalk a young baseballer might walk by in his uniform, and right away I knew the baseball player was the real athlete and the kid I was giving the lesson to was just playing tennis because he wasn't good enough to be a baseball star (or more typically, because he wasn't even good enough to make the team.)

I knew this from experience, after all, I too had played organized baseball as a kid. I was only a fair hitter, but I was a fast base runner and a hot fielder. I once pulled off an unassisted triple play at shortstop. I played center field too and was selected for a number of all-star teams. Nonetheless, I quit in the middle of a Babe Ruth season and gave it all up for tennis. The lure of the racket sport had attracted me; not the glitter, but just the physical aspects of the game. Tennis was more exciting — you got to hit, run, pitch, catch — and you got to do it all the time. You didn't have to wait around for your ups or for something to happen in the outfield. Funny though, now in my dreams, sometimes I get a whiff of the grass in the outfield and I wake up wishing I could just stand around smelling it again (which is a lot easier than running around the tennis court like a madman all the time.)

And so, I occasionally wonder what my life would have been like if I had stuck with baseball. But then I come to my senses and realize that tennis has a gigantic perk. I mean, how many former major leaguers can make a living teaching housewives how to hit a fast ball? And as a tennis player you don't even have to make it to the majors, all you have to do is put on the right clothes and round up the ladies. Try doing that in a catcher's mask!

At the risk of destroying a global myth, however, it must be said that teaching tennis is not as sexy as it appears, and you've actually got to rely on a lot more than just fancy clothes and a cute smile.

Not surprisingly, there were some talented Little Leaguer types in my neighborhood tennis program. And they showed up without their parents, which was perfect. And yet, when I did see their folks, it was with great pleasure. They greeted me warmly, respectfully, and that was about it; they said absolutely nothing about the tennis. But you could tell they approved with every fiber in their bodies. Sheldeen's dad, for instance, was a big black guy in overalls. Occasionally he'd pass by the court with his dog and a smile that was so affable I felt as if he were putting his arm around me. Then he and his dog would go sit under a tree that was so far away he could hardly see his kid hit the ball. That was the type of tennis parent I thrived on, and if it meant giving away the lesson, then so be it. There was no substitute for that kind of trust.

To have such an easygoing father must have been a godsend for Sheldeen, too, and it was surely the reason the kid was so balanced, physically and mentally. He was a rare athlete, the kind of boy who could grow up to win Wimbledon some day, if somehow the rest of the training package were provided. I just hoped he'd stick with tennis and not get drawn into basketball or baseball.

But as much as I liked Sheldeen and the kids in our flatland neighborhood, most of my teaching was up in the hills where I worked with more affluent people. These students paid me the going rate, which was a welcome adjunct to my limited income while in graduate school. The lessons came mostly by referral, though some were holdovers from the old club out near Lafayette, and others were longtime students from before that job, like twelve-year-old Danny who had been with me since the age of four. He had a national ranking now, and with a scholarship and a possible pro career on the line, his folks were smart enough not to mess with the chemistry between us. Of course, for every situation like that there were a dozen other parents who were looking for a new magical coach around every bend in the tennis journey, anxious parents who meant well but knew too much and too little at the same time. Unwittingly, they hampered the development of their offspring and injured both coach and protégé in the process. And to think, all they had to do was let go and allow their hopefuls to be empowered by the unfulfilled dreams of a coach, rather than the dissatisfactions of their own frustrated desires.

I became more in sync with myself after those two little kids from the neighborhood came to my door. My life in the Berkeley flatlands began to take shape again. I found myself thinking about nine-year-old Sheldeen; I wished his dad had the kind of money Danny's father had. Sure, Danny was good for a twelve-year-old, but he didn't have greatness in him like Sheldeen had. Danny was good because he had been groomed like a thoroughbred. Eventually, as he moved into the fourteens, the sixteens, and then the eighteens, other kids were bound to pass him by. His parents, dissatisfied with his performance in those older age groups, would probably decide to find another coach. Even now, I was distancing myself from Danny a little at a time, letting go, I could feel it, getting ready for the big crunch when his folks kissed me off. I tried not to think about him too much. I liked the kid just fine, a lot in fact; that was the problem, a breakup would be hard to take. Sheldeen was a different story; there was nothing his parents would do to take him away; he'd always have a place inside of me.

There were also the guys on the JC team. Even though it was the off-season we stayed in close contact, both on and off the court. And that was rewarding; it was nice to have some older kids around. And, of course, there was school; the professors were great, and a lot of that psych stuff was downright fascinating. I was looking forward to class resuming in a few days. Now that I was settling back into my life in Berkeley, the tennis nomad in me that had been awakened in Montana was going back to sleep again.

I thought I'd call Evonne and Hitch. My sense of withdrawal from the road had diminished, and I figured I could tell them how Todd and I did without feeling too bad about being stuck at home. They'd get a kick about Todd's hammock, and I knew Hitch would want to hear about the fishing. I wasn't sure if I would mention anything about Bonnie. Anyway, I wondered what was up with them.

Nobody was home when I called, so I left a message. Evonne telephoned excitedly the next morning to say they were having a party on the weekend and she was glad we were back in town. I gave her the bad news about Todd still being out there in the badlands of tennis, and she sounded disappointed. But then I told her about Montana, that we had won the dubs. I told her about everything, even Todd's reborn socks, and her laughter howled through the receiver. Then Hitch came on the line, apparently he had just got back from South America. I gave him every detail about trout fishing with Buckskin Charley. I could tell he was into it, he asked a lot of questions. He said some time he and I would fly out to Alaska in his friend's plane and fish for Arctic char and King salmon. Now it truly did feel good to be back. My homies had cured me. Maybe Bonnie will come to their party with me, I thought, as I hung up the phone. The trauma of the funeral should be over by then.

Chapter Twelve

Tenis Envy

And what a great get-together that was! Leave it to Hitch and Evonne to throw a good shindig, not that it was as big as their engagement party — it was just shy of what you might call a crowd. There was a nice sense of group intimacy as we frolicked at their place in the hills with drinks in our hands and nothing in our minds. We danced to oldies and then later as the evening wore on, found ourselves lounging around the living room listening to jazz.

When I had first walked in the door with Bonnie, Hitch was taken aback. "Wow! Where'd you get that?" he exclaimed. "You tennis pros sure know how to pick out the babes."

I could feel my cheeks turning red, I wanted to get inside to a dim corner. "This is a friend of mine from Portland," I said as I moved with Bonnie toward the action in the main room. She was wearing a smart-looking black pants suit, her ponytail unfurled now in buoyant golden brown waves that dropped down over her shoulders. I too was stunned when I picked her up at the BART station. And she smelled so lovely, not perfumey or powdery, but just fresh and airy like a garden after a rain. With her arm in mine and Hitch trailing, we walked in and I introduced Bonnie to Evonne and some of the people I knew from the old club.

The bubbly Evonne was at her best, mingling energetically with friends, many who, like myself, were relatively new in her life. She'd disappear into the kitchen occasionally to reload snack trays or get somebody a drink, then she'd return and join in new pieces of conversation just like she'd been there all along. And she liked Bonnie; the two of them really hit it off. Now in a corner of the room, they were comparing notes as Hitch and I squared off on the green felt of his pool table. Through the talk and music, I heard Todd's name mentioned a couple of times, and mine, and I figured Evonne was describing how she and Hitch had got acquainted down in the hole during her umpiring debut, and of course afterward in the bar. The two of them giggled like school children with martinis in their hands.

"Evonne tells me you're quite a matchmaker," Bonnie said as we walked out to the patio for a breather. In the distance across the dark bay were the sparkling jewels of a San Francisco night, while directly below us in the flats of Berkeley were the dim bulbs of my neighborhood. Suddenly, I felt out of place up there in the lush hills with such a beautiful woman by my side. I tried not to analyze it; what would Hammer do? I thought. Just go with the flow. Yeah, flow with it, man.

"It's not like we planned every detail," I said, "I mean, we knew Evonne would meet Hitchcock but we didn't know it would end up like this, with her and Hitch getting engaged. It was basically a tennis experiment we couldn't resist."

"Spoken like a true scientist." Bonnie looked up at me with amusement. Her arms were around my neck; we were dancing on the dark patio. I wasn't sure how that happened, although we had danced some fast ones earlier with the other couples in the house. Am I dancing

OK? I thought, as we moved to the lingering sound of *Chances Are,* the old Johnny Mathis tune that was coming from inside. Our bodies brushed temptingly time and again as we swayed to the music.

"I suppose you're wondering about my husband," Bonnie said, looking up at me innocently.

"No, actually I was wondering about you. And the music. I don't think I've danced to Johnny Mathis since junior high school."

"This is one of my favorites," she said warmly. "Chances are ... ," she sang along for a while. "Chances are ..." Her delicate voice was just below my ear. The moment was perfect. I knew if I lowered my head her soft cheek would come to mine.

"There's something you should know," she whispered. "It's about Harold and me." I didn't say anything.

"Let me put it this way, he's seeing somebody."

"I'm sorry."

"Don't be. It's a relief, really. It kind of frees me to ..."

"To have an affair, too?"

"Well, yes, I guess so. But it's more than that, it frees me to live. It's like I can think of me first now and I don't have to worry about Harold, for even trifling things. It's like a cloud has been lifted from my mind. Do you know what I mean?"

"I think so. Anyway, I'm glad you're taking it so well."

She pulled away and looked into my eyes for a while without saying anything. "Don't think I'm doing this just to get even," she said finally, "I'm just trying to be me again after all these years."

Her face was inches away. Now in the night her blue eyes held only a vague suggestion of their daytime glimmering, and yet they were magical, temptingly inviting, as was the buoyant promise of her lips and the cool smooth skin at the well of her neck. I felt like ...

Suddenly I became aware that the lingering Johnny Mathis tune had dissipated into the night. Everything was still for a long moment. Then came cheers from inside as Chubby Checker's voice belted out *The Twist.* Bonnie and I broke our embrace and laughed.

"Should we join the others?" I asked.

"Whatever you want," she said. Whatever I want? She took my hand, and as we walked back inside I realized that what I want and what I do are usually two different things. I chided myself for not being truer to my actual feelings; I should have stayed out there on the patio. You need to honor your impulses, I told myself, and not disregard them just because they are impulses. Flow with your feelings, don't be so analytical, be more like Hammer.

While some couples relived the old days twisting to Chubby Checker, we talked it up in the living room with Hitch and Evonne and the rest of the gang. We all sat on the rug around a long coffee table with our backs against various pieces of furniture. Three half-filled bottles of wine and a mix of pretzels and nuts were on the table, while above it, conversations crisscrossed rapidly.

"I hear you came down from Oregon on business," Hitchcock said to Bonnie.

"Well, not exactly business, family matters. A funeral, actually."

"Oh, I'm sorry," Hitch said quickly, "that's always kind of a drag, I guess."

"It's kind of heavy, as they say." She sat up a little straighter. "But it does have its good points. It's a family gathering. You get to see people you haven't seen in a while."

"You mean like Thanksgiving?" Hitch said with a goofy grin.

Bonnie laughed. "Yes, like Thanksgiving, I suppose. Though it's a little more somber. I'll tell you what the real benefit is ..." She interrupted herself to lift her wine glass and collect her thoughts. "The real benefit of funerals is that they are reminders. Reminders of what's important. Reminders that life is short. That you're not going to get another shot at it, and that you've got to live now. Really live. Because, after all, you're going to be dead for a long time. A very long time."

I began to think about long spans of time, about people who had died ages ago and were obviously still dead, guys like Aristotle and Plato, Shakespeare, Isaac Newton. Smart dudes, who died nonetheless, hundreds of years ago, and they would be dead for a long time yet to come. Then I thought about Jesus and Biblical times; I imagined being alive back then, wearing a robe and sandals, even to formal occasions, probably even into the grave. I thought about the dinosaurs and being a pitiful cave man during the stone age, dying naked in some mishap, perhaps in a tar pit. Then the big bang exploded in my mind, brilliantly, some 14 billion years ago. Now that was a long time ago! And yet, in reality it was nothing. After all, there was the future, too.

And what if I multiplied all that by infinity; that was more like death, an incalculable sleep from which I would never wake up. Ever. No matter what happened.

Bonnie was right, we would be dead for a long-ass time. I could remember going to my mother's funeral and thinking those same things, that life is too short and all, but then gradually over the years I began to take being alive for granted again. Now I had been reminded once again of death.

"I'll drink to that." Evonne held up her glass and drained it voraciously. "You've got to live, really live. Life is definitely too short. You only get one shot and you've got to live it to the hilt. Don't hold back. That's why Hitch and I got engaged, and that's why we're not getting married right away, not because we don't want to be married, but because we want to savor our engagement. You're only engaged once so you might as well enjoy it. No sense rushing into marriage."

"Of course," Evonne continued, "we're living together, why reserve that for marriage? If anybody doesn't approve, that's their problem. Right? Besides, I want to make sure my future husband can fix a leaky faucet and change a light bulb. You know, in case something ever happens to me."

"Yeah," Hitch chuckled, "and I wanted to make sure she can fry an egg, just in case I fall in a hole in a place like Kazakhstan. So naturally we have to be living together."

"Hear, hear! Cheers! Here's to living together. Here's to Thanksgiving. Here's to funerals!" Various chants of agreement broke forth in good humor from our well lubricated crowd around the coffee table. "You've got to live now! Go for it!"

There was, however, one lady at the other end of the table who didn't give her blessing to our hedonistic commandments (though her husband didn't seem to object.) She argued that it would be an improper example for young people if we all just lived together before getting married, that it would be almost as bad as same-sex marriages.

"Hear, hear! Here's to same-sex marriages!" came from our end of the table.

"What's proper is proper," the lady insisted with a distinct New England accent. Now I remembered her from the club. She was an uppity CQ, the type of tennis player who uses a ra*cq*uet and not a ra*ck*et. As for me and Hammer, we play exclusively with rackets, so naturally we're CK's and proud of it. Hell, if we're going to hit the ball, we're going to hit it with a racket, a well-built, powerful tennis racket, not some dainty aberration of one that needs to be reminded of hoity-toity French society every time it twits the ball.

Anyway, the lady was a hardcore CQ, the type who pranced around the court and poked at the ball with a racquet (pronounced *rakwet*.) She probably thought the most important duty of a tennis player was to keep one's shoes white.

"CQ," I whispered, leaning across the coffee table to Hitch. He knew what I was talking about. "CQ all the way, baby!" he replied through the lady's prolonged and properly enunciated argument for not living in sin.

"I think she polishes her tennis shoes," I told him.

"Yeah," he said, "she probably throws them in the washing machine with her undies after every match." The goofy side of Hitch was obviously gaining momentum, and I was glad my date was embroiled in dialogue with Evonne.

"That's pretty extreme," I told Hitch. "Besides, even the best tennis shoes would come apart after all that washing."

"Well, OK," he slurred, "maybe she doesn't wash them that often, how am I supposed to know? We could ask Warren." Apparently, the CQ was the wife of Hitch's friend, Warren. I think he felt sorry for him. "Hey, Warren! Drink up, buddy. Here's to Thanksgiving!"

"Cool it, Hitch," I said in a serious tone, "she might come over here and hit you with her rakwet."

"Ouch!" he mocked with an effeminate hand gesture.

Across the coffee table from each other, Evonne and Bonnie were into something deep now, something deep and obviously worth sharing. "Hey, everybody, listen," Evonne announced enthusiastically. "We figured it out, we finally figured out what tennis is all about, why everybody is playing. Why they try to prove how good they are, you know, in tournaments and leagues and all that." She had gained our attention and talk around the table began to subside.

"Or, do you want to tell them, Bonnie?"

My date laughed. "No, you're the hostess, this one's your baby. Anyway, I'm not really a tennis player."

All eyes were on Evonne. "OK then," she said, "most people are playing tennis because they're suffering from a disease — it's called Tennis Envy." The women at the table laughed, followed by belated chuckles from the men. It was a well educated crowd; surely all of us knew something about Freudian psychology. Tennis envy? Perhaps she was right.

"It's true," Evonne went on, "it doesn't matter if you're a man or a woman, everybody wants a bigger, better tennis game. Isn't that right, Bonnie?"

"Looks that way to me, and I've been around a lot of fanatical tennis players, believe me."

Hitch picked up his drink. "Tennis envy," he chortled, "here's to tennis envy, but it's not spelled like that, there's only one N in tenis envy." He wrote it down on a piece of paper and held it up so everyone could appreciate how cleverly the true spelling fit the nature of the ailment.

"Hear, hear! Tenis envy, here's to tenis envy! Hip, hip, hooray! Bravo for tenis envy!" Everyone was pleased, although there was some disagreement as to how to pronounce it. Was it ten us, as in tennis, or was it teenus?

It was decided that the deviation in spelling was sufficient, but that to stray in pronunciation would not adequately identify the sport, especially in casual conversation with those who had never heard of the disorder. So, even though an N would be missing, "tennis" envy would remain the official pronunciation.

"Yes, we all suffer from tenis envy," proclaimed Warren. His wife, the CQ with the New England accent, was in total agreement. She thought it was a wonderful concept, but she probably thought she was one of the few unblemished by it since she wasn't that concerned with winning. In truth, though, she was stricken with a rare form of the ailment, a subtle aberration focused not so much on having a bigger game as with having, perhaps, a whiter game.

Evonne was probably the only one who was not inflicted with tenis envy. She was into the sport primarily for exercise and recreation; if she improved, she improved. Sure, she took lessons, but for her it was basically fun — she wasn't consumed by tennis, she didn't go to bed at night thinking about a particular shot she had hit or a change she needed to make in her backhand. But most everybody else on the planet wanted desperately to be better than they were. They entered tournaments and leagues anxiously, often wanting to be in higher divisions than they were ready for; unless of course, they were sandbagging, in which case they opted for lower divisions so they could win more and enjoy the celebrity of their imaginary omnipotence. In short, they fell victim to the sport, and in so doing, exhibited varying degrees of tenis envy.

An inebriated discussion ensued that night in the Berkeley hills. Was it a true medical condition? What would Freud have said? Would he have just been amused, or would he have lit his cigar and held it high, a curiously enlightened expression on his neatly bearded face? "Ah yes, tenis envy. I'll have to tell Jung about this."

I thought the discovery was rather clever, and I was proud of my date for having a hand in it. I realized how much she and Evonne had hit the nail on the head (and they did it with the butt end of a tennis racket.)

It was 2 am when I escorted Bonnie up the steep San Francisco stairs to her dead aunt's house. The family members from Nebraska were asleep, so we stood on the fog-swept porch and agreed to meet in a couple of days. She gave me a peck on the cheek and that was it.

As I started up the old Dodge Dart, I realized the gas tank was on empty and I needed to get across the bay. My concern mounted as I drove further away from downtown with the engine giving off an occasional hiccup. But then conveniently, an all-night gas station appeared on the corner of 4th and Harrison, just before the onramp to the freeway. I got out and began to fuel up. Then I noticed the automatic hold latch on the pump was broken. That meant I'd have to squeeze the handle the entire time and inhale toxic petro fumes from close up. I coughed just thinking about it.

Handily, I kept an old tennis ball in the glove compartment for just such occasions. I wedged the pliable yellow ball into the pump handle so it held the trigger at full throttle. Then I stepped away from the nearly visible fumes and watched as the noisy pump clicked away. Numbers scrolled across its face like a slot machine that didn't know when to quit.

I was glad I didn't have to squeeze the pump handle. I was nursing an elbow problem and was trying to be as careful as possible with my arm; so it wasn't just a matter of avoiding toxic fumes. That handy tennis ball was looking out for my arm too. I admired the fact that it was such a useful implement.

Suddenly the old Dart had had enough and the ball popped out of the handle. It bounced into the foggy San Francisco night and began to roll down 4th Street, against the sporadic late night traffic. I watched as the ball gathered momentum and sped downhill in all its dim yellow glory. A dead Penn 4, a good ball that had seen better days and was now spinning out of control down the wide boulevard of 4th Street. The ball careened off an oncoming tire as if it were in a great pinball machine, and then it shot out of sight.

I felt good about the ball. With a little luck some kid would find it. The right kid would keep it. He'd put it in his baseball glove. Or in the closet with his frisbee. Or maybe the ball would end up on his dog's bed. Then one day it would be gone, because in a city of steep streets like San Francisco, a ball was hard to hold on to.

The old Dart ran smoothly as it negotiated the lower span of the Bay Bridge with a full tank of gas in its belly. In the green darkness below, mesmerizing lines of white-caps pulsed in the choppy bay. I had heard of people jumping off the bridge, down into those cold white-caps. I wondered what hitting the water would feel like; and then suddenly I felt drenched. I shivered behind the wheel and immediately thought of Bonnie, her warm body, how good it would feel, her smooth warm flesh against mine.

It had been quite an evening. And though Bonnie didn't really play tennis, she was obviously a keen observer of those who did. Together, she and Evonne had discovered tenis envy (with some assistance from Hitch, I suppose.) Not that it took much insight to realize that tennis players want a bigger, better game; the genius came not so much in diagnosing as in naming the neurosis.

I was anxious to tell Hammer about it. I could see him now, nodding his head thoughtfully, the grin widening. "Tenis envy, that's deep. Very deep, dude. Evonne? And the chick from Portland? That's deep too."

In Todd's absence, however, and in an effort to keep from falling asleep at the wheel, I embarked on a one-sided conversation on the subject with the old Dart. I rambled, elaborated, and expanded, imagining I were Freud himself. I saw the big picture, indeed, the very big picture of tenis envy. "You see," I put down my cigar and explained, "whether tennis players are male or female, they suffer equally from the disorder, something that would certainly be viewed as an imbalance, were it not the energizing force behind the entire industry."

Yes, and it wasn't just the players — the manufacturers too wanted a bigger game. I could see it all clearly now. That's why they made bigger, better rackets, rackets that were more expensive and satisfied temporarily the urge to hit the ball harder. At the same time, of course, jealousies were provoked among rival manufacturers who were quick to howl that they too had the most recent additions to the periodic table in their equipment. A jockstrap, for example, with the right atoms in it, could make a serve-and-volleyer out of a baseliner; or perhaps it was a sport bra that would magically transforms one's game (depending on whether one was playing Davis Cup or Federation Cup, I suppose.) Never mind technique, it's all in the molecules, invisible molecules that can make you bigger, badder, better, if only you get them in your underwear, or at least on your tennis racket.

Then I thought about the clubs and tennis associations — they too are inflicted with the disorder. Yes, even the USTA suffers from tenis envy. The USTA is tired of being the short kid on the block of professional sports. It feels shrimpy compared to basketball and football and would dearly like to be as big, for instance, as Major League Baseball.

"The USTA especially wants a bigger game," I told my Dodge Dart. "Why do you think they made decimal points out of us?"

Decimal points?

"Yeah, remember the days," I said, "not so long ago when tennis life was simple, when we were all just classified by letters of the alphabet? Remember? We were simply A players, B players, or C players." There was an Open division too, but that was the same as the A class. (Later, the USTA changed that, separating the Opens; and the A players became the division that was previously labeled as *the B's*.)

My car was a good listener, so I rambled on. "Or, you could have been a D player, god forbid. Remember that time a D player sat in the back seat? I don't think you liked it much. But how would you like to have an algebraic equation as a passenger? It could happen — you might get stuck with a 3.5 or a 2.0, or any other number for that matter. Even Hammer and I are numbers now! For crissake, you'd think the twenty-six letters of the alphabet would have provided enough classifications for the rating of tennis players! But no! Not at all — not even the infinite supply of whole numbers is sufficient! The USTA needs twice that many!" I shouted at the windshield at seventy miles an hour. "It is for this reason they have chosen to use decimal points, so they can put some players in the class between two of the numbers, as in 4.5, which lies between 4.0 and 5.0 and has the further encumbrance of converting us all into decimal points. In other words," I yelled out the window for the whole world to hear, "we can't just be a three or a four — that would be too simple — we have to be a three POINT 0 or a four POINT 0!"

I calmed down, realizing then the advantage of the decimal points — yes, the opportunity to double the number of available divisions could be crucial, were the infinite supply of whole numbers to suddenly run out.

"Like I said," I told a guy in a bakery truck who was passing me on the bridge, "I would have thought the twenty-six letters of the alphabet would have been enough." But secretly I knew that the letters had their disadvantages, since nobody would ever really want to be known as a D player, except maybe the guy who was an F player. In short, the numbers were a subtle way of camouflaging abilities; after all, the difference between a 5.0 and a 2.5 sounds much less than the difference between an A and an F.

My car coughed as it bounced over the railroad tracks; ah yes, we were home now. Goofy and drunken with sleep deprivation, I pulled up alongside the cracked curb in front of my sad little Berkeley apartment. I longed for the old days. I wished we hadn't turned into decimal points.

Chapter Thirteen

Good Vibes

I was groggy Saturday morning when Sheldeen came by. I hadn't had much sleep, considering Evonne's party and returning Bonnie to San Francisco and all. I got back so late, in fact, that my midnight freighter had already made her 3AM rounds past my little 2nd Street pad, and the last of her distant moans had long since dissipated over the bayside flatlands. So now it was almost noon and I stood dazed, holding the front door open for Sheldeen and his older brother and a friend of his brother's. The friend was a long-haired white boy who was into going barefoot and wearing jeans with big flappy holes in the knees.

I shut the door after them and noticed a distinct musty odor. I knew it was coming from the hippie-looking white kid, because both Sheldeen and his brother had been over before and the place never smelled like that. Personal experience told me it was the smell of clothing that had been around too much pot smoking.

The four of us sat around my little kitchen table not saying too much. Suddenly, and with a graceful show of his hand, the hippie kid reached into his shirt pocket and pulled out a hand-rolled cigarette. He put it in the middle of the table. The rich skunky aroma brought back memories, some good, some bad. It's definitely the real thing, I thought.

"It's purple-haired skunk," Sheldeen's brother said enthusiastically, "made from Thai seeds, homegrown right here in Berkeley. You want some?"

I longed for the old days, the days when I didn't know better, the days when I thought I could play better stoned (even though I could never keep the score straight.) "No thanks," I said, "that stuff gets me too confused and I can't get anything done. Then I'm tired as hell the next day. Plus there's the cancer risk. You know it is smoke, after all."

Nobody said anything, but all eyes were on the joint. "Worst of all," I added, "it cuts into my wind, and an athlete depends on his wind. I end up panting and gasping on the court. I suppose you guys wouldn't know about that."

"I know about that," Sheldeen said.

I knew Sheldeen's brother had come over with the hippie kid because he thought I was cool and he wanted me to think he was cool. My coolness was probably slipping away fast. "Don't get me wrong," I said, "I think it's a fascinating high, it's just that it's counterproductive. I'm good for one or two tokes a year, max. That's about it, and only if the time is right. This is definitely not the right time, as much as I wish it were. And just wishing it were the right time isn't enough to make it the right time. That's just common sense, wouldn't you agree?"

Sheldeen's older brother looked sadly at me. "I know what you mean," he said, "It's not always the right time."

"It's never going to be the right time for me," Sheldeen said casually, and I knew he was right, that inside his little nine-year-old brain were thoughts of conviction, thoughts that wouldn't be swayed by peer pressure or idle curiosity — ever. Sheldeen was the type of kid who wanted to do things the right way, the way that worked best, the way that would make a winner out of him. At an early age he had learned that it was more than strength, speed, and size that gave a guy an edge. He had those things in abundance, so naturally, he found himself competing against older boys, big boys who would always be stronger and faster. And so, Sheldeen learned to rely on skill and cunning as much as his awesome athletic ability. This is why on the tennis court with me he was so technique-conscious, always wanting to make sure he was doing it right. And yet, Sheldeen could tolerate the weakness of his friends — if they wanted to goof around on the court, he didn't admonish them. But if he sensed they really wanted to hit the ball right, he'd help them out.

Now in my apartment with his thirteen-year-old brother and his brother's friend, he knew better than to say too much. "Go ahead if you want to," he told his brother, "but I'm not having any." Sheldeen would let his example do the talking. In that sense he was a natural leader, especially on the sports field, a place where actions speak louder than words. It occurred to me that at the opposite end of the spectrum was the political arena, a boundless field where the smallest word could overshadow the greatest of deeds. I doubted Sheldeen would ever be comfortable there, even though he seemed like the kind of guy you'd want in public office some day, when he was retired from his life as an athlete.

The hippie kid picked up the joint from the kitchen table with less fanfare than he had presented it, and he dropped it into his musty shirt pocket.

"Okay, pro, we'll catch you later." Sheldeen's brother gave me a nod, and the three of them got up and dragged their feet to the front door. Sheldeen stopped momentarily to admire an action picture of a youngster I had on top of a bookcase — it was Danny, my nationally ranked twelve-year-old.

"Who's this guy?" he asked, "he looks pretty good."

Indeed, it was a shot taken of Danny at the Fiesta Bowl, in mid-air on a leaping overhead. And yes, he did look pretty damn good, like a miniature Davis Cupper, in fact.

"That's Danny," I said, "he's a little older than you are."

"When I'm older, maybe you'll have a picture of me, too."

"You bet your ass I'll have a picture of you, probably a lot sooner than you think."

Sheldeen went over to the stationary bike I had in the front room; he stroked the smooth cushioned seat. "You can stay and ride, if you like," I told him, "I'm not going anywhere."

"That's okay," he said, and he went out the door with the others. I knew he'd be alright, despite the drugs, the lack of money, and all the other things that came with the neighborhood. Sheldeen had a goal, and that would keep him straight. He was going to be a champion and he knew it. He just wasn't sure it would be in tennis; he liked basketball too.

"Hey, Coach," he called back from the walkway, "see you tomorrow in church." (That was our little joke about my Sunday tennis clinics.)

"I'll bring the balls," I replied, and his face lit up with a white-toothed grin.

Having picked up some required reading at the University bookstore, I spent a few hours trying to get a jump on my coursework, which would begin in a few days. Because I was never able to sit still for very long, I found this task difficult, although it was becoming easier as I slowed down with age. The other thing that made it difficult was that my mind tended to wander, especially if the material was boring. Thankfully, the Psych and Social Psych courses I was enrolled in were interesting, so my daydreaming was limited to sporadic thoughts about Fernando and Hammer, who were still out on the road. Okay, I confess, I also had occasional thoughts about Bonnie. Actually, they were more than occasional — her presence was on every page, in the middle of each line, in fact. Nonetheless, I succeeded in downing a chapter in both books. Then I went out to teach tennis for a couple of hours on a private court in the hills, a regular Saturday afternoon gig.

After my lessons, I stopped on the north side of campus to see what was going on at the Berkeley Rose Garden. That great flowery expanse is tiered like an amphitheater, and there are tennis courts in it. I often taught there on weekdays. I walked downward, in among the trees and blossoms, where the scent of tall evergreens mixed with the delicate fragrance of roses. Unable to resist, I sat down to watch a wedding in progress. A tall bearded fellow delivered the words as melodic fluttering sounds came from a woman who strummed a harp in a kneeling position alongside the bride and groom. They were all wearing shorts and hiking boots and looked like they might have been out for an afternoon walk together, when suddenly, two of them decided to get married. Such is the inspirational setting of the Rose Garden, with its leafy canopies and its soulful view of San Francisco and the Bay.

On the upper tennis court were two players I recognized immediately. They were professors from the University with below average games but very appealing European accents. Even their grunts and groans had a worldly flavor to them and seemed to suggest they were better players than they actually were. I imagined for a moment I too had a foreign accent. I figured I could charge another ten bucks an hour for tennis lessons with a French accent, for instance. But then I wasn't sure if maybe I wouldn't prefer an Australian accent. I settled finally on a blend, imagining I were a Frenchman who had perfected his English in Melbourne, perhaps having remained there on a year-long fling after a good showing in the Australian Open. Yes! I would sound like a cross between Jean-Claude Killy and Crocodile Dundee. It wouldn't matter what I was talking about, so long as it was on a tennis court, even the experts would pay top dollar to wait in line and hear me tell it. And the women! By god, how the ladies would gather 'round me; and for them the presence of a tennis court would be irrelevant, perhaps even an obstruction, a cumbersome barricade between the feathers of my voice and their delicate ears.

The foreign professors continued their exotic grunts and groans, while just below, on the Garden's middle court, some mixed-up doubles was going on (two girls against two guys.) Below this casual battle of the sexes was a concrete backboard, which was really handy despite being not quite high enough to keep the ball from flying over once in a while. Unoccupied, the wall beckoned to me. I checked out the other nearby court, where two men were swatting the ball awkwardly at an accomplished lefty lady. I was hungry to hit the wall, to get the stiffness from teaching out of my body, but I knew if I stepped out there, that threesome would ask me to play doubles. I wouldn't have minded getting a groove going with the smooth-hitting lady, but jumping around in spasmodic doubles with the two hacks was out of the question. If they asked me to play I would claim an injury, which wasn't so far from the truth, since I had some major kinks that needed to be worked out. A rhythm of overheads on the wall, for instance, would give my back a chance to stretch out nicely. Besides, being the strongest player in a pickup doubles game is usually a drag because they never hit the ball to you, and it becomes more like a game of keep-away. All you do is stand around wearing out your knees for nothing. (I wince when I say that because both my knees have been operated on and their time on the court is eroding away.)

"Care to join us?" one of the hacks called out just as I was easing into a series of sweet forehands against the wall.

"Thanks, but I'm not up to it today," I replied without missing a stroke, "I've got some things to work out here. Another time, if you don't mind."

The two hacks stood and watched me for a while, then they resumed their erratic attempts against the smooth-hitting lady. I knew she would have wanted to hit with me as much as I would have liked to hit with her, but we were both stuck, she with the hacks and me with the wall. I definitely had the better deal.

It felt good to be hanging out at the Rose Garden on that sunny Berkeley afternoon, just hitting the wall and stretching around with the fragrance of roses in the air and the distant view of San Francisco between the limbs of evergreens. But soon it would cool off. So I made the ascent back up to street level to get my sweats out of the old Dart.

I could feel my hamstrings tighten as I bent to it and trudged up the steep trail. When I got to the top, a car rolled lazily by the curb. Suddenly I was inspired, perhaps like a cocker spaniel, and I jogged a mile or so up the meandering curves of Euclid Avenue imagining I could keep up with a Volkswagen bus.

The return trip was all downhill. Thank god! Breathing deeply, I sat down on the deck of the Rose Garden, feeling exhausted and energized at the same time (an endorphin high, I suppose.) People were beginning to show up for the sunset viewing ritual — mostly couples and people walking their dogs, dogs who obviously enjoyed the serene view of San Francisco Bay darkening in the pink glow of a sinking sun. I wondered if dogs had endorphins. Then I felt the need to be with someone; I fought off a chill of loneliness as I noticed the growing number of couples, couples of all ages, some with skateboards and acne, others with canes and gray hair. No matter, they all held hands, or they just sat quietly leaning against each other, their minds connected by the vibes, vibes that seemed to connect all of us together. I thought about Bonnie. I would bring her here, I decided. For some tennis. For the roses and the view. And for the sunset. I wanted her to see the people, to feel the vibes, vibes that were unmistakably Berkeley vibes.

Chapter Fourteen

A Center Strap Kind Of Day

The net was droopy in church Sunday morning, as it always was. Hell, sometimes it was flat on the court, so a little low was no problem, particularly when I could take a ratchet out of the trunk of my car and crank it up. But today I felt too lazy to bother with that. I had the kids in mind, I told myself — if I left the net low, tennis would be easier and they would feel more satisfied with the way they were playing. It would build their confidence. On the other hand, if I raised the net that would actually be better training. It was a tough call. Sheldeen was probably the only one who would notice the net wasn't up to regulation. I wondered how much a low net would bother him, deciding in the end, that even though he would go along with it for the group's sake, it would trouble him, particularly if he thought it could be fixed. And yet, if the crank mechanism were broken or I didn't have a ratchet, Sheldeen would accept the condition and not give it a second thought. He would simply make the best of it, like the way a smart player plays in the wind. I thought of telling him my ratchet wasn't in my car, that I had lent it to a friend.

"Hey, Preacher (another joke between us) I see the net is low. Real low. Better give me your keys and I'll go get the ratchet." Sheldeen had been the first to arrive.

"Good idea," I said.

He came back with the ratchet in one hand and a center strap in the other. "How'd you know about that?" I asked, referring to the spare center strap I always kept in my trunk for serious tournament practice.

"That's how they play on TV, they put this in the middle of the net." He held up the long white strap.

"Okay, dude, I'll raise the net and you put on the center strap." I figured those strange dangling buckles would keep a nine-year-old busy for a while.

I sat down on our benchless court in the park and watched as the other kids began to trickle in. Across the wide grass field, Jenna and Mei Mei were skipping toward us. On the nearby blacktop, Joe and Zoran suddenly broke away from a basketball game and picked up their rackets. And now, Sarah and Raul were coming through the gate with rackets damn near as big as they were. Rinku, Samantha, Jill — all three glided in on skateboards.

What a happy, motley crew they were — about a dozen kids — black, white, Chicano, Asian, and others I hadn't quite figured out yet. This youthful microcosm of the globe included representatives from Croatia, Palestine, Kenya, the Soviet Union, and probably every major religion in the world. I was convinced that if they could do the talking for the rest of us, harmony would prevail on the planet. Such was the ease with which these youngsters got along with each other. Of course they didn't have things like money to get in the way of their sense of right and wrong.

"Okay, Coach, I got it." I looked up to see Sheldeen looking proudly at our droopy net, an old ragged thing that was now adorned with a spiffy white stripe in the center.

"I didn't think you could do it," I told him. "Now loosen that strap a little so I can make it higher." I figured this being a special center strap kind of a day, I'd work the ratchet and raise the net to its exact height and not to the extra two inches I usually put on it.

A teaching pro at a club usually has a shopping cart (or something akin to it) to wheel around a supply of tennis balls during the course of a lesson. But a freelancer with no equipment shack is limited to what can fit into the trunk of a car. I used a large laundry basket, which sat now in the middle of the court. But a shopping cart would have been a lot better.

Shopping carts were great — big, stainless steel, and indestructible. The average shopping cart could hold several hundred tennis balls, plus extras like rackets, water jugs, sweats, you name it. Of course, their greatest asset was that they rolled — if suddenly you wanted to work on the other side of the net, you didn't have to lug a crate of balls over there. And because the carts were high off the ground, a lot of unnecessary strain on the back was avoided. (Try pitching balls sometime from a bucket sitting directly on the court. After a couple of hours, you might not be able to stand up straight.)

For decades, the big shiny shopping cart was the unsung hero of the tennis instruction industry. For the teaching pro, it was vital as racket and ball. It was like an old friend; when you got tired, you could lean against it. You could even ride it and pretend you were still just a kid in a supermarket parking lot.

Naturally, I would have loved using a shopping cart on our cracked up old court; and there were certainly plenty of them around in the neighborhood alleys. But I would have had to chain it to the fence when I went home, and even then it probably would have disappeared. So instead, I made do with a big plastic laundry basket.

Of course, the kids didn't know the difference. Overflowing with worn-out tennis balls, our scuffed-up laundry basket was admired by all as it sat dutifully in the middle of the tennis court. With it in place, Sunday morning training was officially underway.

We did the usual reviewing of stroke patterns, primarily for the benefit of the newest members of our congregation, and then we began pitching drills, where two kids pitched balls underhand to two hitters. Two others practiced their strokes, shadowing behind the two hitters, as if they too were hitting the ball. There was also a station on the side of the court where two youngsters rested and did stretching exercises. The remainder of the group picked up balls; and I kept the whole thing rolling by rotating players through the circuit. If a kid faded early, he knew enough to sit quietly on the side of the court; and then when he was ready to jump back in he would work his way through the various ball-collection positions and then to the pitching and shadowing stations, until at last he arrived as a hitter. But we kept a lively pace and the entire loop could be completed in a matter of minutes, even with a dozen kids on the court.

Naturally it would have been nice to spread out across two tennis courts, but the other court had long since been converted to a basketball court. Anyway, one court in a neighborhood is a lot better than none. With as many kids as we had on it, that single court taught patience and teamwork, and the value of safety.

Having learned the hard way that a tennis racket is actually a lethal weapon not unlike an axe, I considered wearing a football helmet during the early days of our junior program. But not wanting to frighten off my disciples, I decided simply to keep ice on hand for injuries. I also decreed that only four players would be allowed to wield their battle axes at any given time. The rest of the rackets would remain in a pile on the side of the court. This greatly reduced accidents. Nonetheless, hundreds of balls were flying during the course of the hour, and soft as they were, even a fuzz nug could be deadly if it shot somebody between the legs, for instance, in which case icing the injury could prove awkward.

Stroke-production drills were the core of the lesson, but afterward students were allowed to "play catch" with each other from up close at the service lines, where one kid hit the ball to a partner who simply caught it after it bounced. The receiver would then hit the ball gently back and the other guy would catch it. With this mastered, the player and his partner would graduate to hitting two in a row before catching the ball. After success at two, players would try for three hits and a catch, and then four and a catch, and so on. The ball would always have to be caught properly before going on to the next number in the series. And no numbers could be skipped! If one was attempting four in a row, for example, after four successive hits, the ball was to be stopped and caught no matter how easy it would have been to hit that fifth ball.

Players were also required to call out loud their numbers as they hit each ball, something that greatly increased the focus and overall success of these beginner rallies. That Sunday, Sheldeen and Mei Mei were able to work their way up to ten in a row using this basic *progression drill*. A couple of the other kids also got to ten, but they had the advantage of having me as a partner.

Such a progression drill is an exceptional tool, whether one's partner is a friend, a pickup game, or just the backboard. Or even a fellow pro. The key is discipline — to hold back and stop at the designated number no matter how much the desire to keep hitting might be. And to count the numbers out loud. Then once ten in a row is achieved, two players have arrived — they should feel free to extend the rally to whatever number possible, without stopping to catch the ball at each interval. However, it is still a good idea to count out loud.

Players willing to use such a routine often find themselves getting rallies that far exceed what they would have attained otherwise. That day in church, Mei Mei and I got thirty-three in a row, and Sheldeen and I reached twenty-seven in these mini-tennis rallies inside the service boxes (also known as short-court.) Sheldeen was actually the better player, but because he hit more firmly than Mei Mei, I had more difficulty controlling his ball. Mei Mei's delicate touch allowed me to return her groundstrokes indefinitely, but at thirty-three I figured it was time to give somebody else a turn, so I netted a ball.

"Mei Mei's a real good player," Sheldeen said, complimenting her in earnest after class. "Do you want to practice tomorrow?" he asked her. She smiled shyly and looked away, holding her precious racket to her chest.

I told her Sheldeen would pick her up at ten. "Won't you, Sheldeen?"

"Sure will."

"I have twelve tennis balls," the little Chinese girl said, and she skipped happily off the court. She joined half a dozen others who were walking away in a pack, dragging their rackets across the big grass field.

Now it was just Sheldeen and me, something we had both been waiting for. He set up behind the baseline, and I fed him a series of forehands from across the net. I knew as important as it was to teach a youngster the correct strokes and not to over-hit, it was also important to let a kid like Sheldeen have the fun of hitting the ball hard. Really hard. Otherwise, there was the risk that baseball or basketball could steal him away, and he would forever see tennis as a wussy sport. So I let him nail a few, without worrying a lot about control. To my surprise, most of the balls landed in the court, as long as I kept the feed low. That classic, high follow-through we had built into his groundstrokes was working. The ball zoomed like a bullet over the net, pulling down into the court with topspin. Little, or rather, big nine-year-old Sheldeen was elated, and come to think of it, so was I.

After awhile I sat down on the court in order to keep both of our hungers alive, I told myself. But actually, I was tired, and Sheldeen sensed it. He undid the net strap and brought it to me. "Come on, Preacher," he said, still beaming, "let's put the balls in your car."

He didn't say a word about how good it felt to hit the ball hard, and I respected that — he just wanted to savor it, to feel it and not think about it. He knew what it was to ride the moment, to be there in that special part of himself, and he knew the kind of consciousness that would pull him away from that place. He probably didn't know he knew these things; he just knew them. So I didn't say anything, either, about the big groundies he had just hit. But I did remind him to practice with Mei Mei. "Tomorrow at ten," I said. He was still smiling.

We loaded the big basket of balls into the trunk of my old Dart, and I was glad Sheldeen was there to lend a hand. (A huge laundry basket filled with tennis balls is heavier than one might suspect.) The tall basket didn't quite allow the trunk to close, so I fastened it down with a bungee cord I kept wrapped around the bumper for just that purpose. Then I asked Sheldeen if he wanted a ride home. "Or, are you going to stay and play basketball?"

"I'm gonna run home," he said cheerfully, and he took off with his tennis racket and that big grin still on his face.

I made a mental note to bring a camera sometime so I could get a picture of Sheldeen to put on the bookshelf next to Danny's.

Chapter Fifteen

Going Pro

My mind kept replaying that slow Johnny Mathis number I danced with Bonnie on Hitch's patio, how she looked at me and how our bodies brushed and then came together in the darkness. I felt like calling her. I had the phone number for her dead aunt's house in San Francisco, but I wasn't sure she wanted me calling her with the relatives from Nebraska still there doing the things people do with other people's stuff once the owner is no longer around to have a say in the matter. (I figured they were probably arguing about it very politely so as not to irritate the deceased, whose presence was no doubt felt every time wisps of fog blew up against the windowpanes.)

At any rate, the plan was for Bonnie to call me. In a couple of days, she had said. Was it a couple of days, yet? I wondered. A couple is usually two, but then again, it can actually be three or even more. According to the dictionary, a couple can be construed to mean several or a few, something I wish I had known as a kid when I used to sneak into the cookie jar. "I only took a couple," I told my mother, rationalizing that I did only take a couple (a couple in each hand.) I ate them quickly (chocolate chip, my favorite) feeling guilty for lying. Ah, but if I had only known I was telling the truth! Damn, I might have snuck back into the kitchen for a couple more.

I pictured Bonnie as a kid, her ponytail in place as she reached into the cookie jar. She probably liked chocolate chip too, I figured. Hell, who didn't? I wished she would call. After all, it had been a couple of days, in the strict sense, anyway. But then I guess it depended on who was counting. Maybe she was using the more casual cookie-stealing definition, in which case it might be a couple more days before I heard from her. My stomach fluttered in anticipation. I imagined us together at the Rose Garden. That would be the perfect spot for a rendezvous, for a tryst, in fact, if I dared call it that.

As I went through my morning stretching ritual, I thought about Sheldeen. I recalled some of those forehands he had teed off on; they were already as hard as Danny's, and Danny was three years older. I imagined what they would look like when Sheldeen was as big as his dad. A guy that size could do damage on the pro tour, provided he could run, too. And Sheldeen could run, there was no question about that. He definitely had potential. Maybe I would introduce him to some of the guys on the JC team, let him watch them work out, give him a taste of some real tennis. He was psyched up, to be sure, but I wanted to take that young athlete and hook him to the bone. I wanted to see him win one of the big ones in ten years. Unfortunately, that would depend on more than just desire and ability; he would need to be on the court with somebody like me every day of the week.

As it happened, some of my JC guys were playing in the Oakland City Tennis Championships, which had just begun, so I invited Sheldeen to come along. I thought about bringing Danny too, but I knew his control-freak parents wouldn't allow it.

Sheldeen was to get permission from his dad and meet me at my place. He was at the door now, very much excited. His friend Pedro, who was not so excited, stood by his side. Pedro was an eleven-year-old brown kid who was unquestionably king of the playground. All day long, Pedro hung out at the school yard kicking butt in pickup baseball, basketball, and football games. Like Sheldeen, he was poor to the point that fees for organized sports were a burden. There would be no traveling across town to a Little League game for Pedro. The school playground was his domain, and there he was king. He had taken a liking to Sheldeen; he probably saw him as a younger version of himself. But unlike Sheldeen, Pedro had no interest in our tennis program. I was surprised to see him standing at Sheldeen's side, a wry smile on his face.

The three of us piled into the front seat of the old Dart and headed over to Davie Tennis Stadium out near Lake Merritt. Davie Stadium is home to the most serious public tennis players in the East Bay. Hometown hero, Tom Edlefsen, used to train there; actually, he grew up in one of the nice little houses nearby. And then there was the legendary Frank Kovacs, a former professional champion. Kovacs seldom came by Davie anymore; after all, he was getting older, and besides, he had a posh home in the Oakland hills with his own tennis court. But goofy Art Larsen did show up, and frequently. A previous national champion, Larsen had been cripped up and couldn't play anymore since his motor scooter accident, but still, he liked to see what was going on.

For these players and countless others, Davie Stadium is Northern California's hidden tennis sanctuary. Indeed, nestled in eucalyptus trees and set within the base of a former rock quarry, the place is nearly invisible until one is pretty much upon it. The tall wall of rock that surrounds the back of the courts offers protection from the elements and makes it easier to concentrate, kind of like playing indoors. The big natural backdrop also modifies sounds, creating a stunted echo that seems to deepen the sound of a tennis ball being hit, all of which adds to the mystique of playing there.

The Oakland City Championships were always held at Davie Stadium. And now, Sheldeen and Pedro were tagging along as I checked out the draw and made my way through the crowd to the stadium court. The number one guy on my team had just walked out there with his opponent, a player currently holding down the number two spot in the open rankings. This was Davie's court in the hole, and it was a damn nice hole, boxed in with concrete walls and tiered seating that wasn't too high and kept us all close to the action. Overhanging limbs and shrubbery were all around. Behind the end of the court, a curtain of tall eucalyptus trees grew up against the wall of the quarry.

In the sunken battle ground below, my guy appeared to be on his way to an upset victory, having cruised through the first set; and up in the stands with me another upset was in the making — it was Pedro. He sat next to Sheldeen, cheering enthusiastically amidst the resounding percussion sounds of a tennis ball being annihilated in the hole at Davie Stadium. The two kids shrieked and hollered with fists pumping; and then when our man fell short, they badgered the opposition. All of which was quite refreshing, considering the fact that most people watch a tennis match with great inhibition, afraid to so much as clap at the wrong moment. Yes, I thought, let these youngsters teach us the kind of spectating tennis players deserve, it's time for tennis to come out of the tea room!

The other guy didn't have a chance, having to go up against Pedro and Sheldeen, to say nothing of an opponent who was most definitely in the zone and looked like he could win the State JC Championships with his eyes closed. After the match our guy sat in the hole for a while and let it all sink in. He had just beat the number one seed, the guy who was expected to win the tournament and walk away with a thousand dollars in his pocket. Hopefully, he wouldn't think too much about that — a tricky subject for a kid who wouldn't be able to take a penny because he had entered as an amateur in order to keep his collegiate eligibility. Sometimes the money could go indirectly to the kid by way of tuition, equipment or books, and I figured it was time for me to talk to the tournament director about that. After all, the kid looked sharp enough to win the whole thing (which would have been serious work even for a player like Hammer.) The kid waved up at us, and we went down into the hole to congratulate him.

"Good game, bro!" little Pedro blurted out, "I didn't know tennis players hit the ball so hard. That was awesome, man." The champion-in-making extended his hand and each boy shook it with a thumbs-up clasp.

We all sat on the bench with the kid for a while and looked up at the now empty stands. It was pleasant and sunny down there in the hole, and as the warmth soaked in, memories grew vivid in my mind. After all, I had won a few down there in that very hole. And now I was here again, and though I wasn't playing, I was psyched up to be there with my player and two green but very enthusiastic juniors. I realized that as well as my JC star had played that afternoon, little Sheldeen would be capable of a lot more one day (if things fell into place.) I didn't know what to make of Pedro. He had the right spirit, but at eleven years old, it was probably too late for him, though he would certainly make a good training partner for Sheldeen, if his interest kept up.

"Man, I bet you're gonna go pro," Sheldeen said, figuring our man was headed for the Major Leagues. "Yeah, you ought to go pro," Pedro put in.

"Anything's possible," the kid replied with an amused look. He knew these youngsters were as naive as they were enthusiastic. They thought going pro was something you did in tennis just like you did in other sports, where you were suddenly chosen from out of the masses; and then voilà — you were in the big time — you went pro.

The only thing Sheldeen and Pedro knew about tennis was how the points were played. I don't think they even knew there were junior tournaments. They knew there were high school teams and college teams (which have nothing at all to do with becoming a pro, except for the fact that a college team can be a good training ground for a year or so.) And they had heard of Wimbledon and the US Open, of course, but that was about it; they had no idea about the structure of the pro circuit, where individual tournaments are linked in a tough, ruthless system that weeds out all but only the most capable tennis players in the world; and of those thousand or so, only the top seventy-five really make a decent living.

But at least the system is fair — there is no selection process — it's all a matter of points (ATP points) based on performance in tournaments, small tournaments at first. Then, as you accumulate more points, you're eligible for larger tournaments where the prize money is greater, and finally, one day you might wake up and realize, hey, I'm a pro, I'm making a living at this game. It's a gradual process, you work your way up, you evolve — you aren't suddenly chosen to be a pro. If you are selected to be on Davis Cup, for instance, or on one of the few professional teams out there, it's because you are already a pro — that's why they want you, they know you can do the job and they want the crowd you can draw.

Sheldeen and Pedro led the way as we walked away from the hole and escorted our guy to Davie's clubhouse, a modest place that always reminded me more of a mountain cabin than a lounge at a tennis club. Come to think of it, it was a lot like Buckskin Charley's setup in Rock Creek, Montana, but everything here was on a smaller scale. I especially liked the porch stairs, where you could sit out front and watch the action on court four. In fact, another one of my guys was out there right now, in the middle of a third set, so I sat down on the steps with Sheldeen and Pedro to cheer him on (power style.) Despite vociferous encouragement, our man lost. But he had put on an excellent showing for a number five player, and my confidence in the team grew suddenly stronger.

As we left that old rock quarry, we passed by a small crowd that had gathered on the end court. An old man smoking a pipe clung to the fence, his fingers laced through the chain link as he watched the match in progress. Apparently, a small dark-haired kid was giving fits to the tournament's third seed; it was a guy about twice his size.

The pint-size little kid didn't look like he was old enough to be in junior high school. But he displayed excellent feel and remarkably clever shot-making ability. On the dead run now, he suddenly threaded a backhand precisely down the stripe of the line for a winning passing shot. His gargantuan opponent stood at the net amazed, clapping his hands in disbelief, but the kid just marched over to the bench for the side change and sat down like it was no big deal.

The old man turned from the fence and caught my eye as we walked by. "Bradley's gonna be a good one," he said, and he lit his pipe with a proud, contented look. He puffed on it until the side change was over, and then he resumed his fence-clinging gaze.

Later, as it turned out, that feisty little kid would climb his way out of the quarry in Davie Stadium and scale his way to the very top of the tennis mountain. He would grow to become a big man himself, one day, and stand even taller as the number four player in the world! Who would have known? Maybe the old man with the pipe knew. Maybe little Brad Gilbert knew all along, after all, he had been clawing and scratching his way past the odds ever since he could remember.

In shadows cast by tall eucalyptus trees, Sheldeen and Pedro stood in the leafy parking lot with me as I spoke with my two college players. We talked for a while in the pungent eucalyptus air, and then it was time to go.

"See ya later, nice playing," little Pedro said, genuinely impressed with my star.

"Yeah, good luck tomorrow," Sheldeen put in, and then to the other guy he offered consolation — "You'll get him next time." (No doubt, Sheldeen had it together for a nine-year-old.)

The two older boys got in their car, and then the three of us jumped into the front seat of the old Dart and drove off. "That guy really creams the ball," Pedro said, still excited about my guy. "I think he's gonna go pro."

Sheldeen turned innocently to me. "Hey, Coach, when did you go pro?"

He had me there. When did I go pro? Hell, I didn't remember ever going pro. And actually, I never really thought of myself as a pro, but rather as a guy trying to become one. I was a teaching pro, or a tennis professional, in the broader sense. But I wasn't the real thing — I wasn't a pro tennis *player*. Sure, I made a few grand over the years in tournaments, but for the most part the tournaments were a struggle. I suppose, during the actual week of a tourney I might have thought of myself as a pro, but that was primarily to get myself psyched up, like in Montana. The truth is, there on that lowest tier of "the circuit" we were all wannabe pros. Though talented enough to beat some of the best in the world on a good day, our lot was ragged and penniless; we scraped by from tournament to tournament chasing the dream, always the dream. For me it was largely a matter of making money teaching, then taking time off to go out and play the tournaments. Then I'd come back broke and teach some more in order to save up for the tournaments again. Teaching had always been the real bread and butter.

Of course, that's all some guys ever wanted — to teach. They knew they weren't cut out for the big time, and as such they didn't feel the lure or the frustration of the tournaments. I envied them at times. They just concentrated on their teaching careers, and in some ways they were better for it. But for those of us who were players at heart, there were invaluable lessons to be learned from the fray, things that went beyond technique and training tips — these were lessons of attitude, discipline, desire, and accomplishment — lessons of life, and given the chance, we would pass them on to our students.

I wasn't sure how to answer Sheldeen — when did I go pro? It was true, some tennis teachers thought of themselves as going pro the moment they made their first nickel giving a lesson, but that wasn't the way I saw it. Even if you made big bucks instructing, you were still only a teaching pro, not a player. Sure, you were a tennis "professional," but to those of us seared by the flame of competition, teaching for a living was not being a tennis pro.

For most of us, for guys like me and Hammer, the idea was to play tournaments for a living, and a dollar earned out there in the wilds of tennis was worth about a thousand made on the teaching court. Such was the power of the dream.

"Is he a player?" Hammer had asked me one day, referring to the guy who had replaced me as head pro at the old club. I knew what he meant, and I knew what he would have liked the answer to be. "I don't think so," I said, and we left it at that.

As I cruised with Sheldeen and Pedro back into the flats of Berkeley, I thought about the JC team I was coaching; there was definitely some potential. The kid at the top was a dynamo capable of anything, as evidenced by the way he handled the number one seed, ripping him apart in the hole at Davie Stadium. And we obviously had some depth; the number five guy didn't exactly roll over and die. The two youngsters in my charge were still talking about it.

"Hey, coach?" Sheldeen had been patient, but he still wanted an answer. "When did you go pro? It was before I was even born. Right?"

"Right," I said, "those guys we saw sure do hit the ball hard, don't they?" (I felt cheap, as if I had just hit him a drop shot.)

"Yeah," Pedro responded quickly, "remember when that ball got stuck in the fence and the other guy couldn't even pull it out. That was funny."

"Yeah, that was cool," Sheldeen giggled. Then he nudged Pedro. "What about when that skinny old man told you to pipe down, that was the best part."

"Just because the guy he was rooting for was losing." Pedro's voice rose up. "That's why he was sore, and I told him so."

"You sure did," I said with some emphasis. The boys laughed.

Their dialogue become more and more rambunctious as they described bits and pieces of the power tennis they had seen that day. The loser of the match had smashed his racket somewhat privately behind the back wall of the court, and I was glad they hadn't seen that. Although, it might have been just the thing to really turn Pedro on to the sport, kind of like when a rock star pulverizes his guitar at the end of a concert on MTV, in which case it would have been more fitting, perhaps, for the *winner* of the match to smash his racket. But tennis hasn't quite gotten there yet. Even at the big time, the most you'll see is a guy take his shirt off and throw it into the crowd; you'll never see him light his racket on fire and fling it into the stands.

I drove into our sad little Berkeley neighborhood, still wondering if I was a pro. Was I ever a pro? Then I wondered when tennis itself would go pro, I mean really go pro. Would it ever make it to the big time, the really big time of professional sports? Would it ever be like Major League Baseball, or the NFL? Or would it remain in the tea room, afraid of itself forever?

I let the boys off in front of their building. Sheldeen thanked me; then he hustled over to his dad who was waiting out front with the dog. The big man in overalls looked at me appreciatively with tired eyes. He gave his son a pat on the back with his broad palm and they walked off together, with Pedro and the dog trailing. I wondered if Pedro had a father, I hadn't thought to ask.

"Okay, pro," the spunky Pedro called back to me, "see ya later."

Well, OK, maybe I was a pro. A part-time pro.

Chapter Sixteen

21st Century Team Tennis

I almost called Bonnie that night, but thought better of it and lay in bed trying to think about other things. My mind drifted in and around Sheldeen and Pedro and the tennis we had seen at Davie Stadium. Then as sleep drew near, the future of tennis itself settled across my temples like a big fuzzy question mark. I knew something was wrong, and as much as I longed for the old days, I knew there would have to be a lot of restructuring if tennis was ever to take its place at the table of big-time professional sports. There had to be an answer, something that would make the game more appealing to the masses. And the solution had to be professional teams, lots of new teams, teams that were much different than those few currently in place.

As I dozed off, I imagined alternative team scenarios, formats that would make the sport exciting for kids like Pedro who would much prefer to make a diving catch for a football, for instance, or tackle the guy who made that catch. And as my blasphemous new tennis thoughts played out, I hopped on my midnight freighter and rolled into the future, where I lived near my pillow in a dream.

It was the year 2053, for some odd reason. It was as if I were narrating a futuristic movie, where life was much as we know it, yet with the kind of high-tech advances one would expect half a century to provide. And amazingly, the game of tennis had changed! Old-fashioned tennis was still played on occasion, but mostly by older folks. In that respect the old stuff was like golf. Sometimes a couple of youngsters would get on a court and do points with each other, but that was no more tennis than two guys playing catch on a front lawn was a game of baseball. Today, in the middle of the twenty-first century, kids wanted to be on tennis teams just like they wanted to be on baseball and football teams. And going pro meant being on a team; that was the only kind of professional tennis there was. There were no more tournaments for individuals; the days of the nomadic solo player were over.

And the teams weren't like the old team attempts before the turn of the century. No, that wasn't team tennis at all, that was just old-fashioned tennis played with backup players who could substitute, one boring guy against another, with a few teetotalers watching from an unfilled grandstand. Now it was the real thing — a team sport where five guys played at once against five others guys on the same tennis court. Traditional one-on-one singles was still the foundation of the game, but as one guy played the point through to completion, the other four players were an integral part of the action. There was a post man near the net, and there were two sidemen who moved up and down the out-of-bounds where the old doubles alleys used to be. And there was a man in back in *the box* ready to jump in and serve the next point in the allotted six seconds which ticked off in big digits on electronic scoreboards as soon as the previous point ended. One of the sidemen could run over and serve, but it was more efficient to fire the ball to the box man and let him step up to the line.

All five players of a team were required to serve a point. Consequently, a team served through its five-man lineup. And then the other team served, and in doing so it could arrange its lineup in an order that was different from the last time it served. With only six seconds to get the ball in play, most squads had a man who hadn't served yet in the box, where after taking the relay, he could step up and serve quickly to either side he chose — that is, he could serve into what they used to call the deuce court, or if he wanted, he could serve into the ad court, on any first or second serve. This kept the receiving team on its toes and forced them to have a man guarding each service square, all of which was further complicated by the fact that each of the five points had to be returned by a different player. Which meant there was a returning rotation, and the receiving team shifted its men accordingly, in a fluid manner, both during and between points.

Naturally, the last man to return serve had the disadvantage of having to cover both service boxes, so it was generally best to reserve the fastest guy for that job, which meant straddling the center mark, and more often than not, lunging desperately to one side or the other.

Once in play, the battle was between the player who served and the one who returned the ball. The others fanned out to their positions off the playing surface, but that was their choice, and if a player wanted, he could remain in an on-court area for strategic reasons or simply to distract the opposition. The risk for such an inactive to be on the playing surface was not just that he might interfere with the movement or vision of his teammate who was trying to play the point; the greater consequence was that he now became fair game for the opponent, who could strike him with the ball and receive three bonus points. Of course, there were nimble players who taunted the opposition, like the acrobatic Hector Mentabe of the Indiana Hitmen who could float ten feet from a guy lining up an overhead smash. Mentabe invariably drew the smash to himself, and then he dodged the ball, often causing the opponent to miss the shot altogether. If the ball did stay in-bounds, Mentabe's teammate would be there to retrieve it. Of course, there were times when Mentabe took it in the gut, accompanied by great groaning sounds from the crowd. But that was to be expected; it was all part of the fun.

Today, in the year 2053, tennis had the best of all worlds. Its longtime similarities to pitching and hitting in baseball had combined with high-powered teamwork not unlike the constant interdependence of players on a basketball court. With this integration, tennis had launched itself into the big time, and along with football, it was now a major sport which towered over golf and other pastimes for the elderly.

Most teams had fifteen men on the traveling squad, all of whom were in superb physical condition. They had to be. There was a continuous sense of urgency, always a place to run to, even in the intervals between points, which were short and not stagnant like in the old days. There was no time for a player to slack off or go whacko.

And the spectators loved it! They especially liked watching the women play. Whether they were in the stadium or in their living rooms, people always got their money's worth watching the tennis games. And the sponsors got more than their money's worth, with all the world-wide television coverage the games were getting. Everybody prospered, especially the players; they had learned a lot since the old ATP and WTA days. Most teams were owned by player co-operatives, and the players controlled the league. One of the things they insisted on was an open challenge system which allowed even a neighborhood team the chance to bump and replace the worst team in the league each year.

There was no doubles at the games, and nobody missed it. Old-style doubles was a thing of the past. Even in the old days people didn't go to matches to see the doubles; doubles didn't make heroes or sell tickets, and it certainly didn't sell TV advertising.

But some things were still the same — the court, its surface and dimensions, and the equipment. Yes, rackets and strokes were pretty much the same (although a few guys were using a double handled racket that allowed them instant use of either hand and a chance at the ball when caught in an awkward position.) Indeed, even the balls were the same, but they were supplied vertically through the columns of the two hollow net posts. There was always a ball atop each post for a player to relay to his teammate who was about to serve before the sound of the six-second buzzer. Similarly, a ball from the post had to be used for a second serve, at which time six additional seconds began to tick off on the big digital scoreboards at either end of the stadium.

Naturally there were no referees; all lines were called by electric eye. Nor were there any ballboys; the balls were fed into the base of the net posts by powerful vacuum ducts at the edges of the court. Once the point was over, it was the responsibility of team members to send the ball to the periphery of the court where it would be sucked into the vacuum system, only to reappear a few seconds later atop a net post.

Exchanges were often long and accented with thrashing groundstrokes, deft halfvolleys, and acrobatic overheads; but even between points, the action was fast and captivating. Occasionally a post man would fire the ball to a teammate who had just stepped up to the line to serve into the right court, for instance, but that player would fake the serve and flip the ball around his back to another teammate who would serve quickly for an ace to the left court. The fluidity of such a move was not unlike the completion of a successful double-play in baseball, and the spectators gasped in approval. Then normal cheering and chatter would resume as the next point got underway. Such was the action — continuous, dramatic, unpredictable — until twenty minutes later when the first quarter was over and all play stopped, regardless of the score or who was serving or diving for the ball.

As in baseball and basketball, heckling and shouting were part of the game. Opposing team members would also taunt each other. There was no such thing as a $10,000 fine for abusing an umpire — there were no umpires! Two technicians ran the scoreboard for the night, and they were miles away monitoring the game on a wall of flat screens. As far as the players and fans were concerned, the electronic scoreboard called the game, and its word was final, even when it announced a penalty shot for an infraction such as serving or receiving out of order, or an improper substitution.

And how the crowd loved penalty shots! Penalty shots created a tension as keen as the most gladiatorial moments in ice hockey. The violating team member was placed in what used to be referred to as no-man's land. In the same area on the other side of the net stood three opponents, each armed with racket and ball. At the shrill sound of the electric whistle, the three shooters would strike at the offending culprit, who was protected by a face mask. He could also deflect balls with his racket. And so, the action was like dodgeball, or more precisely, battleball, where a player could deflect a ball to a teammate who might then attempt a retaliation strike against any opposing player, and that player could, in turn, deflect the ball again, or indeed, field it to rest on his own strings and fire back at the opposition. A hit was worth three points, and the attempt usually took the form of a slashing forehand or a sidearm service motion. With nine points potentially at stake and three balls flying simultaneously, all players became fair game after the initial rifling barrage. Therefore, during a penalty shoot-out, each man was required to wear a face mask, even though most of them thought it a childish precaution.

Today was a World League playoff match between the New York Skidmarks and the Argentine Pulsars. John McEnroe was watching from a celebrity box. He never missed a Skidmark home match, and he still even managed to get to a few on other parts of the globe. McEnroe sat upright, attentive as ever, all of his ninety-four years entranced by the action in front of him. If only tennis had been like this back in his day! He knew the freedom to let loose like these guys would have taken his talents to even greater heights. He gripped the handle of his cane with his left hand and jerked it instinctively in a crosscourt direction as his man hit a deft angle volley for a winner. "Yes!"

Racket strokes had been developing for a long, long time, ever since the ancients in the pre-Christian era first batted a crude ball around. Now, some twenty-five hundred years later, those strokes had evolved to their most advanced limits — there was nothing more to learn about how to hit the ball; there would be no more biomechanical changes in the game. Unless of course, the human body evolved into something else. The gamut had been run, except for trick shots and crowd pleasing stunts, which became ever more spectacular during half-time shows.

Although the overall format was more interactive, and the pace unrelenting, from McEnroe's vantage point in his box seat, the singles exchanges below looked pretty much the same as they had in old-fashioned tennis during the last third of the twentieth century. That had been when the final advances of style were etched into the game. It began with Bjorn Borg, the first of the topspin kings. Borg showed the world how to hit an open-stanced forehand, how to really hit it, especially when deep in the backhand corner where one could hit inside-out to the opponent's backhand. Then, from that same position, Borg could slam the ball down-the-line and send the opponent running. Borg also helped display the superiority of the two-handed backhand, a trend which was for the most part created by Jimmy Connors and Chris Evert.

Aside from the open-stanced forehand and the two-hander, other changes were taking place in the game during that time. A few years before Borg, a fellow named Roscoe Tanner went on record as having the fastest serve in the world. And Tanner was not what you would call a big man. There was something different Tanner was doing with the serve — with his feet together, he launched his body dramatically up into the ball, and in so doing he relied not just on lift from his back leg, but he also got thrust from his front leg. In addition, Tanner had a delayed ball toss which could be kept to an all-time low, making his serve very hard to read, especially considering its swift delivery. But shortly after, it was John McEnroe, the old man in the stands who really gave the public a serving lesson.

During his reign of terror, John McEnroe incorporated the key parts of the Tanner motion, but he used a slow, deliberate style which was easy to observe — everybody could see the powerful thrust that came from his greatly exaggerated front knee bend. And McEnroe's initial racket lift was so premature, almost to the point of being stationary, that he maximized the ability to delay the ball toss and prepare his body for the strike. More than once during his reign, McEnroe was voted as having the best serve in the world, and he also was not a big man.

It was also McEnroe who taught tennis players how to hit a proper low volley. The classic low volley had always been described as getting down low with a lot of knee bend and keeping the head of the racket up with a more or less cocked wrist. But McEnroe showed the world the true meaning of efficiency; if the ball was low, he dropped the racket head downward, without cocking his wrist or hardly bending his knees. And to this day that is how a low volley is hit, from a more or less upright posture with the racket head down. McEnroe's left hand flicked upwards on the handle of his cane now as he watched one of his beloved New York Skidmarks volley a ball off his shin. "Yes!" In a sense, it was he who had taught that player how to hit such a ball, but the thought never occurred to McEnroe. He just sat there mesmerized, wishing he could have been out there now — now that tennis had finally become tennis.

The score was tied at 88 to 88 near the end of the fourth quarter. "Shit," old man McEnroe grumbled as one of his Skidmarks missed an easy three-point shot at a rowdy inactive who was up near the net. McEnroe had mellowed in old age; there wasn't much anger left. But still, mortality annoyed the hell out of him, and it was that reality that drew the vulgarity from his lips. "Shit," he repeated as he observed the nimble, youthful energy on the court below; he realized that he was at the other end of the spectrum, that he was in fact, on the way out. On the way out of everything. And McEnroe didn't want to go.

He wasn't sure he would attend another Skidmark match. Just getting to the stadium had been an ordeal in itself — first finding a reliable driver, then parking and fighting the crowd. Hell, they didn't even announce his presence to the fans anymore. He tried to remember the last time he held a microphone in his hand and said a few words to the crowd. Yes, it was in '27, during the warm-up for World Cup IX , the Skidmarks were playing against the ...

"It's time to go now, sir. Before the crowd tramples us." McEnroe's young, well-built chauffeur took his arm and guided him into the aisle.

"You know, I used to play with the big boys, too," McEnroe said, taking fast little steps alongside the chauffeur. He usually didn't talk about it.

"Yeah, I heard all about that, my boss told me, you played in the old days, you were one of the gunslingers from before, before pro teams came along."

As the two of them walked down the long indoor corridor that led away from the arena, McEnroe with his quick little footsteps, used the tip of his cane to tap at a discarded cup and a crumpled-up food wrapper. He played field hockey with them, bumping the discards into each other, dribbling them deftly along the floor with the cane in his left hand.

"Sir?"

"Sir?" the chauffeur repeated.

"What is it?" McEnroe asked; his cane continued to work the two pieces of litter along the floor.

"Well, sir. It's just that you must have been pretty damn good at that old style tennis."

McEnroe smiled briefly. "I wasn't too shabby, if that's what you mean." The crowd roared suddenly, and then there were great stirring sounds from inside the arena. McEnroe gave one final tap of his cane at the discarded cup, and my hand jerked up into my bedsheet — for it was my hand now that held the cane, and I was the one taking quick little footsteps. I turned to the chauffeur and saw that it was Hammer, and then I woke up with my heart racing. For in my dream my hand had been McEnroe's hand, and his cane had been my cane as I walked away from the tennis games in the middle of the twenty-first century.

The phone was ringing; I cursed it, knowing that it had woken me, that it had transported me back to this unenlightened decade. I let it ring again and again; I figured the recorder could deal with whoever wanted to talk this early in the morning. I looked at the clock; it was six-thirty. Then Bonnie's voice came through the answering machine. I threw off the covers and reached for the receiver.

"It's me. Sorry to be so early, but I wanted to call before everyone here got up."

"You're at your aunt's? In San Francisco?" My mind was beginning to take hold of reality (and enjoying it.) "I'm glad you called," I said.

We spoke briefly, making plans to spend the day together; I was to meet her at the BART station at ten. So I went back to sleep, thinking about things that were even more exciting than being a ninety-four-year-old John McEnroe; although I must admit, that futuristic tennis was pretty wild. I made some notes about it on a piece of paper so I wouldn't forget.

It was still overcast at ten in the morning, but the world was wide awake and happening in an easy Berkeley sort of way. Bonnie was out in front of the BART station, looking elegant and lady-like. She was standing alongside her luggage. Her luggage! That meant she would be spending the night here! Or maybe leaving today? Butterflies began to flutter down low in my stomach. I walked up and she put her arms around me, and the butterflies swirled up into my chest.

I put her stuff in back of the old Dart, and we headed north on Shattuck Avenue to find something to eat. We pulled up alongside a quaint little coffee shop, a place where they wouldn't just throw a bill on our table and expect us to scoot out in the middle of the last swallow. (Of course, if the place got too successful, there was no telling what could happen to its laid-back demeanor.)

Inside were antique wooden tables, leather books, and old-style lamps fitted with dim electric bulbs. The music was drifty and inviting, and the place wasn't crowded; I was sure we could hang out and even digest a little if we felt like it.

We ordered coffee and bagels — real bagels, chewy bagels — the kind that are boiled and not just sprayed with mist like in those phony bagel shops. So we chewed and sipped and stole looks at each other. We ventured into small talk, and then eventually real conversation.

"You finished up your business at your aunt's?" I asked, trying to get a bearing on any romantic inclinations that might have to be postponed indefinitely, if not forever.

"Everything's settled," she said, "my aunt's brother from Nebraska is taking over. He wants to rent the house out, at least for now. Too bad she didn't have any kids. Her doctor and her attorney came out smelling like roses, strange how that seems to happen. Anyway, I'm leaving on Thursday."

"Thursday? That's the day after tomorrow," I said nervously.

"You can get me to the airport, can't you?"

"No problem, but, uh, where will you be staying?" I stuttered.

"At your place, of course." The butterflies in my stomach took flight again.

"Unless that's a problem for you," Bonnie said with apologetic eyes.

"Oh no. It's just that I have a very small place." And now I got worried; she would see the way I really live. I visualized the unkempt parts of my apartment — all the old tennis shoes that were lying around, too worn out to use on a regular basis, but too good to throw away; and the various piles of clothes that were not quite dirty enough to warrant a trip to the laundromat. "Don't expect too much," I told her.

"Anything's Ok. Really. The sofa, the floor, whatever. Really."

"Well then," I said, "as they say in the old country, my shack is your castle." Bonnie's blue eyes sparkled.

"I've got to warn you, though, the chambermaid quit two months ago."

"No problem," she said happily, "I'm not one for absolute tidiness. I like a place that's more livable than lookable."

"Well, then you won't be disappointed, because my place is definitely more livable than lookable." She laughed, adding that a little functional messiness was good for the soul. Functional messiness, I liked that.

I got us each a refill of Antiguan from the self-serve coffee bar and set the cups down at our table. Wonderful full-bodied coffee aroma rose up in swirls of disappearing vapor.

I felt like telling Bonnie about my dream, about the future of professional tennis, but I thought better of it. It was pretty weird, after all, and weird was not how I wanted to be perceived right then.

"I hear Oregon's a great place to live," I offered, for want of something to say.

"It is," she replied. "It's a little ahead of the game, politically and environmentally. In general, there's a type of awareness up there that's hard to beat. And Portland's fine, but there are other places too. Something smaller like Eugene would be nice."

"Hammer's got a friend who really likes Eugene, says there are only three places he'd ever consider living — Eugene, Boulder, or Berkeley."

Bonnie laughed. "The guy must be a real granola-head."

"Yeah, I guess so. He thinks those three towns form a spiritual triangle, says if you're not connected to one of them you're out of touch."

"He might be right." She took my hand on top of the coffee table. "And Berkeley is the true apex of that triangle, don't you think?"

"You mean the vibes start here in Berkeley and then they go to Boulder and Eugene?"

"I'm sure there's some back and forth flow, kind of a cross-pollination effect, but basically, yes, things emanate from Berkeley." This lady was a lot deeper and more hip than I had realized, and her hand was a lot smoother and warmer than I could have imagined. She seemed content just to sit with me, to sip coffee and talk, and watch through the window as the mid-morning humanity of Berkeley walked by on the sidewalk.

But things were busting to get out of my head — all that stuff about five-man teams, the quick-paced teamwork, penalty shoot-outs, and the roar of the crowd at the tennis games in the middle of the twenty-first century. My new companion might have some interesting things to say about it. So I risked telling Bonnie my dream, about everything, even how the balls popped up out of the net posts.

"Well, what do you think?" I said. She smiled pleasantly, thoughtfully, and told me that maybe I was clairvoyant.

"You don't believe in that psychic stuff, do you?" I asked, not knowing where she was coming from.

"Not exactly, but it's true that some people are more clear than others, they have a better handle on the direction things are going. You had a vision. Like a prophet."

"You mean like a religious prophet?"

"Exactly."

"So you think I'm a tennis prophet?" I chuckled and thought of Sheldeen and how we liked to pretend Sunday morning tennis was our church. A tennis prophet, yes, that would suit me just fine.

"Anyway," I said, "maybe you're the one who's clairvoyant — you knew I had a dream and you wanted me to know about it. So you woke me up just at the right time. Yes, I think so, you're here like some sort of angel."

"Just as long as you don't have me fluttering between this world and another, being an angel is fine with me. Especially being your angel. But remember," she added with a serious face, "it was your dream, I simply turned you on to it."

"Now come on," I said, "tell me what you really think about it, what's your take on ten guys being in on the action on a single tennis court?"

"It would be exciting, that's for sure. To tell you the truth, I always found tennis a little boring to watch, not being a tennis player myself. It's not as bad as golf or bowling, but still, it's a little slow compared to something like basketball or football."

"Baseball is slow too," I said, "but there are eighteen guys out there held together by the drama of somebody creaming the ball out of the ballpark. That's hard to beat. Tennis doesn't have that kind of tension."

Bonnie told me she liked the idea of penalty shots and the dodgeball free-for-all. Her eyes sparkled. "It's pretty far out," she said. "But the public's bound to really go for it."

I had the distinct impression that non-tennis players would have a greater affinity for my futuristic vision than those who were currently playing the game and hung up on it. On this latter point, the conversation shifted to tenis envy, and then momentarily to Evonne and Hitch. And Hammer. And then eventually, to Bonnie's husband.

She stroked my hand tenderly and told me that they had both been in graduate school at the University of Oregon when they got married. Then she dropped out to put him through dental school. And that was that; they moved to Portland where she raised two girls, a golden retriever, and one husband. And now she was in Berkeley with me. Blown together by random winds, we were two small feathers whose paths had crossed in the vast sky, and now we were sitting on the same branch like lovebirds, taking comfort in each other's melodies.

Though her love for husband had vanished, Bonnie said she felt sorry for him, that she saw him as a fool. He was having an affair with his hygienist, and all the girl was interested in was the money. "You ought to see the size of her paycheck," she said without the slightest hint of indignation. "You'd think she was another dentist."

"The man's a fool," she added, "he might as well be going to a brothel."

"Why go when you can have the brothel come to you?" I offered.

"Good point. But I'm sure Harold thinks there's more to it than that, that their relationship is going somewhere."

"Does he know you know?" I asked curiously.

"No. I didn't want to confront him, I thought maybe the thing would die down on its own. But ... What can I say? The man's a fool."

"A fool with, apparently, money to burn."

"That's exactly it. Harold made some good investments years ago. He could quit his practice if he wanted to, but now he's more eager than ever to get to the office." There was no bitterness in Bonnie's voice, and I wondered if I would be as well adjusted if I were her.

"You seem to be taking the whole thing very well," I said.

"You've got to go with it, it's just like when you have kids," she said. "If there's one thing having children taught me, it's that you can't control other people. The baby wants to wake up at 2 AM and that's that. If baby wants to eat in the middle of the night, that's the way it's going to be."

"And if baby wants to sleep with the hygienist, that's the way it's going to be?"

"Okay, I admit it was hard at first, but then I got used to it. I mean, you can't just be a control freak about everything, not with your kids, and especially not with your husband. If you do, you won't survive, you'll be a nervous wreck."

"Well, I guess I'm kind of glad it happened," I said, "if that's OK with you."

"I'll take that as a compliment," she said, stroking my forearm with her fingertips. She looked directly into my eyes. "But I want you to remember, I'm not trying to get even with Harold. It's just that the rules have changed. I'm actually a very monogamous person."

"And I'll take that as a compliment," I said.

Hand in hand, we sipped our coffee and looked out the window as interesting looking Berkeley types walked by on the sidewalk. I figured after a while we'd leave the coffee shop, walk over to campus and get lost on some woodsy path. I had a place in mind, a small bridge with water trickling under it. There, leaning against a wooden rail, we'd listen to the quiet sound of water, to the timeless wisdom trickling beneath our feet.

Then we'd take Bonnie's luggage back to my place. I was uneasy about showing her the pad, but I'd have to face up to it sooner or later. Anyway, she'd probably want to freshen up, eat a sandwich, maybe even have a nap. A nap, for crissake, I can't believe I even thought of that. I scolded myself, saying it was just wishful thinking on my part and that no respectful suitor would be having such bedroom thoughts so early in the game.

After the nap we could hang out at the Rose Garden. The sun would still be out and I could give Bonnie a tennis lesson, if she wanted. San Francisco would be glimmering between the limbs of trees, all those shiny little buildings on the other side of the bay, and the bay itself, wide and gray and mixing with ocean below the distant arches of the Golden Gate Bridge. I envisioned the pink glow of sunset spreading across the darkening water, and as I did I felt my palm close over Bonnie's hand. Her fingers responded, and I knew the two of us would remain on the deck of the Rose Garden long after the other couples had disappeared into the night.

Chapter Seventeen

Womb Theory

"First, when you're a kid, it's just a matter of improving; then later it's a matter of improving faster than the next guy, since everybody else is improving too, which means you've got to practice faster than the next guy. So it's a mad race. Then as you get older, for guys like us, it's mostly a matter of staying fit, not getting too far out of shape."

Hammer was more suntanned than ever, but there were also a few more wrinkles around his eyes. I wasn't sure if they were personality marks from his smiley outlook on life or if they were creases that had been etched into his face from squinting while trying to return serve in the sun. He had just blown into town, and as usual, there was a lot of post-tournament philosophizing to do. So I let him lay it on me.

"I can see it all clearly now," he said. "I'm not in the race to improve anymore. And it feels good, not to be so frantic. My job is simply to stay tuned, physically and mentally, and to stay in touch with the racket. Those young punks can practice all day if they want to. I don't need to, I've got the game pretty well figured out. Of course, there are always little things to work on if you've got time. But who's got the time? As you get older you've got to spend more time off the court taking care of your body so you won't get injured. Right?"

"I know what you mean," I said.

It would have been natural to pop open a brewski or two, but it was too early in the day. Todd had come in last night by Greyhound, figuring, I suppose, not to waste any of his precious prize money on airfare.

In the morning his grandfather had dropped him off at my place, and then the old man went to get some parts for a neighbor's vacuum cleaner. Now in my little apartment in the sad gray flats of Berkeley, Hammer and I had some catching up to do.

I let him talk first, because it was his nature to lead the way, and also because I was curious about the two fringe tournaments in Louisiana he and Fernando had played. They had won the doubles in both, and he and Fernando had each won a singles, but interestingly, they never met in the finals like they had in Montana. In the first tourney Todd got bumped in the quarters by a free-spirited tennis player we both knew named Clutch Strafford. Then in the second tournament, the guy knocked Fernando out of the semis. So Clutch was obviously still playing some pretty good tennis.

"Clutch knows how to hit the ball," I said.

"Yeah, well a lot of guys know how to hit the ball," Hammer said matter-of-factly. "Clutch knows how to win matches, too, that's the difference. He's tough, especially when he's down, that's why they call him Clutch. He's tough in the clutch, tough in the clutch Clutch. I had him 5-3 in the third, my serve, and he stepped up his game to another level. It was incredible, the better I hit, the better he hit. What's amazing though, is that he pooped out in the finals. Both times ."

"Clutch used to be able to go all day," I offered. "I guess he's getting old. Like the rest of us."

"That's only part of it. He doesn't train as much now, he's preoccupied with other stuff, so his conditioning suffers. Remember how he used to party, sometimes first thing in the morning, but then he'd go out and train all afternoon? Well, now he's got a different focus."

"What could be more important to Clutch than winning tennis matches?" I asked.

"Are you ready for this? He's into womb theory."

"Womb theory?" I wasn't sure I was hearing right.

"Yeah," Todd repeated, "womb theory. As in wooman."

"Oh, you mean chicks. Good old Clutch is giving up tennis for chicks now?"

"Not exactly, he's into womb theory, like I said. You know how Clutch is, how he's always into some sort of quasi-religion or philosophy or something? Well now he's got this theory and it's taken over his life."

"A theory about women?"

"No, actually it's a theory about men." Now I was really confused.

"Yeah," Hammer explained, "it goes something like this. Men are born coming out of the womb and then they spend their whole lives trying to get back in there. It's like they're trying to get back home or something. There's a circularity to it. Birth, life, death, it's all part of womb theory."

"What about women?"

"That's just it, they come out of the womb too, but they're not trying to get back in there. Not generally speaking. They don't have the circularity, they're more linear, producing offspring and caring for them and all that. Men are more self-centered; they just want to do their own thing, which is to go back home, if you really analyze it. According to womb theory, anyway."

"I suppose Clutch figured all this out for himself?"

"No, actually there's a former Pakistani Davis Cupper who turned him on to it. A guy named Rameesh. It's like a religion for them. They're both really gone with it. The two of them light incense and trip out on womb theory for hours."

"Too much sitting around thinking will get a guy out of shape," I said, remembering how Clutch used to do a lot of long-distance running. If he lost a match, he'd punish himself with a ten-mile run as casually as other guys down a bottle of beer.

"Yeah," Hammer said, "sitting around thinking is bad, but sitting around not thinking can have major benefits, if you know what you're doing."

"Too bad about Clutch," I said, "he used to play some pretty good ball."

"Yeah well, he's still good, I told you he slid past me and Fernando. It's just kind of a shame, he's good enough to beat a guy out for hors d'oevres in the early rounds, but later in the week, when it's time to sit down for the main course he can't even hang on to his fork."

"All because of womb theory?"

"Pretty much. Oh well," Todd rationalized, "a guy's got to have something else besides tennis, right? Especially as you get older. I mean for some guys it's golf, for others it's poetry or Buddhism. For you it's school, right? Well, for Clutch it's womb theory."

"I guess womb theory's not so bad, now that you put it like that. Just don't expect me to get into it. I mean I'll practice it alright, trying to get back in there and all, I'm just not going to try to figure it out, if you know what I mean."

"Yeah," Todd said, "womb theory's not for everybody, at least not in the devout sense."

Suddenly I remembered Evonne's theory, about tenis envy. "I've got something that beats womb theory," I said. "Try this on for size."

"Tennis envy?" Hammer smiled.

"Yeah, and it's spelled with only one N."

"That's deep, dude. Very deep."

"I knew you'd think so."

"Tenis envy, I like that. Where'd it come from?"

"You'll never believe this. It was Evonne."

"Evonne? You're kidding."

"Yeah, her and the lady from Portland."

"The lady from Portland? You mean the dentist's wife? What was she doing with Evonne?"

Hammer's eyes grew wide as I told him what had transpired in his absence, how Bonnie had come down for the funeral and how we had been seeing each other.

"Stretch, you sly dog. I guess I can't even leave you alone for a couple of weeks without you going and falling in love on me. Just tell me this, can I be your best man? I mean, after all, if it wasn't for me dragging your butt off to Montana you never would have met her."

"Dude, who said anything about marriage? Besides, it's not that simple, there are complications. For all I know I may never see her again."

But I knew I had to see her again. I remembered how wonderful it was to wake up that one morning and realize that it wasn't a dream, that Bonnie really was lying by my side, the subtle rise and fall of the blanket, her quiet breath. A few misplaced strands of hair.

"Don't sweat the small stuff," Hammer said, and he extracted himself from his lotus position in order to better digest the news at hand. He leaned back on his arms and grinned, his head nodding introspectively. "Tenis envy, that's deep," he said. "You and the chick from Portland, that's deep too."

"I knew you'd feel that way."

"I think I'll tell Clutch about tenis envy next time I see him," Todd said with a wry smile, "he'll get a kick out of it."

"Maybe it belongs in womb theory somewhere," I suggested, "like a special sect or something, for frustrated tennis players."

Hammer laughed. "I'm not sure it really fits the serious tone of his jigsaw puzzle, but after a few sticks of incense and a couple of whiffs of whatever, there's no telling about Clutch." Todd looked amused. His head moved up and down in that slow pensive way.

I imagined Clutch and Rameesh in a darkened room lit only by candles and the red glow of incense, the two of them kneeling before a Buddha with nice tits. Then I began to think about Bonnie, how we had parted a few days before, how it had felt — good actually, to have those kinds of feelings again. Side by side at the boarding gate we waited for her plane. Then she lined up with the other passengers and filed into the corridor of the jetway; but just before she disappeared inside, she turned around. Our eyes met briefly, for a fraction of a second only. And it was in that instant that everything was said, and also not said. This was the stuff of love — anticipation of absence, one last futile look.

"Dude," Hammer's humorous voice came slowly into my head. "Stretch, dude, you've really got a bad case of it, don't you?"

"Me? Oh, no, I was just thinking about ..." I paused for a moment to regroup my thoughts. What the hell, I could tell Todd the truth, after all, he was a friend, a lifelong friend, and if I couldn't tell him, who could I tell?

"I feel kind of responsible for the team, that's all," I said. "We've got good strength at the top this year and now everyone will expect us to win. You should have seen the way Statler played at Davie Stadium, he ripped

Groyan apart, and Groyan's number two in Nor Cal. You know, there's a type of pressure that comes with having that kind of talent on board."

"You say you got her on board, alright?" Hammer knew me too well. So I gave up trying to hide my true feelings.

"Her? Oh, her. Bonnie. Yeah, she called a couple of nights ago from Portland. Before her husband picked her up at the airport." That last thought shut us both up.

"Now remember," Hammer said after a while, "don't sweat the small stuff." Then his eyes lit up. "Let's go hit some balls," he said, "my game's running pretty good, but I've got to keep it oiled up. Got a tourney next week, something private Clutch turned me on to. He won't even tell me where it is, the deal is that good. The TD's sending me a plane ticket in the mail, and then I'm outa here."

"The money must be unreal," I offered, "it's not like Clutch to be so secretive."

I wondered if I would get pangs to hit the tournament trail again, to join Hammer and Clutch for an adventure, and make some money to boot. But the call of the tennis wilds remained at bay as I thought about school, Sheldeen and Pedro, the guys on the team. Then I pictured Bonnie, and butterflies rose up in my stomach. I couldn't imagine traveling anywhere, unless it was to meet her. Maybe I was cured for good.

"You know I'd go with you," I told Todd as I grabbed my racket, "but I can't afford to get behind at the University."

"Your mind's not on the game right now, anyway," Hammer said. He helped himself to a jar of fuzz nugs from a case on the floor, and I followed him out the door.

We drove over to the Berkeley Tennis Club. Todd knew the manager pretty well and I knew the pro, so it was no problem getting on the courts. Anyway, it was a quiet time of day for them. As it turned out, the number one guy for Cal was there just hanging out, so we talked with him about his team. We recalled past greats, guys like Chuck Darley, Gene Cantin, and Jim McManus. And who could forget Doug Sykes, one of the best black players in the country at the time (second only to UCLA's Arthur Ashe.)

When we got tired of shooting the breeze, the Cal guy joined us for some very solid two-on-one stuff. Hammer and he rotated being the guy on the solo end of the court. I was feeling a bit lazy to work that hard; besides, as Todd said, my mind was elsewhere.

Then later when he had a break from his lessons, the pro came over to where we were on the stadium court. Although he was just a club professional, he had been on the tour and was definitely a "pro," even though now he was just pitching balls for a living. So the four of us did some doubles. Some rather excellent doubles.

My mind may have been elsewhere, but that actually worked to my advantage and kept me from over-concentrating during the match. I played loose and was more offensive than usual, something that didn't go unnoticed to my partner. He stared at me midway through the set.

"Stretch, dude, I see you've finally got your head screwed on right to play this game."

"Or unscrewed right," I suggested.

"Right on," he said. "Maybe you better come to the tourney with me and Clutch before her charm wears off."

"Why should anything wear off?"

"It will, trust me. Soon you'll be worried about the relationship and all the complications. Now you're riding the high, and it suits you well, that's for sure. I've never seen you hit the ball better. Hell, you might be able to ride the high indefinitely, but that's unlikely, especially for somebody like you who has to worry about everything."

He was right. The reason I was playing so well is that I had no second thoughts; I was in a true performance mentality; my go-for-it had kicked in. I had made up my mind to pursue Bonnie, not to let her get away (as I had other women in my life) and so I had become, in a sense, more aggressive. I was being driven by the notion of *he who hesitates is lost*. I was flowing with it. SHE had filled my heart, and those feelings had pumped into every part of my body, believe me, even my fingertips, which pulsed now around the handle of my tennis racket with a new sense of pride and assertiveness. And yet, all this was happening in a rather non-conscious way as we played our doubles.

There, at the Berkeley Tennis Club, on its old-style stadium court, the action with the pro and the Cal guy was fast-paced and satisfying. Hammer and I were up a break in the second set. Occasionally between points I looked up the hill to the white majesty of the Claremont Hotel, while immediately around us in the empty wooden grandstands, I sensed the stirring of hundreds of spectators — people who over the years had watched the likes of Kramer, Gonzales, Laver — Ashe, Smith, Pasarell — MacKay, Trabert — Osuna, Santana. There were so many. Gibson, Connolly, Budge, Hard, Wills — Bueno, King. Newcombe and Emerson,

Rosewall, Connors, Borg. They had all played here and hit the ball much like we were doing that day.

It was my turn to serve. I delivered a couple of unreturnables for a thirty-love lead. I stepped up to the line again, thought about Bonnie, and hit an ace.

"Hell, maybe you'll be able to ride this thing for a while," Hammer said as he turned to me with a hand-signal to cross against his chest.

"Don't bother moving," I said, and I popped another ace.

Chapter Eighteen

Pez Tennis

I was playing so confidently I figured I'd enter a tournament. After all, Hammer was out on the road with Clutch, and I needed something to do, something that wouldn't interfere with my constant daydreaming about Bonnie. A tournament would be perfect, and the sooner the better. I knew it would be too late for this weekend, but then again, maybe somebody had pulled out of an event and there would be an open slot.

I decided to call Peter Herb to find out what was going on. Peter was a clever little player who also happened to be the Northern California Tennis Director. But he told me everything was locked up. Then pleasantly, just before he hung up, he mentioned an unofficial tournament on the other side of the bay.

Two days later I was on my way to a little public park event in Palo Alto with no prize money. I knew no guys from Dick Gould's Stanford team would be wasting their time playing it, even though it was practically in their backyard; and that was too bad, because it would have been a good test of my new Bonnie enhanced game.

I imagined Bonnie was by my side as I drove across the Bay to the Rinconada Park Tennis Center in Palo Alto. And I got off to a great start that first weekend, cruising comfortably through the first three rounds. Then the following weekend I flew through the semis; I was gliding actually, on a big billowy cloud. I parachuted down onto the finals in absolute confidence. But then strangely, I found myself playing erratically, which was odd, because my opponent was not as good as the guy I had in the semis, or even the quarters, for that matter. I was hitting the ball soundly, but a lot of shots were slightly out of control. My halfvolleys in particular were landing just beyond the baseline. It wasn't that I was having trouble hitting them; on the contrary, the racket moved easily in my hand, too easily in fact, giving the racket face too much lift at contact. My low volleys were going long too. And yet, my high volleys were short of their mark, or even worse, landing in the net tape. Thank god I had the little Pez candy dispenser in my bag. The side change was coming up; I'd wrap my hand around that little gem and hold it as I sat on the bench. For good measure I might even put the little Pez dispenser in my pocket where I could get to it between points.

Pez tennis is something Hammer and I stumbled onto a number of years ago at a tournament in Spokane, Washington. We had both lost disappointingly early in the singles, and we did just as poorly in doubles, so with several days left in the tournament, we were on idle. We'd probably hang out and watch the other guys, I figured. It was either that or just split for home, and neither of us was that anxious to leave. We were enjoying Spokane. Or maybe it was just that we were enjoying being on the road.

Conveniently, the tournament director made us an offer we couldn't refuse. "I know you guys didn't make much money," he said, "but if you stick around, there's a way to score some pretty good dough. That is, if you're willing to work."

It seems the TD's brother had a big plumbing supply company, and he was relocating it to the other side of town. The relocation was a major ordeal, and now the guy only had a couple of days left to complete the move, so he was hiring extra workers. Apparently, he didn't have anything against tennis players. "Mostly you'll be loading stuff onto trucks," he told us, "pays a hundred bucks for a morning's work."

"Sounds good to me," Todd said, "Stretch, here, just sleeps in the mornings anyway, so as long as he can do the work with his eyes closed, he should be okay."

And so it was settled, we'd stick around Spokane a couple more days and fatten our wallets before heading back to the Bay Area. The TD's brother even paid our motel for two more nights.

The work was plenty hard, but worse, it was tedious. We were assigned to move several tons of galvanized pipe. The silvery pipe was stacked waist-high in twenty-foot lengths. The idea was to restack it onto big iron racks. The racks would then be hoisted onto a huge flatbed truck that sat ominously nearby.

Each section of pipe was as big around as a jar of tennis balls, so moving those twenty-foot lengths was definitely not a one-man job. Actually, if truth be told, it felt more like a four-man job. It had been a cool morning, but when it was over, Hammer and I were half dead. Sweat-drenched, we sat and gazed at the big flatbed rig, which was loaded now with our work — a mountainous cargo of glistening pipe. Then we each got our hundred bucks in crisp green and hightailed it back to the club to clean up and hit some balls.

And that was the weird part — hitting those first few balls. "My racket feels like a toothpick," Todd called out from his side of the net. Mine didn't feel quite that small. "My racket feels more like a pencil," I told him. Indeed, handling those big metal pipes all morning had changed the sensation in our hands, so now our racket handles felt smaller, and as we swung at the ball we were, in fact, too wristy. It was as if our hands had grown larger. We both felt like we needed our grips to be a size or two bigger to steady the racket.

Immediately, Hammer sat down and wrapped two overgrips onto his Pro Staff. "There," he said, laying into the ball, "now that's more like my regular butt-kicking forehand." Meanwhile, I was enjoying playing with my tiny grip; I felt like I could do more intricate things with the racket. But my timing was early, which is naturally the case when using a smaller grip, since the hand gets thrown into motion more quickly.

As bad luck would have it, the next morning when we reported to work at the Spokane plumbing yard, we were assigned another mountain of pipe to restack. But this time, the hideous pipe, though in the same twenty-foot lengths, was only three-quarters of an inch in diameter. And that made the job a lot easier. Cocky at first, we tried to handle two of the twenty-foot sections at a time, but after nearly crushing Hammer's big toe, we wised up and lifted each pipe individually. "This pipe may be skinny," Todd said, limping slightly, "but it's still really long." I was too tired to reply; we'd been at it for over an hour, and yet, it didn't look like we'd even put a dent in the huge stack of pipe. I figured the stuff was skinny alright, but that was part of the problem — there were a lot more of them in what appeared to be the same size area.

At last we were finished. Breathing deeply and dripping sweat again, we gazed out at the ominous flatbed and its gleaming cargo of galvanized pipe. And again, it had been worth it. We each got another hundred, and now with two-hundred bucks in my pocket, I felt rich, almost as if I had gotten to the quarters, I suppose. We held our heads high at the Spokane club that afternoon as we strutted onto an open court to hit some balls.

"Hey, my racket feels like a telephone pole," Todd exclaimed. Mine felt huge too! It was remarkable — the day before our rackets were too small, and now they were too big. Our fingers were so used to handling those hundreds of skinny pipes at the plumbing yard that even our normal $4^{1/2}$ grips seemed gigantic in our palms. And guess what, we stroked the ball heavier, with less wrist, which felt pretty good, especially on the groundstrokes. But on the serve we were a bit clumsy. Our hands were also less precise in dealing with stretch volleys.

"Just goes to show," Todd said brightly, "that everything is relative, even the grips on our tennis rackets. I mean if your grip suddenly feels too big in the middle of a match, all you have to do is hold something bigger for a while. A jar of tennis balls would be perfect." He demonstrated by gripping his hand around a jar of balls for about thirty seconds, and then he slipped his fingers back onto his racket handle.

"There," he said, "now my racket feels small again and I'll be able to snap it better."

Professor Hammer went on. "On the other hand, if you're playing too wristy and spraying the ball all over the place, you need the racket to feel bigger, more stable in your palm. So before the very next point, all you do is grab something small, like the index finger of your left hand and hold it for a while." He demonstrated, and then he slid his hand back onto his racket handle. "There. Now the racket feels bigger in my palm, and I'll get more stability on the hit."

Hammer explained that the phenomenon had to do with muscle memory and that it was not just psychological. That is, you could truly get the effect of playing with a smaller grip, simply by fooling your hand into believing it was holding a smaller grip. Similarly, you could get the benefits of a larger grip, when needed, by tricking your hand into believing it was playing with a larger grip. "Everything is relative," he said, "even grip sizes."

I'm still not sure how accurate Hammer's theory of grip relativity is, but one thing is certain — I always make a point to have a small handle in my tennis bag in case my strokes need stabilizing. An empty Pez dispenser works great, and so does an old style travel toothbrush. Those are perfect things to hold during a side change if your grip suddenly feels too small. The Pez dispenser is my favorite, even though I don't care much for the candy. It's saved my ass in many a match. Sometimes I even put the little handle in my pocket during play. (The split throat of the modern racket frame can also do in a pinch, and that's something that is always available!)

On the contrary, I don't often worry about packing along something large, in the event my grip suddenly feels too big. The reason is, there is usually a jar of tennis balls nearby, and if not, a net post is an awesome column to wrap one's fingers around (and that can be done at any a side change.) Grabbing hold of the left forearm for a while is perhaps the most instantaneous way of accomplishing the same thing, in which case one needs only to wipe the sweat off the palm before resuming play. And shirts work great for that.

That plumbing yard in Spokane, Washington, gave us a lifelong lesson in grip relativity. We savored what we had learned as we drove back to California in the old Dart (which was not so old then.) We had also volunteered to transport a friend of Clutch's back to Portland. The guy had gotten to the semis in the tournament and seemed very interested in our newly discovered theory of grip relativity.

"So," he called out from the back seat, "let me get this straight. When I get home, I should have my wife hold something small like a crayon for a while. That way I'll seem bigger than before."

"Exactly," Todd said, "a cute little crayon, whatever color she likes."

Chapter Nineteen

Spiraling In Control

I ended up winning the public park tournament in Palo Alto, and that little Pez dispenser helped pull me through; it stabilized my hand when the racket handle felt suddenly too small in my grip. And as psychological as the effect might have been, it worked! But it was really Bonnie who was behind my victory; it was she who had set my game in motion.

And now the trophy from Rinconada Park was on my bookshelf.

Typically, I would have preferred a little prize money, since I usually just changed the name plate on the trophies and gave them to the kids, but this one I would keep. It seemed odd at first — a female victory goddess with her arms arched overhead. But it was made of polished brass, and I became attached to it quickly. The attractive little lady stood on a wooden pedestal, and I knew she would always remind me of Bonnie. I studied the finely polished curves of her tiny body as I listened to the soft sound of September rain falling on the roof. It had been a good rain, kind of fun, as the first ones of the season always are. But soon it would become dissipating mist, then gray skies and wet tennis courts.

Hammer and I had planned to hit some balls, but clouds were huddled over the entire Bay Area and the courts would be wet all afternoon. So I drove over to get him and make alternative plans. When I arrived at his grandfather's little house on Vine Street, I found Todd on his back, staring up at the ceiling. Actually, he was focused on a ceiling fan that had been installed in the living room for the sole purpose of doing eyeball exercises. Lying on his back, Hammer had one eye covered while the other followed the circular movement of a fan blade that had been marked with a spot of bright yellow tape. Then Todd worked the other eye. I knew his routine; he had already done both eyes together, and in a moment he would stand up and flip the switch on the fan motor so his eyeballs could reverse the direction of their workout. Then, depending on his mood, he might switch the fan to a faster speed, or even reposition the spot of yellow tape toward the center of the blade where he would have to perform more rapid eye movement.

Ceiling fans were not very common in Berkeley, the weather being generally so mild, but Todd's grandfather stuck a nice one up there to insure the development of a typically ignored tennis muscle — a player's eye. The fan also came in handy if the old man happened to burn something in the kitchen, in which case he would open the windows and put the motor on top speed, thereby swooshing air throughout the house. But usually those big blades turned around slowly, or indeed not at all, since Todd was rarely at home and not always in the mood for eye calisthenics.

When he had finished with the fan, Hammer offered it to me. So I lay there on my back and rotated my eyeballs in circles for a while. I could feel them flexing, like little biceps in the middle of my forehead. I was ready to strike out at the opponent with them, or at least watch the ball with more pinpointed aggression. I imagined myself in the heat of battle, tracking the ball furiously with my freshly pumped eyeballs. But then we got bored with the fan and went on to other things.

"Yeah, man" Todd said, "let's go hit some balls, that was a good rain we had this morning. It should be fun." I knew what he was getting at.

So we put our gear in the old Dodge Dart and headed over to some really fast courts near campus that stood on top of a parking lot. Nobody was on them, and with good reason, considering the puddles. But not wanting to skimp on training, and more importantly, wanting to have some fun, we slipped into our old shoes and went at it with a couple of nylon-strung rackets I had in the trunk.

We were not after regular tennis, anyway. The idea was to practice footwork, special footwork, the kind of footwork that would be used on slippery clay, where one had to slide into the ball first before hitting it. Not having any clay courts around, Hammer and I had discovered years ago that we could prepare for the clay, at least to some degree, by skidding and sliding on wet hardcourts. This was especially handy during a damp Bay Area winter, when we were tempted to take off on a moment's notice for the sunny dirt courts of Mexico.

Now above a Berkeley parking lot, on a court filled with puddles, we imagined it was the old days and we were headed south of the border. As a training exercise, we kept both feet down on the wet surface at all times and skated around the slick court, figuring all that shuffling and sliding would pay off when we got to the sandy clay in Mexico and had to skid into shots from a dead run.

"Hey, man, my socks are soaked," Todd called out from his side of the court.

"Don't be a sissy," I replied, "we're not even half way through the set!" But I was feeling it too. Every time I put my weight down my shoes squeaked as water squished out the midsoles. But the worst was trying to serve, when water from the nap of the ball sprayed across my face.

"OK," I said, "just a few more points."

So we wrapped it up and threw our waterlogged gear into the trunk of the old Dart, and now Todd and I were strolling down Telegraph Avenue with no socks on our feet. It felt a bit odd, but at least we were wearing dry shoes. I marched along imagining it was still the old days and I was a gunslinger ready to ride into the badlands of Mexico and carve a few more notches into the handle of my tennis racket.

And there were plenty of senoritas, too, right there in Berkeley, although they didn't wear such wide brimmed hats. Actually most didn't wear hats, or undergarments in some cases, and that kept our eyes propped open wide as we flowed along the busy commerce of tattooed orange juice entrepreneurs and barefooted jewelry makers who lined the sidewalks of Telegraph Avenue. Half the hippies in the country were there selling their wares — paintings, earrings, wood carvings, freshly created antiques, you name it. We were, after all, at Telegraph and Bancroft Avenues, innovation hub of the universe, and here on the sidewalks all were welcome — professors and dropouts from all over the world, potheads, preachers, suits, bikinis. Yes, even wandering minstrels, who now having arrived at the great center of learning, wandered less and sang out more as they sought to maintain their spots at various enclaves along the street.

The sun wasn't out, but the sidewalk had dried off and the air was fresh and clean, causing my sense of smell to become suddenly acute as we walked along. We passed the open door of a bakery, and I took a deep satisfying whiff of freshly baked bread. Then from the sidewalk came the subtle but distinct aroma of leather goods, and then candles, cute little candles floating in dishes. The candles smelled like vanilla. I wanted Bonnie to see them. I wished she were with us.

The delicate sound of intricate string music was like an orchestra singing in the otherwise ill-bred noise of the street. It was coming from the overhang of a doorway where a ragged violinist and her bedraggled cellist stood reading sheet music. On the ground between their music stands was the open case of his cello, beckoning like a big velvet mouth. Occasional passersby pitched in quarters and half dollars, but most of the take was a thin scattering of dimes and nickels. A few flimsy dollar bills stood out conspicuously in the middle of the case, probably put there by the cellist, himself.

Having a poor background in music, I had no idea if they were playing Beethoven or Mozart, or even Bach, for that matter. But the ups and downs of quick-paced scales were intriguing, and I noticed the duo had attracted a nice little crowd for their concert. So I stood there for a while with Bonnie in my mind and Hammer by my side.

Todd nudged me with his elbow. "Isn't that Jeff Borowiak?" he said out of the corner of his mouth. He gestured with his chin in the direction of the musicians. And then, yes, I saw him. It was Borowiak, tall and suntanned, standing directly behind the girl on the violin; he was peering over her shoulder, reading the sheet music as her arm flew dramatically this way and that in its various melodic offerings. Borowiak's head bobbed gently and approvingly with the music as he stood behind the violinist, but then every once in a while he winced and his eyebrows would rise momentarily, and then they would flatten back down and the bobbing and weaving of his head would resume.

He must have spotted us; he cracked a brief smile, and the next time the violinist reached out to turn a page of her sheet music, he stepped away from her and came over.

"She took a few liberties with the score," he said, gesturing toward the violinist. "She's bound to improve, but she's got her work cut out, some of those crescendoing triplets are pretty tough. So what are you guys up to?"

Hammer looked amused. "Just out for a little rainy day tennis," he replied.

"We're training, too," Borowiak said, "Torben and I were out doing a little road work when we stopped to check out the music."

"So where's Torben?" I asked. Then I saw him with his long hair and beard, sitting cross-legged at the foot of the cellist. He blended in so well I had thought he was just a local mystic.

But Torben Ulrich was a Davis Cupper from Copenhagen. They called him The Great Dane, because he had set a record for number of Davis Cup matches played. He was Borowiak's guru buddy, and they apparently had a break from the tour, so they were hanging out at Borowiak's place in Berkeley. I recalled that early in his career, the tall smooth-playing Borowiak had wins over Connors and Borg, when those guys were at their prime. Of course, he was expected to do big things, after all, he had won the NCAA's no problem while at UCLA, and then in his first year on the pro tour he beat guys like Newcombe and Smith.

But there was more than tennis for the multi-talented Borowiak and his Danish buddy, Ulrich. They were music aficionados, and performers as well, each being proficient at several instruments. The handsome Borowiak, in particular, was so much a performer that on the tennis court he tended to *conduct* matches rather than just play them. And often in a somewhat choreographed manner, where he projected the elegance of a dancer, so smooth and unrushed were his movements.

Standing taller and a bit slimmer than Hammer, Borowiak was wearing a blue UCLA sweatshirt and old-style cotton sweat pants. "Why don't you guys come along," he said through all the hubbub of the street and the singing of the violin, "we're going up the hill to work our legs." He stepped over to get Torben, who was still cross-legged on the sidewalk near the big velvet interior of the cello case. With a flip of his wrist, Borowiak dealt a five dollar bill down toward the coins that lay in the case. I watched as the bill floated down slowly, gliding first one way and then the other, so smooth and Borowiak-like, and landing at last near the coins.

We followed them along the congested sidewalk, past Larry Blake's Restaurant and over to Durant Avenue, where we turned up the hill and hiked to a large sports field that sat below the big Cal coliseum. Borowiak and the bearded Ulrich started to jog the perimeter of the field, so Hammer and I fell in right behind them and got our sockless feet going.

Running comfortably now, we were about halfway around the big field when an errant football came tumbling along the grass in our direction. Without breaking his stride, the tall Borowiak swooped up the football with one hand; he took a couple of quick steps and punted it into the air, where it spiraled like a sideways bullet high in the gray sky. Fifty yards downfield, some football players in jerseys watched with craned necks as the ball sailed skywards above them. It hovered for a moment before beginning its near vertical descent back to earth; and though it landed in the grass only a few yards from where they stood, the football players made no attempt to catch it. They watched as we jogged on around their end of the field. Time and again, during the course of our workout, they'd break from their huddle and watch as we cruised by.

I wasn't in the best of shape and was having trouble keeping up, when conveniently, we stopped to rest and do leg stretches in the damp grass. From various yoga postures, Borowiak and the sage-like Ulrich began to talk about music, local rock and jazz groups mostly. The intricacy of their conversation was inspiring, but being somewhat lacking on the subject, I could appreciate almost none of it and tended to just sit there daydreaming about Bonnie. Hammer, on the other hand, kept up with the dialogue and even added interesting tidbits about Thelonious Monk and John Coltrane.

They told us they had tickets to see The Grateful Dead at the Fillmore that night and would have to get rolling soon because they had to pick up a friend. Shielding his eyes as if he were holding a pair of binoculars, the bearded Ulrich hunted for the elusive position of the sun in the overcast sky. And then he found it. "It is now time for bed in Denmark," he said, pointing at the horizon, "I must now call my wife and Lars." He told us his thirteen-year-old son, Lars, was a tennis player and that he had just got his first drum set. "I am very much interested to hear about the drums," he said.

We walked with them back toward the hub of the University, then watched as they squeezed themselves into Borowiak's little VW Bug. The car started up audibly and puttered away from the curb. It meandered slowly down the busy street, nosing back toward the curb here and there in search of a pay phone, so Ulrich could call his kid.

I envied those guys. They were real pros, touring pros who traveled the world. They were in the newspaper on a regular basis and on national TV at least a few times a year. Their next stop after this little Bay Area sojourn would be Cologne. Even Hammer was in awe.

"I hear when Borowiak's in Europe he sneaks into a cathedral in the middle of the night and plays the organ," Todd said. I had heard that too. Apparently he would give concerts for the insomniac winos of the village, and whoever else might be up at that wee hour; a distraught housewife or mistress, perhaps, with her pillow by the window and the other side of her bed empty.

"He plays the flute, too," Hammer said, "of course, that's mostly just because it's so convenient to carry. What he really likes to do is get his fingers on a keyboard."

I thought about that spiral kick Borowiak had booted up into the sky, how it lofted and seemed to hang up there indefinitely. That was amazing considering the guy probably hadn't kicked a football in years. He and his buddy were probably at a pay phone right about now so they could call Denmark and check on Ulrich's kid, Lars, who was at home training to be a Davis Cupper, and now also a drummer.

And what a drummer he would become! For as it later turned out, little Lars would end up beating his drum for the whole world to hear. Who would have expected that? Perhaps his sage-like father sensed it coming, for as young Lars grew over the years, the rectangular surface of the tennis court morphed into the circular surface of his drum, and there he ran around on it, thrashing forehands and backhands relentlessly until he became drummer for the rock band, Metallica.

Chapter Twenty

Tennis Ball Shoes

It was evening when we got back to Todd's place. A distinct humming sound was coming from the basement, so we went down the stairs to check it out. It was Todd's grandfather.

The old man was bent over his grinder; a familiar whirring vibration filled the room as he held a tennis shoe against the revolving stone. He worked quickly, carefully grinding the yellow fuzz off a piece of tennis ball he had just glued onto the toe of one of Todd's worn-out shoes. It might have seemed odd that the old man would patch his grandson's shoe with a tennis ball, but then again, the shoe was beginning to look like new.

And so, a tennis ball can be used to extend the life of a tennis shoe. I always thought that was rather convenient. Not only that, but according to Todd's grandfather, nobody will ever come up with a material better suited for the job. For beneath the felt surface of a tennis ball is durable rubber, rubber that is pliable and has a natural curvature for wrapping around the toe of a shoe.

The procedure is simple — just take an old tennis ball and cut along the seam. If you cut the entire seam, you end up with two skinny kidney-shaped pieces of tennis ball. Half of one is more than enough. Simply trim it to cover the worn part of your shoe, which is typically the edge near the big toe and the ball of the foot. Then glue it on and you're ready to go.

Grinding off the yellow ball-fuzz isn't necessary because it will wear off on its own, though it can be a little slippery until it does. And it can look somewhat eccentric to be a member of the yellow-toe elite, but hell, there was a time when all our friends went around with fuzz nug on their shoes. Then Hammer's grandfather volunteered to grind the yellow stuff off for everybody and you couldn't even tell we'd done repair jobs. He also used the grinder to bevel the edges of the patch, which again isn't necessary, but it provides a nicer feel at first.

Down in the old man's basement on Vine Street, we watched as he worked on three pairs of tennis shoes that had been out on the road with Todd. Two of them were being re-patched, so Todd's grandfather had to scrape off what was left of the old tennis ball first. Then he gave that area a light sanding to make sure it was clean. Likewise, he took a piece of sandpaper to the section of tennis ball that was to be attached. Then he glued the two together using contact cement, which takes about ten minutes to set up. That's probably the best adhesive for the job, but sometimes Hammer and I use Crazy Glue, especially if we need to work quickly, during a side change, for instance. But the problem with Crazy Glue is that if you use one drop too much, the patch won't stick. And even if it does, it may be only temporary since the stuff isn't made to handle the constant flexing of a tennis shoe. And yet, the worst problem of all is that you absolutely cannot afford to be sloppy with Crazy Glue; if you get an unnoticed drop of it on your palm or your finger, you may have to tear the racket out of your hand. So generally speaking, Crazy Glue is not worth the risk, although a drop or two on the opponent's chair can prove advantageous if applied correctly at the changeover.

Since most players wear through the inside edge of the forefoot before the rest of the shoe shows any wear at all, such patch jobs can add months of life to otherwise unusable tennis shoes. Not only that, but the shoes, being nicely broken in, allow the ultimate in maneuverability on the court. At the same time, of course, the repairs save you a small fortune over the years.

However, if you are going to patch your shoes, don't wait until you get a gaping hole clean through the sole. Do it when the worn area is getting thin, that way you have a surface to glue onto. And use a tennis ball! Any tennis ball. Hammer and I have tried Shoo Goo, Shoe Renew and all the other repair goops on the market; they take too long to dry and they only last for a set or two. When we patch our shoes we want them to last!

In the basement now, Todd's grandfather put the finishing touches on the final pair of tennis shoes. He bent over the grinder, carefully beveling the edges of the patch, then he put the shoes on the workbench alongside the others. He took off his close-up specs and stood back to admire his handiwork. His handsome old head moved up and down, leathery wrinkles and all. "An old shoe fixed is a new fortune made," he said, obviously pleased with the three repair jobs.

"Right on," I offered, "we may get a good deal on them, but it's still about forty bucks a pop for shoes like those."

"Yeah," Todd said, "if we didn't fix them, I'd have to get a new pair every other week, and that adds up. Besides I always play my best in tennis-ball shoes, they're nice and broken in."

I gazed enviously at Todd's shoes — they looked clean and plenty new enough, but the edges of the soles had been rounded from hard play, and at the toe of each was a new section of rubber that blended perfectly with the worn contour of the forefoot, thus assuring hours more play with unencumbered mobility. Nobody would have guessed the shoes had been patched.

Todd high-fived the old man. "Nice work, Pop," he announced, and he gathered up the shoes in his arms. (Ever since I had known Hammer, he had called his grandfather Pop, even when his grandmother was still alive, though he had always addressed her as Grandma.)

Pop went up the steps first, followed by Todd with his armload of shoes, and then me as we marched up the narrow staircase that led out of the basement.

In the living room now, with our feet still in our minds, we talked about tennis shoes for a while. They were like everything else these days, too many bells and whistles for their own good, which made them heavy and difficult to break in. "For crissake," Hammer complained, "tennis shoes should be light, like running shoes. After all, that's what tennis is all about. Running."

"Yeah," I put in, "Tom Stow used to say a tough tennis match is like a five-mile run. So why should we do it with weights on our feet?"

"It's all a marketing thing," Todd said. Meanwhile the old man's head was nodding in agreement. "Light is right," he said.

"Light is definitely right," I said, "you'd think they'd have figured that out by now. But oh no. And then just when you find a shoe you like, they replace it with another style."

"Hell," Todd whined, "if I could, I'd wear a women's shoe, they're a lot lighter. Only trouble is they're not wide enough."

"Blaine Turner wears women's shoes."

"Blaine who?"

"Turner. You know, that kid from Minnesota. The one who came out of the qualies and won in Palm Springs."

"Oh, that guy. I read about him. I hear he's got a big serve, even on the soft stuff. Lucky guy, he's probably blessed with narrow feet."

And so our conversation shifted from tennis shoes to tennis players, a topic that included Fernando, Clutch, McEnroe, Borg, even Hitch and Evonne. "That was some punt," Hammer said, referring to the spiral kick Jeff Borowiak had sent into the clouds earlier in the day. I envisioned Torben Ulrich, his long hair and beard.

"By the way, how's that kid doing? You know, your star twelve-year-old. Danny what's-his-name?"

He would have to ask. It was just yesterday that the kid's mother had called to tell me he'd be taking a break from the lessons for a while. I knew it was coming, I just didn't know it'd be so soon.

"He lost to a couple of guys he was ahead of in the rankings," I said, "so he's kind of depressed."

"You mean his father is depressed."

"That's exactly it, it's his parents who are freaked, the kid is even-keeled, a realist, if someone beats him he shakes the guy's hand and he's done with it. He knows other guys are going to catch up to him sooner or later. It's his dad who can't face the writing on the wall."

I thought about parents and their kids and what Billie Jean King had said about athletes, that they have a chip on their shoulders, a need to prove themselves, and that's what drives them to succeed. And she was right, for the most part. Hell, I knew it was true about me, at least early on when I was still trying to prove to everybody how great I was. Of course, I also enjoyed hitting the ball, and running, and the pressure of competition; it was all wrapped up together.

But nowadays with so much money in the game, a chip on the shoulder isn't always necessary. Perfectly well-adjusted individuals can be driven to succeed at tennis simply as a career choice, just like they might methodically choose to be lawyers, doctors, or engineers. Given athletic ability, coaching, and an early start, this happens. That's why we see more and more big men in the game, guys like Stan Smith, Pete Sampras, and Boris Becker. Big men who don't necessarily grow up with a chip on their shoulders, just guys who know they can do it and they set their sights high. Guys, actually, like Hammer, who could have made it in any sport; kids who are natural, self-contented winners, and they aren't just running around the playground because they have a deep-seated need to prove themselves.

But what Billie Jean King said is still largely true, especially when you include parents in the mix. So many parents are steaming quietly in the background with big invisible chips on their shoulders. Others sit closer, on courtside benches, with smoke coming out of their ears.

There, in Pop's little living room on Vine Street, I thought about Danny's departure. It was not something I really wanted to talk about, but it wasn't going to go away. I had to face up to it.

"So," Hammer suggested, "the doctor had his wife make the call?"

"Yeah, she was the one who called, the surgeon doesn't like to mess up his hands doing the dirty work, but you can bet your butt he does the dialing when it comes to hiring another coach."

It was a hard situation to walk away from. It was like being an uncle or a big brother, and then suddenly after all those years, being asked to go away. It hurt.

In order to help the wound heal, I had taken Danny's picture off the top of my bookcase and put it in a drawer for safekeeping. But still, I could see him hitting that perfectly executed leaping overhead every time I looked at the shelf.

"Well, at least you've got Sheldeen," Todd said. "He's got more potential anyway."

"Yeah, too bad the world doesn't run on potential. Oh well, got to go with the flow, right?"

"Right on, bro." Hammer commended me; he was pleased I could see it that way. "It's too bad," he said, "but that's the way it is, the better those juniors get, the more likely they are to abandon you."

I didn't feel like talking about it anymore, and Hammer picked up on that, so he switched the subject to food and invited me to join him and Pop for dinner. Then he went back down into the basement to get us a bottle of wine.

The handsome old man did the cooking (something he had always enjoyed, even when his wife was still around.) He tinkered curiously in the kitchen, lifting lids off pots and smelling the various vapors that rose up from his rattling stove. Occasionally he'd poke a fork into something and taste it. "A little too much cayenne," he said, with eyebrows raised high; then he put the lid back down onto the gurgling pan.

All the while, Hammer and I sat in the adjacent dining room, sipping red wine and munching on sourdough a lady friend of the old man's had made. The house was on the first rise of the hills, and though the view wasn't the greatest, through the window we could see the dim bulbs of the Berkeley flatlands as they spread out and disappeared near the edge of the Bay. Across the dark water, pieces of San Francisco sparkled in the night. We looked through the windowpanes, sipping our wine and listening to the music of the old man's cooking. Warm savory aromas wafted into the room. It felt good and homey.

Shortly, Pop brought in a tossed green salad with a dressing made of vinegar and flax seed oil. "Here's to your health," he said. Then he set a platter of hot food on the table and sat down to join us. I thought about

Bonnie when she was just the dentist's wife to me, and how nice it was to eat dinner with all of them up in Portland — her husband and the two giggly girls. I wondered what they were having tonight; probably nothing fancy, I figured, and then I dug in and scarfed down with Pop and Hammer.

"Don't be shy," the old man said when he saw I had finished what was on my plate. "There's plenty more where that came from."

"Yeah, and it's even cooked," Todd quipped, "so help yourself." He passed me the plate of sautéed celery root, and then he helped himself. I couldn't believe how good it tasted. That darn root was just a vegetable, but it had the chewy texture of steak, and damn near the flavor, too, thanks to the old man's doctoring. If I hadn't known better I would have thought I was eating steak.

"It's good for your nerves," Pop said. "I know it tastes like meat, but you boys'll get your protein from the casserole." He shoved the dish of brown rice and lentils toward us. He had prepared it with bell pepper and onion, and it was downright tasty.

Now on thirds, Todd stuck his head down hungrily and cleaned his plate like a dog with a fork. I thought he was going to lick at the remaining tidbits, but he mopped them up with a piece of sourdough. Then he drained his glass of wine and leaned back in his chair with an audible sigh. He pretended to be gazing out the window, but he was really studying the old man.

"Well, Stretch, what do you think?" he said, "do you think we checked into the right hotel this time?"

"You got that right," I said, "there's nothing like home cooking. This is as good as it gets."

Now Pop leaned back in his chair. He, too, pretended to be looking out the window. His head moved up and down with great satisfaction. I began to think about my father; he had moved back East after my mother's death, to try to forget, I suppose. I wondered if we would have gotten along if he had stuck around, if he would have been mellow like Pop. Probably not, I figured, a grandparent was always more mellow.

"You boys run along now and have some fun," Pop said, "before the night gets old. Go on, get out of here." He shooed us away with his hand.

So we headed out to Kip's, a burger joint near campus, to have a piece of pie, and as Hammer put it, to see what the coeds looked like these days. And guess what? They looked pretty good, very good actually, and in an authentic sort of way that was unblemished by things like too much makeup, or in some cases, bra straps.

The air grew thick with the smell of French fries and char from the grill as we made our way into the crowd at the back of Kip's. We settled in a booth that gave us a good vantage point. "Most of these chicks are going to Cal," Hammer said, "so you know they're smart. I kind of like them. It's nice when their hairdos don't get in the way of their brains, if you know what I mean."

"I know exactly what you mean. These chicks are the type that can understand what you're talking about, even when you can't."

"That's it, they're the type who can appreciate you for more than your body. They have minds too, and they understand about philosophy and religion. And they have poetry, beautiful poetry in their souls." He was eyeballing one particularly striking coed. "And sometimes the poetry is on their lips, and at the end of their delicate little fingertips. And then they don't even know they are writing, but their poetry goes straight to the heart."

Soon we were all sittin' on the *Dock of the Bay* as Otis Redding came through the juke box and filled the burger joint with the laziness of a balmy afternoon. Hammer's head, like so many others in the place, swayed to the easy buoyancy of the music.

Todd had had several glasses of wine at home, and now, though he was only having pie and coffee, he was in fine form. I figured it was time to tell him about my vision of tennis, about the futuristic dream I had where the game was fast and furious, with five men in simultaneous battle against five other men. It was either that or pine out loud over Bonnie. I opted for the new pro teams. I could pine after that.

"Dude," I said, "did you ever wonder what would happen if there were more guys on a tennis court? I mean a lot more, and playing singles too?" My partner looked at me sadly with a wrinkled forehead, as if he didn't know who was more confused, me or him. I realized I had lost him.

"Let me put it this way," I said, "I had a dream the other night. It was about pro teams. Of the future. Check this out."

So I told him everything — about my hand on McEnroe's cane, then striking the bedsheet with it — about the fact that there weren't tournaments anymore, but just head-to-head team matches; and how those teams were made up. How players could serve to either box, provided they rotated through the lineup. There was also the receiving rotation. I told him about the ball-delivering net posts, the peripheral vacuum system, the 6-second clock, the electronic umpires. I described how you could get bonus points for striking an inactive player; and then saving the best part for last, I told him about the battleball frenzy of a penalty shoot-out.

Hammer didn't say anything for a long time. After a while his head started to move up and down, slowly, as if he were painting the far wall of the hamburger joint with his mind. Then the corners of his mouth widened into a broad smile; his eyes lit up.

"Stretch, dude, I think you're onto something. Now that you mention it, those rainy days in high school when we used to go in the gym and play battleball were a blast! All that dodging and retaliating, it was a real battlefront, ducking and diving and firing balls at the enemy until nobody was left standing. Heroes were made on those wet days. Man, I'd rather play battleball than just about anything!"

"It was my favorite thing too," I told him, "so with the older boys, I let them have a ball war at the end of their tennis lesson, if the parents aren't around. It's kind of a treat if they're well behaved. It kind of brings tennis down to its most basic elements, I guess. Instead of outstroking the opponent, you simply get to shoot him."

"That's it!," Todd said enthusiastically, "it's the instinct of the hunt, the wild west, cowboys and Indians, all that. But tell me, this futuristic stuff, how did you figure it out? You just dreamed it? Just like that?"

"Yeah, more or less. If Bonnie hadn't called and woke me up it might have gone unnoticed. You know, most of our dreams we never even get to know about."

"Well I hope you thanked the fine lady for your dream." I didn't reply; I was too busy imagining what it was like to hold her, her cheek next to mine, the smell of her hair.

"Your team concept is intriguing," Todd said, "you've got elements of various sports in it. But tell me, when you're in the middle of a shoot-out and you're firing the ball at the other guys, can you use your free hand to toss the ball, or aren't you allowed to touch it with your hand?"

I hadn't thought about not tossing the ball. "Now that you mention it, maybe it would be interesting to restrict use of the hand. Guys could just flip the ball up from the strings like the way One-Armed Joe serves."

We always used to see One-Armed Joe out at Golden Gate Park. When Hammer and I were younger, we'd go out there a lot to get our butts kicked by the veteran Tom Brown, even though he was about twice our age. Brown had been a Wimbledon finalist, and we never did beat his wicked, sliding forehand back then, but One-Armed Joe would always be there trying to give us tips. He's the one who taught us how to practice lobs by rallying over the tops of tall eucalyptus trees.

"Good old One-Armed Joe. Haven't seen him in a while," Hammer said dreamily. "I guess he's still playing out at Golden Gate Park."

"Yeah, and he's probably still wearing those white boxer shorts."

"Hey, if his missing arm and his black teeth don't psyche you out, his boxer shorts will. They make him look like more of a hack, and he loves that. It helps him get odds."

"Dude. One-Armed Joe doesn't need any odds. I've never seen him pick a bet with a player he couldn't beat straight up."

"Yeah, but he always makes it look real close. Then he drags his victim into the clubhouse and he takes the rest of the guy's money playing cards."

"Which is actually peanuts compared to all the money he made betting on Rosemary Casals when she was a kid. He used to call her *The Rose*, and especially when she won big for him. Remember?"

Sometimes as a way of offering condolences, One-Armed-Joe would hand a single red rose to one of his marks after taking the guy's money. "The Rose wanted you to have this," he'd say.

I pictured Rosemary Casals preparing to hit an overhead, and I became suddenly mesmerized. No single moment combines the power and beauty of the sport so well as Casals poised to hit an overhead. Her brown muscular legs stand firmly apart; a slightly paler skin color visible beneath the miniature parachute of her white tennis skirt, the pleats now dropping as her arms and racket rise, ready to strike.

Exquisitely compact, The Rose was superbly speedy, and those who played her felt the repeated sting of darting little feet that lay like tiny thorns all along the vine of her game. One-Armed-Joe made a lot of money betting on The Rose, first when she was a kid and nobody knew how good she was, and then later when she had a reputation there was always some guy who thought he could knock her off. But now with Casals on tour and at the Park less, One-Armed-Joe had to rely more on his other bets and card games.

Sitting across from Hammer in the burger joint, I laughed out loud just thinking about One-Armed-Joe. He was definitely one of the more colorful characters at the Golden Gate Park tennis courts. Actually, it was surprising he could serve so well, considering his missing arm. And I figured Hammer did have a point about my futuristic teams; restricting use of the hand had its merits; it would probably develop more racket artistry. "It's certainly worth thinking about," I told him as a bevy of sorority types squeezed past our table on their way out.

Todd was still eyeballing the coed in the next booth, a slender brunette who was drinking a milkshake and reading what appeared to be a biology book. "Stretch, I'll tell you what." His eyes were on the girl as he spoke. "I'll talk to Clutch at the tournament. We'll get some of the guys to come through town and give your hyper team tennis a try. I think you're on to something."

"Don't forget to tell him about tenis envy," I said.

"Oh shit!" Hammer laughed. "Tenis envy! I almost forgot. Thanks for reminding me. I wouldn't want to forget about tenis envy."

Todd's ticket had come in the mail from the TD. He was flying out in the morning to join Clutch in Vancouver for a small but lucrative tournament with good first round guarantees, so tonight was kind of a farewell get-together. I could tell by the way he looked at the coed that he was getting tired of the road, that he was tired of being the Lone Ranger, leaving behind silver bullets wherever he went. He needed a chance to make special friends. At least he had an excellent home base with his grandfather and all.

He turned to me with a serious face. "When are you going to see her again?"

"Her?"

"Yeah, HER!"

"Oh, her. Bonnie. She's supposed to drop me a line with a secret address for me to write her at. Then we'll figure something out."

"'Absence makes the heart grow fonder,'" he said.

"It sure does, only trouble is I'm fond enough already. If I get any fonder ..."

"Don't sweat the small stuff," Todd cut in, "just ride the high, go with the flow, remember?"

"Oh yeah, go with the flow."

And so we talked about everything from tennis of the future to true love to old times, old times being the best part of the conversation. Hell, there were even oldies coming through the speakers in the hamburger joint, sounds that made us feel like kids again.

With our spirits high we talked about the time Evonne climbed into the umpire chair at the old club. That had been a superb moment. "We did a lot for a lot of people," Todd remarked with a dreamy look.

"Right on," I said, and we high-fived each other above the table

Todd had a plane to catch to Vancouver early in the morning, so we finished our pie and left the place with the coed still reading her biology book.

"It must be nice to be back in school," Todd said, sounding rather melancholy as we slid into the front seat of the old Dart.

"It has its moments," I said, and I started up the car. "Babes and books, that's a hard combination to beat But then again, there's nothing like hitting the tournament trail, is there?"

"Well, no, I guess not. Now that you mention it." Hammer nodded slowly, pensively, the smile forming at the corners of his mouth. We drove in silence, but I knew what he was thinking — that it *was* good being a tennis pro, a real one, one who didn't have to teach. A real pro who hit winners and didn't just stand around on a court all day pitching balls. And it wasn't just about fame and money. Hell, Hammer had already given up on the big time. It was simply the game — tennis — and the satisfaction that comes from playing it well. Christ, if all Todd cared about was money, he wouldn't be wandering around all over the country with a faded Wilson bag and a bunch of scraped up Pro Staffs. No, it was a lot more than bucks and glory; it was the whole package. It was the energized high and the meditative calm. It was the independence, the travel, and the feel of the ball. And the crowd in a stadium court.

I tried to keep things in perspective, but my ears were ringing with the sound of applause as I relived a warm afternoon on a stadium court in Mexico. It was a club in the mountains with a huge arena and brown-skinned ballboys who worked every day and not only when the pros came to town. The ballboys were just poor peasant kids, but they had the potential to climb the tennis ladder all the way to the top; and there they could transform into wealthy aristocrats. But whether they were to become Davis Cuppers, trainers, or just club groundskeepers, now these youngsters were content to run around in the hot sun for a few pesos. Eagerly, they would scoot across the sandy clay and deliver the ball with big eyes and a warm smile. Always the smile. A smile that helped me through matches when the chips were down. How their cheerful brown faces kept me cool! Even now, I sometimes picture those happy Mexican ballboys if I get a case of the nerves.

Man, would I have liked to hit the road with Todd and Clutch and see some strange new sights! There would be no ballboys up in Canada, at least not the real kind who worked year round. But I had heard it was nice in Vancouver, real green.

As the old Dart ascended the dimly lit streets back to Pop's place, I thought about Bonnie, too. And the team. Pedro and Sheldeen. And the Masters Degree I was working toward at the University. These were important things in my life, but they each had their uncertainties and thinking about them made me suddenly uneasy. I felt the need to connect outside of myself, about anything.

"Be sure to tell Clutch about tenis envy," I offered through the puttering sound of the car.

Hammer chuckled. "Yeah, if his head isn't too far into womb theory. I'll lay it on him for sure. And I'll tell him about your dream, too, about those hot new pro teams."

"Thanks," I said, "but could you please not tell him it was a dream? How about just telling him it was an idea, an idea of ours?"

"No problem. If that's the way you want it, Stretch. You and me. We have this idea, right?"

"Yeah, it's better that way, makes it sound more serious."

I pulled up in front of his grandfather's little place on Vine Street and Todd got out. He stood there in the dark not saying anything, with the car door halfway open. He knew I would have liked to go to Vancouver with him. He told me Pop had enjoyed having me over for dinner, that it really made the old man's day. Then he ducked into the car and clasped my hand.

"Remember," he said, "you're still my partner, it's you and me. I'll tell Clutch it was our idea."

Chapter Twenty-One

Courtside Entomology

I was worried I wouldn't hear from Bonnie again. I was just about to give up hope, in fact, when I got a postcard. It was a color shot of Mount Hood draped in its winter whites. On the other side of the mountain, next to my address, were the words, "Thinking of you." That was it. She hadn't even signed the card, which made it even more romantic I suppose, though I can remember feeling slighted. Why hadn't she written more? Oh well, she had certainly gotten to the point. I mean, what other three words could have been more meaningful?

I tried not to think about it.

"Just flow, dude." Hammer's voice was clear as a bell. If I hadn't known he was in Vancouver, I would have sworn he was standing behind me.

"Some things aren't meant to be analyzed," the voice said calmly from somewhere in my cerebral cortex.

"Good idea," I replied, and I put the postcard under my pillow for safekeeping.

But first I studied the perfectly parallel slope of Bonnie's handwriting, the gentle curves and overall beauty of the script. *Thinking of you.* I wanted to kiss the very words. But with Hammer so near, I only sniffed at the ink, instantly detecting a Venetian leather scent that reminded me of my mother's purse when I was just a child.

According to our plan, I was to write Bonnie at an as yet undetermined address, so any official reply of mine would have to wait. I imagined sending her an equally brief soliloquy. Perhaps just a comma and an exclamation mark. Why not? I mean, after all, it's what's between the lines that counts. Why send the lines at all?

Then the next time around I could send a note that says, "Less is more." That is, if she hadn't already sent that one to me. I had a habit of this — entertaining myself with goofy thoughts at times of frustration or boredom. And now that both Todd and Bonnie were missing from my life, my brain was working overtime trying to fill the void.

Thankfully, my classes at the University helped keep me occupied. I also had the guys on the junior college team; we were meeting twice a week now for unofficial practice. And then there was church on Sunday with Sheldeen and the gang, although I usually bumped into Sheldeen somewhere in the neighborhood before then, or he might just drop by for a visit.

A handful of private lessons completed my work week, and I wondered if I was working hard or hardly working. Actually, I felt busy and behind all the time; it was just that my mind tended to wander, which I suppose made me busier and got me even more behind. It was a vicious cycle of tardiness, though certainly entertaining and useful in its own right. Even now I was racing to the Rose Garden in the old Dart because I was late for a tennis lesson. Then suddenly I got the idea to invite Sheldeen along, so I did a U-turn.

I figured little Sheldeen deserved something special, and he had never been to the Rose Garden. What a good time he would have hanging out while I did my teaching! It was a good cause and would only make me a few minutes later. Handily, the kid was out front when I drove by. He ran inside, grabbed his racket, and hopped in the car with a big grin on his face.

The lesson I had was with a lawyer and his son. The lawyer bought an hour slot from me (instead of the usual half hour) so I didn't mind going out for just the one lesson. Besides, I liked the Rose Garden; it was the perfect place to set the mind at ease and let it wander around without worrying that it needed to be reeled back in all the time.

When Sheldeen and I arrived, the lawyer was hitting with a friend on the lower court, and his kid was hanging around looking for moths and other insects in the weeds near the backboard. His son was about Sheldeen's age, but smaller and obviously more interested in things other than tennis, though this was primarily the fault of his father. Not that entomology isn't a valuable discipline, mind you, it's just that I felt the kid was poking around in the weeds out of boredom. I blamed his father for this, who always found someone for himself to hit with when he arrived at the courts, but he ignored his son. He just let the kid dangle along dragging his tennis racket. It never occurred to the attorney to dink around with his kid for a while. And even during the lesson, the kid only got a few minutes from me, usually at the end of the hour when his father needed to rest before jumping into a doubles game, at which time the kid would go hunting for insects again, while his father hacked around for yet another hour. "He's got a good deal," the attorney once told me, "heck, when I was a kid I didn't even have a tennis racket."

While I worked with the attorney, Sheldeen hit the backboard. The idea of an official backboard thrilled him, his prior experience being limited to a cracked concrete wall behind his apartment building.

Sheldeen was in high spirits. He made himself at home hitting the backboard while the attorney's kid fiddled around less enthusiastically in the nearby weeds.

Rather than haul my huge basket of balls down into the depths of the Rose Garden, I had put about three dozen nugs into a plastic bucket and carried that down. So few balls would mean stopping to collect them more often, a definite negative, but the up side was that the chore would go much faster. Most students, however, didn't appreciate that latter benefit — they simply got annoyed every time we stopped to reload. I knew Sheldeen would volunteer to help pick up the attorney's balls, but in the car on the way over I had told him not to, that I would call him over if I needed him. Working with the attorney was a royal pain in the butt, and I always looked forward to those temporary breaks when we picked up the tennis balls; I certainly didn't want any of that precious time to go by more quickly. "Besides," I told Sheldeen, "that way you'll have more time to practice on the backboard."

The attorney was not a typical hacker; he was well beyond that. Though armed with the most powerful racket available and all the latest tennis attire, his style of play was not something found in a store, or anywhere else, for that matter. He was the ultimate hardcore, do-it-yourself, idiosyncratic, argumentative hack from the most agonizingly stubborn part of hell; and I don't even know why he was buying lessons from me, except that somehow he felt better for it. Certainly it wasn't to groom his son for Wimbledon, although even now, hunched over in the weeds, the kid looked more like a player than the father did.

Laughably bizarre, the attorney's serve was composed of a double windmill wind-up, followed by a short straight-arm shove at the ball. That last effort being accompanied by a one-footed hop.

"He serves kind of funny," Sheldeen whispered through the fence, having come over on the pretense of retrieving a stray ball.

"Try not to look at it," I told him, "it's bad for your game."

Sometimes during the lesson I would fix part of the attorney's serve, but then the next week the guy would show up with the same god-awful delivery. At this point I had given up changing any part of his game. I let him teach his own lesson, as it were. So for me, picking up the balls had become the most enjoyable part of the hour.

But there was a time when I did my damndest to excise the hack from his game. "After all," I told him months ago, "you want to be the best player possible, that's what you're paying me for. Right?"

"I don't have any delusions about going pro or anything," he said, "I started too late for that. But sure, yeah, I want to be the best I can."

"Well, then," I said, "the first thing you'll have to learn is to hit the serve with a service grip and not with a forehand grip. Does that make sense to you?"

"Yeah, it makes sense — that must be why they call it a serve grip. The serve grip is for the serve and the forehand grip is for the forehand."

"You'll also have to stop using your forehand grip for volleys," I said. "That is, if you want to become more than a public park hack."

"Man, do I hate playing with hackers," he said.

Naturally, he had great misconceptions about his own game, as all hacks do. It's almost as if when the average hack watches a pro on TV he thinks he is looking in a mirror. It doesn't even occur to the hack that the guy on television is doing EVERYTHING differently, with the possible exception of keeping score.

On that particular occasion, I tried for about the umpteenth time, to work on the attorney's serve using a continental grip, which is standard for the serve. And, by golly, twenty minutes later he was pronating his wrist and actually imparting a little spin to the ball. Of course, it went short and too far to the left, and the spin was more slice than overspin, but hey. "That's the first step," I told him.

I had him stand up close, a few feet in front of the baseline as he served with that new and extremely uncomfortable grip. That way he could at least get the ball over the net. Then later, as he got more depth, I would have him stand further and further back (which is a lot more satisfying than serving from the normal position and watching the ball hit the bottom of the net.) I advised him to practice that way until I saw him again, even though it meant he'd be committing a rather serious footfault. "Expect to turn some heads," I said, "but trust me, you'll get the last laugh."

The very next week, however, when the attorney showed up for his lesson, he had reverted to his old serve. "Sure I want to improve," he announced, "but I want to allow for my own creativity, too."

I began to feel nauseous.

"You know, there are always exceptions to the rule," he said, "that's what law is all about. Differences, loopholes, exceptions, that's how attorneys get rich."

"Well, tennis players get rich by hitting the serve with a service grip."

"Come on," he argued, "you can't tell me there aren't different styles."

"There may be variations in style, but when it comes to the serve there are certain fundamental things that 100% of the top players do. And using a proper service grip is one of them."

"Are you telling me that all the pros serve the same way?"

"I'm telling you they may not serve exactly the same way, but they all use a service grip. And there isn't one of them who uses a forehand grip."

"You never know," he said, leading with his jaw, "maybe someone will come along with a successful new style."

"They may have a successful new style, but they'll be hitting the serve with a service grip, I can assure you."

I was starting to get irritated and knew this guy would end up driving me nuts, so I did what I always do. I imagined the attorney was standing there in diapers instead of his fancy new tennis shorts, and that relaxed me a bit.

"Watch this," he announced smugly, and he let loose with his double windmill straight-arm hop with the frying pan grip. "There," he said, "what do you think about that?"

He looked good in diapers, so I pretended they were soiled, and by god, his serve looked even better.

"There." He hit another one. "Well, what's so bad about that?" he asked.

"It's just that it doesn't go very fast. And if you miss the first one, you'll really have to let up on the second one and you'll get killed."

"I hardly ever miss the first one," he argued.

"Let me put it this way," I said, giving reason one final try. "Everyone uses a serve grip. Not 99% of the players, but 100%! Every one of the top 10,000 players in the world, both in the men's game and the women's game, hits a serve with a service grip. Does that tell you something? Or do you still want to try to figure it out for yourself?"

"There are always exceptions," the attorney said confidently.

"Those are really nice tennis shorts," I said, imagining him now with a pacifier and a bib.

"Yeah, ordered 'em out of a catalogue," he said proudly. "They're real comfortable, I move better in them."

"You have better movements in them?" I said, feeling even more relieved.

And then an idea came out of his shorts, something I could live with, kind of a compromise — I asked the attorney if he wouldn't mind wearing a sign on his back that said he didn't take lessons from me.

The attorney looked confused.

I told him he didn't have to wear it all the time. "Just when you're playing tennis, that way people won't get the wrong idea. I just don't want them to think I taught you how to play."

The attorney laughed. He probably thought I was making a joke. Then looking very determined, he served out the rest of the balls surprisingly accurately in his god-awful style, imagining I suppose, that he was Pete Sampras on a good day.

"Too bad it only goes forty-two miles an hour," I said when one of his serves hit the fence after three bounces.

It's true that learning a proper service grip is the most difficult thing a tennis player goes through, but it must be done if one is to be able to play at all. It's kind of like putting braces on a kid's teeth — they're uncomfortable and awkward as hell for some time, but when it's finally over there's a beautiful smile. So I did have some empathy for the attorney; it's just that I had a job to do. That was before. Like I said, now I let him give himself the tennis lesson. I see myself as an expensive warmup partner, that's all. Which is okay, I just pretend he's wearing diapers and has that sign on the back of his shirt.

If you're going to be so selfish about your tennis, I felt like telling him, why not do it right? Of course, that's typical of hacks — they are selfish about their games, to the point of being counter-productive. They're so narrowly into *their* tennis that they can't focus on the correct way to hit the ball because that's somebody else's tennis. And they certainly don't have the time, let alone the knowledge, to give the gift of tennis to their kids.

I first made the attorney's acquaintance about a year ago, at the drinking fountain at the Rose Garden. For fear he might suck it dry, I made some throat-clearing noises behind him. One thing led to another, and we got to talking.

"Recognizing you're a hacker is the first step to becoming a player," I told him. "The second step is deciding you're going to do something about it." And so the guy put me on the payroll; but he still hadn't made that decision, not really. The fact is, he was probably secretly denying he was a hacker all along, and so he hadn't even got the first part right.

Of course, the irony of it is that the attorney is a big man with decent hand-eye coordination. If he had allowed me to do my job, in six months he would have been able to step up to the line and even a tour player would have taken his serve seriously. As it is now, his strange antics give him away from afar, and his fellow hackers can be heard arguing about who has to play with him when a fourth is needed.

I noticed Sheldeen had taken the attorney's kid over to the Rose Garden's middle court. They were playing mini-tennis from inside the service boxes and seemed to be getting some pretty good rallies. "Well what do you know," I said to the attorney, "look at those two, they're actually hitting the ball back and forth."

"Isn't that something," the attorney said.

"You ought to dink around with your boy like that," I suggested.

"Maybe I'll let him return my serve sometime," the attorney said. "That should give him a thrill."

"He doesn't need a thrill right now, he just needs to develop his eye. And also his enthusiasm for the game."

"Well maybe next time," the attorney said, and he looked at his watch. "We've got to get over to the Cal courts. Got some doubles to play."

I felt sorry for the kid. He was being dragged off now and he didn't even get a chance to be on the court with me. At least he got to play with Sheldeen.

"See ya next time," Sheldeen called out. The boy, trailing his father, turned around and waved; then the two of them hiked out of the Rose Garden.

There was plenty of daylight left. I sat down on the bench for a while to rest my legs and watch Sheldeen hit the nearby wall. He was really getting the hang of it. Taking my advice, he had started with a progression drill on each side and worked his way up from one to ten in a row, first with the backhand and then with the forehand. That was before he played with the attorney's kid. Now he was more or less on a free hit with both backhands and forehands, trying to extend the rally. He was driving the ball with an impressive rhythm, and I can remember thinking he was ready to learn how to hit overheads on the wall. Man, would he be able to get into that!

I took a camera out of my tennis bag, an old 35 millimeter I had borrowed from one of the guys on the JC team. I snapped a few of Sheldeen, focusing as best I could with the zoom lens. I got a close-up of the look on his face, that relaxed determination, the stuff that would make a champion out of him. If everything else fell into place.

Suddenly, Sheldeen stopped hitting and made ready to catch the ball as it came back off the wall. Quickly, I shoved the camera back into my bag. "Hey, Coach," he turned to me, "are you ready to play yet? How about some mini-tennis?"

"I think you already had your mini-tennis for today," I said in a low tone. Sheldeen looked disappointed.

"Oh come on, Preacher. I'm real warmed up now."

I knew how desperately young Sheldeen wanted to play, but at the same time I was enjoying his patience, so I went into a stretching routine. Shortly, I stood up. "Forget the mini-tennis," I said, "you're ready for the real thing. Let's play ball."

Sheldeen's cocoa skin and broad smile reminded me of those eager ballboys south of the Rio Grande, and suddenly I felt good all over. I took out of my pocket the two twenty dollar bills the attorney had given me and I put them in my billfold. Sure, the money would come in handy, but now I would do what I had come here for — to hang out at the Rose Garden and laze around in the mild Berkeley sun and enjoy the view of the bay, and to do my part in the making of a tennis champion.

When we were ready to leave, there was an hour of daylight left; a last rush of players was descending into the Garden. Some I recognized as quite decent older guys who knew what they were doing. "You know," I told Sheldeen, "you might be able to take the bus up here some time and find somebody to practice with. It'd only take a couple of transfers."

"It still costs money," he said matter-of-factly.

I told him we would figure something out. "It shouldn't be too hard, the real problem's going to be when you start going through shoes every month."

"My feet have been growin' two sizes a year since I was six years old," he said proudly.

"That makes it even worse. Or a lot better," I remarked, "depending on how you look at it."

Chapter Twenty-Two

Sipping Commas

Well, that's more like it. The mailman had just delivered a thick envelope with a Portland postmark. There were several sheets of fine stationery inside, each inscribed with line after line of absolutely perfect handwriting. "Dearest ..." Before I read another word I put the semi-transparent pages up to my nose and savored the delicate aroma, which was again like the fresh leather scent of my mother's purse, but this time mixed with a light blossom fragrance.

In order to be absolutely positive the letter was from Bonnie, I turned quickly to the end where the word *Love* stood by itself at the bottom of the last page. That was it! Nothing else — just *Love*. Perhaps this lady was too romantic for me. But then, becoming suddenly paranoid, I wondered if the letter was indeed from her, so I scanned the pages looking for that special address where I could write her.

Yes! Certainty at last! Her name was in the middle of a page, printed in fact, alongside a quaint street — Bonnie Lindview, 1278 Oak Leaf Lane. But wait! That was her home address! Apparently she had decided that because the mail came at noon, right about the time her husband was playing around with the hygienist, that sending my letters to the house would be okay. (Even fitting, I suppose.)

I sat down at the kitchen table and read slowly, digesting every word as if it were a rare delicacy, every comma as if it were a sip of fine wine. My stomach ached for her, or maybe it was my chest, I couldn't tell. I imagined her patiently writing that long letter to me, probably by candlelight, I figured, in a cozy corner of her house. But then I realized she wouldn't be lighting candles at night with her husband around (at least, I hoped not.) So I decided those precious pages were scripted in daylight, perhaps on the back porch in the serenity of mid-morning when the sun was lifting over cedars and tall pines.

Not wanting to be outdone, I decided to take a notepad to the Rose Garden and write her back from there as the sun was setting. I'd go directly after my session with the college team.

As I cruised to the junior college, reflections of Bonnie drifted here and there in the eddies of my mind — her sparkling eyes, her lips, buoyant and cool, the smooth, taut well of her neck. I buried myself in her hair, the soft clean scent of her hair. I was daydreaming, rather pleasantly in fact, when suddenly, a red light popped up out of nowhere in the middle of San Pablo Avenue. The old Dart lurched to a stop as if it had a mind of its own; it came to rest a tenth of an inch from the back of a brand-new pickup truck. Then strangely, through the truck's rear window, I saw the back of my father's head. Boy, did that surprise me! It was his head, alright; I could tell by the shape, and there was that familiar streak of gray hair. From behind, his ears looked a little droopy, but hey, that's what happens when you get older, and I hadn't seen him in years. What my father was doing in a pickup truck was beyond me. Indeed, what he was doing back in Berkeley was really the question.

When the light turned green, I passed stealthily alongside the pickup truck and stole a look at my father out of the corner of my eye. My heart was beating rapidly; I could hear it. But then I saw that it wasn't my father at all — it was a Mexican guy with a large moustache and a red bandanna around his neck!

As the calm of relief settled in, I realized that my dad was on my mind a lot. So much that I occasionally saw the back of his head through the windshield, or maybe it would be while I was walking down the sidewalk or shopping in some store. My mother, on the other hand, was someone I had been a lot closer to; and yet, I never mistakenly saw the back of her head. Of course, she was dead and I guess even the deep recesses of my mind knew that.

Without mishap, I drove the rest of the way to the junior college. The institution was old and the courts were nothing special, but they had been resurfaced in green and red a couple of years ago and they played pretty well. There were two rows of five, with narrow sit-down benches between them. A portable three-tiered bleacher, well suited for team meetings, was at the near end; it would also accommodate the few spectators the college matches might attract. Three of the guys were already hitting with each other when I arrived.

After a while, four other players who were new to the team showed up. Statler, my number one, wasn't there. He had won the Oakland City Championships a couple of weeks ago, so he was in more demand than ever. He probably had a match lined up for himself, and I could hardly blame him. Anyway, this was optional pre-season training. Hell, even during the regular season, I'd want him to skip practice occasionally if he had something better. I knew not all coaches felt that way, but that was my philosophy — to make the best player better too, and not simply to use him as fodder to bring up the bottom end of the team. So when Statler was there we'd be putting two guys on him a lot, to fine tune his every move.

As a coach you don't want to ignore your weaker players, but if you keep the guys at the top happy, you'd be surprised how those vibes trickle down into the games of the guys at the bottom. Overall, it's a matter of give-and-take, but when you have a superstar, it's easy to forget about him and spend more time trying to improve the rest of the lot, and that is a serious mistake. It's that guy at the top who's going to keep morale up and attract other quality players to the team.

On two of the courts, I set up backcourt drills, where you had to grind it out from the baseline and you couldn't come to the net unless the other guy's ball bounced in front of the service line. Then on another court I had one guy work his volleys against two groundstrokers, the object being for the volleyer to hang back a little where he would have to deal with more low balls and halfvolleys. Occasional lobs were mixed in, not just to test the overhead, but to sharpen that crucial transition between the overhead and a subsequent volley. (A volley that follows an overhead is often overhit, and understandably, since one is going from perhaps the loosest shot in the game to the tightest, and many players, especially at lower levels, forget to tighten up for the upcoming volley; that big, loose swing of the overhead still lingers in their bodies.)

After the drills, we all ran a mile together, doing some sideskips and backpedaling. And then we paired up for doubles, just to keep everything sociable, so we could all get to know each other better. I played with the three worst guys, not wanting to put too much pressure on either myself or the top end, and it worked out just fine.

Though Statler, our number one guy was missing, he still picked up everybody's spirit and was a vibrant part of conversation. We all went home feeling good about the team.

And now, with Bonnie on my mind and her letter stashed carefully in my racket cover, I headed over to the Rose Garden, as planned. Sunset wasn't for at least an hour, so I dropped by Cody's Books on the way. I browsed in the big bookstore feeling more intelligent, and also more ignorant at the same time. Then, I cruised over to the north side of campus and ended up, not surprisingly, at the little coffee shop where Bonnie and I had had our first real talk. Boy, did I miss her! There were about a dozen customers inside, just reading and sipping quietly with one another, but the place felt vacant without her. I got that empty feeling, that aching in my stomach again; it's a good thing I'm not sitting at our table, I thought. But then I looked over and saw a young couple sitting there, holding hands as we had done, and the feeling got worse. Pleasantly, as I began to reread her letter, butterflies fluttered inside, crowding out and lifting away the emptiness. It was as though she had suddenly put her arms around me.

Bonnie wrote that she missed me; she reminded me of all the things we had done together. She said she had felt something for me on that very first night Hammer and I had stayed at their place in Portland. It was then that she knew something was missing in her life, and that it was not just a matter of preferences — something real and significant was absent. She wrote that, "there is supposed to be more than obligation, tolerance, patience, numbness."

And I guess I felt the same way. Of course, I always knew something was missing in my life, at least in terms of romance; but hell, I figured that's the way it's supposed to be, that's what makes the world go round — people chasing other people, everybody trying to find the person missing from their lives. It's as if life is one big jigsaw puzzle and we're all down to the last piece; but it's not even on the table!

Though in my case, I must admit, it was not so much a matter of actually playing the game, but rather, dreaming about it. I was too passive about the whole thing, figuring the puzzle would just kind of come together on its own. Now I could see there's a point where you have to act; it isn't enough just to sing along as Bobby Darin pines over the airwaves: *Dream lover / where are you / I need a love / a love so true.* You could sing that oldie all day long, and though it might seem comforting, it would actually get in the way; it would pacify you, slow you down, diffuse your desires. There's a point where you have to take action if you're going to make a relationship happen.

Bonnie's letter went on to say that her girls, who were very adult-like now, were a great joy to her, and that the golden retriever was almost as much of a joy. She said she liked the dog a lot better than her husband, but that she had an indelible sense of appreciation for the man, for their past and everything he had provided or been a part of. She was generally numb around him, but sometimes he would inadvertently brush up against her and she would feel nauseous (which I was very happy to hear.)

In order to savor that last thought, I stopped reading for a while and looked out the coffee shop window. People were beginning to get off work. They were shuffling about in greater numbers now, feeling free I suppose, like school children at the end of the day. It was time for me to get up to the Garden, to catch the sunset and pen some sentiments of my own. I folded her letter with care, as if it were written in gold dust, and put it back in my racket cover.

As I puttered up Euclid Avenue in the old Dart, I kept thinking how convenient it was that Bonnie's aunt had lived in nearby San Francisco, how convenient it was, in fact, that the old lady had died. I felt a twinge of guilt, just like I felt a twinge of guilt when I thought about how convenient it was that Bonnie's husband had stepped out on her.

"Dude." It was Hammer's voice, from out of nowhere. "Remember, Dude, just ride the high. Don't analyze it."

"Okay, okay," I mumbled as I parallel parked, not without difficulty, in the shadows alongside the deck of the Rose Garden. People were beginning to gather in the fading daylight, so I got out and moved quickly to the edge of the main bench where I could jot down sentimental tidbits somewhat inconspicuously. It would be an orange sunset with pink streaks, I heard someone say. "No," another countered, "it'll be pink with orange streaks." Whichever, I knew I would be there past the time of all color, when the gray of sky and the dark of bay blended and a bejeweled San Francisco lit up the night horizon. A whiff of pot drifted by; it was probably the long-haired guy who looked like a musician. Or, it might have been the elderly gentleman with the pipe. Yes, it was the old man; he passed the pipe to his wife, a rather elegant looking woman, and then she passed it back.

And so, I wrote to Bonnie in the cool evening air, becoming ever more prolific as the crowd dispersed. I scarcely stopped to lift the pen or rethink thoughts. Then the notepad vanished in the darkness and I could only feel it on my lap. Now I was truly at my best; I figured I wouldn't be able to decipher the stuff in the morning, anyway. The most remarkable innuendoes of life and love disappeared into the page.

I let the letter age for a couple of days before mailing it. It was better that way, it gave me a chance to extract potentially corny stuff. Besides, I didn't want to put undue pressure on Bonnie, to force her to write another lengthy missive so soon.

Maybe she would call when she got my reply, after all, she wrote that she longed to hear my voice, and to touch me. (That was my favorite part, along with the part about her husband making her nauseous.) Yes, I thought, as I heard my precarious sentiments fall to the bottom of the mailbox, she probably will call, she just wants to get my letter first, to see how serious I am about the whole thing.

Chapter Twenty-Three

Ballboys, A Dying Breed

The Wilson rep came by in the morning with some rackets for me and Todd. A tall, good-looking guy with wavy hair, he usually dropped in about twice a year.

"Hammer's out of town, up in Canada," I said, "but he told me he needed a couple of frames."

"Hammer?"

"Yeah, Hammer, you know, Todd. We call him Hammer now, on account of he carried a hammer with him to Montana."

The rep laughed. "Oh yeah, I heard you guys rode the rails out to Montana, what'd he take the hammer for, protection or what?"

"No, man, it was to help him sleep." The rep looked perplexed, but then I told him about the hammock, and also about Todd's lucky socks, and of course, that he got to the finals and that we won the dubs.

"Todd, I mean Hammer, must be playing well," the rep said. "I hear he won something out in Louisiana too."

"Yeah, won a singles and two doubles, played with Fernando Vasquez. You remember Fernando?"

The rep nodded, and then he stared off into space with an amused look. "It must be nice," he said, "seems like Todd … uh … I mean Hammer, really knows how to pick his tournaments."

"Hammer manages, that's for sure."

"Here," the handsome rep handed me half a dozen pairs of socks, "you guys take these too, we don't want any of our people trying to play without socks."

He left three frames for Todd, knowing how hard he was on them. I only took one since mine were still in pretty good shape. It was free shoes we both could have really used, but we only got a promotional deal on those. Hell, neither of us used Wilson shoes, anyway. Hammer used Prince and I used adidas, not that the Wilsons weren't good or anything; it was just a matter of individual foot shapes.

The Wilson rep left with a smile on his face and the future of his company in mind. "Hammer, I kind of like that," he said, "I think I'll mention it to my boss, he's got a thing about names."

It was three weeks later when Todd returned from Canada with Clutch. After the tournament they had traveled into British Columbia with a couple of chicks they met in Vancouver, which I suppose gave Clutch a chance to practice womb theory, at least in the more casual sense. His usual partner, Rameesh, had gone back to Pakistan to cremate his father the week of the tournament, which is why he needed Hammer for the gig.

They had done pretty well, winning the doubles; and Todd won the singles too, so he was in fine spirits now. The kind of spirits that come from having a little extra cash in the back pocket and a little womb theory in the front pocket.

The girls from Canada had driven them all the way back to Berkeley. Cruising in an executive-gray Cadillac El Dorado, they dropped Clutch and Hammer off at my place, and then promising to return on the way home, they went down to check out the scene in LA, where one of them knew a big-shot film producer.

Travel-weary now, the two tennis players were sprawled out on my living room rug with their baggage. Clutch lay on his back, using his tour bag as a pillow; more upright, Hammer leaned back on his elbows. I got down too and leaned against the sofa. We all just kicked back for a while.

"Canada's good people," Todd said, reflecting on the trip. "They're more refined or something up there."

"I like Vancouver," Clutch put in, "that's why I play that one. Let me know if you want in next year. You too, Stretch, and I'll talk to the TD. He owes me some favors."

I knew that Hammer, having won this year, would get an automatic invite next year, but I wasn't so sure there'd be a slot for me.

"Count me in," I said, feeling like it was the old days and I was still a gunslinger ready to head into the badlands of tennis. After all, I would be finished at the University next year.

"But only if the guarantees are hot," I added, knowing I probably wouldn't do it without plane fare and hospitality.

"You got it," Clutch said, eyeing Todd, "just see to it that your old buddy Hammer, here, comes and we'll cut you both a deal."

Todd looked ever so slightly amused. "I'll do my best," he said. But we all knew that in the world of independent pro tennis it was hard to commit too far into the future, especially for somebody as talented as Todd. Anything could happen. Hell, once when he was in the middle of a tournament, Hammer got a call from a guy who wanted him to play another event right then. The guy, it seemed, was a millionaire whose kid was in a tournament, and the kid needed a confidence builder. The plan was for Hammer to enter as an unknown and knock out the top seed, conveniently getting injured in the process, which would then leave the door wide open for the guy's son on the other half of the draw. Apparently the kid was a pretty decent player, but the top guy was just too good. Anyway, the kid needed a confidence builder, and there's nothing like winning a tournament to build one's confidence. The TD and the kid's father were the only ones who knew that a regulator had been hired. And all Hammer had to do was play the one match, since they were going to pair him with the seed in the opening round. So they flew him out there, paid him three grand under the table, and watched him go to work. It was a pretty sweet deal all the way around. The kid ended up winning the whole thing, and the tourney Hammer ducked out of got rained on for two days, so he got back there in time to make another couple thou. The point being, I guess, is that you never know until you know, especially when dealing with outlaw tennis players and renegade tournament directors who don't have to comply with the laws of organized circuits and player associations.

It felt like old times with Clutch and Hammer as we sat around my little flatland pad talking about Canada and babes, and to some extent, tennis and world peace. But now it had gotten well into evening, so I drove Todd and Clutch over to Pop's. Clutch would be crashing there, along with another guy from the tournament who was fishing his way down from the Pacific Northwest. He was due to blow into town any time smelling like fish guts and beer.

I parked in front of Pop's place on Vine Street, and we all got out of the car and stood wearily under the street lamp. After a while, Hammer took Clutch in to get him settled, and then Hammer came back out to lean against the side of the old Dart with me.

"How's the little lady doing?" he asked.

"Not bad, I guess. We've been writing each other, talking on the phone now and then. But there are complications, you know."

"Now remember, Stretch ..."

"I know, I know, just go with the flow, don't analyze it. And above all, don't sweat the small stuff."

Todd laughed. "I'm proud of you, Stretch, you're learning. Now if you could only utilize what you've learned you'd be in great shape."

He was right. Though I hated to admit it, I still needed to *be* in that frame of mind, an awareness of it wasn't enough. But it was a step in the right direction.

It felt good to have Todd back in town. He was a true soul brother. Initially, I thought of him as a soul mate, which indeed he was, but then a part of me got homophobic and immediately recategorized him as a soul brother, which another part of my mind, though relieved at not being bisexual, felt was a possible affront to our black brethren. In either case, I was more complete now that Hammer was around, and even the void left by Bonnie's absence and Danny's quitting on me seemed bearable as I drove back down to my pad in the flatlands.

True to his word, Todd had returned with Clutch. Then Clutch's fisherman friend showed up smelling like a bait shop, and now we were all on our way to a private court in the hills to experiment with what Todd called my *hyper team tennis.* I recruited a few players from the junior college to join us, including Statler, and also the pro at the Berkeley Tennis Club who convinced the Cal guy to come along.

Because we needed a clock man and Sheldeen was handy, he came too, armed with a squeeze horn he took off the handlebars of his dad's old bicycle. Now in the front seat of the old Dart, Sheldeen tested the horn at select opportunities on the way over, making great goose-honk sounds out the window. Behind us in the back seat, the guys from the JC team howled every time the head of an adjacent driver spun around or an unsuspecting pedestrian jumped.

With such a bizarre mission about to unfold on their tennis court, it was a relief that the family was out of town when all ten of us (grown men mostly) began to swat balls at each other at the goose-honk of Sheldeen's bicycle horn, which signaled the shoot-out at the start of the match.

Balls were flying every which way. I scored a hit on Clutch's thigh and immediately felt the sting of a shot to my forearm. Across the net,

Statler was smiling — it must have been him; and then he jumped like a stung rabbit when Hammer landed one on his right butt cheek.

"Squawnk!" came the horrible honk of Sheldeen's horn. Apparently all balls had touched down and were therefore out-of-play now.

Everybody who had been hit raised their hands sheepishly, and we tallied up. Three on our side, and two on theirs, which made the score nine to six since we were giving three points for connecting in a shoot-out.

That was pretty wild, the score was nine to six and nobody had even served yet; though one of the five guys on the other side was about to. Their post man relayed to Statler, who was at the center mark going into a service motion (to which one of our service boxes? I wondered.) I was behind one and Hammer was at the other, so either way we were covered.

Statler rolled it deep into the left court, where Todd stood coiled to hit a backhand; but the serve was long. Immediately, Statler slid to the other side of center and hit his second serve at me, which the rules permitted. I returned deep and Statler stayed back. Hammer, getting into the spirit of things, began zigzagging around on our side of the court to distract the opposition; handily, he flattened out on the ground each time I took a swing at the ball.

Finally, Statler missed; point to us. At the side of the court, Sheldeen stared closely at his Mickey Mouse wrist watch; with lips moving and fingers poised around the bulb of his horn, he began his count (which we, being mere amateurs, had instructed him to extend to eight seconds instead of the six which players in the new millennium would be allotted between points.)

Now Statler ran to the post and the Cal guy began to serve, since a rotation was required for each point. I too moved off the court, because I had just returned and a receiving rotation was also required. Hammer stood ready to return again, along with a long-armed JC kid, who was slow in getting into position. The Cal guy served into the unguarded box, but the kid stretched out his lanky arm and snagged it, sending up a sky ball which the Cal guy patiently let bounce, and then he popped an overhead into the corner; but the kid stretched out his long limbs and again he sent up a lob, this one much weaker, which the Cal guy came in to crush; and yet, at the same time, Todd rushed directly at him kamikaze-style. With overhead cocked and ready at the net, the Cal guy aimed for Todd, which would garner three bonus points for his team. POW! The ball pounded the court and bounced up at Hammer, who tried admirably to get out of the way, but the ball brushed his shirt with the sound of a flag flapping in the wind.

"OK," Clutch bellowed, "that's four more points for us."

"Four points? What d'ya mean, four points?" Hammer argued amicably. "The ball only hit my shirt, and it bounced first. Do ya get four points for that?"

"Three bonus points," said Clutch, "plus the point for winning the rally." Clutch cheered on his teammates. "Isn't that right, guys?"

Our men objected, just as a matter of principle, and a heated discussion ensued. "The ball bounced! Shirts aren't good! Shirts are good, but they're not worth the full three points! When you get bonus points in the middle of a rally, the point for winning the rally is NOT allowed!" SQUAWNK — Sheldeen signaled that the eight seconds to get the ball in play were up. "Talk all you want," the pro from the Berkeley Tennis Club said, "but we get a penalty shot now because you guys failed to serve in the allotted time."

Silence. Everybody looked at Sheldeen, who sat on the bench with his hand on his horn, looking very innocent. "Time out! Time out!" somebody yelled. All eyes shifted to me.

It was obvious I hadn't thought out all the details. "Yeah, I guess that's right," I said, trying to assess the situation. I figured the bouncer was good, since the point wasn't actually over yet. And clothing counted, for sure. I suggested we should always give a point for winning the rally, or bonus points for hitting an inactive wouldn't really be bonus points.

Then I paused to reconsider. "But I am willing to modify the system if you guys think we should." Nobody said anything. "Okay then, that makes four more for you guys, which makes the score ..." Now I was truly at a loss.

"It's thirteen to seven," the Cal guy announced, casually confirming what everyone already suspected, that he was probably the brains of the outfit. He went on to explain that it was 9/6 after the initial shoot-out, then 9/7 after the first point, and now since the second play was worth four points, it was 13/7.

Thirteen to seven and we hadn't even played the third point of the match! "Let's play to fifty," somebody said. "Time for lunch," another guy shouted. "Yeah, let's play for lunch, each team serves through its rotation, twice, and that's it."

So it was settled, we'd each serve twice, which meant returning twice, as well, and then we'd go chow down, with the loser paying. This modest wager put new life into the future of hyper team tennis, creating an attitude typical of what we were used to at the tournaments. Now it was as if the other guy was about to steal our food. And we couldn't let that happen. It wasn't that we didn't want it to happen; it couldn't happen! Because if it did, we'd go away hungry (and maybe even have to sleep in the car.)

It was decided to begin the match afresh, and also to discuss the rules more thoroughly, now that there was so much riding on it. Naturally, there would be penalty shoot-outs for all infractions.

We broke out brand-new nugs for the occasion (our favorites, plain unflavored Penns) but decided to use only one ball, which meant that if a first serve missed, that ball would have to be relayed back for the second delivery and the clock would start over. If a faulted serve ended up on the other side of the net, the receiving team would have five seconds to place the ball at the base of a net post, and then the eight-second clock would start again. (It was obvious the clock man had the most difficult job, it also being his responsibility to call foot-faults and over-rule bad line calls.)

So we put nine-year-old Sheldeen in charge; after all, he had the bicycle horn. There would be no arguing with him, his honk was final.

The next half hour produced some of the most amazing moments in tennis history, which were too extraordinary to even highlight, except to say that there were leaps and dives, relays, handoffs, players picked off like targets at a shooting gallery, and of course, standard ordinary great points of all kinds. I mean after all, we were dealing with a bunch of gifted athletes, who also happened to be among the most free-spirited and innovative individuals on the planet.

On the last point of the match, Clutch's fisherman friend, whose clothes still smelled like salmon eggs, edged his way up to the service position unseen, as if he were sneaking up on a trout stream. Clutch fired him the ball and he plunked it over the net for the soggiest ace I'd ever seen, while our team, still trying to figure out who's turn it was to return, stood by and watched the ball dribble to rest in the service box.

SQUAWNK! SQUAW SQUAWNK! Great goose-honks called out in all directions over the Berkeley hills. Indeed, now that the battle was over, Sheldeen's horn was set free in a victory of its own.

We knew who won — it was the other guys — Statler, Clutch, and the Cal guy. And that damn fisherman, though his final point didn't make any difference one way or the other; it was just the icing on the cake, a cake those guys would get to eat. (I guess, we'd get to eat it too, after all, we'd be paying for it.) To make it official, the Cal guy announced the score was 26 to 14 in this first ever Hyper Team Championships.

Someone suggested La Val's, a joint on the north side of campus, so all eleven of us rolled down the hill to present awards and poison ourselves with pizza and beer. The JC guys were particularly enthusiastic. They were under age, and now in the back seat of my car I could hear them discussing the best way to conceal beer, which was apparently in a red and white Coke cup (which had accidentally been refilled with beer.) Or, we could ask to have our Cokes served in mugs, just like the beer. Either way, it wouldn't be difficult; we'd march into the pizza joint and take over an area in the back. Pitchers of beer and Coke would arrive at our table. With so many glasses shuffling about, only we tennis players would know which pitcher was being poured where, or indeed, whose lips were on what glass. Hell, Sheldeen was the only one I felt obliged to look after, and he'd look after himself, I was sure of that. None of us would get too soused, anyway; it was still early in the day and we were an active lot, preferring to be on the move until nightfall.

As it turned out, we ordered two pitchers of dark Lowenbrau and a pitcher of Coke — so we were home free! Those two liquids looked so much the same, when they arrived at our table, even we had trouble telling them apart. More than once we had to stick our noses into the mist to tell one from the other.

Warm savory Italian aromas weaved in among us, teasing our rumbling stomachs as we sat in the back of the pizza joint reeling to the sound of Janis Joplin belting it out from the jukebox. Then came Santana's *Black Magic Woman,* and my mind lifted and swirled on wide lingering guitar riffs, until Credence cut in with *Proud Mary* and *Down On The Corner,* back to back. We talked about CCR for a while, after all, Fogerty and the boys grew up in nearby El Cerrito. Then, just in the nick of time, four giant pizzas arrived, one with everything, two everythings without anchovies, and one with pineapple and Canadian bacon.

Because we were starved, the pizzas were that much more satisfying. "Anything that tastes this good has to be bad for you," Todd announced after inhaling a wedge of pineapple and Canadian bacon. The crusts were chewy, and some were topped with cheddar instead of the more bland mozzarella. Both were hot as molten lava. But that didn't stop us; we just doused our singed tongues in coke and beer.

The pro from the Berkeley Tennis Club downed a couple of pieces hurriedly; he thanked us and split. Back at the club, he had a full afternoon of lessons on the books. But even without him, we were the largest group in the place, and our boisterous ramblings rose up over the dwindling lunch crowd, particularly when a memorable tennis adventure came to the forefront, or an especially good-looking coed walked into the place. Much of the discussion was, in fact, about chicks, women, babes, or poontang; depending on who was doing the talking. Then the subject of gay tennis players came up and lingered so casually, I thought the JC kids, with their freshly lit cerebellums, might wonder if some of us dudes preferred young boys. They got kind of quiet, and Hammer picked up on it.

"How's your girlfriend doing?" he asked me loudly, as he poured himself another from what I assumed to be the pitcher of Lowenbrau.

"I miss the hell out of her," I replied, hoping to straighten out any possible confusion as to my sexual orientation.

Todd chuckled. "I didn't ask how you were doing, I asked how she was doing."

"She's okay, but according to her letters, she'd like to get back to California, maybe settle in the Bay Area in a couple of years, you know, when the girls are both away at college."

Wups, maybe I shouldn't have said anything; across the table from me, the lanky JC kid raised his eyebrows. I knew what he was thinking, what's my coach doing, dating an old woman or something? I was probably older than he thought, but still, a chick with a kid in college, that was old! It even seemed old to me now, but then I pictured Bonnie's face and I knew that if she were to suddenly walk into the joint, every guy in the place would freeze like a bird dog on a pheasant, especially those young JC studs.

Between casually chewed mouthfuls, Clutch told us he had decided that the most beautiful women in the world were in Barcelona. I wasn't about to argue with him; he was probably right. Hammer and I had been to Spain, once in fact, with Clutch, and as I recalled, the women in Barcelona were strikingly statuesque.

"Yeah," Clutch said, "it's kind of a class thing. The rich men want the good-looking women, and those guys can afford to be picky, believe me. And the best looking women want the richest men. Each succeeding generation has the potential to become more and more beautiful. Beauty is kind of bred, you might say."

"Ah, but the middle class in Spain is growing," Hammer volunteered thoughtfully, "which means that the rich upper class is getting smaller, and though it still retains its ability to attract the most outrageous females, there will be fewer matings, and therefore a decline in the number of beautiful offspring."

"Well, maybe there will be fewer of them, but they will be more beautiful than ever," Clutch countered, "because with only so many super-rich dudes, only the very best looking chicks will land one. And their kids will be better looking than ever."

That sounded logical enough. But I noticed an amused look on Todd's face, so I wasn't sure. In either case, Hammer was right, the middle class in Spain was growing. Whether or not it would affect the looks of Barcelona women, I could only guess; but one thing I was sure of, it was taking its toll on the ballboys.

That ever expanding middle class was interested in something new — saving a buck (or a peseta, to be more precise.) So now at the tennis clubs, there were more and more members who would just as soon pick up their own balls. No longer was there a reason to keep the eager peasant boys around, no longer would they live day in and day out on the clay, chasing balls, and eventually honing their own games. Yes, in years past, every decade or so, Spain had produced a world champion, a player who had worked his way up the ranks, from ballboy to Davis Cupper, from lowly peasant to pride of the upper class. And pride it was — such a champion would marry into the elite ruling class as easily as if he were seeking the hand of the village washerwoman. I thought of Manolo Santana and Manuel Orantes, two greats who had sprouted right up out of the dirt. There was also Higueras. And then Luna and Muñoz. They were all Davis Cuppers. And each had begun as a poor boy working at the club, shagging balls for the wealthy. In their downtime they would hit the wall, and if they were lucky, they'd get a tip from the pro. They were schooled at the club too, so they also had to make time for studies. No, life wasn't easy for these little working men, but for the right kid the day was a reward in itself. And more importantly, it was a path. A route to tournaments and travel; an entrance actually, to the entire world!

But sadly, the ballboys of Spain were doomed, for with the growth of the middle class came the end of a subsidized ballboy program. I wondered if that small country would still produce world champions on a regular basis For sure, there would be greater numbers of good players, and certainly more women.

It was up to Mexico, perhaps, to remain as the one country where a dirt poor kid could climb the tennis ladder all the way to the top of society. Although in comparison to Spain, Mexico had produced very few world champions over the years. I guess they didn't take that much of an interest in their youngsters down there. Although there was Joaquin Loyo-Mayo, the little lefty who began as a ballboy in Veracruz and ended up playing for USC, where he won the NCAA singles and doubles titles. He married well, became a Davis Cupper, and traveled the world for a dozen years on the wings of his tennis racket. Not bad for a barefooted little kid from Mexico!

There was also Ecuador, where Pancho Segura was from. He started as a ballboy and became one of the greatest tennis legends of our time.

"I'm going to play in Spain this summer," Statler, my JC star said, a slice of pizza hanging limp in his hand.

"You'll have a good time," Clutch told him.

"Yeah," Hammer agreed, "cheap living, good tennis, and pretty women. France is good, too. Or, you can just go to France in the winter and play indoors."

"I'll be in school in the winter," Statler said.

"That's even better," Hammer offered enthusiastically, "cheap living, good tennis, and books. Plus, you'll have babes who speak English. Although there's nothing like a French accent to turn you on."

"I kind of like the girls in northern Europe," the Cal guy put in. (He'd played the circuit every summer since his freshman year.) "You know, Denmark, Norway, Sweden. The women are more sophisticated up there, more independent, they give you a little breathing room, they don't just stick to you like a shadow."

"Good point," Clutch conceded.

"But are you sure sex is okay? I mean for sports?" the lanky JC kid asked sheepishly from across the table. "My dad says you're not supposed to mix athletics and women."

"Just don't do it in the middle of a race," Hammer told him. "Anyway, that's what the track guys say. And they should know."

"I like to knock one off first thing in the morning," Clutch said, "unless I'm playing a tournament. For doubles, it doesn't matter, so long as you're not still in there when you're supposed to be on the court." I wondered if that was one of the tenets of womb theory or just the wisdom of a practical tennis player.

"I like girls who play tennis," the lanky kid volunteered.

"Let me tell you," Clutch offered with the tone of a big brother, "sometimes it's best if they don't play tennis, at least not too seriously. The worst thing is to have a chick who thinks her tennis is more important than yours."

"Yeah," Todd said, "it's kind of nice when they're content just to tag along and watch you play." And I had to agree, a woman who could appreciate tennis was one thing, but one who was hung up on it was quite another.

Clutch's fisherman friend was a skinny guy with a shaggy beard and a deceptively tough game. He was a deep thinker, kind of like Todd, but even more laid-back. At last he cast his thoughts out into the stream. "I like a girl who sweats," he said.

"You mean on the court?" one of the JC kids asked. Laughter exploded at their end of the table, along with some Coke that was about to fizz out the nose of one of them. He held his nostrils so as not to mess up the table, and I wondered if it was, in fact, Coke. I figured the Lowenbrau would be better for his sinuses.

"Yeah well, everybody sweats," Hammer chuckled.

"You know what I mean," the fisherman clarified, "a chick who doesn't mind sweating. I like to go hiking and camping, so she has to be in good shape. So long as she's still soft where it counts." That was probably my style too, a girl who had kind of a tomboy edge but was still feminine at the core.

In the restaurant now, the skinny fisherman smelled a lot better. His clothes, in fact, seemed to add to the many savory aromas in the place. "A little sweat on a woman can be a nice thing," he said.

"Well in that case, I've got just the chick for you," Clutch volunteered. "She's so sexy you won't want to stop, and the two of you will be perspiring so much you'll look like you're in a synchronized swimming contest."

Feverish moans and warbling catcalls played out like high lobs over our table, while elsewhere in the restaurant, heads spun around, and then they turned back to the chewy business of their own mushrooms and molten cheeses. Yes, the Lowenbrau was doing its job, washing down crust and giving us a midday buzz that took our conversation to new heights (or perhaps lows, since it had now dropped into the street.)

"Boys, boys," the bearded fisherman held up his glass. "Gentlemen," he warned in a low tone, "better skip the details. Young ears are best kept clean, if you know what I mean." He nodded toward Sheldeen who hadn't said a word, though he appeared to be enjoying his meal as much as anybody.

"My brother's friends talk about pussy all the time," Sheldeen said matter-of-factly. "I know what's going on."

Faces froze with various looks of pride at our young companion; but

I think Sheldeen thought we were about to laugh at him. "You don't believe me?" he said quickly. "It's true. I could have plenty of booty if I wanted. Girls are always chasing me around the house. I let one get me once, I thought she was going to swallow me up!"

More than a few pairs of eyebrows went up; some of the JC guys giggled; they were probably virgins. They were from up in the hills where things were sheltered, more hung-up. Hell, Sheldeen was from down in the flats, where your folks might come home from work and boogie to the funky chicken on the front porch if they felt like it. Things were out front in his neighborhood, less inhibited. Life itself was more natural, more expressive. It made perfect sense that nine-year old Sheldeen could have gotten it on at his tender age. Besides, he was more grown-up than most.

"Like I said," the skinny fisherman raised his glass again, "it's best to start them young, that way they can get over it and focus on the more important things in life."

And so, much of our conversation in the pizza place was about women, but it was, to be truthful, a misleading perception. For in order to get as good as we all had at tennis, there had been little or no time for matters of women. That part of our lives had been, in a sense, deprived. That's why we talked about it so much; it was a sort of wish-fulfillment. Sure, some players were natural Romeos, and a few of the guys had long-standing girlfriends or were married. But as much as one-night-stands and even relationships might have been available, most of us indulged very little. We were too entrenched in the war, the very battles of tennis and the restrictions those battles imposed. As we got older, however, the war became less important; the battles became further apart, and that left some time for romancing more than the racket and ball.

During his short stay in Berkeley, Clutch never did say anything about tenis envy. I figured Todd had probably forgotten to mention it to him in Vancouver, what with all the distractions involved in winning a tennis tournament and touring the countryside with a couple of babes in their Cadillac. Either that, or maybe Hammer did bring it up and Clutch was offended by the suggestion that tenis envy should be included in the elaborate and important workings of womb theory; after all, one was just a modern day neurosis for those of us who liked to jump around in a giant playpen in our spare time; the other was a foundation for human interaction since the first bipedals rose up on their hind legs and walked out of the jungle erect (in search of, I suppose, a womb big enough to sleep in.) I thought both subjects were best left untouched at present.

We had a good couple of days with Clutch and his friend. They complimented me on my innovative team tennis, said they'd be thinking about it and would forward any new ideas. "Even if it's imperfect, it's a lot more fun," Clutch said. "It really spices up the game. And it allows teams to have a lot more guys. Sponsors would be very interested in a league like that."

"Indeed, the formative stages are fascinating," the skinny fisherman said, tugging at his beard. Then the two of them jumped into the back seat of the Cadillac El Dorado. True to their word, the chicks from Vancouver had returned from LA. They looked wistfully at Hammer as their car idled; you could tell they wished he were going with them.

"See ya later," he said.

"Yeah, come up and visit sometime," they offered.

"Okay. Bon voyage." We waved as that expensive-looking car glided away from the sad flats of Berkeley with our pals in the back. Clutch flashed a peace sign through the rear window; he would be dropped off in Seattle, where he had another tennis gig. His buddy, now wearing freshly washed clothes, was destined for a creek in the Cascades, where as he put it, he could practice his serve and fly casting at the same time.

Chapter Twenty-Four

Juicy Fruit

I often felt guilty that I didn't know enough about politics. Hammer knew a lot more than I did, but we were both consumed with tennis and had little time for the government. To be sure, we wanted the species to survive, and if that meant a cleaner environment and a simpler tax form, then so be it — we'd cast a vote. But basically, we just let other people do the work. We'd be the last people on the planet to jump up and down on a street corner waving our tennis rackets in protest. Capital punishment, on the other hand, was a subject Todd had very strong feelings about. And I didn't even know it. That is, not until after Clutch left and we got invited to play in a fundraiser in Beverly Hills.

I guess I figured Todd didn't believe in capital punishment, not that I ever thought about it. But apparently there were special circumstances in which he did support the death penalty, for instance, when somebody leaves gum on a tennis court. Especially on a tennis court in Beverly Hills! This all came to light during the fundraiser, which was just a little eight-man singles gig, but they gave excellent guarantee money for both Saturday and Sunday, so we hopped in the old Dart and headed to the southland.

I got bumped in the opening round, but Hammer was hot and he made it to the final, where amidst all the pomp and glory, he began to hit spectacular winners, much to the admiration of an awestruck crowd. Then, during the fourth sidechange, he stepped into a big blob of chewing gum. Concealed beneath the bench, the gum lay there like a tar pit just waiting for a tennis player to fall into its glue-like mess. I had never heard Hammer scream such a profanity before, at least not at a fancy tennis club, and yet there was a certain charm to it, a sort of pitiful shriek that even won over the umpire who was kind enough to offer Todd his left shoe. Todd accepted, and the crowd, which included more than a few film stars, applauded excitedly.

I caught a glimpse of Dustin Hoffman out of the corner of my eye. At least, I thought it was him; he looked rather serious. I had heard he was, hands down, the best celebrity tennis player.

So now I was sitting on the side of the court thinking about Dustin Hoffman and Bonnie and trying to pry off stretchy pieces of what smelled like Juicy Fruit that had worked their way into every possible crevice on the bottom of Todd's shoe. After a while, the smell started to get to me and I thought maybe I would have preferred Doublemint. And then Hammer got broken — he had lost some obvious agility out there with the umpire's shoe on his left foot. I tried to work more quickly, but the tar-like Juicy Fruit was not giving up easily. I had gotten most of it off, but gum still lay wedged deep in the grid of the sole, which made the shoe a bit heavy, and yet at this point I figured Todd would be better off wearing it. The umpire's shoe, though almost the right size, was brand new and clumsy, not to mention the fact that it was a Fila and Todd was used to riding Prince. Besides, I knew the umpire would be pleased to get his shoe back — up in the chair, he looked a little funny with just a sock on that one foot. And his film industry buddies wouldn't let him forget it; they snickered like school children every time he announced the score.

Todd untied his shoelaces eagerly at the next sidechange when he saw me approaching with his preferred left shoe. Equally excited, the umpire sat up a little straighter in his chair. And so, the shoe re-swap was executed, swiftly and unnoticeably, and yet the crowd, keen as they were, gave thunderous applause for the event.

Now with his proper foot gear, and the roar of the crowd ringing in his ears, Hammer began to regain his balance, just in the nick of time. He eked out the match. Barely. Though actually, he looked quite nimble in the third set. But it wasn't until we got back home in Berkeley that his victory against the Juicy Fruit was complete. Acting on a tip he got from Pop, Todd had placed the troublesome shoe in the freezer overnight to make the stubborn goop more brittle. And now, hunched over a workbench in the basement, he pried a screwdriver into the bottom of the cold shoe. Meticulously, he lifted out the foul smelling Juicy Fruit from Beverly Hills, one sliver at a time. It took a while to de-gum the whole shoe.

"People who throw gum away on the street should be arrested," I told Todd.

"Yeah," he said, "and if they leave it on a tennis court, they should be executed." He was relieved now that the ordeal was over, but he was still in favor of capital punishment for this one special circumstance.

"Well, at least they should get a public caning like in Singapore," he said, feeling less vindictive now.

"Yeah, and they should have to wear orange jumpsuits, too, and pick up litter all weekend," I suggested.

"I'm going to write my congressman," Todd exclaimed, and he high-fived me. I wondered which congressman he would write to, and then I felt a sudden twinge of guilt, because I didn't even know for sure who my congressman was. Hell, I barely knew who the Vice President of the United States was. I hung my head in shame as I followed him up the narrow staircase that led out of Pop's basement.

Chapter Twenty-Five

The Leftophobe

My mother was wearing a long camel-colored coat. She and my father had just returned from a rare night out. They had gone to Spenger's for dinner, and then they saw a movie — *The Apartment.* Now Mom was vibrant despite her illness. "Jack Lemmon and Shirley MacLaine were just terrific," she announced with a sparkle in her eyes I hadn't seen in months. With a little rouge on her cheeks, she looked good in that soft camel-colored coat. My father was more anxious; he wanted to know if we children had been behaving in his absence.

I knew the question was directed at me and my little brother, since my sister spent all her time studying and behaving. Besides, my father was looking right at me. I had shown my little brother my BB gun, but I knew that wouldn't be a good thing to tell my dad. In fact, just to keep my brother from bugging me, I often let him handle my BB gun; I even let him take it into his room all by himself. I hoped my brother wouldn't say anything about the gun.

"Daddy, when can I have a BB gun?" my brother asked in a surprisingly mature voice.

"When you can read better, in a few years, then you can memorize the hunter safety book."

"But I want a BB gun now." But I want a BB gun now, but I want a BB gun now, the words seemed to echo over the bay as I stood on the deck above the Rose Garden waiting for Todd to show up. The haze had lifted; I could see the shore of San Francisco and a sprinkling of white sailboats on the gray-blue water.

My little brother got to shoot a lot more than a BB gun in Central America and the Middle East. Each time he went out on one of his secret assignments, I felt as if I had sent him there. It might have been my fault that he ended up in army special operations in the first place. After all, I had practically given him his first gun, a gun that teased him as he stroked its dark wooden stock and shot at imaginary enemies beyond the walls of his little bedroom. All those times I needed him not to bug me so I could cram for a test or catch up on my homework — all the times I shut him up by letting him sneak my BB gun into his room. My brother even hid pages from gun magazines in his school books, he had developed such a great love for the mystery of guns.

But now he wasn't so anxious to squeeze the trigger anymore. At least he was still in one piece, which was a lot better than some of his buddies ended up. But he wasn't the same. Last I heard, he had quit his elite army career and was working at a gas station in Texas.

I wondered if my sister was in touch with him. But she was entrenched in her own family woes in South Carolina. I doubt she even saw much of my dad, even though she was always his favorite. She and I exchanged Christmas cards, that was about it.

Everybody had left, but I was still out here in Berkeley, still holding onto the past, and my tennis racket. My grip was beginning to loosen on my racket, I could feel it, but as the image of my mother in her long camel-colored coat loomed over San Francisco bay, I realized that the past had a hold on me that wouldn't let go.

I began to feel less guilty about my brother after Todd arrived and we horsed around up there on the deck at the Rose Garden. With our hands in our pockets and the indifferent Berkeley sun at our backs, we looked out at the wide bay in the distance and talked tennis.

Todd was excited. "Five hundred bucks for one match is a good deal," he said.

"What if you lose?" I asked.

"Then I only get two hundred, which isn't too bad. Anyway, it doesn't cost me a cent, so it's a good deal."

"Not bad," I said, imagining how nice it would be to make five hundred dollars for just playing a couple of sets. For me to come by that kind of money meant pitching balls all day long for the better part of a week.

Hammer told me his opponent was a kid from Argentina who had won the juniors at Wimbledon a couple of years ago. But it seemed he hadn't lived up to expectations. The kid was in San Francisco visiting relatives; his agent had called.

"The guy must be loaded," I said.

"Not exactly, he's just got a good sponsor, some real estate development group in Buenos Aires, they're the ones putting up the money. They want him sharp. He's got some sort of Davis Cup try-out when he gets home. So they're paying good money up front."

"That's good money, alright."

"There's only one problem," Todd said with a goofy smile. "The kid's lefthanded."

Actually, that was a problem. Hammer and I both had a habit of losing to lefties. I was particularly bad with them, having lost to four lefties in a row one season, and one was just a junior.

We often talked about the advantages of being lefthanded; we both knew we'd be playing better singles and certainly better doubles if one of us were lefthanded. And actually, when a lefthanded friend of ours was hanging out in Berkeley, we were sharper than ever, even though the guy wasn't quite up to our level. Working out with him had prepared us for hitting to different parts of the court, and it made the occasional lefty we would run into seem like nothing out of the ordinary. But now it had been a while since either of us worked out with a lefty.

The idea that Todd had a money match with a lefthander made me anxious, even though he would be the one facing the culprit. I guess I had always been somewhat of a leftophobe, and I couldn't seem to shake it.

Yes, I knew only too well about lefties. I had never known a lefty who didn't have a criminal mind, or at least the potential for one. I could feel the phobia setting in now, creeping around like little lefthanded rodents in my brain, little smiling lefthanded rodents.

And no, the seemingly benign lefty is not to be trusted! Indeed, even if he is bumbling with clumsiness off the court, leave it to the lefty to have a smooth backhand and a deft half-volley. Yes, and if his serve is not ferocious, it is nonetheless loaded with trickery.

I remembered uneasily how the phobia really struck that one year when I lost to all those lefties. The fear of lefties had rotted my brain. Even the pen in the hand of a lefthanded bank clerk was enough to make me queasy. Then it got suddenly worse in the quarters of Amarillo when that lefty greased my hand with peanut butter during the initial handshake. He said he had just finished lunch and was sorry, but screw that! It wasn't enough that his backhand was not in the usual place, he had to slap me up with peanut butter at the start of the match, something that probably didn't even bother his service toss, and yet I, as a righthander, was not even able to grip the racket! I wiped my hand as best I could, but that peanut butter smell lingered on my racket handle throughout the match, disrupting my concentration.

"You can't trust a lefty you don't know," I told Todd, my mind still in the jar of Skippy.

"Just relax, Stretch, I don't play the guy until Thursday."

"That's the day after tomorrow!" I exclaimed.

"Stretch, dude, just relax. Anyway, I have a plan."

Hammer told me not to sweat the small stuff, that it was just a fact of life that lefties have an advantage. "That's what makes the challenge," he said.

Dr. Hammer went on to give me an advanced seminar on the subject right there on the deck of the Rose Garden. He spoke with an air of distinguished authority, as if he were standing behind a podium, at Oxford, perhaps.

"Certainly," he said, "lefthanders always have an advantage in any kind of man-to-man combat, whether it's tennis or actual warfare. Aside from the natural ambidexterity that society encourages in them, lefties have an advantage in all physical encounters where the opposition must react." He paused momentarily to look over the heads of those attending his lecture.

Then he went on. "Generally speaking, when the vast majority of any competitor pool is one way, the differing minority will have the advantage of imposing a non-routine, and therefore, less perfected, maneuver on an opponent who is trying to react. This is more or less, the element of surprise."

Dr. Hammer told me to imagine a jungle scene where two enemy soldiers armed only with knives are about to encounter each other. One soldier happens to be lefthanded, and the other, though trained for combat against the occasional lefty, is not immediately primed to go up against one (that is, he is more tuned to perform against the far more common righthanded soldier.) The lefthander, similarly, is more fine-tuned for an encounter with a righthanded enemy, like the one who just met him face to face in the brush. A powerful rush of adrenaline surges through each man's body. They are about to go for their knives!

"Which soldier would you prefer to be?" Todd asked in a very serious tone.

"Well, I guess the lefthander," I said. "I just wouldn't be sneaky about it, I'd stab the guy and get it over with."

Hammer laughed. "Anyway, I have a plan," he announced, and with that he pulled a mirror out of his pocket, a flat little mirror about the size of the Ace of Diamonds. The silvery rectangle flashed in his hand as we stood there in the sunlight above the Rose Garden.

Since Todd wasn't much into primping, I wondered if he was planning to deflect the sun into the opponent's eyes with the mirror, or if he was going to receive flash signals from one of the spectators. Me? Maybe I would be the guy signaling him from the periphery. Don't forget the guy is lefthanded, I could tell him, aiming the little mirror as best I could.

"Come on," he said, and I followed him down into the flowery depths of the Rose Garden. The court at the bottom was open, but Hammer stopped alongside the first one, where some hackers were playing doubles. One of the players happened to be lefthanded, and he actually looked a little better than the righthanders, even though in reality he might have been a little worse.

"It's not fair," I said, "lefties even look better than the rest of us."

"Let's stand on our heads for a while and look at them," Hammer suggested. "It's interesting to see what tennis players look like upside-down." He was eager and went right into a headstand next to the court.

While I knew the extra blood flow to my brain might be beneficial, I was feeling too lazy to do a headstand. So I lay on my back on a nearby picnic bench and let my head hang backwards over the end of the bench, thus assuring Hammer that I would get an upside-down view of the action on the court. "Incredible!" Todd said with his feet up in the air.

I noticed, now that I was upside-down, that the three righthanders suddenly looked lefthanded, and the lefty looked righthanded. "I see what you mean," I said, my head still dangling over the end of the bench. And damned if those three new lefties didn't look better than the new righty! "It's not fair," I repeated, "there's something about being lefthanded that just looks better."

After a while, Hammer dropped down from his headstand and stood up. "Or, you can do it another way," he said. With his feet wide apart like a guy hiking a football, he bent over and looked under his butt at the foursome. "They look reversed again," he noted, and he studied them like that for a while.

"Yeah, well, they may be reversed alright, but you look perverse."

Hammer extracted his head out from under his butt and assumed a more normal posture. "That's where this little mirror comes in," he said proudly. He held the mirror out at arm's length and looked into it. Now with his back to the doubles game, he could see over his shoulder at the reflections of the men as they played their short-lived points. "Ah, yes," he sighed with pleasure, "now these dudes are reversed again, and I'm not even upside-down. They're right-side-up. This is definitely the way to go. It's a handy way to see a lot of lefties. I'm going to use it for sure, it's a lot more convenient than standing on my head."

"Or shoving your head in your butt," I added.

Then Todd told me the rest of his plan. He wouldn't practice much today; he would just do some loose points with me, mostly playing my forehand side to prepare for hitting to the Argentine's backhand. And tomorrow, the day before the big match, he wouldn't even set foot on the court. No, he would simply look at the reflections of tennis players, all day long. He would go to the Cal courts and also the Berkeley Tennis Club. He would use the little mirror all the way up until the moment of his match, imagining that all tennis players were lefthanded. Yes, and when he went into a restaurant or a coffee shop, he would hold the little mirror discreetly and spy on the tables behind him, watching as the customers, every last one of them, picked up their forks with their left hands. Hammer's whole world was about to become lefthanded!

"It's all a mental thing," he said. "When that Argentine kid walks out there and stands on the other side of the net, I don't want to even notice that he's lefthanded. Of course, he's going to be lefthanded, everybody on the planet's going to be lefthanded!"

It was just as well that Todd was preoccupied with the mirror, because the day before his match was busy for me and I wouldn't have been able to workout with him. I had the JC team in the afternoon and classes at the University all morning. One of my classes was an upper division psychology class, and I was friendly with the professor, a very low-key guy named Rudolph I bumped into occasionally at the campus Espresso shop. So after class I asked Rudolph about the lefty phenomenon; I wanted to know why a lefthanded tennis player could look better than a righthanded player, even if he wasn't.

Rudolph pondered a bit. "Very interesting," he said, "I haven't considered perception changes in terms of sports before." He reminded me about the black and white drawing of the old lady that is usually included in an introductory psych book — the picture of the old lady that suddenly becomes seen as a young lady. "One image is in the foreground, the other image is in the background," Rudolph explained. "Then after a while, the eye allows the foreground and the background to switch, and the other woman appears."

Rudolph said this switch in perception can be voluntary, but that it was more interesting when it's accidental, which suggests a type of limited focus or attention span. "Or even possibly," he said, "it's a matter of nerve cells becoming saturated, and then becoming overwhelmingly more receptive to the other image. Which means," he suggested, looking somewhat worried, "that there's a biological capacity for boredom."

"And a biological remedy for it," I put in.

"That's right."

"So the grass is always going to be greener on the other side of the fence?" I asked.

"That's a definite possibility," he said, and we walked out of the classroom together.

I asked him if that meant I'd always be jealous of lefthanded tennis players.

"Not necessarily," he said, as we made our way down the near empty hallway. "You see, on a cellular level you're saturated with righthanders, which makes a run of the mill lefthander look more refreshing to you. You interpret it as if the lefthander has better form."

That was great, now at least I had some explanation, and some reason to believe lefties weren't so good, after all. It was simply a matter of perception, and a false perception at that, triggered by the biological capacity for boredom.

Rudolph thought the mirror was a good tool for Todd, but that the upside-down image as seen during a headstand or a chin-under-butt view might waver, as that lefthandedness is a matter of interpretation by the cerebral cortex. "With a mirror, there is a reverse image on the retina, the appearance of lefthandedness will be constant," he said.

Everything was set for the day of the big match. Hammer was supposed to play the lefthanded Argentine star at Golden Gate Park at noon. There would be a decent crowd there, too. San Francisco's Golden Gate Park always had good lunch time matches, players like Tom Brown and Gil Howard, Bob Murio and Greg Shephard. And Rosie Casals, of course. Occasionally Whitney Reed tiptoed over from across the Bay, and sometimes Gary Rose would show up. Maybe Garth O'Malley. There were always plenty of aficionados and passersby around, so when a player like Hammer was warming up, spectators gathered on the rising benches behind the courts. Guys like One-Armed-Joe began to place bets.

Unfortunately, I wouldn't be there for the excitement; I had a stack of afternoon lessons at the Rose Garden. By the time I got to the city, I'd only have to turn around and go home. All I'd get to see would be the warmup.

And so I ended up thinking about Todd and his mirror all the while I was teaching. I wondered what the Argentine lefty looked like and how wicked his slice serve was. Sometimes a lefty could run you into the fence with that serve on the backhand side, and then with almost the same delivery, he could hook it in at you, jamming your forehand. Of course, a righthander could do the same thing to a lefty; it's just that a righty isn't as well rehearsed at it. A righthander is more used to playing fellow righthanders and delivering kick serves.

As I completed my teaching at the Rose Garden, clouds drifted high over the Bay, dimming the late afternoon sun. I knew Todd would be finished with the Argentine by now, or quite possibly, the Argentine would be finished with Todd. I kind of half expected him to drop in at the Garden and give me a first-hand report of the match, but then I figured he could have just as easily drifted over to Hippie Hill, which was only a few hundred yards away from the Golden Gate Park tennis courts. He might have hung out there after the match. Win or lose, it would make no difference; Hammer would sit in the buoyant grass on Hippie Hill and roll his head to the music. There would be the beat of conga drums and tambourines, an occasional flute solo. There would be other tennis players in the colorful crowd, too, blending in, listening to the beat, not caring if they'd won or lost.

It was nightfall when Todd finally showed up at my little place in the Berkeley flatlands. Submarine sandwiches and a six-pack of Heineken were a welcome sight; he took them out of his big tennis bag and put them on my kitchen table. We began to shoot the breeze. I was right, he had gone over to Hippie Hill after the match. "Yeah, man," he said, "it was nice. I just kicked back for a while and smelled the grass, if you know what I mean."

Not much of our talk was about tennis; most of the discussion was, in fact, about poetry and music, which meant that Hammer did most of the discussing and I did most of the listening. He got into some deep philosophical stuff, but eventually, after a few brewskis, the sound of Hammer's voice lost all its meaning and his words became the music he was talking about, low pulsing tones that blended in with the humming of the city night, the rumble of Harleys, and the occasional sound of a siren.

Then Hammer's music dissipated altogether and all that was left was the wide stillness of the night. Thoughts of Bonnie drifted through my mind, nagging sadly. I felt suddenly alone.

"You can crash here, if you like," I said, feeling the need for company.

"Naw man, that's okay. I've got to get Pop's car back."

Drowsily, Hammer pushed himself away from my little kitchen table. "By the way, the kid was pretty good for a lefty," he said. With wallet in hand, he thumbed quickly through five crisp one-hundred dollar bills; he took one out and slapped it down on the table as if he had just dealt me the Queen of Hearts.

"That's your share," he said, and he walked out the door with his tour bag shouldered and the little mirror tucked safely inside.

Chapter Twenty-Six

Amphibian Tennis

Who said winning isn't everything?! Probably one of those new-age mental softness coaches. And of course, in the overall existential scheme of things, winning is pretty irrelevant. On the other hand, it's 110% of the stuff that matters, even in casual competition. It's a whole lot better than losing, no matter how you look at it; so now, two weeks later, Todd was in a different frame of mind. He had just been bumped from the first round of San Francisco's annual Grand Prix event. A big Australian with a HUGE serve had done him in straights, and now Hammer had some things to think about, and he needed to be alone. Actually, he had done very well for a guy thirty-five years old, and he made a nice chunk of change to boot.

But still, he was haunted by the match. It wasn't that Todd was giving up on tennis, hell, he had already done that, at least as far as big-time stardom was concerned. It was just that he had worked his way through all of the qualifying rounds in the tournament, only to lose to a guy who he felt he could have beaten, if only he had returned serve better. Sure, the guy had a huge serve, and he disguised it well, but still, there had to be a way to prepare faster, more efficiently, and do more than just block the ball back at the guy's feet or push up a lob to his backhand. It wasn't that Todd had lost, it was the challenge of improving that had taken hold of his mind and wouldn't let go.

He escaped into the deep green solitude of Muir Woods, just north of San Francisco, to think things over, and as he put it, get down with his game. There had been a good rain the night before, causing little ponds to form in a marshy area of the woods. Hammer's return of serve dilemma drew him ankle-deep into the tiny marsh; he got down on his haunches and squatted attentively over salamanders and tadpoles. He was especially intrigued by the darting movements of tadpoles. He imagined they were all wet little tennis players. Then bigger, more vocal amphibians began to croak at him from all around the pond, and he had a sudden brainstorm about leaping into position like a frog. He raced home to tell me about it.

"It was like it was meant to be," he said as he dragged me off to the little one-court park in Berkeley where I teach the neighborhood kids.

Dilapidated as that court was, the weeds that grew through it reminded me of various public courts I had played on in my youth. There were great fissures in the blacktop and the net was dangling by threads, and yet, that didn't matter at all. In fact, I went back in time and soon felt like a carefree kid on a summer day.

The other nice thing about that crummy court was that we could be completely anonymous on there — nobody from the world of tennis proper would be around to distract Hammer as he tried out his new frog-leap return.

He figured that was just what he needed. So I fed him balls from my giant laundry basket. I hit simulated serves from a few feet inside the baseline in order to save my arm, and Hammer returned them using his new frog leap. "Did you see that one?" he said eagerly, "I don't think I could have set up as quickly with regular footwork."

I served to the extreme backhand corner, thereby stretching the limits of his frog-leap. Todd wasn't worried about his forehand; he figured he could handle just about any serve on that side. It was the backhand that gave him problems, particularly if he wanted to drive the return. He felt he was often late in turning and stepping into the ball after making a sudden lateral move; so now he did all that in the air, and he landed in perfect form, like a well coached bullfrog.

The difficulty came in judging exactly where to land, and though he shanked quite a few, Todd was connecting better and better with each subsequent return. Indeed, some of those frog leaps were incredible, and I complimented him appropriately, with a low croaking sound from deep in my throat. He croaked back in an unrushed manner, like a bullfrog calling out from a lily pond.

It would have been something if Hammer could have made those returns in actual competition, but I knew that wouldn't be in the immediate future. He was smart enough to separate the game he was working on from the one he would use in a match. After all, there was one's practice game, and then there was one's performance game, and the successful players were able to distinguish between the two.

"I kind of like this funky old court," Todd croaked, after one particularly springy frog leap. "It reminds me of the old days, the real old days."

"I know what you mean," I croaked back, and I fed him another ball.

"By the way," he asked, "how's our little buddy, Sheldeen, doing?"

"He still talks about the day he was clockman, says he's not putting the horn back on his dad's bike for a while, just in case we need him."

"And he's hitting great," I added. "He's even recruited another guy, Pedro, an older kid. They practice together a little. I just wish they had the bucks to get more exposure. I mean, there's only so much I can do by myself."

"It's too bad. But that's the way it is," Hammer said, "if a kid doesn't live near a happening public facility, then he's got to have bucks."

"Yeah, and a taxi driver for a mom."

"You got that right. And it's best if she's a better taxi driver than a tennis player, if you get my drift."

"For sure," I agreed. "If she's too good at tennis she may be too into her own game. And if she does care about the kid's game, she might think she knows all the answers, and then the kid's screwed for sure."

Hammer said he was lucky he grew up near Recreation Park in Long Beach. "There were always old-timers hanging out at the courts," he said. "I'd skateboard over, borrowed a racket every day for a month until one of the old guys finally broke down and gave me his. That was the old days when the tennis was still free." I could tell it made him a little sad thinking about it.

I told him when I was a kid I didn't live too far from the Cal courts, that I'd walk over and watch the guys on the team. But he already knew that because we had been reminding each other about our tennis beginnings ever since we met. "Then sometimes I'd hike up to the Rose Garden and hit the wall," I said. "It's still free there. And there are some pretty decent old-timers hanging out."

"Yeah, and you're one of them," Todd chuckled, adding a frightening new thought to my recollections. Actually, the idea pissed me off, probably because there was some truth to it. I got angrier with each step as I marched back to the baseline to serve another ball to his goddamn frog leap.

"I may be too old to hop around the court like a frog," I countered, gearing up now to serve the ball as hard as possible at him. "But that doesn't make me an old-timer. At least not yet." This time I went for an ace.

Instantly, Hammer was in the air, his legs apart. With my ball upon him, he landed and simultaneously ripped a winning backhand; then he dropped down the rest of the way onto his haunches as if stuck in the ooze of the court. "Don't take things so personal," he said, and he let loose with a deep, bellowing "C-R-O-A-K."

Strangely, that cracked old court suited us just fine. It was excellent for our purposes, perhaps even better than a nicer court. It was as if because the court was so bad, our mission had become that much more serious, after all, it wasn't the kind of place we'd have played at for sheer enjoyment (although there was some pleasure in belching out those primitive amphibian sounds.) And like all public facilities, occasional passersby made it interesting, much more so than if we were behind the bars of a private club, for instance. But school was back in session now and the park was deserted, except for a grandparent walking a toddler and a couple of bums sharing a bottle in a brown paper bag. And two longhairs on a tennis court croaking at each other.

In the cool autumn air, golden leaves were beginning to fall and float dreamily to our feet. They looked good in the cracks of the blacktop, and I knew that as crummy as that court was, there were plenty of places in the world where it would have been the best court in the land. I figured there were probably half a dozen guys on the tour right now who grew up hitting balls on a worse court. Guys like Damian Tong who had to hike for miles just to see a fishing net strung out three feet high across a section of flat dirt. Two old men would be waiting to hit the ball at him when he got there. And the winds would be fierce. But Tong would let the old men ride the blow and he would fight it, pounding groundstroke after groundstroke into the gale. Hour after hour, Tong would lay into the ball on that crude dirt court. Then he would run back to his village, making sure his time afoot was better than the day before.

And so the quality of a court didn't matter much, so long as there was somebody there to help. Of course, all that was really needed was the knowledge. And desire. Take the case of Figar Horthpeungh, who had never even set foot on a tennis court until he entered his first junior tournament at the age of fifteen. Figar did it all alone on the back of a barn. It was just him and those big wooden planks. And the pictures in an old tennis magazine. Now, some ten years later, Figar is twenty-eight in the world and living like royalty. But he still gets back to milk the cows and feed the chickens when he has a break from the tour. It's his idea of a vacation. Besides, he says it keeps him from going soft.

As dilapidated as that court in the Berkeley flatlands was, it worked out well, enabling Hammer to advance his theory about returning serve like a frog. But later, back at my apartment, he confided that his knees were a little tender from all that hopping, so he'd have to think it over before incorporating the maneuver into his game. "I think I'll call up our old friend, Vic Braden, and see what he has to say about it," Todd said. "Who knows, Vic may have already analyzed it in his tennis lab."

Hammer was kneading the inside of his right knee. He looked a little disappointed. He told me he really liked the potential of the frog leap, but danger lay in trying to shift the weight forward while landing sideways. "The human knee isn't made for the kind of abuse the rest of the body can lay on it," he said sadly, "which is kind of strange, considering those millions of years of evolution and all."

"Tell me about it," I said, "I've had both my knees operated on and I never did so much as one frog-leap return in my life. The knee just isn't up to the rest of the joints."

"Maybe we grew too tall as a species or something," Todd shouted over the noise of the shower. He had helped himself to my place as if it were a locker room and I was just the guy handing out towels, which was okay with me because he extended the same kind of hospitality to me. Once he even lent me clean underwear, which is something one dude doesn't often do for another.

Freshly cleaned up, we were in the front room now. Hammer turned to my bookcase, as he often did, to see if I had anything new. He couldn't help notice the photo of Danny was missing and that it had been replaced by one of Sheldeen. Gracious as ever, Hammer never said a word about my former student.

"Your protégé looks good," he said, pointing to the picture of Sheldeen, who in fact, did look pretty good. With both feet slightly off the ground, he had just clocked one of his big forehands.

Bzzz — the plea of the telephone came suddenly, discordant and nagging. It was Evonne. I hadn't heard from her in a while; she wanted us to come over, for some reason I didn't quite understand. So we took one last look at Sheldeen's forehand and drove out of the sad gray flats and up into the lush Berkeley hills

Evonne was always a kick, and since Todd hadn't seen her since her engagement party, he was looking forward to the visit. "I'll have to congratulate her on her discovery of tenis envy," he said as we strolled up the flagstone walkway to her front porch.

She was at the door, wearing sunglasses that were so big they covered her cheekbones. Indeed, most of her face was hidden.

She greeted us, but she wasn't her normal cheery self. "What have you two been up to?" she said from behind the huge sunglasses.

"The usual," I volunteered, "how have you and Hitch been doing?"

Evonne hung her head. "Don't even mention his name, that dirty rotten son of a bitch."

"Are you okay?" Hammer asked, obviously perplexed.

"I don't know how to tell you boys this, but it's over. The whole thing. Us. The engagement. Everything is over." She raised her head and carefully removed the big sunglasses, revealing two purpley blackened eyes and an ugly laceration across the side of her nose.

"Hitch did that to you?!" Todd exclaimed.

"The son of a bitch won't be doing any more of it," she said sheepishly. "At least not until he gets out of jail. But that's okay, because I've got a gun."

"Hitch is in jail?!"

"You've got a gun!?"

Dumbfounded, we stood motionless on the porch. "This is all hard to believe," I said.

Evonne put her sunglasses back over her brutalized face. "Come in and I'll tell you all about it."

I wasn't sure I wanted to know the details, but I felt awful for Evonne.

Hammer and I followed her into the living room, a grand place with lots of glass and a panoramic view of San Francisco and the Bay. It was night the last time I was in there, and music filled the room. Bonnie was by my side. Things were popping. But now everything was dead, like in a museum. The normally effervescent Evonne sat curled up in an armchair, dark sunglasses hiding her face. Todd and I sat on the edge of the couch and looked at her feet.

She whimpered like she was going to cry. Then we heard a noise from the other room and Hitch came barreling in. Evonne jumped to her feet. She began to bawl hysterically. No wait, she was laughing! Hitch was laughing too. They took each other's hands and danced around in apparent ecstasy.

"You're not in jail?!" Hammer protested.

"Yeah, what's going on!?"

I sat upright with a confused grin as the happy couple embraced; their intertwined bodies shook spasmodically with laughter. Between convulsions Evonne spoke to us in gasps. She said that Hitch hadn't really beaten her up, she had slipped on the tennis court and rammed herself with her own racket, right between the eyes. It was a freak accident caused by a wet court, she explained.

"You're not supposed to play on wet courts," I said, wondering if she was telling the truth. (Over the years, I'd seen plenty of hackers running around with big goose eggs on their foreheads, and of course, knots on their shins. Hell, I'd even inflicted a few leg wounds on myself. But never had I seen such a scraped and blackened face.)

"It's true," Evonne insisted, "I didn't know the court was so slippery. It was the end court, you know, the one where the sprinklers overshoot. Anyway, we rolled off the puddle and it just looked a little damp near the alley, so we began our doubles. Marge and I were against Kendra and Doreen. We were still in the warmup when I went down."

"Let me guess," Todd said, "you slipped on the line?"

"Boy did I!" Evonne seemed proud, almost pleased with her accident. "I had jumped up for an overhead," she said happily, "and when I came down — blam! That was it. I didn't even know what happened. I was seeing stars, if you know what I mean."

"I know exactly what you mean," I said, remembering the spray of stars I had seen when I got knocked out in a football game in junior high school.

The spunky Evonne said she put a bandage on her nose and finished the match with a bit of a headache. It wasn't until the next day that she really looked beat-up. So she and Hitch decided to pull a fast one on us.

"Yeah, they let me out for good behavior," Hitch bellowed, savoring the beauty of their prank.

Todd's grin began to form in earnest now that he knew what was going on. He turned to Evonne. "You've got to watch out for the lines," he said with some emphasis, "even on a completely dry surface the lines on a hardcourt can be like ice. Half the time they skimp and don't add any sand when they mix that white paint. Haven't you ever noticed the way the ball skids when it hits the lines sometimes?"

"It always seems like it's skidding to me," Evonne said cheerfully. "But I'll be more careful from now on, you can bet your booty."

"Do men have booties?" Hitch asked, genuinely curious. "Not that I'd be interested or anything. I like my fiancée's just fine."

"Sure they've got booties," Evonne was quick to reply, "it's just that we women don't go around talking about them."

"Why should you?" Hammer said, "all you have to do is shake yours and we men come crawling. Booty and all."

"Care for something to drink?" Hitch set four of his big tankards on the coffee table and filled them from a bottle of chilled White Zinfandel. He told us he had picked up a case of the stuff on an excursion to the Napa Valley. (What the hell, the day was almost over and I didn't have class in the morning.)

"You guys are staying for dinner, aren't you?" Evonne asked eagerly from behind her dark lenses?"

"Why not?" Todd replied, "it's not often we get to dine with the person who discovered tenis envy."

"It was nothing, really," Evonne giggled. "I couldn't help stumbling onto it. I mean the disease is rampant in the suburbs. I think even golfers have it."

"Yeah," said Todd, "they have it alright, but they sure as hell don't want to know about it, especially if they think they might have caught it from a tennis player."

It was true, golfers were even more snobbish than tennis players, to the point, in fact, where they often looked down on us tennis players as if we were ruffians, untidy riffraff in short shorts and T-shirts who couldn't afford to play their more gentlemanly game. I suppose their manliness (their gentle-manliness) felt threatened by our relative rowdiness much in the way that we tennis players were intimidated by swimmers who paraded around the club pool more or less naked while we marched by in stiff white clothing secretly admiring their golden tans. Fear of the lusty swimmer was so great, in fact, that at one time it came to be understood that doing laps was bad for tennis. Now, of course, the opposite has been shown to be the case. It's all a survival response — the fear of losing one's woman or one's station in life — and it became generalized into kind of a class thing. At least, that's what Rudolph, my professor friend told me.

"Golfers are the most elitist," Evonne said, continuing our well lubricated discussion. "They're too stuffy. All they really want to do is lounge around the bar and talk about the lengths of their drives, but we know what's really on their minds, don't we?"

"Their putters?" Todd suggested.

"I'll drink to that," Hitch offered, holding up his tankard. "Here's to our putters. Tennis players have the best putters, everybody knows that."

"Hey, you guys," I said, becoming suddenly serious, "I know it's all a matter of degrees, and there are exceptions, but have you ever noticed that tenis envy is more prevalent at the lower levels?"

"But then I guess that only makes sense," I added.

"Naturally, the worst players have the worst cases of it," Hammer said.

"Watch it," Hitch warned with surprising gravity, "you're talking about me now. I know I've got a bad case of it, but I'll show you guys, you'll see. Some day my game's gonna be bigger than yours. A lot bigger."

"That'd be pretty big then," Todd said with modest nonchalance like he was John Wayne and had just stepped off his horse.

Hitch pointed his finger. "Mark my words fella, you best keep a yardstick on that horse a yours, because I'm gonna be showin' you what big is all about."

"Boys, boys," Evonne chided unseen from back in the kitchen, "do we always have to be comparing the sizes of our games?"

"He started it," Hitch chuckled as he poured more White Zin into Todd's tankard. Then Todd excused himself to call Pop and tell him he wouldn't be home for dinner.

My mind drifted upwards, northwards, over the California-Oregon border. It landed in Portland, where Bonnie was. I imagined her with us now, seated next to me, her soothing voice, the feel of her arm against mine. And then I realized that these people — Todd, Evonne, Hitch — they were special, the people I was closest to. Bonnie was the only one missing, and though I missed her sorely, it was still good to be here. To have friends near.

At eye level now, two big tankards were coming at me. They were inches away; I raised mine up in self-defense. "To your butts," said Hitch with Hammer repeating, "Yeah, to your ..." CLONK!

The vibration in my hand felt good — good and solid — like the clean feel of a perfect overhead.

"Come on, boys, let's eat," Evonne called out, her words mixing angelically with memories of Bonnie calling us in to dinner in Portland.

Dazed and still pining, I followed Hitch into the dining room. Behind me was Hammer, his voice next to my ear, or maybe I was just imagining it. "Now remember, Stretch ..."

Chapter Twenty-Seven

On Break And Proud Of It

So now, Todd and I were about to dine with Evonne and Hitch, after the feigned wife-beating incident. Technically, it would have been a case of fiancée-beating, in as much as they weren't married yet. They did, however, take great pride in announcing that a date had been set; the ceremony was to be some time next summer, probably in July. Or August, according to Hitch, who had other plans for the summer as well, some of which were dependent on last minute variables like Alaskan fishing conditions and the lead-up to who might get into the World Series.

Because it was such a special occasion (with the marriage date and all) Evonne had put real wine glasses on the table. They looked a little fragile compared to those big tankards, but their tall thin necks went nicely with the long-stemmed roses from Hitch and two candles that flickered in pewter holders. A large salad bowl sat on the table, alongside teriyaki salmon and sweet smelling basmati rice.

When she first sat down to join us, Evonne took off her big sunglasses, though not without some hesitation. Now in the candlelight, the tennis accident in her face didn't look so bad. We got used to it as if it were just a birthmark and we were all in nursery school together.

And our conversation was no less childish; it slipped musically from this to that as if its general direction was of no real importance other than to produce pleasurable sound effects to go with our food and wine. And oh, that wine! But then Hitch got hung up on Evonne's tennis game and we gained some focus. "Her serve is too weak," he complained. "You should see the ladies she plays with, they never hold their serves, not even in doubles."

"Hey, we're on break, and proud of it," Evonne announced enthusiastically. "When we say we held serve, we mean we held the other guy's serve."

Hammer chuckled. "On break and proud of it. I like that."

It was true that serving was not necessarily an advantage for women, especially at Evonne's level. Hell, even in the pros, the ladies had such big groundstrokes they could cream the average serve and send the server scrambling into a corner. It was a wonder they held serve as often as they did.

I could see Hitch wanted his fiancée to have a classy game and not just be another dainty housewife with a powder-puff serve. I told him not to worry. "She's doing okay, she's got the right grip and she's getting spin. And, she's hitting the first and second balls exactly the same, which is extremely important. Her serve will get nothing but better."

Hammer was nodding in agreement, slowly, pensively. "Look at the top women," he said, "they can crunch any short ball, and for many of them the serve *is* the first short ball."

Evonne extended her wine glass across the table to us. "On break and proud of it," she declared. And we responded. "On break and proud of it." CLINK. CLINK CLINK.

Reluctantly, Hitch brought his glass up, but then he mumbled something about Evonne's forehand. "Well, at least her forehand should be better," he slurred. "It's not normal to have a better backhand than a forehand, is it guys?"

"Sometimes the two-hander can be better than the forehand," I said, "especially with juniors and novice women. But, no, in a sense Hitch is right, the forehand always has the potential to be stronger, even more lethal than the two-hander." I thought about what Big Bill Tilden used to say about the forehand, that more could be done with it than with any other stroke. And of course, he was right. Even at the big time, if the pros were fast enough, sometimes they could pound out a match without hitting hardly any backhands at all.

Evonne's forehand always began with a straight backswing. I knew she would gain more versatility with a loop backswing, when she was ready for it, but since I was only working with her occasionally now, I hesitated to suggest any changes in her game. Todd, on the other hand, seized the opportunity and began a lengthy discourse on the advantages of the loop backswing.

"It'll loosen you up," he told her from across the dinner table, "and give you natural momentum going into the hit. Plus, you'll get more topspin." With his hand above the plate of salmon, he began to demonstrate the stroke in the air, creating a breeze that caused the candles on the table to flicker every time he hit an imaginary ball. With his elbow leading upwards and back, and then down toward the table, he emphasized the circularity of the loop backswing and its proclivity for knocking over wine glasses. "A bit of a loop in the backswing is a nice thing, wups, sorry about that." A large pink spot the color of the salmon formed on the tablecloth.

Hitch seemed almost delighted. "Yeah, you're a sorry ass, alright," he chuckled, as Evonne reached over in a futile attempt to soak up half a glass of White Zin with her napkin. She told Todd not to worry, that it was an old tablecloth and that she would definitely try the loop backswing. But not until she was on a tennis court.

"Sorry about that," Hammer repeated sheepishly.

"Yeah," Hitch laughed, "you're a sorry ass, alright."

Todd's eyes brightened suddenly, as if a switch had been flipped on the back of his head. "Dude, we're all sorry asses," he announced. Then the pensive smile took over, that slow introspective nod, and I knew we were in for something deep. Although it was a while in coming.

It wasn't until the end of the evening, when Hammer had settled on how best to describe it, that he finally explained his insight to us. And what an amazing insight it was! Though not quite as humorous as tenis envy, it gave us a lot to think about and was probably more fascinating than any other generalization one could make about tennis players.

In a nutshell, the notion goes something like this: Tennis players are always apologizing to their warmup partners (when they fail to hit the ball back properly) and to their doubles partners (when they miss a shot.) They are always saying sorry, wups my fault, sorry about that, or whatever. Now then, if one tallies all these tennis apologies, the numbers become startling on any given day (throughout a particular state, for example.) Nationwide the numbers of apologies are astounding, and worldwide they are astronomical, especially when considering play for several weeks or more. If one starts counting from the very beginning, for instance, since the inception of the sport, the numbers of tennis apologies are practically infinite. Conclusion: Tennis players as a group have said they're sorry more times than any other group or class of peoples since the utterance of the first spoken word by primitive man.

Now on the living room rug, Hammer leaned back on his elbows and smiled. "What a sorry lot we are," he said, with that amused look.

"Sheuwh! That was a mouthful." Evonne was the first to say anything. "Now that you mention it, I guess we tennis players do apologize to each other a lot. But you think it's excessive?"

"Hell, I do it once in a while, myself," Todd admitted. "I'm just saying that overall there must have been millions of apologies made on the tennis court, which is a strange thing. Especially for a sport."

"There must be more sorries than aces!" I blurted out. Then thinking about it, I added, "at least at the lower levels that must be true."

"The number of apologies at the lower levels are great enough to offset the number of aces at the upper levels," Todd said thoughtfully.

"I told you guys you're a bunch of sorry asses," Hitch slurred from his armchair, wine glass in hand.

"The overall numbers might reach a billion," Todd suggested.

"Billions and billions," Hitch proclaimed in a nasally tone as if he were a tipsy Carl Sagan describing the infinite universe.

"So, what do you think?" Hammer asked Evonne, "do you want a loop backswing or not?"

"I wouldn't be caught without one," she replied. "Now that I've seen what it can get out of half a glass of wine."

"You won't be sorry," Todd said with a wink.

We decided to test Hammer's hypothesis over the weekend by counting the number of apologies launched at some of the local tennis facilities. We would extrapolate statewide numbers from there and then project a count for the entire northern hemisphere. We would also work on Evonne's new forehand.

We discussed using tape recorders to gather our data, and possibly Hitch's video camera, deciding in the end that not even notepads would be necessary. "We're not trying to launch a space shuttle," Evonne suggested, "we just need to get a casual inventory of apologies. We'll do it Saturday morning at prime time. Hitch and I will hit our club and two others in the area. You and Todd can go to some of the public courts."

The idea was to spend about a half hour at each place, observing, if possible, the warmup and the first set. Each of us would be able to keep an eye (or an ear) on two courts. We would focus primarily on doubles.

"Just remember the totals you get at each place," Evonne said, as she and Hitch walked us out to the curb in the cool night air. In the light of a street lamp, the old Dart looked out of place in front of their elegant house.

Evonne handed Todd two paper plates covered with aluminum foil, and we were off. The leftovers, that mix of teriyaki salmon and basmati rice, emitted an inviting odor in the cold air that seemed to warm the interior of the car. "Look, midnight snacks," Todd said, holding the plates up as we cruised down the dark hill.

Chapter Twenty-Eight

The Sorry Coefficient

When Saturday morning arrived I didn't feel like getting out of bed, at least not just to see a bunch of sorry-ass loser tennis players apologize to each other when they sprayed the ball all over the court. But alas, there were important contributions to be made to the fields of social psychology, cultural anthropology, linguistics, possibly even archeology if Leake or somebody could find an apologetic-looking skeleton beneath the stadium court at Roland Garros. Besides, I knew Evonne and Hitch would be out doing their part for our scholarly endeavor, so I crawled out of bed and drove over to pick up Dr. Hammer.

In the Dart now, Todd was eager as we headed to the Cal courts, where a lot of Berkeley locals played. "There'll be a lot of hacks there," he said, "I bet we get at least a dozen sorries per half hour on each court."

"There's no sense going to the Berkeley Tennis Club," I said, "they're better players there, they probably don't apologize to each other very much."

"But it would make an excellent comparison, for another study sometime," Dr. Hammer noted.

Today, we decided, we would go for big numbers, so we would hit the Cal courts, Berkeley High School, and the Rose Garden. Davie Stadium, the premier East Bay public facility, would be a possibility if we had time.

I told Todd that Golden Gate Park would be the perfect place to do our sorry survey. "It's big enough and they have all levels of play. You, me, Hitch, Evonne, we could all go out there together and get some great data. We could get One-Armed Joe and give him a couple of bucks to help with the counting. Too bad it's so far away."

"Yeah. We'll have to save it for a follow-up sometime, just to check our numbers."

"Good idea," I said as I pulled up alongside the tennis courts at Berkeley High School, having decided to hit the Cal courts next, and then head up to the Rose Garden after that.

On one of the courts a ladies doubles game was in progress; two other courts were occupied by singles hitters who were just rallying. Handily, a foursome of old timers was approaching one of the three vacant courts, so our plan to tally from start of warmup to end of set looked intact.

"Okay," Todd said, "I'll take these old fogies and the two guys slapping the ball around next to them. You can have the babes on the other side and whatever else comes along." He winked at me.

The women were 3.0/C player types who mistakenly thought successful doubles meant running up to the net whenever possible, even at their level (which was more or less defined by not having a volley, an overhead, or a second serve.) At every opportunity, they ran up to poke at the ball in the air and miss shots and tell each other how sorry they were.

"Oh, sorry, Wilma."

"My fault."

"Sorry about that."

"Wups, sorry, Gracie."

Their voices rang out pleasantly with apologies as if it were simply a part of calling the score. "Deuce, sorry, your ad, my fault."

With surprising vigor they jumped around and cut each other's balls off, as it were, dumping volleys and rolling halfvolleys into the net. They spent so much time in no man's land, they must have thought it was a place where only women should be.

I felt like screaming at them to STAY BACK more and not to hog the ball, especially the low ball down the middle, which was an easy groundstroke for the partner who by some miracle happened to still be in the backcourt.

And yet, I kept the count going (seven apologies so far in three games.) I stood there by the fence smiling politely and inspiring them, I suppose, to run up to the net and miss even more.

After a while, Todd came over to my court. "Let's get out of here," he said, "I can't take much more of this." He never was much of a spectator; even when it came to better players, Hammer wasn't a watcher. He didn't even look at tennis or football on TV. "Sports are something to participate in, not watch," he once told me.

"What kind of numbers did your old timers produce?" I asked him with genuine interest.

"Six sorries in the warmup, then five more with the score at 3/2 in the first. I figure half a set's enough, we can estimate the rest. But check this out, the two guys just stroking on the next court scored fifteen. Strange, isn't it? But I guess there's a logic to it. How are the baberonas doing?"

"Eight so far, wups, make that nine sorries in three and a half games."

So we split the Berkeley High scene somewhat prematurely, but not without results that couldn't be parlayed into meaningful data, data that would confirm what we already knew — that we were all just a bunch of sorry-ass tennis players.

We headed over to the Cal courts, and then we went up to the Rose Garden to take a final count. By now our census had evolved into an efficient system that was not dependent on doubles, warming up, or even sets; largely because we found apologies everywhere and we lacked the patience for more than a quick sampling. We simply parked on a court for ten minutes, got a total, and converted that to a per minute reading which subsequently became known as *The Sorry Coefficient.*

One court at the Rose Garden had a sorry coefficient of 3, a record high for the day, and yet it was produced by just two people! And one was a pretty good guy! The fellow was hitting, it seemed, with a woman he was interested in, so every time his ball strayed from her in the least he apologized, being the chivalrous type. Strangely, when he really missed his mark, his sorry seemed less sincere, more casual, as if it weren't really an apology at all, but rather a statement of how he was actually a much better player than his poor shot had demonstrated — "sahhhreee," his voice rang out as if he were calling a dog.

Of course, his partner also misdirected some nugs, but only when it was a bizarre misfire did she vocalize an apology. For the most part, the couple's high sorry coefficient was due to his chivalry and air of superiority. Their ten minute total was 30, for a coefficient of 3 per minute.

In general, ten minutes produced under 10 apologies, a coefficient of less than 1 per minute. Typically, the coefficient was something like .6 or so. Averaging out our data for the morning, we got .8 at the high school, .5 at the Cal courts, and 1.8 at the Rose Garden (which was unusually high for the reasons mentioned.)

Todd and I were burned out on apologies. Having completed our survey, we sat beneath an overhang of yellow and white blooms at the bottom of the Rose Garden. "I wonder how Hitch and Evonne are doing," he said, "they can probably stand this sort of thing more than we can."

"It's not exactly my favorite thing, either," I told him, "but in the interest of science, I figure I can watch some hackers now and then."

"You watched? Hey, I just shut my eyes and listened. It's better that way."

"Good idea, I'll try that next time."

From the colorful depths of the Garden we hiked back up to the top to stretch around and shoot the breeze up there on the deck. The midday sun was breaking through the haze; over the bay, clouds were beginning to lift, expanding our view to the near edges of San Francisco. I thought about Bonnie. I felt like writing her again from up there, right then, in fact. But with Hammer at my side, I chickened out. "Yeah," I told him, "we should call Hitch, see what kind of numbers they came up with."

"Maybe Evonne will invite us over for lunch," he said.

Chapter Twenty-Nine

A Serious Side Change

Of all on-court situations, singles points will resonate with fewest audible regrets because one doesn't normally apologize to the opponent for blowing a shot in the middle of a match. Although I have seen it done by an arrogant Hungarian who specialized in psyching out the opponent and going back to the old country every year to hunt unsuccessfully for a young bride.

It is usually just in the warmup that one apologizes in singles, or between points when one might inadvertently (or not so inadvertently) hit a ball to the far corner — "sahhhreee." Doubles play, on the other hand, has a high sorry coefficient because there is a partner on the same side of the net whose main job is to tell you not to worry about it every time you say you're sorry. The ideal scenario goes something like this: You blow an easy ball, hang your head and say "sorry."

"We'll get them next time," your partner offers in a delicate priest-like voice, as if the match weren't really over and you were just a child whose shoelace had simply come undone.

Such a passive approach was never the case with Todd, however. Once, early in our careers, we were playing for what seemed like a lot of money at the time, four hundred dollars; the winner of the match would also get hospitality for the week. It was, as they say, a huge match. We were down a set and losing in the second when I apologized again for missing yet another ball. (Unfortunately, this one happened to be on game point.) At the side change, Todd sat there with an agonized look.

"Let me ask you this," he said, "if you were playing singles and you missed that same shot, would you say you were sorry?"

"Of course not, there would be nobody to apologize to, except myself."

"Well, why not apologize to yourself?"

"Hell, I'd probably just get mad at myself."

"And that's my point! In singles you'd get pissed off and dig in immediately. But in doubles, your first response is to hang your head and feel bad about missing the ball. If you want to play doubles with me, I don't give a shit how many balls you miss, but I want you mad at the opposition, or mad at yourself, or even me, whatever works. I don't want you feeling sorry for anybody, and especially not me. Deal?" He extended his hand, a genuine grin on his face.

Now I saw the light. "You got it," I said, and our hands met in a thumbs-up clasp. We got up from that bench and kicked their royal butts all over the court. Sure, I still missed a few, but when I did, I tried to feel the anger, the motivation of rage and not the inhibition of regret.

Hammer had shown me that an apologetic attitude, no matter how well intended, diminishes one's competitive spirit. Besides, there are other things to think about in the middle of a match (like maybe how not to miss the ball next time.) There is also energy to be conserved by not getting caught up in the apology syndrome. We made a pact on that day never to apologize to each other on the court again, not even in practice, a ploy that would help tone our tournament demeanor.

And so, the notion of apologies had been something that was buried in Hammer's mind for some time. There it fermented over the years, flowing out suddenly well-aged when he tipped over that wine onto Evonne's tablecloth. And now in the same dining room, this time while lunching on turkey sandwiches, we compared our data to that gathered by Evonne and Hitch.

Evonne was excited. "I never would have thought there would be so many apologies made on the tennis court," she said. "It *is* rather bizarre."

We showed them how to convert their numbers to our standard per minute measure — the sorry coefficient.

"The sorry coefficient, I like that," Evonne said approvingly. I thought of Rudolph, my psych professor, and wondered what he would think of the sorry coefficient.

"It's more like a sorry-ass coefficient," Hitch griped with a disgusted look. "Hell, I must have heard the word sorry more times today than I have in my whole life!"

"Sorry about that," Hammer chuckled. "But I guarantee, we got the heaviest dose of it." He went on to tell them about the couple at the Rose Garden who apologized thirty times in ten minutes.

Hitch put down his turkey sandwich. "Well, bless my booty!" He was truly amazed. "A sorry-ass coefficient of three! That's going to be hard to beat."

In general, though, their results were pretty much like ours. We all agreed that people just hitting had the highest coefficients, and that doubles play produced higher numbers than singles play. Naturally, better players usually had lower coefficients than worse players.

However, as we observed the phenomenon over the next few weeks, we found an exception to the rule. Some really green beginners didn't apologize in situations where better players would have, because they didn't know enough to apologize. If they were just trying to rally back and forth, for instance, they might have thought that since the ball was basically in the court, that was just fine, even though one of them had to race to the far corner to retrieve it. And in a sense, they were right (raw beginners, sheer novices ahead of their times, instinctively taking the wuss out of the game.) For them, the very notion of a warmup, of delivering the ball on a silver platter to the opponent, did not exist. Who's to say? They might have been raw beginners, but when it came to their sorry coefficients, they had the low numbers of world class players.

As it turns out, golfers also have very low sorry coefficients, largely I suppose, because people struck by those hard white balls are usually out of sight, and rather than wonder if an apology is necessary, the expert golfer has simply learned to yell "fore" to the horizon.

Chapter Thirty

The California Standard

As winter approached, Todd became neurotic about more than just the weather forecast. He was troubled by the notion he would be forever known as a sorry-ass wimp tennis player. So now, as if in an effort to prove we weren't all just a bunch of losers, Todd was still at it, casually collecting sorry coefficients from various tennis facilities the way some people collect matchbooks from restaurants; after a while he had a whole pile of the colorful things and wasn't sure exactly what to do with them. So he spread them out on my kitchen table.

After looking at them for some time through the lens of a perfectly focused Heineken microscope, he got sensible. First, he threw out all the numbers that were unusually high, and then he tossed out the extreme lows. Professor Hammer then took an average of what was left, in order to calculate what would hereafter be known as the California Standard. This number was determined to be .6, which means that on the average, when a tennis court has people on it, somebody apologizes to somebody else slightly more often than every two minutes. And not just in California!

The California Standard was to be considered the measure for the industry, in as much as California tennis players usually lead the way (even though that point is argued occasionally in Florida.) Now we would be able to project the number of apologies in the entire United States, simply by applying the California Standard. But first we would need to get the latest figures on tennis court usage.

Handily, Hammer and I had a friend who worked for the USTA in New Jersey. His name was Brewski, although his parents still thought his name was Horace Brewer. (In case you hadn't noticed, all tennis players, indeed, all athletes worth their salt, acquire nicknames. My name, for instance, is Stefan, Stefan Dubitski, but like I said, most people just call me Stretch.)

So we telephoned our old pal Brewski back at the USTA office and laid it on him. Brewski said he envied our not having to put on a tie every morning, that he was in the middle of a staff meeting, and that he'd get back to us regarding our research project.

It took him a few days, but by the end of the week we had our numbers. It seemed there were approximately 50,000 tennis courts in the country registered with the USTA and at least another 50,000 not registered; and Americans ran around on them for a minimum of 11 million hours last year. Hammer put down the phone, his eyes bulging like flexed biceps. "Dude," he said, "what's 11 million hours worth of the California Standard?"

Let's see, first convert to minutes. Yes. "There are sixty minutes in an hour," I volunteered, feeling like Einstein. "What's sixty times 11 million?" I asked, feeling suddenly less brilliant.

"Six hundred sixty million minutes," Todd said after a moment, with his finger in the air as if he had just called a let serve but wasn't sure if he had really heard anything.

Okay then, six hundred sixty million minutes times the California Standard (which is .6, but we decided to drop it to .5 just to get a quick estimate.) "It's more than ..."

"Three hundred thirty million," we said simultaneously. Three hundred thirty million apologies!

"And that's just last year," Hammer said, "and just in the United States." Man, are we a bunch of sorry asses, I thought, I can't wait to see the look on Hitch's face when those numbers slap him on the back of the head.

From the USTA office, Brewski had advised that the numbers he had given us were low, if anything. In a follow-up call he sounded intrigued with the project, said he would get back to us with court time for the last one hundred years, but to go back before then would be difficult.

And so, Brewski, the former Horace Brewer, who graduated Phi Beta Kappa from Wisconsin in theoretical physics and won the Big Ten singles title that same year, had come through for us. He told us a conservative estimate of total U.S. court time for the last one hundred years was something like three hundred fifty million hours, give or take a few dozen here and there.

In terms of international play, Brewski suggested 10% of U.S. numbers, as a rule of thumb. So, by adding another 10% we would approximate worldwide hours of court usage for the century, which we would then pleasantly convert to minutes and multiply by the California Standard. Since our calculators didn't have room for that many numbers on them, we had to sharpen pencils and suck on the erasers for a while to make sure we got the figures right. After all, thirteen billion eight hundred sixty million is a number that demands to be double-checked. It looks like this (13,860,000,000) and is the kind of number Carl Sagan would have been proud of. Actually, he would have been tickled pink, because that same number is almost exactly the age of the universe! I wondered if he was a tennis player. On TV he always looked like such a humble guy; he probably had a fairly high sorry coefficient, I figured.

For the sake of simplicity, we rounded off our big number to 14 billion and designated it modestly as the *Global Grand Total* of all apologies made on the tennis court since the beginning of time (not counting sorrowful pleas for non-tennis purposes, by reconciling lovers, for instance, who might have enjoyed the privacy of an old-style ivy-enclosed court.)

We realized the 14 billion Global Grand Total, the GGT as we came to call it, made up a big chunk of mankind's apologies in general and distinguished tennis players as the greatest single contributors to sorrow and also the most sorry-assed people on the face of the planet.

"It doesn't take a statistician to figure it out," Todd said, one lazy afternoon as we sat with Hitch and Evonne on a courtside bench at the old club. "With a GGT like that, we're obviously a bunch of wusses, that's all there is to it." He went on to talk about the warmup in tennis and asked us if we could think of any other sport where you actually warm up with your opponent before the start of battle. "Try to imagine a couple of heavyweight boxers stepping into the ring and warming up with each other," he said.

"Yeah," Hitch held up his fists in an effeminate manner, his nose turned prudishly in the air. "Just give me a few left hooks to the jaw and I'll be ready," he said with a noticeable lisp.

"That's what I mean," Hammer chuckled, "they ought to abolish the warmup in tournaments. All you need is your own warmup partner, not the opponent. In doubles it's easy enough, since you've already got a partner, one by the way, who should know your prematch needs and be good at satisfying them."

"What about feeling out the opponent?" Evonne said, realizing now she had really opened herself up with that one.

"Yeah, I like to give them a quick feel," Hitch quipped, "especially in mixed."

"Come on, you know what I mean. Isn't the warmup a good chance to check up on the opponent?"

"You mean give them a checkup, like in the doctor's office?" Hitch looked absolutely serious. "No wonder some of those old guys bring their stethoscopes to the courts, and I thought it was in case somebody got a heart attack or something."

"And to think I fell for him because he was funny," Evonne complained.

We sat on the side of the court and thought about it, but the only other sports we could think of with an opponent warmup were ping pong, racketball, badminton and squash; and they were all very minor sports, though to their credit, they appeared to have much lower sorry coefficients than tennis.

"I think they ought to abolish the damn warmup," Todd said. "If you want to check out the opponent, go watch him play somebody else. There's no sense wasting points you win in the warmup, they should count toward the match. You can step onto the court with your own warmup partner, that's all. Take your five minutes with somebody who can do the job right."

"And let the fans scream and shout in the middle of points," I suggested, now that we were beginning to escort tennis out of the tea room.

"Yeah, and fine their sorry asses if they apologize to each other," Hitch said. "We can't have a bunch of wusses wreckin' the game for everybody else."

"Right on," Todd declared. "And no dress code either, if you want to go out there covered in nothing but tattoos and a jock strap, that's okay, so long as you're wearing tennis shoes."

"And I suppose the women can go topless?" Evonne asked with an amused look.

"That's it," I cheered, "let's take the damn game out of the tea room. If the Duchess of Kent wants to watch, then she can sit in the bleachers and belch and cuss and pull peanut shells out of her hair just like everybody else."

"Man, you guys are relentless," Evonne said, realizing now that it wasn't just the trimmings, but all of tennis etiquette was about to vanish into thin air.

"It's for the good of the game," I volunteered. "If tennis is to survive, it can't be a class thing anymore. It can't be strawberries and cream forever, it's got to be chips and beer. And if it's to grow into more of a big-time sport, then it's due for some huge changes."

With that, Hammer and I told them about hyper team tennis, our futuristic vision where the game is spiced up with human targets and shoot-out frenzies. We told them about our on-court experiment with Clutch and the guys. "It was basically a success," Hammer said.

Hitch was keen, he was ready to jump into in the fray. "That would really put me on my toes," he said, "plus you get bonus points. I like the idea of not dillydallying around the court like a bunch of wussies."

"If the idea is to draw bigger crowds, then I guess all that excitement would do it," Evonne said with some reluctance. "It would make the game a real live team event, I suppose. But since I'm still learning, I think I'll stick to the regular stuff for a while, if you guys don't mind."

"Do what you want, Hon," Hitch said, "but on my team I'm going to have some real hot players, guys who can pick a fly off a player's nose from fifty feet."

"If they can do that, the rest of their games should be pretty good, too," Todd offered.

Evonne still had second thoughts. "Anyway," she said, "who wants to get hit with a tennis ball?"

"Oh, come on, Hon, it doesn't even hurt, it's not like getting tackled or being hit with a baseball. Or a hockey stick."

"Yeah," Todd chuckled, "it's still pretty wimpy compared to all that."

It was a gorgeous day at the old club and we were content just to sit there and shoot the breeze. But now I was getting the urge to hit the ball.

Evonne stood up momentarily. "Come on you guys, let's work on my new forehand, that's what I came here for."

"I came here to kick your butt." Hitch gave Hammer a wry smile.

"You're on," Todd said, and they slid over to the next court to whack a few, leaving Evonne's new forehand to me, which was fine.

Over the years, I had spent as many hours teaching players as I had trying to beat their brains out, and looking back, it wasn't the victories I remembered most, it was the games I had molded, the strokes I produced, the people I helped; especially the juniors, and oddly enough, the players I had helped for free. It took me a while to learn it, but basically, tennis players (particularly worse ones) don't want to hear about things that will improve their games (even if it comes FREE from a known expert who normally charges a million dollars an hour!)

So over time I learned to control my tennis doctoring instincts, keeping any worthwhile tips to myself (unless actually doing a paid lesson.) If I sensed even a stranger was receptive, however, I might venture forth with some small suggestion. Later, when observing that same player, if I saw the suggestion was taken to heart and the player was actually trying to do what I had told him, I would open up my doctor bag again. And it didn't matter if the patient couldn't afford the medicine; like I said, many of the players I remembered were the ones I had helped for free. They had a trust for my knowledge, and I had a trust for their commitment. I knew they would do what I told them, even if it meant their games would suffer for a while for it. It was all a matter of trust. It could have been a public parker in torn sweats or a CEO clubby in a three piece suit, it made no difference. If the attitude was right, the subject of money was secondary.

Evonne was one of those students who trusted me implicitly, and I trusted her. I could have told her to stand on her head for the entire lesson and she would have done it, if she thought I was serious. She was in good shape, fun to be with, and nice to look at. I recalled her memorable umpiring debut at the old club, down in that rambunctious hole when she was just a raw beginner. What a good sport she had been! That was almost a year ago. Even if we hadn't become such good friends, she would have been impossible to forget.

So while Hammer toyed with Hitch on the next court, Evonne and I hit. I could see her forehand had indeed begun to take shape as she made a conscious effort to loop the backswing. Occasionally, she was late for the hit, but that was to be expected.

On a previous occasion I had shown her how to make the loop, bringing the racket back over an imaginary wagon wheel, and then coming down around the back of the wheel and up into contact with the ball. "Be sure to get to the bottom of the wheel," I reminded her, "before going into the hit."

Now she was ready to compact the circularity of the backswing, so I showed her how to make the loop more efficient, to elongate it into a more horizontal egg-like pattern. "You see," I said, "it's not that different from your old backswing, it's just more fluid and relaxed."

"I like it," she said, after timing a particularly effective crosscourt shot. "It's got more topspin, alright."

"Wait 'til you really start hitting it."

"Maybe I'll beat his booty one of these days." Evonne gestured at Hitch who was walking to our court with his head hanging. "Hammer bageled me," Hitch complained in a sour tone, "and all he did was hit dink shots." (Hitchcock was a good club player, but he was nowhere in the class of a seasoned pro like Todd who could either crush him with power, or simply put him on the operating table and dissect him.)

Looking dejected, a sweat-drenched Hitch sat down on the bench while Evonne and I finished up. She promised to practice her new egg-shaped backswing at home (but not at the dinner table.) "Do it in front of a mirror," I said, "put some music on and get a good rhythm going. Do sets of one hundred, three times a day, and your new forehand will kick butt in a week."

"Did you hear that, Hon," Evonne said, trying to cheer up Hitch, "I'm going to kick your butt in a week!"

"I could believe it," he groaned, "and if I've got any butt left after that, I'll kick it, myself."

"Hey, give yourself a break," I said, "Todd's a world class player. What did you expect?"

"Hell, he didn't play like one. He only hit a couple of regular serves, the rest were underhand. He just yo-yoed me around and drop-shotted me to death, and when he wasn't doing that he hit skyscraper lobs." I knew how Hitch felt; it wasn't just that he got beat, he felt humiliated. But that was his problem, Hammer had a right to play however he chose.

"Maybe Todd wanted to have some fun too," I said, "to do some of the things with his racket he doesn't get to do against better players."

Hammer had gathered up his things and was coming over. He stood before us now looking fresh as a daisy. "Look at him, he didn't even break a sweat!" Hitch griped.

"Hey, if there's one thing I've learned about tennis, it's not to waste energy," Todd said cheerfully. "If you can win playing easy, then that's what you do. There's plenty of things to save your energy for." He looked at Hitch. "Dude, you don't drop a nuclear bomb when a slingshot will do. Right?"

"But you beat me with a pea shooter," Hitch mumbled, his humiliation beginning to lighten in his mind.

"Tenis envy strikes again," Evonne offered enthusiastically. "Hey, maybe there's a tenis envy coefficient!"

"For sure there's an envy factor," Todd put in, "only thing is, it's a lot harder to measure than the sorry coefficient."

"There's probably some correlation between the two," I suggested.

Todd sat down with us on the bench, put his chin in his palm, and stared at the smooth Laykold finish of the court. Finally, he looked up. "The envy factor and the sorry coefficient are interrelated," he said, "and they can be inversely proportional. Although usually they are proportional."

Hitch screwed up his face.

"Now, Hon, don't be impolite to the professor," Evonne scolded playfully, "he's talking about you."

Indeed, this was all very complicated stuff, in as much as we were embarking into previously uncharted frontiers of tennis psychology. Todd tried to explain it to us. As he put it, a player with a humble demeanor could have a high sorry coefficient, and yet he might also be fairly content with his game, something that would yield a low tenis envy factor. And so the two would be inversely proportional. But then again, a high envy player who is extremely dissatisfied with his game, might be so aware of his own shortcomings that he apologizes to his partner all the time, which would make the sorry coefficient and the tenis envy factor proportional.

"What about the guy with high envy who is too pissed off to apologize to anyone, which again inverses the proportionality?" Evonne suggested.

To be sure, it was all very confusing. In general though, we decided that a good player will have a realistic outlook on his game and therefore a low sorry coefficient and also a low envy factor. A poor player could easily have high envy, and being caught up in his own failings, he could be excessively apologetic, as well. We therefore postulated that there is a tenis envy factor to one's game which isn't necessarily, but is usually, proportional to a player's sorry coefficient.

We were beginning to get burned out on the intricacies of what we had gotten into, so taking a suggestion from Hitch, Todd announced that for the time being the envy factor would simply be measured on a scale of 1 to 10. I figured I was probably a 1 or a 2, being pretty content with my game at this point and having other things on my mind that were more important to me than tennis. But I could remember when I was a fanatical youth, wishing desperately I had a better backhand and a powerful serve like the big boys, which would have given me a high envy factor, probably a 7 or an 8. Although I'm sure there were days when I was really feeling it and was a full blown 10.

"The California standard for tenis envy will be 5," Todd announced, and we all headed into the clubhouse.

Chapter Thirty-One

Number 1 Woman

The weather in the Bay Area became unusually damp over the next couple of weeks, prompting Hammer to fly to a tournament in Hawaii, where I envisioned him hanging out on the sunny beach with skimpily clad surfer girls. But I was stuck in Berkeley, where it was gray and drizzly, which I suppose made it easier to sit stapled to a chair in the library and catch up on my studies. (Now that it was near the end of the term, it was obvious that the procrastinator in me was the only one getting ahead.)

The damp weather persisted. But enough! Even when it wasn't raining it was dark and gloomy, and especially in the library where there seemed to be fewer coeds with each passing day. So when Carroll William called, I was primed for action, anything, and the idea that it would be accompanied by sunshine really got my juices flowing. Carroll William, a Fresno teaching pro, was an old friend, and a feared player in his day. Apparently, he had put together a doubles event for local pros and he needed one more guy, so he gave me a call. It was a Sunday round robin with a little prize money, thanks to a local sports surgery center. Berkeley was due for more rain on the weekend, but it looked clear for Fresno, so I said yes.

Carroll William had been a teaching pro at Fresno's Roeding Park for as long as I could remember. He and old Bob Fentayne were always out there. Old Bob was doing mostly group lessons with little kids, and Carroll William had the privates and the more developed youngsters who were tournament bound. Of course it wasn't always like that; when Old Bob was younger he too had energy for one-on-one sessions with serious juniors. But then he slowed down and Carroll William was there to take up the slack. That was the nice thing about a free public facility like Roeding Park; if nobody meddled with it, a first-class instruction program would evolve on its own. Whereas, if the city tried to force a program on the players, a lot would be lost — not just in quality, but in the sense of brotherhood that was holding the place together. Such an intrusion would likely end up in court rental fees. And then it would be over — the "drop-in" mentality of the place would disappear, and instead of being active, the courts would become a concrete wasteland, except for certain times of the day when people with fancy clothes ran around on them.

Because it was near Highway 99, Roeding Park was the perfect site for a traveling tennis player. With fifteen courts and plenty of shade trees, there were always players hanging out, even in the blazing heat of a Fresno summer. On the way to LA, Hammer and I would drop in; and then on the way back we'd stop there too. It was a great way to break up the monotony of the drive. We'd say hi to Carroll William and Old Bob; then we'd sit in the shade of a tall evergreen and shoot the breeze. Maybe we'd hit some balls if we felt like it. Even if it was the dead of night and nobody was there, we'd hop out at Roeding Park and stretch around for a while before climbing back into the old Dart and getting mesmerized by the white line in the middle of Highway 99.

But now it was winter, and the air in Fresno was crisp and sunny. As I pulled off the freeway onto Olive Avenue, things began to look distinctly familiar, especially the tall trees of Roeding Park. I hadn't been to the park in a few years and recalled now its sprawling golf course-like lawns.

My senses sharpened as I drove into the area where pairs of tennis courts were laid out among towering evergreens and great soothing sections of grass. I could see the place hadn't changed much and judging from the number of players hanging around, there was still no fee to play. As I drove around the bend to the far courts, I spotted the ever-bronzed Carroll William leaning against a shopping cart full of tennis balls. Near his little wooden equipment shack, he was talking to a couple of eager high school boys, and then the boys headed off.

I parked the old Dart alongside Carroll William's little shack. He walked over with a long outstretched arm and shook my hand. "Nice timing," he said, "I just finished up. How the hell are ya, Stretch?"

"Good. Now that I'm catching some rays. You know how that is."

"Sure do, brother." It was true that the San Joaquin Valley could have days on end of miserable ground fog and be cold as hell, but according to Carroll William, it had been a pretty good winter so far. "Only had to slosh the frost off my windshield twice," he said, "and one of those times I used a Coors Light."

Carroll William was well humored. A little older than I was, his curly black hair looked thinner than I had remembered. Gray showed at his sideburns now and above his ears, otherwise he had that same lean leathery look. His lanky brown body was all muscle, tendon, and veins.

"So who's my partner for this doubles gig?" I asked him.

"You don't think I'd give you to any of the other guys?"

"Right on, bro," I said, and we stepped onto the near court to hit a few and continue our conversation across the net. He asked me what the "untamed one" was up to.

"The untamed one?"

"You know, your buddy, Todd."

"Oh yeah. He just got back from Hawaii. Now he's in Acapulco playing an exhibition, or maybe it's Guadalajara. I forget which, sometimes he doesn't even know 'til he gets there." Carroll William smiled; I could tell he was thinking about the old days, the days when he, too, would be out there in the badlands of tennis, chasing the dream and seeing the sights.

"Anyway, we call him Hammer now on account of his carrying a hammer all the way to Montana." Naturally, I had to update Carroll William on everything. And he told me about what had been happening in the valley and how there was almost a private takeover of the tennis at the park. "The park players raised hell," he said. "There was stuff in the newspaper and on TV about it. And it wasn't very pretty. But in the end, the Fresno city council vetoed the private takeover. Thank God."

He walked up close to the net and waited for me to come up. His face grew serious. "The most important thing," he said, "is that this place remain free, that's why we have so many people hanging out, and that's why this is one of the best places in the state to find a pick-up game. We wouldn't want anything to happen to that."

Carroll William's leathery face wrinkled up. You could tell it hurt just thinking about it. "Yeah, it was a close call," he said, "some people thought they could make some money, and the city thought they could pass off the maintenance. It was almost a done deal. Anyway, we've got a new Parks and Rec Director now. I think she knows how things are supposed to work. So we should be okay for a while."

I knew what Carroll William was up against. I looked around the place, at all the tennis players, and at those just waiting to play — regular folks carrying tennis rackets, old-timers and peely-nosed juniors. Then I thought about Recreation Park in Long Beach, and how the pay-for-play had wrecked that scene.

"Recreation Park is now called the Billie Jean King Tennis Center," I said, somewhat out of the blue.

"Oh yeah," he said, after thinking for a moment. "Long Beach, right? I hear it's not so good now. Hey, but you know where they've got a good thing going? Up in Seattle. A place called Lower Woodland. They've got ten courts and it's free. A buddy of mine lives up there. He claims it's the best place to find a pick-up game in the country."

With the net between us, we backed away from each other and got into it. We focused more and more on the mission at hand and began to hit harder from deep in the court. "So what are the other teams like?" I called out, "how hard is it going to be to win this thing?"

"Most of the teaching pros around here are soft," Carroll William said between strokes, "so they're not much of a threat. But we did let a team in from Fresno State, and those guys are crunchers."

"I hear Fresno State's got a new coach," I said.

"Yeah, Brad Stine, and he's a real powerhouse. And his guys are good, it'll be tough to beat them. But it doesn't matter, everybody gets a hundred bucks. There's two hundred for the runner-up and three hundred for the winner. We kind of spread the wealth, it's more fun that way."

I could handle that — first-rate doubles and no pressure. There were six teams in, which meant five matches, probably five pro sets. Not a bad way to spend a Sunday afternoon, I thought. Sure beats the hell out of a rained out day in Berkeley.

Carroll William had some Saturday errands to run, so we did a modest tune-up and called it quits. He gave me directions to his house and told me to head over when I was ready; his old lady would let me in. So I stayed on the court and loosened up my service motion for a while, and then I did some stretching exercises on a big wooden picnic table. I could see Old Bob giving a lesson to a group of kids on the court near the backboard. He waved, and I waved back. Then I walked over for a closer look.

His kids were learning the rudiments of the serve. With racket on shoulder, they were practicing the toss. But they weren't tossing the ball at all, which I thought was pretty cool. They were simply moving the arm up through the toss extension, and at the top when they finished, the ball was still held in their fingertips. Old Bob made them hold the ball straight up like that and look at it. He had them do it over and over.

Next, they brought the ball up to that same high position, but this time they were allowed to open and close their fingers briefly at the last moment so the ball jiggled slightly at the apex. One slender Mexican girl with long flowing hair and head tilted skyward looked beautiful as she strained to see the ball jiggle in her outstretched fingertips.

After the lesson, Old Bob told me this miniature ball toss was the key to developing a good serve, since most problems arose when players released the toss early (too low in the motion.) And of course, he was right, because even if it was only a few degrees off, a ball released down low would be way off target by the time it reached the contact zone.

"So, I have them release high and toss tiny," he said. "Then later we allow a taller toss."

Originally from Spain, Old Bob had silver hair and the slightest trace of a Spanish accent. The young Mexican girl I had admired was at his side. "Maria's going to be a good one," he said, his voice worn hoarse from decades on the court.

"I'm going to be number 1," she announced proudly.

"I'll remember your name," I told her, "so in about ten years when you're number 1 woman in the world I can tell everybody I know you."

"I'm going to be number 1, not number 1 woman," she said defiantly. "I'm going to be the best in the world."

"Better than the boys, too?" I asked.

"Better than everybody."

Just then an old cruiser pulled up and idled alongside the courts with the relaxed sound of a seasoned tugboat. It was Maria's uncle. Old Bob gave her a pat on the back and she ran off. Through the car window, Maria flashed us the No. 1 sign with her index finger as the car, moving slowly, chugged its way out of the park.

"She's a cocky one," Old Bob said.

"Cocky is good," I offered. "Anyway, she'll probably settle for number 1 woman when she's about thirteen."

Old Bob chuckled. "Yes, by that time they usually understand the differences."

"No doubt, but the public may not have a clue. I mean it's not like golf."

"It's more like baseball or football," Old Bob agreed. And then his worn voice came alive. "A good sixteen-year-old boy will beat any woman in the world," he said. "That's just the way it is."

But Old Bob told me people could learn a lot by watching the women on TV. "They are not so strong, and they don't move so fast as the men, that is why you can see the strokes better."

The sun arced low behind trees in the southwest, casting great cool shadows on the park as Old Bob and I walked across the grass to our separate cars. I felt suddenly damp and chilled. I was wearing my warmups, but I had broken a sweat hitting earlier, and that was the problem. So I changed into dry clothes as discreetly as possible inside the cramped quarters of the old Dart, and then I headed out to find Carroll William's house.

Having to change a flat tire on the side of the road is a lot better, I suppose, than having to change one in the middle of the road. At least, that's what I told myself when I was about halfway to Carroll William's house and the old Dart limped over to the curb. I wondered if I would have preferred to have the flat tire in Berkeley where somebody driving by might recognize me. But that could prove embarrassing. I mean, after all, how many idiots are dumb enough to get a flat tire? Probably just the idiots dumb enough to be driving an old Dodge Dart, I thought. I got out and looked at the rear tire; it was totally down, well beyond the canister of emergency whipped cream I carried in the trunk. I stood in the street behind my car, staring at the tire. I wondered how hard it would be to change it; I hadn't done that unsavory task in quite a while.

Suddenly a vehicle pulled up right behind me, so close in fact, that I could feel heat coming off the engine. It was a recent model Ford pickup truck. The driver got out. "Nice car," he said, "an old slant-six, right?"

"Uh, yeah, that's right."

Then another pickup pulled up, this time in front of my old heap. A guy with a cowboy hat got out and came over. "Check it out, it's an old slant-six," the first guy told him. "Yeah, an old slant-six with a flat tire," the guy with the cowboy hat said, "let's get this puppy on the road."

The two of them got out tools from the back of their trucks. They made stiff-jawed small talk as they worked on my car. "I see you got a wench on the front a your truck," the one guy said. "Yeah," the other guy replied matter-of-factly, "I always like to keep a wench on the front a my truck. Ya never know when you need a good wench." The guy almost cracked a smile; it must have been an old joke, I figured, that bit about calling a winch a wench.

In a matter of minutes my old heap was jacked up, and the spare I carried in the trunk was swapped out with the left rear tire. "She's ready to roll," the first guy announced, and he tapped at the roof of my car like he was slapping an old friend on the back.

I thanked them as earnestly as I could. "You bet," the one guy said, tugging at the brim of his cowboy hat. He told me I might want to get a new set of tires when I got home. "Them there's purdy durned bald," he said, and he climbed back up into his pickup truck.

"Man, was I glad I didn't have that flat tire in Berkeley," I told Carroll William when I got to his place. "I mean, who would have stopped to help me out there?"

Carroll William laughed. "That's what Fresno's good for, it's a good place to have a flat tire!" He slapped his knee. Then he turned to his wife, "isn't that right, Southerly?" Southerly was a slender thing, who after all the years, had learned to be both friend and mother to Carroll William. She seemed amused, perhaps even relieved, that there was somebody else in the house for him to talk to. She was busy preparing dinner, but she paused now and then to watch us and smile a little.

"I'm telling you, Fresno's got that pioneer ethic," Carroll William said, "that help your neighbor spirit. And everybody here knows how to use tools. It's a great town for a flat tire!" Carroll William slapped his knee again; he couldn't get enough of it, and he elaborated from time to time during the course of our meal. Me, Southerly, and their fourteen-year-old daughter, we all listened patiently at the dinner table as, between mouthfuls, Carroll William described the entire and complex meaning of life in Fresno and how it could be summed up by the changing of a flat tire.

After dinner, his daughter excused herself to go do her homework while we more imaginative elders sat around the crackling fireplace and pretended we were camping. We listened to Southerly play acoustic guitar. Her delicate fingers plucked and strummed with intricate precision, and her once quiet voice grew husky and filled the warm room as she sang out Americana folk songs, one after another. I had visions of Woody Guthrie and the freighters I rode with Hammer, and then my thoughts drifted to Bonnie; or maybe it was her thoughts that drifted into mine. I felt warm, inside and out.

In his chair, Carroll William was asleep now, and the guitar sang more gently. Southerly's voice had become a whisper, its lonely sweetness interrupted only by an occasional muffled crackle from the embers in the fireplace. It was a night I didn't want to end.

I felt well rested at Roeding Park the next afternoon when the tournament was alive with players. A lot of locals had come out after church to watch the action; they lined the grassy edges of the courts, cheering for their favorite club pros. Carroll William in particular had a good following from the park, so we had plenty of yahooing regulars to witness our memorable moments and assist us with calls we might otherwise have been too polite to make in our favor. Among the trees, bedraggled homeless types hung out and spied on us tennis players with the same curious interest they gave to watching squirrels.

Carroll William and I played well together. In fact, in a lot of ways, it was easier to play doubles with him than it was to play with Todd. Carroll William was a solid percentage player; he was also lefthanded, so his heavy slice serve curved naturally toward the opponent's backhand. He took care of business in a very methodical way, without too many surprises. On the other hand, Hammer was less predictable, more magical; so in a sense I had to be more alert while playing with him. But when Hammer and I were on, there was nothing like it. We had knocked off more than a few tour level teams over the years.

Although Carroll William's return was somewhat predictable, the fact that he was lefthanded could be unnerving for the guy serving, since on the very next point the guy would have to shift gears and deal with me as a righthander. And then there was Carroll William's overhead, a lefthanded smash that would suddenly appear full-blown from a place in the sky where you'd expect a righthander to flick hopelessly at an impossibly high backhand volley.

I thought about the little mirror Hammer used to conquer the lefthanded Argentine, and I told Carroll William about it.

"That's brilliant!" he exclaimed. "I think I'll use a mirror too, next time I run into one of those lefthanded sons of a bitch. I can't stand them either."

"But they make great partners," I said, and we high-fived each other.

Between matches we sat in the sunny grass on a blanket Southerly brought. She was at a picnic table now, busily peeling oranges and shelling almonds for the players to eat. Having just lost in a close TB to a predictably tough Fresno State duo, Carroll William and I were heady from an overload of endorphins and tournament vibes that made us feel twenty years younger. That had been our only loss, and with one more match to go, I was close to a two hundred dollar paycheck. But I didn't care that much about the money, not even the hundred bucks I was already guaranteed. It just felt good to be catching the crisp Fresno rays and to be knocking the ball around with other guys who knew what they were doing.

Carroll William told me he had a really special player signed up for the tournament at first, but then something came up. "Yeah, man," he said, "I had Bob Mathias all lined up."

"Bob Mathias? You mean Bob Mathias, the Olympic hero?"

"Yeah, man, the decathlon, two gold medals in a row."

My mind flashed back to *The Bob Mathias Story* I read over and over again in a grammar school primer. Orange Wheaties boxes with Bob Mathias on them flickered by at close range, blocking my view of the nearby trees.

"Yeah," Carroll William said, "Mathias has a place in the mountains near here, grew up in Tulare, you know, just a little ways south." Carroll William told me Mathias just pulled into the courts one day to eat a sandwich. He had come up Highway 99 from LA and was headed to his place in the mountains.

"I didn't know Bob Mathias played tennis," I said, somewhat in awe.

"He doesn't," Carroll William said, "but when I found out who he was, just sitting there eating a sandwich, I had to put a racket in his hand and hit a few balls with the guy. And guess what — even though he's only played a few times — the guy's damn good, especially for his age. He doesn't miss a ball."

"He's only the best athlete in the world," I remarked, "that's got to help."

"Anyway," Carroll William said, "Mathias and I hit every couple of months now, whenever he's passing through. Actually had him recruited to play this thing, but then he had to go to Colorado Springs to see about something at the Olympic Training Center. So I called you."

I felt suddenly dejected. "Oh, I see, I'm not your first choice, you really wanted to play with the best athlete in the world."

But then I thought about it and laughed. Hell, I'd probably play with the guy, too, if I got the chance.

"Can't say that I blame you," I told Carroll William, and our hands raised simultaneously in a high-five salute.

It was awesome hanging with Carroll William. Not only was he a formidable player, but he was also a renowned instructor quick to share subtle insights to the game. And, actually, he hadn't always been into tennis. When he was younger, Carroll William was a first class pole vaulter. But one day he just quit. He liked the traveling, he said, and the skyward rush to the bar. But he preferred his own vaulting stick, and he got tired of lugging that big thing on top of his car. He said he figured a tennis racket would be a lot easier to deal with, especially in airplanes.

So Carroll William might have started late, but because he was a superb athlete, he became an open tennis player inside of three years. Of course, he had some outstanding mentors in his corner, national champions like Larry Huebner and Glenn Hippenstiel who used to play at Roeding Park on a regular basis. Also, Butch Walts and Chris Sylvan were coming up strong out of the juniors, and Carroll William loved to punch it out with them, until they went away to college and made names for themselves on the pro tour.

Carrroll William told me he thought Fresno, being a country setting, was a good training ground for athletes, because as he put it, "the open spaces extend your horizons." He said it was a perspective thing, that it was easier to run long distances in Fresno, for example, since things were more spread out. I recalled how Hammer and I used to train at the horse track at Golden Gate Fields in Albany. Boy, did that giant track extend our horizons! A guy cleaning out the stalls told us each lap around was a mile. Not wanting to get shown up, or more importantly, not wanting to get run over, we'd make sure there weren't any races scheduled when we went over there. And then we'd sneak in at the starting gate and prance down the track excitedly like two-legged stallions. But after the first turn, the novelty wore off and we'd be stuck in the drudgery with our heads bent low like old work horses. One thing, for sure, it was easier to count the number of laps we'd done, after all, a five mile run was just five times around the big track. And then a couple of days later, when we did our usual training at Berkeley High School, we'd go around that little track so fast we almost got dizzy. "Yeah," I told Carroll William, "I know what you mean about open spaces, they do extend your horizons."

"Fresno's good for that," he said, "and face it, the weather is good for sports here, even if it does get a little hot."

Man, did I enjoy the weather we were having that winter day, just warm enough to play in shorts, but cool enough that you needed your sweats during the warmup. I always had mine on between matches when we kicked back on Southerly's blanket and caught the crisp Fresno rays. When we got hungry, we ate almonds by the handful and washed them down with juicy slices of freshly peeled oranges. When we got stiff, we stretched. Actually, Carroll William did Tai Chi, which looked cool as hell and seemed to have a lot in common with tennis movement. Then when we got bored we pretended we were smart and talked about the hole in the ozone and organic farming. Carroll William also talked about nuclear weapons in space. "It's just a matter of time," he said, looking overhead, "hell, they're probably already up there ticking like time bombs." And then he began thinking about that flat tire again.

"These Fresno people may be a little behind the times," he said, "God fearing and all that, but they're solid. There's a lot of pioneer ethic around here — that help your neighbor spirit that changed your tire. That's the stuff that built this country. Of course, there's lightweight city-types too, moving in all the time, just go out to the north end of town and have a look, you wouldn't even know you were in Fresno out there with all those fancy new stores and office buildings."

"You can't stop progress," I offered.

"Progress is great," Carroll William said, "so long as it means cleaner air and water you can drink, and getting the nukes out of space. Hell, when I was a kid you could see the mountains, and you could drink the water. Progress is what fertilizers and pesticides were all about, supposedly. Now look, we're sitting in the most productive agricultural valley in the nation and we can't even drink the water. Hell, half the time we're not even supposed to breathe the air." He gestured overhead, "Wait 'til one of those nukes goes off up there, see what that does to the air."

He took a deep satisfied whiff of the fresh air. "But never mind right now, brother, 'cause we had a good rain a couple days ago and now things are downright tasty. So feel free to suck it in." He took another sensuous snort of the air. Then he pointed to the east, where the peaks in the distance were white. "Look out there, brother. See? You can even see the mountains. You see that snow, that's what it's all about, that's our rivers. Our water. But by the time it gets down here you better be careful about drinking it. Who would've ever thunk it would come to this? Got to buy the stuff in stores now just like it was milk." He pitched me a plastic store-bought bottle. "Here, drink up, brother."

Suddenly we were being called out for our final match, so I took the bottle of water with me. We went to the court near Carroll Williams' little equipment shack and began to square off against a couple of guys from one of the clubs. On the court next to us the Fresno State duo was busy clobbering their opponents. Next to them, two smooth-stroking pros from the historic Fig Garden Club were warming up for their finale.

Roeding Park looked good in its cool greenery of tall trees and sprawling lawns. And now the tennis courts were dressed up with high quality play. Spectators were gathered all around, but mostly near us and two courts over where the Fig Garden pros were playing. I was into it hot and heavy, confident, poised, moving well; when suddenly, play was disrupted. It was a woman, an old bag lady coming noisily onto our tennis court with her shopping cart. She wheeled the cart across both service boxes and headed onto the next court. One of the Fresno State guys froze mid-swing as the old lady rolled her shopping cart onto their court with an air of indisputable superiority. And though her cart had no balls in it, it was brimful with various gadgets and doodads, probably all the latest teaching aids, I thought sarcastically. It was obvious she was a pro. After all, her long tennis dress may have been outdated, but she had that look — that leathery wrinkled look from too many seasons in the sun.

Gravity tugged at her chin with each step as she pushed the rattling cart across the court and mumbled about the old days, about Borg and Connors, Evert and King. Hell, maybe she *was* the real thing! Her eyes were squinty and distrustful; she was someone who had seen too many close calls, too many officials.

Now preferring the other side of the net, the old lady maneuvered her cart around a net post; she guided it deftly with years of familiarity. All she owned was in that rattling cage — not much. But hers was the victory of anonymity, the prize of animal instinct and unshakable confidence. Without a second thought, she rolled right through the action on the last court, and then she bounced over the curb and into the thick grass, where the shopping cart moved in silence. A squirrel sat straight up and watched as the old lady continued her shortcut to the bathroom.

Chapter Thirty-Two

Birth Of A Forehand

Spring came around and so did the junior college tennis season, and then it went, faster than ever, it seemed. We did fair, finishing third in the conference. Statler, apparently partying too much the night before, lost in the semis of the State Championships, which was still good enough to get him a full ride to LSU (something Fernando helped arrange.)

A new summer was already upon us, and Bonnie and I were still on separate continents, or so it seemed. She did come down for a visit a couple of times. We thought it best, for the time being, that I not try to see her in Oregon. Everything was moving so slowly, and yet at the same time, faster than ever.

I finished up my coursework at the University, not with flying colors, but there was a pleasant hue to my performance, which Rudolph, my psych professor, appeared to enjoy. We had became friendly and had lunch a couple of times. He wondered if I was going to get a classroom teaching job somewhere now that I had a Masters Degree, or if I was just going to stick with tennis. I told him I didn't know, that I'd like to do a little of each if possible.

Hammer came and went from his renegade tournaments, pretty much as usual, lying low here and there whenever the mood struck. I went with him to Montana again, this time by air, courtesy of Buckskin Charley. We repeated in doubles and Todd won the singles. When we got back, Hitch and Evonne were tossing wedding dates into the air, most of them for the last Sunday in August.

Then Sheldeen turned ten years old — it was like an alarm clock going off inside my head. He had only a year to prepare before jumping into the increasingly brutal 12-and-unders in Northern California. And he hadn't even played a tournament yet! But he had developed the rudiments of what would eventually become a very good serve, and he was now taking the bus up to the Rose Garden twice a week to hit the wall and practice with the old guys. Sometimes Pedro would join him. But Pedro was less committed; he was primarily there because he liked Mei Mei, who tagged along with her racket now and then. The bus driver liked Mei Mei too, and when the three of them went, he let them ride for free.

After church on Sundays, I usually hit casually with Sheldeen when the rest of the congregation had gone, but now that he was ten years old, reality struck; it was time to get some serious work done. "If you want to play tournaments, you're going to have to learn how to hit a killer moon ball," I told him one day after the other kids had left.

"What's a moon ball?" he asked innocently.

"It's kind of like a lob," I said. "Watch this." Leaving him at the baseline, I went to the other side of the net and arched a high ball to him with a lot of topspin. The ball bounced, climbing quickly over Sheldeen's head. To his credit, he jumped up and glanced it with the tip of his racket.

"Let me try again," he said eagerly, "I bet I can hit it back."

This time I really whipped some nasty, wristy topspin at him. Sheldeen backed up a step. But he didn't have a prayer; he just stood there looking up at the ball as it bounced out of reach. "Hey, cool," he said, "you gonna show me how to do that, Preacher?"

And so the moon ball became the first real weapon we put in Sheldeen's tournament arsenal. It would force the opponent to deal with an extremely high topspinning ball, hopefully on the backhand side where a weak reply would be likely. Then Sheldeen could finish the point with a groundstroke or an easy bounce-overhead. Hell, at his level of play, a good moon ball could win a point outright. Later it would serve as a handy, unrushed approach shot. Eventually it would double as an offensive lob when the kids were older and they came to net more. (It would also be useful when pushed off the court and time was needed to get back in position.)

"It's not a sissy shot," I told him, "and don't let anyone tell you it is, even the pros hit moonies. They just don't do it as much as in the 12's."

I fed him some easy balls and told him to imagine he was hitting the ball over a volleyball net. He got the hang of it quickly on the forehand side, especially when I showed him how to open his stance and be less rigid with the follow-through, allowing the hitting arm to swing up at the ball and then back down as kind of an after-thought. But not wanting to shortchange his game, we worked on developing the shot off his two-hander, too.

I also showed him how to handle the other guy's moonie, by moving toward the spinning ball and catching it before it climbed too high. "If you can hit better moonies than the other guy, you'll beat him," I said, "provided you're also better at returning his."

Of course, the other nice thing about mastering the moon ball is that it tends to let one's groundies out of the closet; it makes the average forehand, for instance, more dynamic. Because it sharpens one's feel for topspin, it becomes easier to hit passing shots and shallow angles with power.

I fed Sheldeen ball after ball, and he hit one arching moon ball after another, essentially emptying my big laundry basket into the air. But he looked troubled as we picked up the balls. "I don't think I got enough topspin," he confided, his young mind comparing the balls he hit with the one I had bounced over his head.

"Who do you want to beat, anyway?" I asked, "a college player or a grammar school kid?"

"Well, okay. A kid, I guess." His confidence had obviously been shaken from trying to loft so many balls and not having total control of the shot. After all, there was a certain delicacy to it; you had to brush the ball just right, especially if you were going to hit hard and not just push a lob back at the guy.

"Forget about the moon ball for now," I said. I told him to grab his racket, that I'd feed him some regular forehands.

"Go ahead and put them away," I insisted, "like you always do, use your normal power forehand."

So Sheldeen let them rip, and sure enough, everything about his forehand was better now — his stance opened up, his body coiled more, and his arm lashed out freely, generating a lot more topspin than he was used to. But the balls landed in the net.

"Hit harder," I told him, "hit as hard as you want."

His eyes lit up. "Really?"

"Yeah, really."

And now the balls zoomed up over the net, and then down into the court, one after the other. It was thrilling. Indeed, we both had so much fun we emptied the big laundry basket again, this time with shots that fired like cannons.

And so, that Sunday, immediately after services, Sheldeen's forehand was born in our funky neighborhood church. It was enough to make a believer out of me.

"I think I'm ready for a tournament," he said.

Bonnie called that night. It was nice to hear from her, except for the fact that she had been planning to come down again but now that school was out her oldest daughter had decided to fall in love for the summer. He was a football player with questionable motives. Bonnie was hesitant to take her eyes off the hot teenager, even for a second.

"I know she's making it with the guy," she told me over the phone, "I can tell. She's more rebellious, in a goofy quiet kind of way. Do you know what I mean?"

"I think so." I said, imagining the exuberant teenager going around the house in silence, the happy secret trying to pop out of her eyes.

Bonnie sounded a little nervous. "I just hope she's smart enough not to get pregnant. I mean it's so easy to get carried away these days, what with the movies on TV and all. I mean how can you trust a guy whose life goal is to dive into the end zone?"

"Yeah, what she needs is a nice wimpy tennis player who's afraid to kiss her."

Bonnie giggled. "That would be a lot more comforting, I'll tell you that."

"What does Harold have to say about all this?"

"He's not concerned in the least, in fact, he likes the boy, sees him as the kind of kid he always wished he could have been. As long as Tammy's home by midnight, everything's fine with him."

"A lot can go on in broad daylight," I offered.

She laughed. "And Harold should know." She was obviously somewhat amused by her husband (and hopefully, still nauseated by him from time to time.)

"Anyway," I said, "I'm sure you've had lots of talks with the girls about the subject."

"It's just that this guy is so ready to score a touchdown."

"Look," I said into the phone, "not everybody gets a tennis nerd, consider yourself lucky."

Bonnie laughed like her old self. I imagined her sparkling eyes, the smooth, cool skin of her cheeks, the hollow at the well of her neck. Man, was I disappointed she wasn't coming down!

"It's good to talk to you," she said softly, and then we said good-byes, our voices transforming into tiny electrical whispers that would meet in the wires somewhere. Perhaps under a pair of doves.

Chapter Thirty-Three

The Living Room Rug

My midnight lover rolled in and snuggled up close. She offered her last dissipating moan in the distant flatlands, but still, I couldn't sleep. When it was time to get up, I had great pains in my chest and stomach. Actually, I'm not sure I even slept. I had to see Bonnie! I had been looking forward so much to her visit, and now an indefinite postponement! I couldn't take it. I festered about all morning; and then I decided to do it. I put my lessons on hold and told Sheldeen to pick up the newspaper so it wouldn't look like I was gone. Then I jumped into the old Dart and split to Oregon, hardly packing or checking to see if the tank had any gas in it. I had tuned up that old slant six the week before and it seemed to be running smoothly, all things considered.

After two hours on the road I was in the middle of the Sacramento Valley and wondering if I was doing the right thing. I was also a bit drowsy. Besides, I felt like being called Honey or Sweetheart, so I pulled into a crossroads coffee shop to be cradled by the waitress.

"Room for cream, Darlin'?" the waitress said tenderly as she poured me a cup of the house brew.

"No thanks, just black," I replied. She was older but nice looking, and her motherly presence was comforting.

"How ya doin', Sugar? Ready for a refill, Darlin'?"

I wondered what Bonnie would end up calling me, later, if we were married and settled in our ways. I kind of preferred Sweetheart. But not all day long, not when she was pouring me a cup of coffee or anything. Just at special moments, when she was kissing me good night, for instance. That would be perfect. "Good night, Sweetheart," she could say, and then I would feel the warm press of her lips. I figured they'd still be soft and buoyant even after all those years.

I finished my coffee and left a fat tip on the table. The coffee wasn't too good, but it did the job, and besides, it was worth it, being called such tender names.

"Drive safe now, Darlin'," the waitress called as I slipped out the door.

What if Bonnie were to call me Darling? I wondered about it as I cruised northward in the old Dart. I figured I'd get used to the name, eventually. But deep inside, I knew that Sweetheart would always be my favorite.

By nightfall I was in Yreka at the top of Northern California and staying at a great motel for just five dollars, a deal I worked out with the manager on the condition that I sleep on top of the bed and not *in* it. She was the type of woman who had a soft spot in her heart for forlorn looking tennis players. I promised her I'd only mess up one towel. "It's okay if you use the bedspread as a blanket," she said, and she handed me the key to the room. I slept peacefully with the windows open, smelling the fresh foresty air.

I pulled out early in the morning and drove down the road to where a big brick Coca-Cola bottling plant sat alongside the railroad tracks. The tracks were beginning to shine in the sun; they seemed to go on forever in both directions. A guy could hop on here and go all the way up to Canada, I figured; or maybe go the other way down into Mexico. I longed to be in a rattling boxcar again. I recalled my trip with Hammer; all those sights, the powerful fresh air rushing in, the smells. I parked the car and let the tennis hobo in me come alive. I wanted the hot Mexican sun; I wanted earthy courts. I wanted brown skinned ballboys, their ever smiling faces. But not a freighter was in sight.

And yet, the Coca-Cola plant was getting ready for one; it was busy as a beehive. On the nearby dock, workers were loading big wooden pallets. One of them spotted me and walked over. Apparently, he also liked forlorn tennis players. "Going to be a hot one," he said, squinting at the low glistening sun. He handed me a couple of six-packs through the open window of the old Dart. He offered me some bud too, but I told him just to toke one up for me some time. Then he flashed me the peace sign and went back to his work.

Now someone was coming from down along the railroad tracks — it was an old-timer wearing a fancy black cowboy hat. He approached my vehicle and peered casually inside. He looked to be about sixty, maybe sixty-five years old. His brown leathery face was trimmed with gray sideburns and a silver handlebar moustache. A flashy bolo tie hung like a pendulum over his red flannel shirt. The stylish old cowboy got right to the point and asked if he could have a ride to "Ory Gon."

"Not going far," he said, "juss ta the other side a the border. Maybe an hour. Jacksonville's where I'm headed, juss a stone's throw from Ashland." He put his cigarette out in the dirt with his boot. "I'll tell ya when we git there," he said, and before I could give him an official invite, the old cowboy was sitting in my car.

Well, why not, he looked harmless enough. Anyway, he was already settled in with his arm resting comfortably on a six-pack of Coke. He told me he usually took the freight back when he came south of the border. "But when I seen you, I figured that'd be the way to go. Them trains can be a while comin'."

"I know what you mean about the freighters," I said, "but they can be a lot better than riding your thumb."

"Yeah" he agreed, "it's not like the old days, nowadays you're mostly juss settin' on your thumb."

Instinctively, the old Dart merged onto the wide open pavement of I-5 and began to pick up speed. It wasn't long before we had cut into the mountains and crossed the border. Great soothing landscapes of green Oregon rolled out in front of the windshield. "See them hills? We're in Ory Gon now," the old-timer said from beneath the brim of his cowboy hat.

"By the way, the name's Ray. Ray Corbin." I told him a little about myself, that I taught tennis and had just got my Masters degree, and he told me he had received an education, too, that he had graduated from Applegate. Applegate University? I couldn't exactly place it.

"I've got good writin'," he explained, "grajeeated from Applegate Grade School. We learnt the Palmer method. It was juss me and three girls that grajeeated. I didn't pass the fifth grade the first time on account a my nines. And on account a my daddy liked ta take me fishin'."

The old guy tapped his fingers on the Coca-Cola from time to time as we drove. He seemed amused. "Yeah," he chuckled, "when I was a kid, Coke was the real thing, it *was* Coca-Cola. Hell nowadays they oughta juss call the stuff *Cola*-Cola, if you get my drift."

"I know what you mean," I said, wondering what it would have been like to have the real *Pause That Refreshes*. That might have come in handy between sets, I figured. I pictured the big red Coca-Cola coolers one always saw at the courts in Mexico, those icy wet bottles, the ever smiling ballboys. Those bright-eyed peasant kids certainly didn't need their spirits lifted any. But their dads, probably their dads could have used a sip of the real stuff now and then.

By the time the old Dart came to his stop at the Jacksonville turnoff, I realized that my passenger was a lot older than I had thought, and apparently, in very good health. I wondered what his secret was.

"I drink and smoke ever day," the old cowboy said, as he hopped out of the car. "And I don't miss a day. But juss two smokes and two beers.

That'll do. Two and two. Two and two is four," he said proudly. "Yes, sir, I'm eighty-three years old. Grew up in these parts. Grajeeated from Applegate. Juss me and three girls. And now, if ya don't mind, I've got ta git ta the saloon."

With his flashy bolo tie reflecting in the sunlight, the old guy looked good in his red flannel shirt and black cowboy hat as he walked down the side of the road. His upper body bobbed with the spirit of a horse that could smell the barn.

I thought maybe I should drink more, maybe even smoke a little. After all, that old-timer was in great shape. But I just couldn't see how the cigarettes were going to help, even in moderation. And then the old cowboy shrank away in my rear view mirror and I thought about Bonnie. More and more I thought about her as I pushed the accelerator down past all those tree-shadowed towns: Medford, Grants Pass, Eugene, Albany, Salem. Finally came the big river city of Portland.

I had made good time. With the windows open, I savored cool damp air as the freeway stretched skyward over the Willamette River. Multiple bridges spanned the great water below me. A few miles ahead would be the monstrous Columbia — I knew I wasn't supposed to go that far — so I merged into an exit lane and dropped down into the city. The Cascades, which had been in full view to the East, disappeared behind the buildings and tall trees of Portland.

I cruised through congested streets for some time, not knowing exactly where I was going. Then the city opened up and a large sprawling park appeared. So I pulled in to collect my nerves and wonder if I was doing the right thing. I mean, maybe Bonnie wouldn't like me visiting.

I contemplated that unpleasant notion as I sat parked beneath the limbs of an old maple tree. Strangely, the tree offered more than its shade, for I was soon distracted by a bunch of small birds who were hopping around on the hood of my car. No, wait, they were eating my car!

At closer inspection I realized the little sparrows were simply eating insects off the old Dart, Oregon insects that had careened off the windshield during the trip and were now spread out like tiny hors d'oeuvres on the bumper and the entire front end. Some were stuck to the headlights and the license plate, but the little sparrows didn't seem too interested in those. When they finished the meal on my car, the little black and brown birds settled back into the limbs of the big tree. They all but disappeared into its husky bark, their camouflage was so uncanny. Indeed, some knotholes I mistook for birds and some birds I mistook for knotholes. The birds had small flecks of white on their shoulders, an observation that finally gave me an advantage in seeking their whereabouts in the tree.

I thought about Charles Darwin for a while and how natural selection had adapted these little creatures so perfectly to their environment. Their camouflage was so exact! Of course, nature, unlike Picasso or Van Gogh, had thousands of years to stumble onto the right colors. I figured Darwin was one very heavy dude to figure out how it all worked. He was right up there with Freud, I supposed. Or maybe Freud was right up there with Darwin, it was hard to say. In life, as in tennis, the difference between number 1 and number 2 was always a very close call.

I knew just enough about Darwin and Freud to feel uneducated for not knowing more. I also knew I was only thinking about them because I was postponing the inevitable, namely, my arrival at Bonnie's place. So I summoned all my courage and started up the old Dart. Twenty minutes later I found Oak Leaf Lane, exactly where a gas station attendant had said it would be. And now I was parked right in front of her house.

It was early afternoon, just about the time Bonnie's husband would be downtown fooling around with his hygienist, and right about the time the mailman might be delivering a letter from me. I wondered if Bonnie would have preferred a letter. Maybe I was blowing it. After all, we had kind of agreed that it was best for her to visit me. But then I reminded myself that you've got to take action if you're going to make a relationship happen.

The neighborhood was old and elegant. Pink-barked dogwoods lined the stone walkway, where intrepidly, I walked up to the front door, wondering if Bonnie was home and where her kids were; and indeed, who else might be home. The drapes were closed, so it was impossible to see in the house.

Butterflies swirled inside as I stood close to that big Portland door listening for some clue. But nothing, not a sound, although I thought I heard a dog bark at the side of the house. Yes, it was a dog, a large dog barking angrily now like there was an intruder at the gate! I decided to ring the bell, even though it was somewhat unnecessary at this point.

Chimes sounded from within, then footsteps, delicate footsteps, a woman's footsteps, I hoped. The door swung open and Bonnie stood there looking as if she had been hit with a stun gun. She threw her arms around me and all the butterflies inside me fluttered to the far corners of the universe, and then they settled back down into my stomach. "Stefan! Wow," she exclaimed, "talk about surprises!" (It was nice to be called by my real name for a change; sometimes I got kind of tired of just being Stretch.)

She led me into the living room and we kissed. It had been a long time, too long. Her lips were buoyant, like little pillows, in fact. But then I drew away and looked around nervously. "Don't worry," she said, pulling at my ear with her teeth, "no one else is home."

There was the quick sound of zippers opening as we slipped each other's clothes off right there in the living room. We stopped only to kiss newly exposed areas and fumble with stubborn buttons. And now we stood a foot apart in our stocking feet. I looked down self-consciously at my nakedness and thought of Henry Miller, his great line about "it" being light and heavy at the same time, like a piece of lead with wings on it. I wondered what Bonnie thought about "it." Her nakedness was certainly appealing to me, supple and pink and surprisingly youthful. She extended her arms with a warm smile, and the gap between us closed.

We slid down into the fluff of the rug and I recalled the tournament in Chico I had played when I was fresh out of college, the girl who had shared her sleeping bag with me on that first night, and her doubles partner who took her place the next night. It was pitch dark. The doubles partner and I were in the middle of it on somebody's living room rug. We could hear snoring in the corner of the room. "Is that okay?" I whispered to the girl, unsure if my piece of lead was meeting her expectations. "Try going in circles," she said. Circles for crissake, what did she mean by circles? Hell, I was having enough trouble just going forward and backward. I settled on a kind of sideways maneuver that seemed to satisfy the girl. "Yeah, like that," she said, and then suddenly I could feel Bonnie moving all around me, pressing in on me, massaging me with a firm yet slippery grasp. I moved against the current of my impulses, and all I could think about was what Tom Robbins said about all the water in the world trying to come out of one tiny pinhole. And then the dormant pump inside of me released itself. In slow motion. Again and again. And then again, the surge of life broke free. Bonnie moaned tenderly and we fell asleep right there on the rug.

Half an hour later we got up and put our clothes back on, neither of us needing the assistance from the other we had apparently required in removing them. "How about something to eat?" Bonnie said, and she fixed some sandwiches. We ate them with iced tea on the back deck, and it was just as I had imagined — redwoods, cedars, and pines all around, moss-covered limbs, lots of ferns. Bonnie's golden retriever, Syd, who had been barking so ferociously before, now lay on the deck alongside us, watching dreamily as squirrels and jays flitted about the brushy hillside.

Bonnie told me she had been doing a lot of painting lately. She led me upstairs to a spacious studio that smelled faintly of turpentine. There were dozens of oil paintings, some on the walls and some still in progress on easels. Mountainscapes, rivers and forests, city scenes, towns with quaint shops, children at play. I was impressed. They had that three-dimensional quality good oil paintings evoke.

"I had no idea you were an artist," I said, somewhat astonished.

"I was an art minor in college," she said, "but I majored in physics and didn't have much time to dabble in it back then."

"Physics!" Now I was really impressed.

"I was going to be a professor, was in my second year of grad school, in fact, when Harold and I got married. Had to quit, get a good paying job to put him through dental school. You know the rest, raised a family and all that."

"It's a shame you had to give it all up."

"Hey, now it's my time," she said, her blue eyes sparkling. "I paint every day."

"What about the physics?" I asked.

"Oh, it's still a part of me. It's kind of a spiritual thing, it gives me an outlook, a foundation for my life. And for my paintings." I must have looked confused.

She explained patiently. "It's like what Einstein said about religion, that dedicated scientific researchers are the most religious of all people, because they believe in a cosmic type of religion." She told me Einstein said it was the most important job of artists and writers to keep that spark of cosmic spirituality alive.

She took my hand. "In my work, that's what I try to do, I try to convey a sense of cosmic spirituality. It's a subtle thing. Sometimes it's more obvious, other times it may not exist in the painting at all, except as the viewpoint I had when I created the work."

I wasn't well versed in art, but I could see she was talented, that the paintings looked real and that she wasn't just feeding a bunch of seagulls on the canvas and trying to pass it off as art.

"A lot of people call themselves artists," I said, "but they can't even draw."

Framed on one wall was a turbulent seascape of jagged whitecaps — powerful sprays thrashed at dark mists and ominous clouds — reflected throughout were thin fiery veins of lightning. No wait, I think it was a scene from outer space! Some sort of storm in space.

"You've got to be able to render detail," Bonnie said, "make it real, you go from there."

She told me she painted on site or from memory, but she never used photographs as they tended to get in the way of her interpretation of things. And I told her I didn't know a lot about Einstein but whatever he said I would definitely go along with. I said I thought her paintings belonged in a museum or something. She hugged me and whispered that she had a show coming up in Seattle. She said that, actually, it was her third show and that the paintings were beginning to sell.

Wow, I thought dizzily, as I followed her down the stairs from her studio, there is a lot to this woman. I mean, she's an artist and she almost became a physicist.

"I was going to be a doctor once," I said somewhat by accident, as we sat down in the living room. Bonnie turned to me with an inquisitive look.

"It wasn't like I had to quit or anything," I told her, "it wasn't like your situation. It was all my choice. And I chose tennis."

"Well, good for you." She actually commended me! "I'm sure you made the right decision."

I was about to tell her I wasn't so sure I had made the right decision, when suddenly there was the sound of a car entering the garage. Then the garage door closed with a thump. I stood up. Bonnie told me not to be concerned, that it was just the girls. "Harold's hardly ever here," she said. "Anyway, he's got the office closed for a few days, he's over in Bend at a rock concert."

"A rock concert? You mean like Woodstock?"

"Yep, a big outdoor rock concert. He's with you-know-who." Bonnie laughed. "I guess he thinks he's a hippie now. I've got a spy in the office next door, she tells me everything."

"Hello," Bonnie called out to the girls as their giggling voices came into the house; and then they came striding into the room. "Guess what, we've got company. You remember our friend, Stefan?"

They froze right over the spot where Bonnie and I had been intertwined. The younger one kept looking down at the rug; I couldn't tell if she was shy or if she thought maybe the rug looked a little flattened down.

Bonnie told them I had just come up from Berkeley, and we sat together and exchanged pleasantries for a while. Apparently, Tammy, the older girl had a part-time job for the summer in a record store. She had just picked up her sister from a photography class she was taking. I told them I was still teaching tennis and also coaching a junior college team.

"What ever happened to that guy, what's-his-name?" Tammy asked. She was the one with the football player boyfriend, and super cute, not that her younger sister wasn't an attractive little lady in her own right.

"Hammer, uh, I mean, Todd," I said. "He's still around, doing his thing, playing tournaments here and there." Mere mention of Todd loosened everybody up and brought giggles back into the room. No doubt the girls remembered his free spirited playfulness, his good looks and flowing rock star hair.

After a while, they looked a little fidgety. "Nice to see you again," Tammy said. "Yeah," the younger one put in bashfully, looking down at the rug, "Mom talks about you all the time." And then they left to go call their boyfriends or something.

Wow, so I guess I wasn't exactly a stranger in the house. Bonnie sat there smiling, looking like the cat that swallowed the canary.

Bonnie thought we should all get to know each other better, so the next day the four of us went for a hike in the foothills below Mount Hood. Actually, there were five of us, counting Syd, who was the unofficial leader of the trek.

It was amazing how that retriever stuck to the trails. He was too smart to beat out a path of his own, although you could see he was tempted to jump into the brush whenever he saw a squirrel or heard something. But he just stood there on the trail watching, until we all passed him by, at which time his instinct to lead took over and he ran again to the head of the pack. I thought about Hammer; I figured if he were with us he'd be racing the dog for top spot.

It felt great to work my legs; I had made good time getting to Portland, but all that driving had stiffened me up. Of course, the main thing was that the old Dart had survived the trip.

We moved at a steady pace as we made our way in and out of sun-streaked forest at the base of the big mountain. Then at last, we stopped to rest at a small but fast moving stream. Yes, the sound of water! I thought about the little wooden bridge in Berkeley at the north end of campus where Bonnie and I had leaned against the rail and listened to the water trickle, to its primordial wisdom. Then I shut my eyes and imagined I was hearing Rock Creek gurgling peacefully in the distance, all the way from Montana. I could hear its wisdom, too. But I longed for the big water Buckskin Charley had shown us in the gorge, that misty spray, wet boulders, the loud rush of waterfalls. Yes! That was water, roaring water with a hoarse voice that called out its wisdom to the far reaches of the universe.

Syd stood by the little stream, where he lapped at the water's edge for some time, perhaps enjoying its modest sound as much as I was. Then Bonnie passed out sandwiches. The girls talked about their boyfriends and college and working at the record store. We all just sat there on stumps and felled logs, checking each other out and eating, and wondering how I fit into the picture, I suppose.

Through the cedars and pines, the rugged top of Mount Hood looked good in the near distance. I was amazed there was still snow on it.

"It's a dormant volcano, eleven thousand feet," Bonnie said.

"Dormant? You mean like Mount St. Helens?" I asked.

"Oh, it's more dormant than that," Tammy giggled.

"Yeah," her younger sister said, "but just don't go sitting on top of it when they tell you to evacuate."

The hike had been a good idea; I was glad I got to know the girls better. They were full of life and laughter and plenty smart. Tammy was transferring to the University at Eugene, where she would be a communications major. And the younger one would join her there; she was getting some sort of scholarship for scoring 800 on her math SAT's.

Back at the house, reality struck that second night. I knew I'd be leaving in the morning. The lavish guest room I had shared with Todd the previous summer felt empty now without him. I wondered if Bonnie would sneak in, or if I would sneak into her bedroom. I figured the living room rug was out of the question. Maybe she'll come in here on the pretense of collecting my laundry, I mused. That would be a good excuse. Anyway, the girls knew what was up; they knew things weren't working out with the old man and I'm sure they realized their mother and I would want to spend some time together.

She came in alright, sooner than expected. We talked about everything — Einstein and religion, my tennis, her paintings, what her daughters thought of me. "They think you're cool," Bonnie said, "especially for an older guy."

"What about Harold?" I asked, "what do they think about their dad?"

"Oh, they still love him. They just think he's being stupid. They gave up arguing with him about it."

"You mean they talk to him about it?"

"Oh, it's out in the open now, we've all done the counseling thing, like one big trying-to-be-happy family. We all sat in a circle with a therapist and listened to Harold explain why he needs the freedom to have a new life."

"And that's it?"

"That's it. He's looking at apartments now. I told you I have a friend in the office next door."

I didn't know what to think. "Would you say things are working out, then?" I asked somewhat uneasily.

Bonnie said she thought so, but that she felt sorry for her husband. "I mean what's he going to do when Ms. Hygienist dumps him? Oh, well, I guess that's his problem." She rolled over on the bed and kissed me. She told me she loved me. The words echoed in my mind, the soft sound of her voice, repeating itself, over and over as I drove down woodsy I-5 the next morning. It was just the old Dart and me, and the delicate sound of Bonnie's voice. And the lingering feel of her skin next to mine.

Chapter Thirty-Four

Defining Quickness

I returned from Oregon feeling a whole lot better. But all too soon my usual routine enveloped me and I missed Bonnie, even more than before (especially at night when that freighter moaned quietly in the distant flatlands.)

It was the same old thing, day after day, week after week. Time kept moving by, quickly, yet slower than ever it seemed. I felt like a spectator stuck in the wake of things streaming by — my classes at the University, the JC season, the Montana tournament; and now Evonne and Hitch were married! It had been a quiet September wedding, with a not so quiet reception.

Winter rains hit as if from out of nowhere, and then spring and the JC tennis season rolled by again so fast I felt as if I had been run over by a truck. When it came time to go to Montana for a third time, I just sat there dazed with tread marks across my forehead.

So Hammer went out there by himself. He met up with Fernando and won the doubles. But he lost the singles final to Statler, who was now playing some pretty good ball for LSU. (I heard Buckskin Charley gave Statler his full prize money in crisp green even though the kid had signed something saying he was an amateur and would only accept hospitality.)

Boy, did I miss Bonnie! She still hadn't officially split with her husband, but at least they weren't living under the same roof. Now that the girls were both away in college, the dentist figured he could take an apartment, just like Bonnie had predicted. And I suppose that was a step in the right direction, but the great distance between us still ached in my gut, especially when I found myself up at the Rose Garden at sunset, or when I was watching a romantic movie on TV. Bonnie came down to Berkeley now and then, and I went up to Portland on occasion, but sweet as those times were, they were too few and far between during the two years we had been lovers. I tried to convince her to enroll the girls at UC or San Francisco State so she could move closer and still keep an eye on them.

As for Sheldeen, he was now in his last official year of the 12's, and his game was coming along well. He had won two tournaments the previous season, finishing with a year-end ranking of thirteen, which wasn't too bad considering he didn't come from a tennis family and his practice matches consisted primarily of Pedro and the old guys at the Rose Garden. I still worked with him after church on Sundays, and also on Wednesday evenings. And now the pro at the Berkeley Tennis Club stepped into the picture, inviting Sheldeen to train with his kids twice a week in a clinic for tournament players. The package was just beginning to come together for Sheldeen, but he still had a long way to go — the goal for this year was to get him ranked in the top five. Then, by the time he was in his second year of the 14's, he would have to be 1 or 2, for it was the juniors who held down the top two spots in Northern California who had a chance at pro careers. Top-tenners got scholarships and had fun traveling with the game for a while, but looking back over the years, it was always the one or two players who consistently dominated their age groups who had a shot at greatness.

I heard through the grapevine that Danny, my former junior star, had quit the game. Apparently, his parents couldn't handle the fact that he was only ranked twenty-second in the sixteens, so they just kind of let tennis fade out of his life. Which was a real shame, because it was only the kid's first year in the sixteens and with the right approach he could have easily cracked the top ten the next season. The poor guy probably figured it was easier not to do tennis than to deal with the anxious trip his parents laid on him. I heard his dad had him serving balls before school every morning on their private court, and that he had switched coaches five times since they left me. Obviously, tennis had become a burden, so Danny quit altogether. Anyway, it was time for the kid to get away from his father's whip, and if that meant giving up a sport he once loved, then so be it. Hopefully, when Danny was older, perhaps as a grown man, there would come a time when he would take his racket out of the closet and hit the ball again, just for himself. It would be kind of like going for a bike ride for the first time in years — those joyous sensations of youth would come back. Surely then, he would rediscover why he had once played the game. In which case, all of his parents' efforts wouldn't have been in vain. Though they probably wouldn't see it that way.

I took Danny's picture out of the drawer where it had been for nearly three years and put it on the bookshelf next to a recent one of Sheldeen. On the timeless court of the bookshelf they were both 12 years old and looked like contemporaries. Danny was up in the air, hitting that perfect leaping overhead; Sheldeen was in follow-through stride, having just clocked one of his big forehands on a run to the net.

I looked at the photos for a moment, and then I went out the door; I had a lunch meeting with the pro at the Berkeley Tennis Club. I needed to make sure we were both on the same track as we fine-tuned Sheldeen's game. I had begun to notice habits he was picking up from the other kids, things I didn't necessarily approve of.

For one, Sheldeen appeared to be volleying with one hand off the backhand even when he wasn't stretched out, using a flimsy one-handed poke when he could have really crunched the ball with two hands. He was also beginning to release the left hand on the groundstroke and go into a one-handed slice backhand when he could have executed the same shot better with two hands.

"It's strange," I told the Berkeley pro as we sat at a quaint cafe on College Avenue, "you'd think the teaching industry would catch up to the cutting edge of tennis. I mean, the superiority of the two-hander is accepted now, but apparently just for topspin. You tell a kid to hit slice and he thinks he's automatically supposed to take one hand off the racket."

"You can blame it on the players at the top," the pro said, "the ones kids see on TV. And their coaches, they're all releasing when they slice the backhand. I think it's a perspective thing. Underspin is inherently a defensive maneuver used for control, so the idea of hitting that same shot powerfully is not something they're even tuned in to."

"Yeah well, when the ball is above the net and you have a straight shot at the court, you might as well let it rip."

"I couldn't agree more," he said. "After all, when a lumberjack chops down a tree with an ax, he is essentially hitting a slice shot, and he sure as shit doesn't do it with a one-handed backhand. If he did, it would be the last tree he ever chopped down." The pro held his arm; he winced as if his elbow had a great pain in it.

"Yeah," I chuckled, "one-handers do have a lot more arm trouble."

"Two hands is definitely the way to go," he said, "for everything off the backhand wing — topspin, slice, volleys, you name it. If you can snag it with two hands then that's the way to go. If it's not in the strike zone for two, then you keep it in play with the one-hander, but that's basically just a backup shot."

I sure was relieved to hear him describe it like that. But then I wondered why so many of his kids released a hand on routine backhand volleys, thereby not generating the power to put the ball away, or even the control to aim it well, for that matter.

"It becomes a judgment thing," he told me, "when to volley with two hands and when to volley with one hand, and most of my kids are lazy. They don't want to have to make the decision, even though in the end it would come as automatic as switching from a forehand to a backhand grip. So they go into the one-hander by default when they're up at the net or going into slice from the backcourt."

"Well, Sheldeen's not a lazy kid." I stressed the point. "And he wants to do it the best way possible. You don't exactly have to get stern with him, just explain which way is better and he'll take over from there."

"I'll show him a picture of Jimmy Connors hitting a high backhand volley with two hands. That should do it."

"Right on," I said. I imagined Connors in mid-air, hitting that big putaway shot. (That same high backhand volley hit with only one hand was, in fact, the weakest shot in the game, but with two hands it became like a mini-overhead. It was a case of the weakest hitting zone transforming into one of the most powerful!)

There were even guys like the South African, Frew McMillan, who used two hands on BOTH sides. I imagined McMillan slashing his way to the net in doubles, wielding his racket with both hands like a medieval axe man gone mad. Once Frew closed in on you, you were done; nobody could keep up with the guy.

"Don't worry about Sheldeen's backhand volley," the Berkeley pro said, "we'll fix it. Anyway he's a good kid, I get a kick out of him, he never leaves the court until every single ball is back in my shopping cart."

"He's the helpful type," I offered.

"I think it's more than that — he just plain hates to leave the court."

He told me the Cal coach was at the club the other day with some of his guys, and he noticed Sheldeen. He was fascinated by Sheldeen's speed and commented that big as Sheldeen was, he moved with the light-footed grace of a more slender athlete.

"The kid's quick," I said.

"Come on, tell it like it is," the pro said, "the kid's quicker than shit."

"Okay then, he's quicker than shit," I said, wondering for a moment how fast actual shit was, and if it was even in the same league as something like piss, for instance. He's really faster than piss, I thought. Which, I suppose, made him faster than shit.

The Berkeley pro asked about Hammer. He said he was looking forward to playing doubles with us again, that he needed it, that it helped him get in touch with his real self.

"There's no substitute for playing," I said.

"Yeah, but you've got to be playing with the right people," he added, and he stood up to go. I had to boogie too, so we went our separate ways.

The thick pedestrian flow alongside College Avenue engulfed me as I came out of the cafe and made my way down the sidewalk. I imagined Bonnie was by my side, her warm hand, her body brushing up against mine. I figured she'd want to stop now and then and check out some of the more artsy stores on the strip. I was also thinking about Sheldeen's game, his power and speed, when suddenly, a very fit looking kid approached from out of the hubbub and extended his arm. We shook hands heartily. He was tall and sinewy and bronzed by the sun, and I didn't know who he was, but he was obviously a tennis player, probably in his early twenties.

Our palms remained clasped for some time.

"Remember me?" he said, as people on the sidewalk maneuvered to get around us. "I'm Ernesto. You taught me and Felipe how to play, remember? It was at that little park behind the rec center."

Now I remembered the kid, vaguely. Ernesto Garza. He was one of six or eight youngsters we put on a summer league team when I was working for the Oakland City recreation department. He was still grasping my hand.

"Hey, man," he said eagerly, "you're the reason I made it, I doubt I would have ever won a match if you hadn't chilled out my serve ten years ago."

Garza? Garza, now that name really rang a bell; there was a Garza knocking guys off in some of the satellites; I read about him in a USTA publication. Ernesto. Yes, Ernesto Garza! He was considerably taller now.

"I never would have recognized you," I said, somewhat dazed.

"Yeah, man, remember, you fixed my serve. Remember, I was always double-faulting. But then you showed me how to get more bite on the ball, so I could hit my second serve hard and still get it in. Remember?" He was looking at me in awe, as if I had just popped up out of a manhole. Finally, he let go of my hand.

"Well, I've been kickin' butt ever since then," he said.

It was satisfying to know I had helped the kid, that I had helped put his serve on track. Of course, he hardly even had a serve back then, but what little there was apparently got off to a good start. The USTA article, in fact, had described Garza's serve as one of the more formidable weapons on the tour. All of which, I suppose, goes to show the importance of building a good second serve.

And yet most players, especially those at lower levels, get carried away with trying to cream a big first serve. But when that understandably wild first serve misses, there is an instinct to let up on the second serve, in fear that it will miss as well. The result is that the second serve never gets a chance to be hit hard. Nor does the first serve get a chance to truly develop! Because the only way to really feel free to take chances with the first serve is to know that if it misses, there is a great second serve ready to back it up. And so, building a big second serve is actually the first step in building a big first serve. But like I said, most people approach it the other way around.

I remembered Dennis Van der Meer; I would always be indebted to him for giving me an authentic *American Twist* second serve when I was a teenager. That hot kicker became the backbone of my game.

The suntanned kid looked confident as hell. "You're only as good as your second serve," he called out with a thumbs-up salute, and then he was swept away by the flow on the sidewalk.

Nice seeing you, Ernesto, I should have said, but I just stood there like a bump on a log, thinking about it all. I felt stunned, as if I had just been aced. By a second serve.

Chapter Thirty-Five

The Motel

When Todd barged into my apartment in the morning, I was up but not exactly awake. I wasn't sure I was ready for all the energy that was coming through my front door.

"We're going to Monterey for a couple of days," he said excitedly, like a school kid on his birthday.

"The Monterey Jazz Festival isn't 'til the fall," I said, vaguely remembering how Hammer would suddenly disappear on that weekend. He always wanted me to go with him, but I could never get away.

"No, man, that's not why we're going. There's a meditation center out there I've been meaning to get to, and Pop's car is in the shop."

Obviously, Hammer needed a lift, and since the old Dart was still alive, I was solicited into the plan. "If I go, I'm just hanging out," I told him. "I don't think I can take all that intense meditation."

"Ok, suit yourself. I'll set you up at Lloyd and Mary's, they have a place in Carmel, you can crash there, and then pick me up when I'm done."

"Or, you could stay at The Motel," he noted.

"You know I couldn't do that, it would spoil everything."

"True," he said pensively. "It's settled then, you're staying at Lloyd and Mary's place. It's a lot more grand than The Motel, anyway."

And so, the next afternoon the old Dart was off and cruising down Highway 1 to the Monterey peninsula. When we got near Carmel, we took the 17 Mile Drive exit and wound our way down the hill to a wooded road near Asilomar State Park. A partially camouflaged sign in the brush said, Buddhist Meditation Center.

"We're here," Todd announced, and he jumped out of the car. "Come get me tomorrow at one o'clock." He looked around excitedly. He told me not to keep Lloyd and Mary up too late. "They're old and they turn in early. But they're good people. You'll like them."

He handed me a piece of paper with their phone number on it. Then he disappeared into the forest carrying only his jacket. The end of his toothbrush stuck out his pants pocket.

The day was far from over, so I had plenty of time to kill before dropping in on my hosts. I toyed with the idea of checking out John Gardiner's fancy tennis ranch in Carmel Valley, where ripe yellow Penn balls fell off apricot trees and sliced backhands went for $10 a tray. Yes, cultivated tennis games for the rich and famous! Maybe I could help out with a serving clinic, or just pour the wine at sidechanges.

Actually, I didn't need to go anywhere at all. I was in Pacific Grove, after all. PG, as they call it. PG was the perfect place to wander around in a melancholy mood and think about the old days. So that's what I did. The little coffee shops and eateries and vistas of Monterey Bay were a welcome mat to the good times past of my life, to those early years before my tennis game had peaked. Indeed, life itself seemed it would go on forever then. Now every time I played there were aches and pains to remind me that it wasn't just my tennis game that would end one day. It would all end at one point. Hopefully, later than sooner.

As I strolled along the sidewalk shops on Lighthouse Boulevard, I tried not to think about Bonnie too much. But there were so many couples walking hand in hand! Occasionally they stopped in doorways to read menus together as steamy aromas slipped past their cheeks into the cool blue air. So I thought about Mexico, years ago when Hammer and I first went down there to show those clay-courters a thing or two about serving and volleying. Those were the days! Big red metal coolers of Coca-Cola on every court. All those icy wet bottles! Swigging them down at sidechanges in that pre-Gatorade era as a big-eyed ballboy stood by with towel in hand. Then swapping for the towel and giving the kid the ok to finish the bottle of Coke. His bright eyes and white smile. The hot sun, the earthy courts, and of course, elegant senoritas all over the place. Admiring and eager, their conflicted minds didn't know what to make of us tennis nomads from the States. But some of their countrymen did, and though we may have taught them a thing or two about volleying, they taught us more than we needed to know about sliding and skidding on that crushed brick surface. In the stadium court now, I could hear the sudden roar of the crowd. I could feel the dry Mexican sun. As I walked along Lighthouse Boulevard, I could even see the lovely senoritas wearing their wide-brimmed hats. But mostly I imagined those brown-skinned ballboys, their big smiles and bright eyes.

Since it was only a few blocks away, I decided to hike down the hill to the water and watch Monterey whitecaps crash against the rocks at Lover's Point. Sea lions would be camouflaged as they sunned themselves on various shoreline rocks, and it would be fun to spot them. But Bonnie wouldn't be with me and that would be tough.

I didn't last long, actually, and retreated back across the street to where Lover's Point Restaurant sat on the inside bend of the road. And there it was, right next door. The Motel! *BORG'S MOTEL,* the sign said in big neon letters. I stared at the sign for a while. Then I scanned the long string of rooms; I took in the overall scene, the cypress trees, the view of the bay. Its simplicity had a calming effect, and Bjorn Borg may as well have owned the place as far as I was concerned. The rooms were plenty adequate and certainly reasonable, considering the area.

Borg's Motel is our favorite motel on the planet, but Todd and I never stay there. The lobby is about as far as we get; we don't ever want to find something wrong with the place, like a leaky faucet, a spot on the rug, or a burned out light bulb. It remains a virgin in our minds, an unblemished reminder of perfect old days and a great champion.

I thought about Borg and McEnroe, Vilas and Nastase as I hoofed back up to where the old Dart was parked on Lighthouse Boulevard. Man, those were the days! Too bad those guys weren't playing much anymore. Of course, when their countries needed them for a big Davis Cup match they still coaxed them out occasionally. Jimmy Connors was another guy who was still in the news, but mostly with his senior tour. And Martina Navratilova continued to compete here and there. So even though it was the end of an era, I still felt connected to it. I would always feel connected to it.

Suddenly, I got an urge to see the little neighborhood tennis center in Pacific Grove. Todd and I used to play tournaments there, but they never seemed to have much prize money, so we gradually stopped going altogether. And yet, I always liked that little PG tennis complex and its cozy stadium court. There were even locker rooms. In fact, I envied kids who lived in the neighborhood and could just walk across the street for the tennis. The only trouble was, Pacific Grove kids were too soft to ever get really good at tennis; they didn't have the burning desire that's bred in the ghetto or in the nearby lettuce fields of Salinas, for instance. PG was a sleepy little town, and likewise, its tennis players were a sleepy lot, friendly and polite, but not made of the stuff that would develop a champion. Over the years, there were some excellent teaching pros at the little PG complex, but they just didn't have the material to work with. And there was one other problem — it cost a few dollars an hour to play there, so even if there was a poor kid with the right hunger, it was unlikely he'd get a chance.

Nobody was at the courts when I cruised by in the coming dusk along Gibson Avenue. The place looked as I remembered it, but strange and lonely in its emptiness. Everything was so quiet, actually kind of eerie, and I knew I'd start thinking about Bonnie if I stuck around, so I didn't even get out of the car. I just drove past the place a couple of times, and then I headed up the hill to Lloyd and Mary's.

The name Morain was etched into a log at the side of the road, so I knew I was there. Tucked away in the tree-limbed hills of Carmel, they had a big spread with a guest cottage and a wide blacktop driveway that looked more like a small airstrip. From up on the front porch I could see the vast blue Pacific; to the south were the low sprawling mountains of Big Sur.

Lloyd wasn't at home when I rang the bell, but Mary let me in and welcomed me with a warm hug. Dressed in clothes from the 50's, she was a frail wrinkled thing with a pleasant New England accent.

"I don't know where Lloyd is," she said. "That's one of the things I learned early on in our sixty years of marriage — don't ask hubby where he's going when he says he's going on an errand."

Papers and pamphlets were scattered throughout every room in the house. And books were everywhere, but there wasn't a bookshelf in sight; like the papers, they were grouped in piles on the floor and on table tops.

"You'll have to excuse the mess," Lloyd said, as he came energetically into the house. "Mary's got papers everywhere, she's even got them in the oven in the guest house."

Mary blushed. "Well, when I finish my research I'll take them out of there."

"You ought to turn on the oven right now and be done with it," Lloyd laughed. Then he turned seriously to me. "No, it's true," he said. "Truly, we've got projects all over the place. I just finished my book last month, you should have seen this place then!"

Actually, Todd had told me that Lloyd was an editor for a national publication and that he and Mary were recently voted philanthropists of the year. But for all the money they had, they hardly spent a dime on themselves, and even so, it was only on bare necessities.

Lloyd's faded old flannel shirt was threadbare at the elbows. He walked up and took hold of my right biceps. He squeezed my arm, kneading the flesh. "A big strong tennis player like you, let's arm wrestle," he suggested.

Before I knew it, we were locked wrist to wrist over the kitchen table. I never was very big on arm wrestling because it tended to aggravate my tennis elbow. But I figured, hey, this guy is almost ninety years old, if it makes him happy, why not?

"It's the skinny guys like you and me who are hardest to put down," Lloyd said, as he slid his palm loosely over mine and jockeyed into position. "The big guys with all the muscles aren't so tough, the strength is in the tendons."

Slowly, I felt the vise of his grip tighten around my hand. And then it was over. I was sure glad there weren't burning coals on the table, like in the days of Ben Hur and the Roman Empire, and I told Lloyd so.

"They don't do that much anymore," he said, "but once in a Romanian peasant village I saw two guys going at it over steaming gruel."

"By the way, don't feel bad," he told me, "I may be twice your age, but just last year I put down a Norwegian champion when Mary and I were setting up a school in China."

"He was from Denmark," Mary corrected from where she stood at the stove.

Apparently, the wiry Lloyd didn't practice or even work out; he simply arm wrestled once in a blue moon when the occasion arrived. Man! I wished I could prep for tennis matches like that.

During the course of our rather modest meal, I tried to blend in unobtrusively, like the tablecloth, so my kind hosts could discuss their more intellectual concerns without having to water it down on my account. But they were bent on teaching, and more than once directed their remarks at me.

Lloyd put down his wine glass and grasped my wrist firmly. "Listen," he said, "if we run out of food on the planet, we'll all be in trouble."

They were both big on *population control*, and much of their writings had to do with educating people about the consequences of overpopulation. The other thing they were deep into was *Humanism,* which as I gathered was a generalized religious outlook which sought to rid itself of anything supernatural.

"But sometimes those religious myths can help people cope," I said, remembering what an Islamic friend had once told me.

"Human beings deserve more than to believe in something that's not true," the elderly Mary said sternly, and she left it at that.

Later, I thought about Bonnie as I drifted off to sleep in their den. I figured Lloyd and Mary were her kind of people, and I wished she could have been there.

In the morning, a wide streak of sunshine broke through the Carmel mist. If it had been a Saturday, I would have rolled down the hill to the old two-court stadium in the woods. At one time, those stone walls were home to the best players on the peninsula. Guys like Treves and Telfer used to hang out all day long, drinking beer and taking on all-comers. Maybe Gillette or Manning would show up. Before he got famous, Timothy Gallwey might even be in there, gliding around on the smoothest strokes in town. (Man, I would have loved warming up with that guy!)

I wasn't sure if the players were still hanging out there. Anyway, it was midweek and the pickings would be slim; so I figured I'd cruise over to Monterey and check out Fisherman's Wharf, maybe Cannery Row and the aquarium.

Not surprisingly, I found myself lazing around the old part of town where it was less touristy. I ended up in a quaint bookstore, browsing contentedly. Next to me in the isle, two people were talking about a Clint Eastwood sighting. They said he came in and played the piano at his Hog's Breath restaurant in Carmel, and then he left. Maybe he sang that night too, I heard he had a nice singing voice. And apparently, he also picked up a tennis racket now and then. I wondered how well he could wield it.

Just then a single Western forehand rifled in the air, kicking up dust in the lonely back alleys of my mind. Eerie desert music from *The Good, The Bad, and The Ugly* filled the recesses of the little bookstore, echoing slyly, and then fading much later, as I walked along a sun-parched Alvarado Street leading my horse and imagining there was nothing in sight but a few white adobe buildings.

Next thing I knew, I was sipping coffee out front at a little sidewalk cafe. I thought about Todd and wondered how he was doing; I figured he was in the ultimate state of Zen mindlessness right about now. Near my table, a steady stream of pedestrians flowed by on the sidewalk. I tried to figure out which ones were Monterey locals and which were tourists. It wasn't always easy. I wondered what the locals thought of me, if they looked at me as one of their own. I mean, I obviously wasn't a tourist, at least not in the normal money-spending sense. I hated thinking of myself as a tourist. I was a visitor, true, but once arrived my intent was to blend in, to be an anonymous part of the locality.

The coffee got me buzzing, and suddenly I felt kinked and bound by the constraints of my chair. So I stood up and stretched my arms skyward. Then I did some leg stretches, right there by the sidewalk. A couple of starchy tourists sitting at the next table gave me a funny look. Hah, I thought, they probably traveled a long way just to see this. Maybe I better get down and do some yoga, too, just so they get their money's worth.

After the yoga, I felt good and loose, and yet just tight enough. I was balanced, poised, ready for action. And I knew Hammer would have been proud of me for having the cojones to get loose right there in front of all the cars on Alvarado Street.

I felt like hitting some balls. The Monterey Tennis Center was only a few blocks away, and I wasn't due to pick up Todd for a couple of hours. I could have walked, but I knew it would be nice to have the old Dart with me; that way I wouldn't waste a lot of time trying to figure out exactly what equipment to take. I'd simply take it all.

I negotiated the traffic and narrow one-way streets, my neck and shoulders undulating to the seductive beat of reggae music — it was Bob Marley wailing through the car radio. I wondered how I would look in dreadlocks, and if I could play tennis with my hair like that. Actually, one of the guys on the junior college team wore dreadlocks and it didn't seem to slow him down. The sound of Van Morrison, his voice plunging then rising, came pleading over the airways just then as I pulled up on Pearl Street alongside the tennis center.

I got out of the car. There was a guy hitting serves on one of the courts. He was about 40 or so and actually looked pretty good. I went to the next court, where there was a small practice wall at one end, and eased into a backboard routine. Now the kinks would really come out!

The guy hitting serves watched me out of the corner of his eye, just as I slyly watched him from time to time. But I was feeling lazy and found myself resting more and hitting less. Soon I was sitting on a very comfortable wooden bench at the side of the court. In fact, the big high-backed bench conformed so well to my body that I had no inclination to get up. I just sat there in the cool Monterey sun admiring the guy's serve on the next court. He was obviously older, but built like a workhorse. He grouped the balls well, pounding one after another into the corners of the service box. He wasn't really nailing the ball, but just hitting it firmly and uniformly, the way a good player warms up. Next thing I knew, he was at the entry to my court. "Mind if I come in?" he asked with an Eastern European accent. That figured, he probably came from some sort of hardy Czech or Yugoslav stock.

"They call me Z," he said. "I live in Napa, but I have rental property in Salinas. After repair I come here."

He told me he had injured his right leg recently in a tournament, so he wasn't really able to play. "For now all I do is serve like baby, just roll the ball, you know." Man, if that was his baby serve, I figured the real thing would probably put holes in the concrete!

"It's just as well you're injured," I said, "I don't feel like getting up. This is the nicest bench I've ever seen on a tennis court."

"It's Vali's bench," he said, "look, you see?" He pointed to the curved wooden backrest where an inscription was etched deep into the wood.

IN MEMORY OF LT. VALI B. MOEZZI
UNITED STATES NAVAL AVIATOR

Moezzi? Vali? Hey, I knew the guy! He had a brother and they were both damn good tennis players. Good looking guy, slim, dark-skinned, played for San Diego State. I was stunned. I remembered Vali's energy, his enthusiasm and gracious manner.

"What a shame," I said, "killed in action, I suppose."

"Not exactly. He was in Navy, yes, but war was over, it was only training mission. Everyone here knows story."

Z told me everything. How Vali was just thirty years old. He was a jet pilot and had been in for seven years. It was just three weeks before he was due to get out; he even had a job waiting for him as a passenger pilot. And then he bit it!

Here the Viet Nam war was over and the guy still gets killed! A mechanical malfunction, they said. What a waste! I wondered what would be better, to go down in action over the Mekong Delta or to buy it in the same plane on a training mission during peace time.

Of course, there never really was a peace time; there was always some sort of war going on. So I guess it didn't matter much — it was just a terrible waste of life, no matter how you looked at it.

There was just an oil slick on the water, Z told me. Apparently, the upper half of the co-pilot's body was found floating nearby. But the two navigators lived; they were found bobbing in the South China Sea about a mile away. Vali had been a quiet hero; he ejected his crew, all three of them, and then he sat there waiting for his turn. But it never came. I couldn't get over it — he became an oil slick on the water.

Z and I stood back and looked at the massive wooden bench. This was the grandstand court at the Monterey Tennis Center. Nearby, the clubhouse deck offered a bird's eye view. I remembered a few years ago when a bunch of locals gathered up there, hoping to see their boys knock off me and Hammer in a three hundred dollar wager.

"The bench, it is nice," Z said, and I followed him off the court.

Three young Asian girls came in as we left and began to do drills with well trained precision. I wondered if they were Vietnamese or Laotian or what. They looked like sisters and were obviously off to a good start. Even their serves looked professional. Their coach, whoever it was, certainly was due credit. Or maybe it was Vali who was due all the credit. I pictured the girls as babies running with their mother through a rice paddy, bombs exploding all around them, their frantic screams, their mud streaked faces. And then nothing. Silence. The raid is over. Because Vali or some other unsung hero has done his job. Three weeks later, babies and mother are on a plane to the US; it could have been a story I read about in the newspaper. But no mention of Vali or anybody else. And yet, without them those kids would never have picked up a tennis racket. The girls were giggling now, creaming the ball, speaking English perfectly with a trace of the old country in their voices.

I figured Hammer and I had a lot to talk about on the way home.

At one o'clock, when I drove over to pick up Todd at the meditation center near Asilomar, he was standing by the bushes at the side of the road looking exactly as he did when I first dropped him off. Even his toothbrush was sticking out of his pants pocket. But his spirit looked dampened.

"What'd you have for breakfast?" he asked as soon as he jumped into the old Dart.

"Not much," I said, "just homemade oatmeal with molasses and raisins. That Lloyd really likes to pour the raisins on. Plus a glass of juice and a slice of melon."

Hammer looked kind of dejected. "Why? What'd you eat?" I asked him.

"A grain of rice. We had the same thing for dinner."

I was astonished. "Just a grain of rice?"

"Well OK, it was a few grains, actually. About half a cup, if you want to know the truth."

"Well, was it at least brown rice?"

"I think so, but it went down so fast it was hard to tell. Then we got a cup of tea to help settle the meal."

"Tea? And rice? For breakfast and dinner?"

Hammer nodded sourly and changed the subject. "What'd you sleep on?' he asked.

"Just an old fold-out couch Lloyd has in his den. Why, what'd you have?"

"A wood floor with a mat on it."

He asked me what I'd been up to. "Not much," I told him, "went down to the water, played a little tennis, walked around, checked out a coffee shop and a couple of bookstores. Why, what'd you do all morning?"

"Sat on a rock."

"Well, what'd they talk about?"

"Talk! We weren't allowed to speak. We just sat there on our rocks listening to each other."

"Oh. That must have been kind of quiet."

"Yeah, well at least we could hear the sound of the surf."

"Waves are cool," I said. "Anyway, you were meditating, right? So your mind is clear now, right?"

"Clearer than ever. And guess what, I'm ready to clutter it up again."

Of course, Todd's idea of a cluttered mind was basic in-the-moment emptiness with a few tennis balls drifting among the clouds and an occasional mermaid porpoising up out of the still blue water.

"Yeah," I told him, "a little clutter is good for the soul. Functional messiness, at least that's what Bonnie calls it." I figured I'd tell him about Vali Moezzi later, after he had a chance to eat something.

We hightailed it away from the meditation center; and now with the old Dart struggling slightly, we were headed up the grade of Munras Avenue to where Crazy Horse restaurant sits nestled against the pines at the top of the hill. The place has a classy salad bar, with soup and rolls, and even slices of real turkey, so it's the perfect spot for a fill-up. Besides, the freeway onramps are right there, so it's a good jumping off point for home or wherever else one might be headed. I parked the car in the lot and shut off the noise of the engine. Hammer's stomach rumbled audibly in the sudden quiet. "If you don't mind," he said, "after we eat, I'd like to go back down the hill and look at The Motel for a few minutes."

Chapter Thirty-Six

Bent Over The Football

Monterey had been a pleasant diversion, and I was glad Todd dragged me along. But that's all it was, a diversion. Almost immediately, I became my usual self-doubting self. I wondered if I could ever end up like that old lady I saw at the courts in Fresno, pushing all of my possessions around in a shopping cart. Hell, at least she had a shopping cart, so in that sense she was ahead of me.

I felt apathetic and immobile, as if I were stuck in the rut of the road, just waiting for a good rain to wash me away into the rest of my life. And there were downpours in the months to come, but a storm of the necessary magnitude never did arrive.

I had coached the JC squad for four seasons, making them the dominant force in the conference, but now a rumor began to circulate that one of the football coaches was going to take over the team. The gossip turned out to be true. The guy had recently become a tennis nut and that was enough, apparently. As the athletic director explained, "It's more efficient to use a coach who's already on campus."

"Even if he doesn't know anything about tennis?" I asked.

"Fraley's got the winningest record of any defensive coach this school's ever had," the A.D. said proudly.

"Then maybe he can teach the tennis players how to tackle their opponents," I cracked, figuring I had nothing to lose.

His lips puckered.

"Besides," I said, "I've got the winningest record of any tennis coach you've ever had."

"It's out of my hands," the A.D. said, rising from his chair. "Paul Fraley's full-time staff, so that's the way it is. I'm sure the school will be happy to keep you in mind if any part-time slots open up in the Psych Department, since you've got a Masters Degree. But if Fraley wants the tennis team, it's his baby."

The guy looked a little flabby, like a pudged-out bowler who was used to having a drink each time he stuck his fingers in the ball. He stood there smiling with his hand extended like he was my best friend or something. I didn't feel like shaking it. "Later," I said, "I've got a pass to catch," and I went out the door.

Well okay, I thought, what's a JC coaching job, anyway? Certainly nothing from a financial standpoint. But there had been a pleasant satisfaction to it; I enjoyed hanging with the guys. It also served as a potential stepping stone to a coaching position at a four-year school, and some of those gigs were beginning to pay decently. Screw it, I thought, let Mr. Football take my guys, we'll see what he does to the team.

It soon became evident that as little as that JC job paid, it had combined with my limited income from private lessons to get me over the hump each month. Clearly, I would need to find something else. Besides, I had too great a vacancy factor in my life, what with Bonnie still up in Oregon and Hammer out on the road so much.

So that winter I tried to peddle my Masters Degree at various Bay Area colleges, something I had never really done with any seriousness before. But everything was sewn up. I was politely put on a list, a list that was probably for show anyway. They already had their people picked, that's the way it worked. If an instructor position opened up, there was a fast behind-the-scenes shuffle. Either that or there was a careful manhunt that went far beyond the scope of the list. Hell, who could blame them? If I were in charge, I'd want to do things my way, too. The problem for me right now was that I hadn't rubbed enough elbows in academia. Rudolph, the one friendly professor I had, was potentially of some help, but he was still small potatoes; he was certainly no ace in the hole. He lay there face up in my hand like the jack of hearts, pleasant enough, but powerless compared to the wild cards that were held by the other players.

I figured my best bet was to work my way into the classroom through tennis, and not the other way around. Of course, that's what I had tried to do in the first place. It was a Catch-22 if there ever was one (although not having read the book, I couldn't be absolutely certain about that.)

I thought maybe I'd take another club job; it would be nice to have some bucks for a change. I just hoped I wouldn't have to relocate. I wasn't ready to say good-by to Sheldeen and the gang, and my handful of private students. There was also the Berkeley campus with its hills and dales. And the Rose Garden. I would miss the Avenues, too — College, Telegraph, Shattuck — all those little restaurants and coffee shops. And the sidewalks, filled with ordinary city people, people who nonetheless looked like they belonged in Berkeley.

I was still floundering a couple of months later when the bombshell hit — it was Todd — he was getting married! Hell, I didn't even know he had a girlfriend. Not only that, but he was starting a job as a stockbroker! He called me from some sort of E. F. Hutton training institute in New York.

"Dude, it's me. I'm a suit now, can you believe it?"

"Well, no, but yes, now that you mention it. And you're getting married! I guess you've always been the spontaneous type."

"It was only spontaneous at first," Hammer said, "when I first met Laura. The rest was a deep, ground-out decision that took about three weeks of figuring out."

"Most people would call three weeks pretty impulsive, at least when it comes to marriage."

"Oh, no, it was total analytical preoccupation. In the end, though, I got to kind of a stalemate, so I went with intuition. It was like hitting a big groundie for a winner when suddenly you know it's time to end the point. If you think too much about it you'll blow the shot, you've got to just go for it. So I let it rip, dude."

"You sure did." I laughed. "Anyway, I can't wait to meet her. Laura, you say?" And you're going to be a stockbroker?"

"Right on, dude, I just kind of fell into it, figured I'd go for the bucks, you know, something to go along with the whole wife and kid thing."

"You're having a kid, too?" I asked, startled.

"Well yeah, not right away or anything, but eventually, isn't that what the whole thing is about?"

"What about tennis?"

"Hell, I'll always be able to kick your butt, that'll be good enough for me. Anyway, I'll play NorCal weekend tourneys, if the bucks are there."

I was somewhat dazed and didn't say anything into the phone right away.

"Dude," Todd said, "I'm thirty-six years old, it's about time I settled down, don't you think?" I couldn't argue with that. Hell, I was almost forty now and really feeling it, not just physically, but emotionally, the need to have someone there (and not a plane trip away.)

"Well, congratulations," I offered as the shock wore off. "She must be some babe."

Two weeks later, Hammer The Suit was in town and commuting to work in Walnut Creek. Laura, his fiancée, was back East finishing up graduate school. When it went through the grapevine that Todd was settling down, he began to get job offers from tennis clubs. But Hammer didn't want to teach tennis. One of the gigs was in Marin County, on the other side of the Bay near San Rafael, and the job sounded pretty good, so Hammer tried to give it to me. "Call the guy, if you're interested," he said, "I already told him about you. It's not too far from Berkeley and you can make some decent money out there. Rudy Herrera was pulling down thirty-five G's and he didn't even go in every day."

"You're sure you don't want the job?" I asked, knowing what the answer would be. For as much as Hammer had done his share of teaching (and a good bit of it with me) he never really liked it. He said it was too much like being a prostitute, going through the motions for someone else. Tennis meant more to him than that. If he wanted to coach someone he would, but he wasn't going to do it as his job. Besides, teaching tennis was bad for the game, it slowed down your reactions and conditioned you to hit into the other guy's rhythm.

"You take a sport like skiing or golf," Todd said, "and when you demonstrate how to make a turn or hit out of a sand trap, or whatever, you're pretty much doing it the way you would normally. But as a tennis teacher you're always doing things that are abnormal to your game. You're hitting short and soft and you take your eye off the ball so you can analyze what the student is doing. Either that, or you're pitching balls stiff-legged, losing your instinct to move on the court. Besides, the good days are over. You've got managers now who want a piece of your action, and a lot of clubs don't even give retainers anymore, at least not like they used to. And, they're into the multi-pro concept at a lot of places, where they let a bunch of people teach, which pretty much dilutes the pot. Hell, it used to be they paid you a chunk just to be who you were, lessons were the gravy. Now they skim your lessons and expect you to pick up the trash and clean the restrooms just for the privilege of being there."

"It's not like that everywhere," I said.

"No, but it's a definite trend, the writing's on the wall. The worst of it is, you're just a worker, expendable. They pretend to like you, but they've always got somebody in the back of their minds they'd like to replace you with. Your only hope is to own the club, and those opportunities are few and far between. Hell, these days, it's better to be the manager than the pro. The managers are salaried and some of them are former teaching pros who take the best lessons for themselves, and then they get their cut of your action too. And you better not complain about it. If you so much as look at them wrong, they'll have the board write you a 'dear pro' letter. Then you're off hunting down another job, and it'll probably be a lot further away than you'd like."

"I guess you're right," I said, "the good days are over." But at the same time I knew the job in Marin County would be a blessing, if I got it. Maybe having more bucks at my disposal would entice Bonnie to move down from Oregon.

"I'll call the guy for sure," I said, "I could use something."

"Go for it, bro. But just don't hire any softies."

Hammer and I had this thing about *softies*, a term we used for a certain type of assistant pro. A softie was not a player with a reputation, but a recreation type whose biggest asset was that he was not a threat to the star stature of the head pro. Because of the inherent insecurity of the profession, a lot of teaching pros used softies as their assistants, even when more appealing heavyweight players and coaches were available. Although often a little short when it came to high-end junior development, the congenial softie insured the longevity of the head pro by making sure no hot-shot assistant could win over the confidence of the members.

Of course, the unfortunate thing about the softie syndrome was that it tended to dilute the quality of club coaching. When the head pro retired from a club, or moved on to something else, it was not uncommon for his assistant, the softie, to take over. After all, everyone knew the guy, and if there was one thing he was good at, it was being well liked. Or, the softie might fill a slot at another club. In either case, the overall result was an evolution of less able types. The scenario was typical at the clubs, but it occurred in college coaching positions, as well. (Although even a proficient softie wouldn't have a prayer when looking into the nostrils of a guy who knew how to bend over a football.)

I savored that last thought as I recalled my talk with the pasty faced athletic director. Then feeling somewhat redundant, I asked Todd if he was sure he didn't want the Marin job.

He looked contented, kind of dreamy. "Naw, man, I'm keeping my tennis for myself, and a few special people. I'm not going to prostitute it. Besides, I kind of like the stockbroker thing. I get a rush off it and there are some pretty big bucks out there. Who knows, maybe Laura and I will own an investment house some day. Did I tell you she's getting her doctorate in international finance?"

"Oh," I said.

Chapter Thirty-Seven

The Club Job

The tennis club was relatively new. Situated in the low green hills of Marin, it was a modest eight-courter with a swimming pool and a clubhouse. Locker rooms, snack bar, pro shop — the usual. Upstairs was the manager's office and a room with an antique pool table. In another room was a long oval table that was vacant most of the time, except for one night a month when the guys on the board met.

There was no court in the hole, but every pair of courts was separated by an elevated redwood deck which allowed viewing to either side. The members weren't into showcasing matches anyway, although like all players, they got psyched up (or psyched out) when people hung out and watched.

And they were pretty cool for the most part, not near as many CQ's playing with rakwets as I would have anticipated (considering the parking lot had so many Lincolns and Mercedes in it.) There didn't appear to be many SW's either, at first; but then one warm Saturday morning after getting trounced in a league playoff match, great numbers of them stuck their heads out of the sand and complained about how they Shoulda Won.

In general the members were a sociable lot, causing the club sorry coefficient to run a little higher than the California Standard. Naturally, there were some raw beginners flopping around, misfiring balls at each other, but there were also more than a few seasoned hacks. This always surprised me, considering they had plenty of money to remove the awkwardness from their games. Oh well, better I suppose to spend the cash on nuclear rackets and invincible stock portfolios. After all, who needs lessons when you can do everything wrong and still hit the ball a million miles an hour!

The overall tenis envy at the club was fairly low, in spite of the fact that a couple of the men were off the charts. These two nervous fanatics played singles with each other every other day, constantly questioning one another's calls. Their grunts and groans and cries of desperation gave the impression that a lot was at stake, perhaps life itself, but in the end they both walked away, the one holding his head a little higher than the other. Then a couple of days later, his head would be hanging and the other guy would be the one walking around with a smug expression on his face.

All in all, the job in Marin was a welcome relief; it was nice to have some bucks for a change. I had the old Dodge Dart rebuilt and planned to take Bonnie to a nice restaurant next time she was in town. Maybe we'd go to Spenger's; after all, that sea-cabin vibe was hard to beat.

There were plenty of lessons at the Marin club, but not so many that I needed an assistant, which kept things from getting complicated. The other nice thing was that the pro shop was minimal and more or less just for show, which was smart because it took a pretty big club to actually turn a profit in a shop. Thank god I wasn't expected to run it. Anyway, the kid who answered the phone at the front desk was there if a member needed to buy a jar of tennis balls or a wristband or something.

I got a small retainer, to get me by on rainy days I suppose. But the best part was that I wasn't expected to hang around the club making myself look busy. I set up my own appointments and got 100% of that action, which included a junior program three days a week, a men's doubles night, and a ladies' group Tuesday mornings.

I was required to run a club tournament twice a year, and that was it. The members didn't want a lot of organized events crowding up their courts. No wonder Hammer had figured it was a good job, not too cumbersome. Apparently, he knew one of the members fairly well and the member was in tight with the manager, a private fellow who stayed upstairs in his office most of the time, whistling like a bird and doing his books. We got along great. He was on the inside, and I was on the outside, along with a gardener-maintenance dude who thought sweeping up around ladies in short skirts was the greatest thing since the invention of the leaf blower.

I commuted across the bridge to Marin pretty much daily that spring, limiting my freelance lessons in Berkeley to select times, which worked out for almost everybody. I ended up having to drop the stubborn attorney whose kid tagged along in the weeds at the Rose Garden. It was not a difficult good-by. Of course, now that I didn't have to fix him, I envisioned the guy as more humorous and less of a pain in the butt. Hell, I'd probably end up with an equally stubborn lesson soon enough at my new job. Anyway, I gave the kid a butterfly net and that was it.

I wanted to tell the boy, I too collected insects when I was his age. I wanted to tell him my special story, about my first butterfly, how I picked it out of the Encyclopedia. It all came back to me then as I handed him the net, how stunning the butterflies in the Encyclopedia were — all those brightly colored wings with their intricate markings! I was captivated by all, but my young eyes kept coming back to one particularly handsome fellow, the buckeye, whose brown wings were trimmed with orange at the edges, while nearer the body, purple-blue rings stood out irresistibly like exotic eyes. Yes, the buckeye was the butterfly for me!

I remember it all so clearly — with net in hand, I marched out of the house on a world quest to find the awesome buckeye, loveliest of all butterflies. I began in the vacant lot at the end of the street and immediately noticed something more or less camouflaged in the dried grass at my feet, something brown with frail wings, wings that had orange trim and beautiful purple-blue rings on them! It was the buckeye, handsomest of all butterflies, right there in my own neighborhood! I was stunned, ecstatic for days, in fact, until I had a very large collection of buckeyes and decided to go after something more exotic, not so common and plain looking as the buckeye, something more elegant like a yellow and black swallowtail. Yes, the swallowtail was the butterfly for me!

The sadness of it all, the beautiful buckeye made ugly by its own abundance, by familiarity. I thought about what my psych professor had said about there being a biological capacity for boredom, and I wondered how many husbands and wives had suffered the fate of the buckeye. I would never feel that way about Bonnie, I knew that. But what about her feelings; would she see me as a dismal buckeye some day?

Anyway, I handed the kid the butterfly net and wondered what sad stories he would capture with it. He was kind of dragging his tennis racket in one hand, but the lighter more magical butterfly net he held higher in the other, swooping at the air as he trudged up out of the Rose

Garden behind his father. I remember wishing he could have been a part of my Sunday morning tennis program in the flatlands. Indeed, church had now become the highlight of my week, even though that funky old court was more cracked and worn than ever. Sheldeen, Pedro, Mei Mei, Zoran — these were also my people, young as they were, and it felt good to be with them. The attorney's kid would have fit in well. But that was like wishing he was poor, or he didn't have a father or something.

As for Sheldeen, he had become a real asset with that Sunday gang; it was like having an assistant pro out there. And he certainly enjoyed helping out. Then afterwards, he and I would do our thing. Occasionally, Sheldeen's dad would walk by with the dog and a big affable smile; then he'd go sit in the grass, too far away to actually see what was going on. But that was enough, his son was on a tennis court, and now there were a dozen trophies at home and articles on the wall from newspapers. The big man in overalls didn't want to get too close to the picture, he didn't want to understand it, he just wanted to gaze out and look at it like some people look at a sunset or a view of the mountains.

His dad was usually gone by the time Sheldeen and I finished our workout. And what a workout it was! At thirteen now, Sheldeen had grown and was hitting so well it became one of my best weekly tune-ups, especially since Hammer was largely unavailable, what with Laura and being a stockbroker and all. Additionally, Hammer was creating his own wedding vows. He was scripting a ceremony that, as he put it, was "very religious, but not linked to dogmatic contemporary mythologies or anything else supernatural." He telephoned across the country every day to give Laura the latest version, which she was happy to go along with, but she drew the line at exchanging vows on a Tibetan mountain top.

Neither Todd nor I went to the Montana tournament that fourth summer, but as soon as school was over we put Sheldeen on a bus and he went out there to help Buckskin Charley with some junior tennis camps for his Spiritual Athletes Foundation. Three weeks later, Sheldeen came back with stories of trout fishing and a can of Championship Wilsons (the real McCoy, a metal can with a sardine-key attached to the bottom.) He had also acquired a bank account with three thousand dollars in it! He showed me the passbook shyly. Startled, I counted the zeros several times. It was three thousand dollars, alright. I called Buckskin Charley immediately to thank him. "The kid's a good worker," he said. "Besides, we had a good year here at The Foundation." He told me the money was to be used for college and tournament expenses.

"The kid's got a future," he said, "he might even have to skip college and hit the circuit, and pogo-sticking around the globe on a tennis racket can get expensive."

So Sheldeen and Buckskin Charley had hit it off; it looked like the kid would be going back to Montana the next few summers. I figured he'd have some serious change on hand by the time he was ready for college, or indeed, the lower levels of pro tennis. And with Charley's foundation committed, I'd have the leverage to land more sponsors. The package for Sheldeen was beginning to take shape.

I had the momentary fantasy Sheldeen was on center court Wimbledon, down on his knees like Borg in victory. I wondered if I would be there with him. As his coach? A friend, perhaps? Or maybe just one of millions watching him on TV. Hell, anything was possible. He was already number five NorCal in his first year 14's, and he was improving fast.

One quiet weekend, Todd went back East with Pop to get married to Laura in a small church in Connecticut where she used to sing in the choir. It was a location he conceded to her, so long as no clergymen were present. I was best man in absentia and rather enjoyed it. I didn't feel like going to a wedding, anyway; it would only make me more aware of the fact that Bonnie and I were still apart. Besides, just the immediate family was there and I probably would have felt like an outsider. Although I'm sure I would have found Hammer's ceremony interesting.

The happy couple spent a week in Hawaii; then they settled into the Bay Area. Todd got transferred from Walnut Creek to the San Francisco financial district, and Laura worked there too, in a Japanese bank. They lived with Pop for two weeks, then found a place in Mill Valley. Her folks helped with the down payment, and they were set, ready to embrace their new lives.

Because Mill Valley was nearby, Todd came over to the Marin club now and then for a quick workout or to hit with some of my juniors, which was a great treat for them. He really liked kids and, actually, had begun to fantasize about being a father. He was already telling me his favorite names for a kid, names like Summit, Hail, Forest; and Sierra if it was a girl. It wasn't that Laura was expecting or anything, Hammer just liked the idea of having a kid, especially a boy. He confided to me that, really, his favorite name was Shade, but that his wife thought it was a little too casual, even for a guy.

"With a name like Shade you're automatically accepted in certain circles," he said, "it gives you an edge."

I told him the name might also keep the kid out of certain other circles.

"Only if the circle is made up of a bunch of squares," he said with a patient smile. "But I suppose that's what life is all about, especially when you have kids — you've got to be ready for the squares. Anyway, Laura doesn't like the name," he said, obviously disappointed.

Chapter Thirty-Eight

Sleeping In The Soup

Occasionally, after checking up on Pop, Todd would drop in unexpectedly at my little pad in the Berkeley flatlands. I cherished those visits, realizing they might eventually disappear altogether. I recalled the last one. Supplemented by Heinekens, it felt like old times as we sat at my little kitchen table. Hammer was flipping through the latest issue of a popular tennis magazine. He was wearing a new business suit, but he had on his old grin, a grin that morphed into a chuckle from time to time as he skimmed through the glossy magazine. Then he really let one loose, and I asked him what was so funny.

"This article about the Western forehand," he said, holding up the magazine, "they're talking about the extreme Western, how it's almost like a sideways service motion."

"So? What about it?"

"That's just it, it's nothing new, but they make it sound like it was just invented."

"Well it's been around for at least a century," I said, "why do you think they used to call it a *buggy whip* forehand."

"Giddyap, yeehaw!" Todd shouted, and he rolled up the magazine and slapped it down at my kitchen table like he was a stagecoach driver and the robbers were in fast pursuit. "Yeehaw!" he cried.

I told him the only new shot I could think of was the between-the-legs backfire Yannick Noah started using, much to the delight of the spectators. Even veteran TV commentator Bud Collins stared through the television screen with popeyes.

"That's a new shot," I said, "not very useful, but at least it's relatively new."

"For sure, the castration shot is a fresh one," Todd laughed. "Every hot dog around is just waiting for the chance to use it, and preferably on national TV."

"Hey, if you're going to become a eunuch, you might as well do it on national TV."

"An audience is good," Hammer said, "you win the point under your balls like that, you get to pick out your harem."

Hammer asked me about the club and how things were going out there, so we talked about the Marin scene for a while. And then he went home, much too early it seemed, but I guess Laura was waiting on the other side of the Bay, so he couldn't just hang out like he used to. He looked quite handsome in his suit as he went out the door.

I felt about as empty as the bottle of beer in my hand. Sure I had a job now, if it could really be called a job in the grand scheme of things. It was really just a glorified gig. A little tennis club gig. But was it the answer? Was tennis even the answer? Hell, I compared myself to Todd; he was married now, and he had a real job; he wasn't just babysitting the grownups during recess.

I considered my uneventful life and popped another Heineken. It went down easily, surprisingly easily. As I began to think things through, I realized that everything was changing around me — people, places, my friends. The world was passing me by, so quietly that I hardly even noticed it until later, it seemed. But there were also times it went by like a speed boat, leaving me bobbing in its wake. And so what I really needed was a lifejacket. Yes! I could wear a lifejacket everywhere. But when I thought about it, I decided I didn't like the colors they came in. And then I had a stroke of genius — a new car! Yes, a new car was the answer, that would be something big in my life, something I could sit in and keep up with the world at its fastest moments. Well, maybe not a brand new car, but just a good used one, something more reliable and up to date than the old Dart. I pictured myself driving a recent model Ford Mustang, and my spirits brightened. In fact, I had seen a sleek yellow Mustang parked out front in a lot on Shattuck Avenue. I imagined cruising in it, leaning back with Bonnie by my side, and my heart soared. But then as I finished another beer, I realized you can't even buy a *used* car anymore. Not at all, you have to buy a *pre-owned* vehicle! And that ticked me off! What a gimmick that was, as if they weren't used cars at all, but something better, something pre-owned. No thanks, I thought, just give me a used car, buddy. A good old-fashioned used car. Give me the yellow Mustang, or maybe something classic like a 57 T-Bird. Yes, I thought, I'll take the T-Bird. And make it a convertible. I envisioned opening the door for Bonnie. I doubt she'd want to get in anything pre-owned anyway. So just lay the used car on me, buddy, and get the hell out of the driveway.

I guess I was getting drunk and kind of irritated. But, hey, is this progressive terminology really progress? Pre-owned for crissake! I remembered that the great fishing writer, John Gierach, complained about political correctness, and how it was sabotaging our language; indeed, our very culture. After all, now we don't even have waiters or waitresses. We have servers! (Because they are supposedly less sexist.) Hell, we don't even have stewardesses, the flight attendants pushed them all out of the airplane!

This is all perfectly convenient for a unisex lifestyle, I suppose. But boring — one neutral word that satisfies both male and female. A bisexual name tag. Ingenious syllables that don't offend and can go both ways if they feel like it.

I guess, in the case of a "pre-owned" automobile, it's not exactly a matter of political correctness, after all, cars can be pretty sexy whether they're neutered or not. Either way, I'd much prefer a used one, and preferably a 57 T-Bird, like I said.

Things were perfectly functional before. But now everybody's got a new name tag. I get one, too, the minute I step out of the house. And sometimes it's okay. For instance, I don't mind being a *guest* at a motel, but not in a restaurant. Call me old-fashioned, but when I'm eating I consider myself a customer, not a guest. If I were sleeping in the soup, that would be different, I suppose.

So, hunched over my fourth Heineken, I sat at my little kitchen table bitching to myself about life. I figured Hammer was probably home in Mill Valley by now. Then suddenly, my IQ rose two-hundred points and everything became crystal clear. I sat bolt upright. Yes, I thought, it's the *appearance* of progress, not progress, that makes the world go 'round. And tennis players are spinning on it along with everybody else. The manufacturers make new mysterious rackets all the time, rackets that are somehow better to play with. And the teaching industry is always trying to come up with a new way of describing something old that gives it the look of being a brand new revelation. First we had good *strokes,* then we got good *technique,* and now we have good *mechanics.*

It used to be if you hit the ball well, you were said to have *good timing.* Then it came to be you had *executed the shot* well. Now, that same player is described as a good *ball striker.* What will be next, I wondered? Perhaps in a couple of years ball strikers will be extinct and vector makers will roam the planet. Then eventually it will probably go full circle and good timing will again be in vogue.

Yes, I thought, everything needs a fancier new name tag, especially teaching pros at tennis clubs. Traditionally, one was either a pro or an assistant pro, and that was it. But then fueled by what Hammer calls the multi-pro concept, things grew more complex. For instance, if a second assistant pro was hired at a club, the original assistant pro might feel slighted and due for some sort of recognition, something that would distinguish him from the new guy. After all, he not only had the seniority, he probably knew a lot more, too.

This scenario is occasionally resolved by not hiring an assistant pro at all. That is, the same guy is brought on board, but he is simply called an *instructor.* And everybody is happy (except, of course, the instructor.) This is a matter of extending the teaching hierarchy at the bottom.

A more common approach, however, is to move everybody upward. When the new assistant pro is hired, the original assistant is elevated to the status of pro, and to keep the balance, the pro now becomes the *head pro.* All this has a fairly nice ring to it.

And yet, if another quality coach comes on board and another upward shift in the hierarchy is necessary, the ring can lose some of it splendor, at least for the head pro, because now he is called the *tennis director.* And though he is the guy at the top, and everybody else is subordinate, he will feel a loss for his old title. For in his heart he is a tennis pro, he will always be a pro, and being a tennis "director" just doesn't cut it.

Hammer and I used to talk about this stuff a lot, sometimes with tongue in cheek, and sometimes with tongue on forehead. We've slurped it with our soup and mashed it in our potatoes, much to the annoyance of the server, although the waiter didn't seem to mind in the least. Another time, while being served a meal in a high chair, Hammer asked a stewardess if it was true that they had all become sexless flight attendants, and she winked at him and gave him her phone number.

Still pining for the old days, I stumbled down the hallway trying not to spill the empty bottle of beer in my hand. The floor seemed to be swaying; indeed, by the time I got to my bedroom I felt as if I were a raft on the high seas. I thought it best to skip brushing my teeth. I also thought it best to keep the old Dart. It'd been running just fine. Sure, I'd be stuck in the slow lane, but that way I'd be able to enjoy the scenery a lot more, so it wouldn't be a problem at all (unless I was trying to get away from a tournament where ballgirls and ballboys had been replaced by ball persons.)

Chapter Thirty-Nine

Origins

In the morning I was in more of a fog than usual. To be sure, I was nursing a rather unpleasant hangover. But then a letter with a Montana postmark arrived, and I felt downright refreshed. The letter contained a plane ticket to Panama and a note from Buckskin Charley asking me to call. So I dialed him up (actually I pressed him in, not having had a rotary phone in some time.)

Charley explained that a friend of his from Costa Rica had called. It seemed there was a big junior tournament in Panama. All the top kids from Europe and South America were going to be there. Charley thought it was a good opportunity for Sheldeen to get to know some of the players he'd be knocking heads with on the pro tour in a few years. "The fourteens is none too early to get psychologically conditioned to the players you'll have to be dealing with for the rest of your career," he said. "Besides, the tournament is on hardcourts, it's a perfect one for the kid to get his feet wet."

Apparently, the U.S. was sending four boys and four girls in the eighteens and the sixteens, but no fourteen-year-old juniors were officially going. Of course, even if they were, it was doubtful Sheldeen would have been selected. He was one of the top kids in Northern California, but he had no national ranking whatsoever. A USTA sponsored berth would have been out of the question.

Nonetheless, it was still likely there would be some American kids in his division. "Usually there are a couple of fourteen-year-olds from Florida at this thing," Charley said, "but what's more important is that Sheldeen will be able to connect with kids from France and Spain and Brazil. And those juniors are the best in the world. Some of them could be dominating the pro circuit in a few years. You never know. Anyway, I got a good deal on the plane ticket. And Sheldeen will be staying with my friend's brother-in-law. All things considered, it's a relatively inexpensive lesson in international tennis."

"He's still got another year in the fourteens," I said, "maybe we should wait 'til then. I'd hate for the kid to get discouraged if he gets bumped early."

"If he exits early he can just hang out and practice with the other juniors, that's one of the perks. He'll love it. Besides, if he zones he could blow through the field, and think what that would do for him."

Sheldeen had been gone all day at a tournament in Sacramento, a sunny tennis town that always produced top-flight juniors, thanks to the dedication of coach Nick Carter. Even though Carter had relocated now, the seeds he planted germinated well, and there would be no lack of good competition for Sheldeen in Sacramento. He had traveled up there with a couple of boys from the Berkeley Tennis Club. They were playing at the historic Sutter Lawn Club, and I was anxious to hear how he did. I also wanted to tell him about Panama, but he hadn't got back yet.

Actually, I kind of expected him to be home by now and drop in like he usually did to give me a detailed account of his results. I saw him play when I could, which wasn't all that often, so typically he'd just come by afterward and lay it on me. But now it was well into evening and I still hadn't heard from him. So I decided to swing by his place to see if he had called his folks; maybe he planned to spend the night in Sacramento.

I grabbed my car keys and went out of the house — and there he was with his tennis gear, sitting on my front step! He looked rather glum. He must have been beaten, and beaten badly to be hanging his head like that.

"Hey, what's up?" I said, somewhat startled.

"Nuthin'."

"Whad'ya mean, nuthin'? How'd you do?"

"I got to the quarters," he mumbled, staring at the ground. "And I beat the guy easy. But then afterward he wouldn't even shake my hand." Sheldeen looked pained.

"Hey, don't worry about it," I said, "there are a lot of babies like that out there." But Sheldeen wouldn't look at me, he just sat there with his head hanging, his handsome features contorted. If I didn't know him better, I would've figured he was about to cry.

"Hey, it's no big deal," I said firmly, but the kid still wouldn't look me in the eye.

"The guy called me a monkey," he blurted out suddenly, "he said I came from an ape."

"Well, we all came from apes," I countered emphatically. "The same ape, in fact!" His head turned towards me.

"Your ancestors just stuck around Africa longer, that's all. You tell that smart-ass his ancestors were black too, but then they moved to a colder place and their skins turned lighter and they became white dudes."

"You mean black people were the first?" Sheldeen looked straight at me, a sheepish grin on his face.

"Of course, the first humans were black, everybody knows that. That's what all the scientists say, and that's good enough for me."

"Me too," Sheldeen said. He stood up with a proud, glowing look.

Ok, so now the kid was back on track; he was more upbeat than ever, actually, and even beat a seed in the semis the next day in Sacramento, which was pretty good, considering he was playing up an age division. I, on the other hand, was haunted by his experience, the sheer ignorance of it, the bigotry. And I didn't feel like talking to anybody about it, not the tournament director, not Hammer, not Bonnie, nobody. I just swallowed it down as best I could; but the aftertaste wouldn't go away. I felt bad for the kid. I figured maybe in a couple of days we'd both be OK and I'd give him the plane ticket Buckskin Charley had sent for Panama.

Chapter Forty

A Limo In The Flats

The fact that Sheldeen was entered in a world event put some focus in my life. I felt almost as if I were going, and that helped fill the void. It gave me something to think about at night besides Bonnie and why Hammer was married and I wasn't. But then Todd was a stockbroker now, and I was still trying to squeeze the juice out of tennis. Maybe that was the problem. Or maybe he was just a lot better at going with his flow.

Sheldeen was due to leave for Panama in a week, so I scheduled two matches a day for him with older juniors. One was actually a girl, the number three eighteen-year-old in Northern California. Her steady, hard-hitting baseline style was perfectly suited to his, and their backcourt points were lengthy and capped with impressive finishing shots. I really couldn't spot any weaknesses in his game — passing shot, moon ball, overhead, volley, serve — it was all there in fine form. But I got out my big laundry basket of balls anyway, and early in the mornings we went down to our funky neighborhood court.

I fed him shots that were more difficult from a standpoint of movement, making him scramble quickly into position, for instance, before executing what would otherwise have been an easy forehand or backhand. We spent a good deal of time fine-tuning his midcourt swinging volley and also his bounce overhead from deep in the court, because those were shots he would have to win the point with if faced with a scrappy rival with a game more or less equal to his.

Hammer made a point to be available in the middle of the week, so I managed to leave the Marin club early and we double-teamed the kid in the Berkeley flatlands. We had been pounding heavy-ass groundstrokes at him for the better part of an hour, when feeling a bit haggard, Todd and I ventured up to the net where we could just volley the ball back. But we made Sheldeen grind it out in the backcourt for another half hour, figuring that was the kind of stuff a world class fourteen-year-old would be doing.

"I kind of like Sheldeen's backhand," Hammer said, as we moved him carefully from side to side with our volleys.

"His forehand is nothing to sneeze at," I volunteered.

"Yeah, well, you're expected to have a good forehand," Hammer said, "it's the backhand that will surprise the opponent."

Sheldeen's groundies had been ricocheting off our string beds in a seemingly endless rhythm.

"The groundstrokes are definitely the backbone of the game," I said. "Anyway, that's what the old timer at the Rose Garden used to tell me."

"For sure," Todd offered, "even on the men's tour, ninety percent of the guys on top are backcourters. Sure, they can do it all, but the groundies are the key. Look at Lendl, Borg, Austin — Evert, Connors — Agassi, Graf, Seles, Courier. They do it with the groundstrokes. Martina, McEnroe, Sampras — they are the exceptions. Sure, they serve well and they can volley, but they are a little weak off the backhand wing."

"Yeah," I said, "when they're backhand to backhand against a two-hander you can see the difference, the one-hander is usually the first to spray the ball, even if his name is McEnroe or Sampras."

Finally, Sheldeen began to miss a few and I knew he was spent. "That's fine for now," I told him, "time to take a breather."

"I think I'll run first," he said, and he put his racket down at the side of the court where there was a big crack in the blacktop.

"Okay, but just ten times around the park." With all the training Sheldeen was doing, I figured, more than two miles would be pushing it.

Instantly, he was off. Hammer and I sat down against the chain link and watched him stride out on the turf. When he got to the far end of the park where the ground was mostly dirt and weeds, he mixed in footwork patterns and short sprints.

"The kid's got what it takes," Todd said, and then we talked more about groundstrokes and the old days and how weird it was that Borg never won a US Open.

"That's kind of strange," I said, "when you consider that Borg was a backcourting, counterpunching groundstroker who won five Wimbledons on a fast grass surface that would have presumably offered itself more to a volleyer. You've got to wonder, why not the US Open on its slower surface?"

But Hammer had a theory. He thought maybe the fast grass of Wimbledon favored Borg's innate quickness by allowing him to respond in movement and shot-making more quickly. "And," he said, "with opponents rushing the net more often, Borg's passing shot got more opportunities at Wimbledon than at the US Open."

That sounded reasonable enough. And yet, during his five straight

Wimbledon victories, Borg's fleet-footed game was comprised of a lot more than whipping topspin groundstrokes. The truth is, he came to the net a good deal of the time. Too much, in fact, at least according to Hammer, who was now deep in thought. Hammer said sadly that Borg might have won a sixth Wimbledon title, or even a seventh. "But he got carried away with hitting volleys."

As Todd explained it, Borg had won the Italian and the French, but the public had grave doubts about whether the young Swedish counterpuncher could win Wimbledon. After all, to win the great grass championships required the tactics of an accomplished serve-and-volleyer. Everyone knew that. It wasn't like the French, where one could slog back in the trenches of a clay court. Or even the relatively safe baseline haven of a hardcourt. No, this was The Big Green, where the ball slid fast and held low. Volleys meant everything. Volleys and serves.

And so Borg became more and more trained in the tidy racketwork of the standard chip volley with each successive Wimbledon title. His devastating swinging volley from midcourt all but disappeared after his third victory. He would cast off the criticism that he was just a scrambling backcourter. And to facilitate his getting to the net, his serve was garnished with more of a forward run.

Sheldeen came chugging by just then like a relaxed locomotive, on what appeared to be his fourth lap around the park. "Yeah, it's a real shame," Hammer continued, "Borg was playing all along the way more and more guys are playing today. He was ahead of his time, forging the way for others, with his big inside-out forehand and his two-handed backhand. He was grinding it out from the baseline, but then everyone criticized him and made him think about the volley too much. Even his serve seemed to diminish."

We often spoke of Borg as *The Great One*. Hammer looked out through the chain link, where Sheldeen grew smaller in the distance. "I'll tell you one thing," he said, "if anybody ever does beat The Great One's record of five Wimbledon's in a row, you can bet they're going to be doing it from the backcourt."

Maybe he was right; after all, there were fewer serve-and-volleyers these days, and it wasn't simply because the courts were slower and the balls were heavier. Hell, the guys had bigger serves than ever, so they could come to the net if they wanted. It's just that everybody's groundstrokes got bigger too, and they became more content to stay in the backcourt. Besides, coming in meant facing the other guy's big groundies from up close, and maybe getting passed. Some guys still came in a lot, but for sure, the days of just flying in on every serve were over. I recalled Arthur Ashe at his prime, how he would serve and run to the net — he'd skid to a stop, legs wide apart, then lunge to the side with his long arm outstretched to volley the return. I pictured Vitas Gerulaitus, too. But he'd be in the backcourt gliding around and then suddenly dash in to sprint right through a volley. He'd be mid-stride when he connected with the ball, his long blond hair trailing in the golden sunlight.

We sat there on the court waiting for Sheldeen to finish running. "It's too bad Borg quit," I said rather dreamily. We always lamented the fact that Borg quit the game shortly after losing to McEnroe in a fateful Wimbledon final. But Hammer insisted Borg wasn't playing his natural game in that match, and that's why Borg always felt he should have won. "Because deep inside," Hammer said, "The Great One knew he could have won. And that bothered him so much he quit after a few more tournaments."

"Anyway, it's just a theory," Todd said. He had been there at the match and remembered it well, even though it was more than a few years ago. He said it was as if the nimble Swede had decided to prove to McEnroe (and to the Duchess of Kent) that he too could serve-and-volley. He went to the net all the time and was hardly in the backcourt. His efforts were admirable, but the result was that McEnroe gradually forged ahead. And at moments when Borg did try to rely on his awesome groundstrokes, they were slightly out of tune; he had lost his feel for the powerful putaway and the perfectly threaded passing shot. It was too late.

"But Johnny Mac played well in that final," I said. "Besides, back then the grass on center court got pretty chewed up and it wasn't repaired all that well. Borg would have had a lot of bad bounces to deal with if he stayed in the backcourt more."

"I still think he would have been better off focusing on groundstrokes and not the volley. Anyway, I'm not saying Johnny Mac didn't play a great match, I'm just saying it might have turned out differently if nobody had messed with The Great One's game. I'm saying if he hadn't been so preoccupied with being a volleyer and had just played his game all those years, he might have won those five Wimbledons and then some."

"Wow," I said, "I would have liked to see The Great One win another Wimbledon, that would have been cool."

"Who knows," Todd offered, the sneaky smile beginning to form at the corners of his mouth, "he might have even won *use soapen*" (that was the way Borg pronounced *US Open*.)

Although we referred to Borg as "The Great One" and McEnroe as simply "Johnny Mac," we both knew that the superiority of one player over the other was nuanced and open ended. In a pinch, the cool-headed Swede could probably get through anything, but when the chips were really down and everything was on the line, McEnroe would get mad as hell, and if he couldn't get to the other side, he'd die trying. He was the kind of guy you wanted on your side. And yet, arguing about these guys was like debating the superiority of a Chevy over a Ford — it came down to instinct. Some people were drawn to Borg's cruise control, but then there were others who lived just to see McEnroe step on the throttle.

Sheldeen burst into the court just then and plopped himself down in the doubles alley near us. His handsome, sternly chiseled features glistened with sweat. He looked more serious, older actually.

He went into a stretching routine, breathing deeply, patiently holding each position for a good minute on the blacktop. Watching him made me feel lazy and old. "Here," I tossed him a towel to wrap around his neck in the cool air.

"Well, kid," Hammer said, "I think you're ready for Panama. But not because you're playing well or because you're in such good shape." Sheldeen looked up curiously.

"It's because of this court, this broken-down old court. They'll probably put first round 14's on something damn near as bad, but you're not a typical spoiled-brat American. You'll be ready. You know what it is to play tennis on a court full of weeds and still kick ass. You'll surprise them."

"Yeah," I said, "there's no telling what conditions they'll lay on you in Central America. They'll try to knock you off any way they can. They'll use the heat, the court, whatever it takes."

"I'll be ready," Sheldeen said calmly, "whatever it takes." I noticed the toe of his right shoe was showing signs of wear. I figured when he got back from the tournament it would be worse, and we'd take it over to Pop's for a repair job.

We had another brief workout the morning Sheldeen was to board the plane for Panama. I gave him a quick overall tune-up, and then I fed him a series of short balls.

"You've got to be ready for the short ball," I told him. "A lot of these foreigners are used to playing on clay and they like to use drop shots, even though they shouldn't on a hardcourt. Just be alert and you'll run up and burn them. You might even want to hang back a little and try to entice them to use the dropper." Sheldeen's speed was phenomenal, especially for a big kid; it would be natural for the opposition to underestimate his ability to retrieve the ball or suddenly dart forward and put one away.

"Don't worry, Coach," Sheldeen said, somewhat amused, "I can get to just about any short ball."

"The problem isn't getting to the ball, it's hitting it with authority when you get there."

In order to demonstrate my point, I had Sheldeen stand at the service line, and I dropped a ball gently over the net. He got to it alright, but with the ball only inches off the ground and the barrier of the net so close, it was no easy task to hit a hard groundstroke into the court. Naturally, Sheldeen just kind of shoved the ball back over the net.

"Come on, hit hard," I said, feeding him more balls, "let them rip. You can't just get these dinkers back, you've got to put them away." So Sheldeen layed into the ball with his topspin forehand, but it either hit the top of the net or went long.

I encouraged him anyway. "You're on the right track," I said, "but you've got to use more hand and wrist, not so much arm. Whip the ball with your hand, a real loose hand." I flapped my hand at him like I was waving good-by. "Like this, you've got to miniaturize the entire stroke into your hand, a floppy loose hand with almost no backswing."

Sheldeen mimicked my exaggerated wrist motion, and soon he was taking those ground-sucking dinkers and whipping them over the net at will. So I put him behind the baseline and had him sprint up to that same short ball before hitting it for a winner.

And now I was mixing it up, feeding him balls of various depths to put away. He didn't miss a one, and he hit them all with power!

"Hey, Preacher," he said with a sly grin as we stopped to pick up the balls, "I think I'm ready for Panama."

"Just be ready for the drop shot," I reminded him at the airport as he was about to board the plane, "Keep your hand loose and let it rip, and you'll do fine."

An excited Buckskin Charley called two days later. "Guess what? The kid knocked off a seed in the second round!" His Costa Rican friend had telephoned from the tournament. Apparently, Sheldeen French fried the guy (6-1, 6-1.)

Charley called again the next day. "Guess what? The kid's zoning, he's in the quarters." He had just beaten a Russian boy in three sets.

Now my every breath was filled with the humid air of Panama. I pictured Sheldeen, the sweat streaming down his taut cheeks.

"He's in the semis!" Charley told me the next day. And then it was "THE FINALS!" Sheldeen was the only American playing on the day of the finals, and all eyes were on him. The USTA coach, who was there with his eighteen-year-olds, now escorted Sheldeen everywhere. Charley's Costa Rican friend called me during the warmup. "He's playing a junior from France," he told me, "a tall boy who is lefthanded. The boy looks very good. In the semis, he hit the most beautiful drop shots."

"From the baseline?" I asked.

"Yes, and from the volley as well."

"Does he have a two-hander?"

"No, he hits the backhand with only one hand."

I was relieved. Okay, I thought, I don't care how good that one-hander is, it is going to crack. Sheldeen will make him hit the high ball, and if that little French tickler thinks he can drop shot on a hardcourt, Sheldeen's going to teach him a lesson he'll never forget.

Charley's friend promised to call back the minute the match was over. I felt a rush of adrenaline as I sat at my little kitchen table in the Berkeley flatlands thinking about Panama and Todd and Montana and Buckskin Charley. Bonnie, Evonne, Hitch, freight trains, everything was speeding through my mind. I pictured Fernando, his ponytail and his poetry. Then I imagined an all-court shoot-out; I knew that if tennis were like that, kids would already be turned on to it, just like football. And yet, at the same time I had visions of the old days, when everything was so simple, before we all became decimal points. Suddenly there was the roar of the crowd in a stadium court — Sheldeen had just crushed a forehand — then came a close-up of his father's smile, a thick warm smile that wouldn't have been any different if the kid had lost in the first round.

The phone was ringing, in the distance at first, then louder, annoying me, stealing me away from my kaleidoscopic daydreams. The man's voice with the Latin accent was at the other end of the line. "He has won in straight sets," the voice said, "six-four, seven-five. Your Sheldeeno has won. The US coach is walking him off the court."

It took a while for it all to sink in. Actually, it wasn't until the next morning that it really hit home.

YOUNG AMERICAN WINS the paper said. It was an Associated

Press release that surely got printed in every major city in the country. Sheldeen had been in the San Francisco Chronicle sports section before, but this was different. He wasn't just mentioned along with the other winners. This was an article not about a tournament, but about an inner city kid from the States, and how he had won the tournament, by beating players from South Africa, Brazil, Russia, Germany, Australia, France; junior players who were number one in their countries and were expected to become Davis Cuppers.

"Unseeded Sheldeen Wagner of Berkeley swept the field in his first ever international attempt," the article said. Then there was a quote from Sheldeen's coach, Neil Foyer, the USTA guy. At least the guy talked like his coach. "He's exceptional for his age, and he works hard. You'll be hearing a lot more about Wagner and other Americans in the future." Foyer went on to say how one of his eighteen-year-old girls lost in the quarters, taking the eventual winner to three sets before bowing out.

The next afternoon Sheldeen arrived in a sleek black limousine, courtesy of a local car dealer. That big long car looked like it had pulled into our little flatland neighborhood for a funeral or something. But then Sheldeen got out very much alive and beaming, a huge silver bowl under his arm.

Pedro and I were waiting out front, along with Mei Mei and Sheldeen's dad. A lot of other people from the neighborhood were there, too. After all, there was a barbecue in the works you could smell a block away. The limousine driver left his car on the street and went in to help himself to a couple of burgers. Then that big black limo made its way out of the Berkeley flatlands.

More and more people continued to crowd into Sheldeen's little house, and all the while, a beautiful voice could be heard singing; it was his mother in the kitchen. A plump jubilant woman, she sang while she prepared extra food for the barbecue. She always sang while she worked, even on less celebrated occasions. Her husband, the big man in overalls, watched contentedly over the grill on their tiny back porch.

Sheldeeno, as the locals had called him during the tournament, was full of interesting details about Panama, which he shared excitedly, like the fact that everyone drank Coca-Cola and smoked Marlboros. He said the traffic cops had machine guns and that there were brightly colored flowers all over the place. Now he was teaching his young neighborhood pals how to keep score in different languages, and also how to swear.

They gathered around him eagerly, the whole gang chanting the most exotic sounding phrases. At any rate, to the untrained ear, those foreign delicacies certainly didn't sound like obscenities. But then Mei Mei joined them, and Sheldeen became reluctant to translate the vulgarities.

By the time evening arrived, Sheldeen looked worn out, perhaps even troubled. He really didn't seem like a kid who had just won a world tournament.

I had to go, so Sheldeen walked with me along the sidewalk for a while, and his dog tagged along. I guess the little fellow missed Sheldeen, after all, he hadn't seen him in a week. Then suddenly remembering something, Sheldeen reached into his pants pocket and pulled out a crumpled-up newspaper article. "Hey!" he blurted out, "you're my coach! Not this guy!"

"I know that," I said, "and you know that. That's what matters, not what other people think." But secretly I hated that article too, and I knew that what other people thought was in fact what mattered, and that there might come a time when other people could take over Sheldeen's life and I would be completely out of the picture, along with Buckskin Charley and the other small sponsors I had found for the kid.

We sat down on the dusky curb for a while and talked. I was happy for him and proud, extremely proud. But I think we were both a little worried about what the future had in store. Hell, he must have gotten half a dozen phone calls during the barbecue — equipment manufacturers, clothing companies, college coaches — they were already hitting the kid up.

"I wouldn't have won if I hadn't kicked ass on the French guy's dropper," he said, his spirits beginning to pick up.

"How bad did you burn him?" I asked.

"Not too bad the first time, but then I really ripped him and he got scared to hit it. Then he got impatient, especially with his backhand and he began to miss."

We stood up to go and shook hands. "Remember," Sheldeen said, "I don't know who that guy is. You're still my coach. You'll always be my coach."

Always? I wondered about that as I walked alone down the sad gray sidewalk. That would be nice. But there were powerful forces out there. Naturally I wanted it all, I wanted to take the kid all the way. But some things might be too hard for him to resist, and that bothered me. Even now, I could feel other people closing in on the kid, stealing him away from me.

I pictured that long black limousine parked in our little flatland neighborhood. A limo that wasn't there for a funeral. Or was it?

I began to feel depressed. I remembered what Hammer had told me — "the better those juniors get the more likely they are to abandon you." I tried to be upbeat; I forced my stride to be light and bouncy, rationalizing that if the powers that be took Sheldeen away, there would always be another kid out there in those endless flatlands. Another poised little athlete with natural talent. He would just be waiting for me. Of course, the trick would be in finding him. And turning him on to tennis.

In the distance behind me I could hear someone calling. "See you Sunday ... in church ... Hey, Preacher ..." It was Sheldeen. The streetlight was out and I could barely see him.

Chapter Forty-One

Hippie Hill

Now that the dust had settled from Sheldeen's international debut, I got back into my rut of thinking about Bonnie at night and wondering why Hammer was married and I wasn't. Hammer the stockbroker, and me, Stretch, still trying to squeeze the juice out of tennis. I wondered how long I'd be pitching balls. Maybe I should get into something else, I thought. Oh well, the little club gig in Marin was going along pretty well. I didn't mind the short commute across the bridge; actually, I found it enjoyable. And now I had a few bucks in my pocket, not that I was getting rich by any means.

But unfortunately, some changes were taking place. The contented whistling of the club manager was no longer heard in the upstairs office. He had accepted a job at a posh resort in Palm Springs. We had gotten along great and I hated to see him go, but he was going to make twice the money in Palm Springs, so he couldn't say no. I wondered if he would whistle like a bird in his new office, or if the big money would dry up his music.

The new manager was a prim and proper middle-aged divorcee who most of the old guys on the board found attractive in spite of her stiff demeanor. Dixie had been dating the president of the club when she was hired. (He was a sixty-year-old widower with silver hair and a pretty good backhand.)

Dixie didn't have what you would call a natural affinity for tennis pros, but she tolerated them, at least the ones at the clubs. The real pros, the ones who traveled the world actually playing the game were of no use to her whatsoever.

I knew from the start Dixie and I weren't going to hit it off, the vibes just weren't there. We never had much to say to each other. And when we did speak, it wasn't like a normal conversation; it was as if she were on the phone and I was just a call she was trying to get rid of. I seldom saw her anyway. She stayed in her office for the most part, but still, it made me uneasy to know she was running the show.

After a while, Dixie began to bug me about my lessons — who I taught and when, how much I charged for the groups, and so on. Then one day she announced that the board had approved a new policy — checks for tennis lessons would be written to the club, not to me. Cash payments would also go to the club. The club, in turn, would take out my deductions and pay me. I knew what was coming — the big skim. Hell, she'd probably take away my little candy-ass retainer, too. Then, showing them how she'd made money for the club, she'd ask for a goddamn raise!

Dixie also made a point to tell me that her nephew, who lived in New Hampshire, was a tennis teacher. She said the kid was anxious to move to California. Apparently he majored in recreation management in college, and though he only played junior high tennis, he learned how to teach it recently during a one-week stay at a tennis resort. (Well, la-di-dah.) She probably figured he'd make a perfect pro for the club.

Now it seemed Dixie always had something to tell me — be sure to pick up all the balls on the teaching court, latch the gate, keep the juniors from being so noisy, let the person at the desk know exactly when you'll be in.

The job was beginning to aggravate me, and Dixie annoyed the hell out of me. The whole atmosphere of the club was changing for the worse. Even the grounds looked sterile and artificial, everything was so perfectly manicured. The natural leafy beauty of the place was disappearing fast, as was the smile on the gardener dude's face. No longer would the sudden turn of his leaf blower accidentally lift the edge of a pretty tennis skirt;

he was too busy trimming this and chopping that and wiping the sweat from his brow.

I wasn't psyched up anymore when I drove across the Richmond-San Rafael Bridge in the mornings. In fact, I found myself scanning the want ads. I even applied for a couple of jobs, just for the hell of it. One actually required a Masters degree in psychology, a personnel supervisor position at a manufacturing plant in Oakland. And it paid great! And guess what?

I got the job! The lady in charge told me I had a lot of experience dealing with people, and that the owner of the plant was a tennis nut. The job was mine if I wanted it. I told her I wasn't sure I could handle going to work in a factory five days a week.

"You get to wear nice clothes, and you'll have your own office," she said.

She leaned toward me and whispered secretively. "You don't have to make up your mind right away, our contract with the temporary person isn't up for a few weeks. Think it over."

I was definitely thinking it over, especially when things with Dixie got bad at the club, or I thought too much about Sheldeen slipping away from me. But then a miracle took place, and things didn't seem so awful. It was Bonnie — she came down from Oregon and moved in, to kind of feel things out, she said. Yet, after a couple of weeks it felt so natural I doubted either of us considered it a trial run any more, especially now that her husband had filed for divorce. It had been a long time coming, more than three years to be exact, but now at last, Bonnie and I were together and living under the same roof.

We moved from my funky apartment in the flats and rented a small cottage nestled in the Berkeley hills about halfway between Pop's place and where Evonne and Hitch lived. It was sweet and woodsy up there and just a short walk to the Rose Garden. We often took that stroll in the evenings with Syd, Bonnie's dog, who she couldn't bear to leave in Portland. She hated to leave the girls too, but they had each other and their boyfriends. She didn't see that much of them, anyway, since they were both away at college in Eugene.

Bonnie and Evonne became real pals. They did a lot together. Then on the weekends, if Hitch was in town, he and I would join them for something — dinner, a movie, whatever. Sometimes Todd and Laura would come along and it really felt like old times, old times that had merged magically into the present.

Bonnie and I rounded up the whole gang one Sunday after church. We decided to do San Francisco. It would be casual, which meant packing our bikes along and riding around Golden Gate Park, which was cool because they closed off the park to cars on Sundays. We would also hit a few balls at the courts there, and then go out to eat in Chinatown.

Actually, we never did the tennis, so pre-occupied were we with riding down to the ocean. When we got back to the park we were bushed; we just pedaled over to Hippie Hill and crashed out with everyone else. All of humanity was there. Flower children, flower parents, flower grandparents, flower aunts and uncles; it was definitely flower power on the cool green grass of Hippie Hill on that sunny San Francisco day. Bonnie pulled out the drawing pad she always carried and began sketching. "Looks like Mardi Gras or something!" Evonne exclaimed. Indeed, there were blue jeans and cut-offs, purple togas, pink bikinis, longhairs, ponytails, dreadlocks, tattoos and earrings, popsicles and frisbees, men, women, children, and all held together by the tribal beat of the conga drums at the base of the hill. There must have been fifteen dudes in a line, all of them bare-chested and sweating as they pounded out the tribal rhythm of ancient Africa into the firmament above Golden Gate Park.

We picked out a spot halfway up the slope of the hill and kicked back. Hammer was in a modified lotus position, lolling his head to the beat while Laura lay in the grass with her head propped up against his thigh.

Meanwhile, the goofball in Hitch had been set free. "Look at all the weirdos," he said. "I bet a lot of these people are suits when they're not pretending to be hippies. And they're probably all gay," he added with an air of feigned superiority. Evonne laughed. "Well why don't you go down there and tell that big black guy with the peace sign on his drum you think he's gay." The guy looked to be about six-eight. Obviously the leader, he was heavily muscled, with a stomach ripped like the bottom of an egg carton. He sat with his big conga drum between his knees, flailing at it as if he were in a trance. His body glistened with sweat. Sweat seeped from his every pore; it flew off his elbows and fingertips. Dripping wet, he looked authentic and primal in his loincloth, as if he were still attached to the very beginning and his bulging veins were actually tributaries of the Congo River. He was linked to the past by the sound of his drum, and the sound of all the other drums, as we all were as we lay around Hippie Hill on that balmy San Francisco day.

"I kind of like the big guy," Hitch said, and then we all just settled in and listened to the beat of the tribe.

Bonnie put down her sketch pad and lay down beside me. In the cool grass, her hand felt warm in mine. We just lay there feeling the rays of the sun on our faces and listening to the continuum of the beat, that ever pulsing tribal beat.

The incessant sound mixed in my head with the miles of rhythmic rattles the freighters had rolled into my mind on the way to Montana. Suddenly there was the forlorn plea of the horn from up front, and I felt Bonnie's hand offer mine a tender squeeze. A wave of incredible oneness with her swept through my being. I felt grounded to the earth and to life, itself. At last.

The peculiar scent of a homegrown cigarette wafted by from time to time, and Hitch would say something like, "Hey, what's that smell?" or "Pass it over here, will ya?" Then the odor would disappear and there would just be the fresh clean smell of the earth. And the relentless sound of the drums.

Small puffs of cloud drifted by overhead as the tribal beat rose up and spread over Golden Gate Park. That incessant beat, primal and omnipotent, like the timeless flow of the Congo River that gushed through the veins of the big man, fueling him as he worked his drum in front of the pack.

The sound of the drums reminded me of the thump of a tennis ball being hit in Davie Stadium, that deep stunted echo. I imagined overheads being hit from within the confines of that old rock quarry, thousands of them — then there was the staccato beat of a hundred tennis players in loincloths rifling volleys at each other. Then the freighter passed through my mind again. There was the sad call of the horn, and I saw Sheldeen waving good-by from the caboose, shrinking into the distance. I squeezed Bonnie's hand and felt her reply, and I knew that everything would be okay.

Eventually, the breeze picked up, chilling those of us in shirtsleeves and stirring the crowd on Hippie Hill. People began to crawl out of their slumbers and drift away in groups. Some, like us, were on bicycles, but most just walked away sadly with their heads bent down as the big congas beckoned for them to stay.

Unable to resist, I spun my bike around and took one last look at the line of bare-chested drummers. The big man was still in front, the Congo still gushing from the well of his neck, its white foam seeping at his nape. With black shoulders glistening, his slick arms jumped in the fading sunlight of Golden Gate Park. He flailed at the drum, over and over, his whole body pulling at the fingertips. Drumming with arched palms and white eyes. Drumming and drumming and drumming. The sound spreading across the dusky park. The white-eyed drummer, waiting, as each beat calls out to its forerunner. Waiting. As the hollow of the next beat rises from between black thighs. Waiting. The primal echo, the arched palms and white eyes waiting, forever waiting for that tribal beat to transport us all back to the banks of the Congo River.

"Hey, let's go, Stefan." Bonnie had circled back on her bike. She looked amused. "It's getting cold, we're going to eat, let's go." The big man had pulled me back in, but the idea of food was a good one.

Chapter Forty-Two

Backwards Tennis

Usually we went to Edsel's place, a little second story dive in Chinatown. Edsel was just the waiter, a somewhat gruff, but very comical waiter. He had kind of a sideways chip on his shoulder, which you'd expect of a Chinese guy named Edsel whose middle name happened to be Ford. Edsel Ford Fung.

We always had a good time at Sam Wo's, where Edsel worked. But they were packed today, so we were trying out another restaurant and eating our own brand of humor. Todd and Laura had discovered the place. Actually, Bonnie and the girls went there for lunch a couple of times, but it was my first visit. It looked typical enough, steamy and sizzly in the kitchen, oriental paintings and lanterns, a big goldfish up front near the register; and smooth-skinned kids helping out here and there amidst a background of high-pitched nasal dialects and elastic oriental music. At the perimeter tables, old Chinese men lifted soup bowls up to their chins. It was definitely the real thing.

Okay, so we pigged out — egg rolls, fried shrimp, sweet and sour spare ribs, almond duck, chow mein, chow yuk, fried rice, black bean fish. Those warm savory aromas! There was scarcely room on the table for it all.

Almost immediately, Evonne proposed a contest which would prove once and for all who was more coordinated, men or women. The idea was that we would all eat with chopsticks. Which wouldn't have been so bad if the bet hadn't been that we had to do it lefthanded. With our stomachs rumbling, Hitch, Hammer, and I balanced precariously tiny amounts of food on our twitching sticks, sometimes actually making it into our mouths with the delicacies, while the women, appearing completely ambidextrous and oriental, fed themselves luxuriously large quantities at a steady pace that was only interrupted by accurate comments about how inept we men were. Our sole consolation during the meal was an occasional swig of Japanese beer.

We conceded halfway through and resorted to forks and right hands, while our women folk continued deftly with chopsticks in their lefts as if they ate that way all the time. "Okay, I'm convinced," Todd announced, "women are more coordinated than men."

"And they're lefthanded, too," Hitch offered with a goofy grin, "that's why they throw so weird righthanded."

"You guys are definitely better at the delicate things," I said. "You'd probably make great surgeons."

"And lovers, too," Todd noted. Then, using his fork as a small shovel, he cleaned his plate in a couple of swipes and helped himself to more.

"Well, life is delicate," Bonnie suggested. "But women are tough too, they're mothers of the earth."

"And they're the original gods of religion," Laura proposed. "That was before Jesus and those other fellows got involved, if you know what I mean."

"It wasn't really Jesus' fault," Hammer said.

"That's true; it was just men in general, I guess, especially the ones holding the purse strings, like the priests."

"I think the ones holding the spears had something to do with it too," Bonnie said.

"Let me get this straight," Hitch said soberly, trying to clarify the point, "you're saying that medicine women were the original medicine men?"

"I couldn't have said it better myself," Laura acknowledged, and she offered her glass of Sapporo out over the table, and we all joined in. CLINK. CLINK, CLINK.

"Bravo! Here's to goddesses."

"And chopsticks."

"Yeah, here's to lefthanded chopsticks."

"And conga drums."

"Here's to freight trains."

"Here's to bicycles."

Yes, now with Bonnie in my life I was more silly, perhaps, but I needed that. And yet, at the same time, I was more serious and aware. In short, I was more complete, I felt as if I belonged. The idea of losing Sheldeen seemed less troublesome, and even my problems with Dixie seemed minor. I searched for Bonnie's hand under the table and took it; it was nice to have it so near.

I leaned back in the booth and listened to the elastic sound of Chinese music that seemed to spread into the far corners of the room. Those stretching tones shrank into themselves, and then they pulled apart again, spiraling and bending to the far reaches of the universe, or so it seemed. It reminded me of psychedelic rock music I heard on the radio every day, and I wondered how far ahead the Chinese were. I mean, did the Chinese always have an expanded consciousness? After all, their music probably hadn't changed much over the last thousand years, and yet hip Westerners, aided by mind-altering substances, were just now beginning to express a similar wide range of consciousness in their music. Contemporary rock music was sounding more Chinese all the time. Religion, too, was becoming a reflection of the Chinese as young people everywhere began to discover the ancient wisdom of Buddhism and Taoism.

Under the table I felt a sudden tug at my hand. It was Bonnie with that amused look again, trying to reel me back in.

It took me a moment to get my bearings, and then I realized the dialogue at the table had drifted into a new bewildering direction. It seems Laura, who had done undergraduate work in linguistics, got everybody interested in palindromes, or *deep* palindromes, as she called them — words or phrases that tend to retain their meaning when read backwards. Symmetrically spelled words like peep, kook, and gag are readily available palindromes. But the letters of a phrase can also be read backwards. *A man, a plan, a canal, Panama!* is the classic palindrome phrase of our time. And yet, *Live Lewd* is more fascinating, because the reversal *(Dwel Evil)* retains meaning by use of different words. Laura said Dick Cavett had recently discussed these unique words on his TV show. She had taken out pen and paper and was giving us a class on the subject right there in the restaurant.

"How about *tennis*?" Evonne suggested, "I think tennis is a deep palindrome." I had had a couple of Sapporos by now and could scarcely tell the difference between the Astrodome and a palindrome, although I did give it a try, trying to read the word "tennis" backwards in my mind. SINNET. No I just didn't see the connection. Hitch was looking at his fiancée with his head tweaked, as if he had just discovered she was an admitted bisexual. "Sinnet!?" he slurred.

"Look, you guys, don't you get it?" Evonne was delighted. Then Bonnie's face lit up. "Yes, tennis *is* a deep palindrome, think about it." She nudged me with her elbow, waiting for me to say something like "yeah, Okay, I get it," but I was still in the Astrodome.

"Sin Net?" Hammer said questioningly. "Yes, that's it!" Laura exclaimed, seeing it now, "sin net, the sin of the net, the sin of hitting the ball in the net.

Hammer smiled with his slow, introspective nod. Wow, I thought, I guess tennis is one of those rare words. All you have to do is read it backwards and the key to playing the percentages will stare you in the face — don't hit the ball in the net!

And so we decided, over Sapporos and almond duck, that the best short tennis lesson in the history of the game is secretly encoded in the word, itself. Laura told us it was an exceptional find. "When you examine just one word, it's rare to find any related meaning at all when you reverse it, unless of course, it's spelled with symmetrical letters."

"What about *ball*?" Todd asked. Hitch raised an eyebrow. "Ba ball, I mean, la labb?"

"That's it," Todd said eagerly, "because when the pressure's on you can always throw up a llab."

"Not bad," Laura said beaming, "I'll have to contact my friends back at the University, tennis definitely deserves to be in their hall of fame. Sin Net, I like that."

And golfers weren't to be left out! Not at all. We declared their sport equally scholarly, after all, the reverse of golf is FLOG. And that summarizes the entire game, perhaps even better than the forward reading. At least as far as we tennis players were concerned; for to golf is to flog, and to flog is to golf, it's all the same. In the end, the ball has that same chopped up look.

The six of us ate our fortune cookies. Teetering slightly, we made our way out past the goldfish at the front of the restaurant.

Chapter Forty-Three

The Wilson Razor

I sure liked living in the woodsy Berkeley hills, and Bonnie certainly seemed to have adjusted well to her move. Though she hadn't been in the Bay Area long, she made friends readily and was always doing something. She even landed work in a San Francisco ad agency, something in the creative department. It wasn't like she needed the money; it was just a part-time job, to keep her connected, she said.

With Syd striding by her side, she ran a couple of miles in the hills every day, so they were both in pretty good shape. And though she hit with Evonne on occasion, and me of course, she had no real interest in tennis, or in even seeing the club in Marin, for that matter. She never mentioned it, but tennis was probably part of the initial rift between her and her husband. There may have been some deep scars there.

Nonetheless, I thought I'd show her the club sometime, let her get used to hanging around the place; eventually then, Dixie would meet her. Surely, Dixie would see what a wonderful person Bonnie was, and things would go more smoothly for me. After all, everyone liked Bonnie. She was smart, nice to look at, and just reserved enough not to rub anybody the wrong way (whereas sometimes a woman with Evonne's exuberance could be too much for a stuffy CQ or a manager with a bug in her butt.) Dixie's bound to like Bonnie, I thought, and that will be a plus.

One of the club tournaments was coming up, the very next weekend, in fact. That was it, I'd have Bonnie help me at the desk. She'd get to meet a lot of members, and though I knew Dixie wouldn't be playing, she'd probably be on the grounds. Her boyfriend, the silver-fox club prez would play for sure.

Organized tournaments were not a priority with the Marin club, but the members loved this one. It was basically social, a mixed doubles event comprised of four pro-sets with rotating partners. Upper and lower divisions were determined by whether you won or lost in the opening round. Accomplished players, hackers, CQ's, CK's, SW's — everybody would come out for the big event. And though they wouldn't admit it, a lot would be on the line for most and their true colors would show as they made tighter calls than usual. Naturally, those who finished on top would get their names engraved on the championship plaque.

The sorry coefficient would probably be higher than usual, I figured, since players would be paired with unfamiliar partners and there would be an instinct to apologize more frequently. And yet, the envy factor might fall as players focused more on the action at hand and less on their own shortcomings. That is, until the event was over and all results were in, results which would brand ability levels on their foreheads until next year's tournament, when perhaps, still haunted by a doublefault on matchpoint, a player might settle his nerves this time with a few ounces of vodka in a water bottle.

Beneath blue skies, mild bay breezes swept over the tops of whitecaps, gently cooling the low green hills in Marin County where the little tennis club stood. In the near distance was Mount Tamalpais; I looked out to it from time to time throughout the course of the morning. By my side at the tournament desk was Bonnie. She had always been willing to help and more or less volunteered for the position when I mentioned I could use a hand. (I got the impression tennis was gradually forging a more favorable spot in her heart.) With everybody romping around on the court, we were halfway through the tournament now and made ourselves busy opening up new balls for the rest of the matches.

One after another, like little bullet shots, the airy sound of new tennis jars being opened created short but satisfying bursts, or tharts, as Hammer liked to call them. The tharts let us know that the balls were, indeed, fresh. A familiar scent filled the air, that gaseous blend of plastic, rubber, and felt.

But then Bonnie almost sliced off her finger trying to open a jar of Wilsons. "Ouch," she squeaked, rather politely, considering the fact that the slit in her finger was deep. She tried to press the flesh together but blood kept coming out. I handed her a towel and ran into the pro shop to get a first-aid kit. Damn! I had forgotten to warn her about that.

I scolded myself for not showing her how to open those awful jars safely. The natural instinct is to hook one's finger through the loop and tear the aluminum lid off without a second thought, but every once in a while a sharp edge will get you. That's why seasoned players learn to tuck their fingers safely out of the way before yanking the top off. But the best method is to put one's thumb against the lid and apply pressure, thus stabilizing it as you pull up on the loop with your finger. Then you can pry the whole thing off slowly and bloodlessly.

I was feeling faint when I returned with the first-aid kit. The sight of blood always made me woozy. I hoped to god I wouldn't pass out there at the tournament desk in front of everybody, and especially not in front of Bonnie. The towel I had given her now had inky red stains on it. Bonnie removed it from her hand and thank god blood wasn't spurting out — her finger just looked kind of pink and pressed in, especially near the slit. But I didn't trust the slit, I knew it could well up with blood any second. I worked quickly despite my wooziness and pulled the skin together with a couple of small butterfly band-aids. Then I put a larger bandage around the whole thing, and I began to feel better.

"Are you OK, Stefan?"

"Yeah, no problem," I said, trying not to look at the red-stained towel. "I should have told you how to open those things. People are always getting cut up."

"You mean I'm not the only clumsy one?"

"Hell, I don't know any serious player who's never drawn blood trying to open a jar of balls. It's as if there's an invisible razor inside. Me, Hammer, Hitch, we've all been sliced. I bet even McEnroe's cut himself. You'd think the manufacturers would have come up with a safe system by now."

"I don't mind, really." She looked cute, somehow even cuter now with a bandage on her finger. I thought of my mother when I was a kid, how she would sometimes appear at the dinner table with a band-aid on her finger.

"It's nice of you to help out," I said.

Just then the silver-haired prez came over to report his scores. Tall and suntanned and immaculately dressed, he looked like something out of a tennis magazine. He noticed Bonnie struggling a bit with the pencil. "Oh, dear, what have we here?" he said, pointing to her hand, "a fresh battle wound?"

Bonnie giggled. "You'd be surprised how dangerous it can be opening up some new tennis balls," she said bashfully.

"No, my dear, I wouldn't be surprised at all. I've been nicked a time or two, believe me." He picked up her hand and examined it. You could tell he thought he had a way with women. "I see you're all doctored up now, you'll be good as new," he said, stroking her hand. He winked at me, then he went off to where a small group of ladies had gathered.

In a moment players were all around us, reporting their scores and figuring out who they were going to play in the next round. The ladies certainly enjoyed seeing Bonnie at the desk, such a fresh new face. And the men, well, even the worst of drubbings didn't seem so bad when reporting scores in her sparkling presence.

Bonnie had made a favorable impression, that was obvious. But still, there was no sign of Dixie. I figured she'd probably show up for the barbecue, and then she could meet Bonnie. A lot of the players were already hanging out in the barbecue area, snacking on chips between their matches.

At last, we wrapped up the tournament and had an awards presentation; and then sure enough, I noticed Dixie at the periphery of the crowd, giving instructions to the grounds guy. Soon the silvery prez was at her side, and they were off, bouncing along through that ever carefree crowd.

Yes, now that the tournament was over and we were enjoying the barbecue, everybody let their hair down. Even the SW's showed themselves. Great numbers of them stuck their heads out of the potato salad and complained about how they Shoulda Won. *We were up 5-2. If only my partner hadn't doublefaulted. If they hadn't called that ball out. If only I hadn't missed that volley. Pass the ketchup, will ya. I told you, my strings were too tight. The sun was in my eyes. My shoulder was sore. They had tri tip last year, I liked that better. Yeah, but I just kept missing, I had a new racket. Anyway, you know how I hate playing against that guy. Then they got a lucky net cord, you should have seen it. And then that ball rolled on our court!*

"There was nothing we could do," someone said, "that Sydney Smith runs like a gazelle."

"Yeah well, he has the backhand of a gazelle, too," a more experienced player replied, "you should have played his backhand."

Bonnie and I just kind of hung out by the pool and let the players came up to us with hamburgers in their hands. "I had to play with you know who in the second round," a lady confided in me. "Yeah," one guy said after getting royally creamed, "they played the big points better than we did." He had been beaten at love, but the match lingered in his mind as if it were a third set tiebreaker.

The two fanatical men who had regular vendetta matches with each other had been paired on opposite sides in the second round, and now they were still talking about it. "I told ya," the one guy said with a crazed look in his eyes, "don't ever tell me it's Break Point! Announcing the score is one thing, but if you ever tell me it's Break Point again I'm gonna kill you!" The other guy just chewed on his hamburger, a very innocent look smeared over his otherwise delighted demeanor.

They were all here — 2.7's, 3.9's, SW's, CQ's, SW/CQ combos, you name it, we even had a few players you couldn't put in a category. There were also about a half dozen highly accomplished players. They stayed in a group pretty much to themselves. But regardless, everyone was having a lot of fun, especially now that the gatorade had been replaced by a keg of beer. And now that our responsibilities were over, Bonnie and I could relax, too.

Suddenly, two 3.5 ladies were standing before us. I had heard their team got to the district finals in USTA league play, and I congratulated them. "Hell," one of them complained, "we should be going to the nationals. We beat the team that's going."

"That's good," I said. "Or, I mean, I guess that's too bad."

"Yeah," her partner chimed in, "the only team that beat us was a bunch of damn lobbers in pukey green shirts. I hate lobbers. You should have seen them, if they got anywhere near the net they turned around and ran right back to the baseline to lob again. Those damn pukey greens aren't near as good as we are, all they know how to do is lob."

Bonnie's blue eyes sparkled. "I thought you were supposed to want the opponents to lob," she offered, "that gives you a chance to hit the smash." And of course, she was right; that is, generally speaking, the object of the entire game is to force the opponent to hit up so you can hit down. The problem is most 3.5 ladies don't have good enough overheads to handle the lob; they don't back up well, nor do they know how to come in from the backcourt to intercept a lob. Hell, if they could, they wouldn't be 3.5 women, they'd be 4.0's, at least.

"I know what you mean about lobbers," I said.

"Yeah," said the lady, "if it weren't for those pukey greens we'd be going to the nationals."

Bonnie and I finished eating and began to mingle freely. But wherever we were, Dixie and the prez seemed to be somewhere else in the crowd. Then finally when the prez did head in our direction, Dixie remained discreetly behind to chat with a couple of CQ's who thought she was just terrific. Standing before us now, the prez complimented me on a well run tournament. He took Bonnie's hand and stroked it. "Young lady, such beautiful hands, you'll be good as new in no time, I'm sure." He was still stroking her injured hand, when out of the corner of his eye, he caught Dixie looking at him. He stammered briefly and went off to get another drink.

It was obvious Dixie had been avoiding us. "I was hoping you'd get to meet the manager," I told Bonnie as we drove home across the Richmond-San Rafael Bridge that evening. Not wanting to give Bonnie a bad taste for the club I hadn't told her how I really felt about Dixie, figuring maybe everything would work itself out if I just gave it more time. "She seemed a little preoccupied," Bonnie said, "her friend, what's-his-name, seemed nice enough. A little flirtatious, though."

"Hey, when you're president of the club you can be as flirtatious as you like, if you know what I mean."

It felt good to have Bonnie sitting next to me as the old Dart negotiated its way up into the dark hills above the Berkeley flatlands. I thanked her for helping out. And then I tried to put the Marin club out of my mind. As I flopped down onto bed beside her, I let my thoughts drift back down to the flats, where I would be in the morning with Sheldeen and the gang.

Chapter Forty-Four

Crossroads

Our bustling congregation was overflowing that Sunday on our little one-court church in the flatlands, but we managed just fine and everybody was improving. We did the usual: progression drills, stroke production, simulated competition, and free play; and now that the other kids had left, Sheldeen and I stood alone and talked. At almost fourteen, he had become quite a young man.

Uncomfortably, he showed me a letter he had received; it was from a big-name Florida pro, a guy with a boarding academy. The guy had seen Sheldeen play in Panama, and now he was offering him a scholarship. Room and board, the works. Immediately, I was irritated. The guy was trying to steal Sheldeen away from me! He wanted the kid as a feather in his cap (a cap that was, by god, fancy enough already!) If he wants to claim a champion, I thought, then by god, let him build his own!

Sheldeen put the letter away, and we hit for a while, neither of us doing too well. The crossroads before us was making us erratic; even our routine groundstrokes didn't know which way to turn. Gradually, though, I settled down and saw the sign that pointed in the right direction.

In Florida, Sheldeen would live and breathe tennis. He would hang out with nationally ranked juniors. And, he would get to hit with touring pros who came through the guy's place on a regular basis. He would also have a good academic program. I summoned him up to the net for a conference, and suddenly I became so happy for the kid that it wiped away the bitterness (and towered far above the emptiness that I would surely feel later.)

"You've got to do it," I told him, "it's your ticket, your chance."

"But I like it here in Berkeley." Sheldeen hung his head. "I don't want to live in Florida,"

"Go!" I almost shouted at him. "You'll be back here a lot, believe me. Then, when you make it to the big time, you can live wherever you want; Switzerland, Berkeley, Monte Carlo, wherever. Of course, by then you'll be living in a different place every week so it won't matter much, I suppose."

"A guy's got to have a home base," he said gloomily.

"Well then Berkeley it is! And guess what?" He looked at me cautiously. "If you can make it back on a Sunday, we'll save a place for you in church."

Sheldeen smiled briefly. "I'll be back every Sunday I can," he said soberly.

"Don't worry about it, I don't expect you to rush back from the French Riviera or somewhere just to hit balls on this beat-up old court."

Eventually, Sheldeen and I resumed our workout. Hitting carefully into each other's rhythm now, we savored the feel of extended exchanges as if each ball were, perhaps, a farewell rally. One hit went on for what seemed like ten minutes.

Later, when it was time to go, we gathered up the stray balls and put the big laundry basket in the trunk of the old Dart. We drove in silence over the tracks and through the neighborhood, past weathered little houses set back on wide roads. Then I let him out in front of his building.

"You'll always be my coach," he said with a concerned look.

"Don't worry about it," I told him, "you haven't even left yet." In truth, though, I too felt uneasy as I drove back up into the hills. The idea of losing Sheldeen was, perhaps, inevitable; I just never dreamed it would happen so soon; I figured the kid would at least be around until he went away to college. I thought about what church would be like without him. Pedro seldom came anymore now that he was older, and when he did show up it was just to eyeball Mei Mei, who had grown into quite a little China doll. She had gotten good enough to play number one for her junior high team, and I suppose, without Sheldeen, she'd be there to lend me a hand, especially with the little kids. She certainly was good at recruiting them into the program, although I still hadn't spotted any prospect with the kind of raw talent Sheldeen had displayed at an early age. But I knew there was a chance the right kid could show up eventually. He was somewhere out there in those endless flats, just waiting for me, whether he knew it or not.

Now that Bonnie and I had a cozy little pad up in the hills, I kind of missed the old flatland neighborhood down below. I never thought I'd long for the freighter that woke me up in the middle of the night, but I did. I guess there would always be a little tennis hobo inside of me.

And I missed running into the neighborhood kids. I imagine they missed me too. And as funky as that old blacktop court was, I missed having it nearby. I was at ease at the park. There was nobody around to tell me what to do. If I felt like sitting down on the court, I did it; if I felt like hitting an old ball over the fence, I blasted it. If the kids wanted to show up in blue jeans, there was nobody to complain they weren't in proper tennis attire. If someone wanted to bring a dog, then we had a dog tethered near the gate, where the bikes and skateboards were parked. Sometimes Bonnie even came along.

And now she was here at the park with her dog, taking a Sunday stroll while I finished up with the kids on the court. Syd was kind of pulling her through the grass. Then occasionally they'd stop and Bonnie would steady her drawing pad to sketch bits of life, I suppose, that only a neighborhood park in the Berkeley flatlands would know about. But church was just about over and the kids were beginning to leave, so she came in and sat down next to me on the blacktop.

We leaned back against the chain link and watched the children go their merry way, led by the ever popular Mei Mei. This was the third time I had taught the group without Sheldeen, who was in Florida now. And though Mei Mei was an able assistant, it wasn't the same. Sheldeen had been my little buddy; not only that but he had been my hope, my link to the big time. He was the reason being at the park was so satisfying. Without him everything we did on the court — all the drills, the stroke production, the stretches, everything — it all seemed somewhat irrelevant. Not that the kids weren't fun or anything; it's just that it wasn't the same without Sheldeen, and my spirit was dampened. Even the neighborhood felt strange without him. I had received a letter a few days after he got to Florida, and that was it. Short as it was, the letter replayed easily in my mind.

> *Hey, Preacher — The clay courts are fun, but I'm not very*
> *good at sliding. I think I'm the only black boy here. I'm not*
> *sure if the other kids really like me. But I made a friend.*
> *A brown boy from Ecuador. His father is real rich. Say*
> *hi to Mei Mei and Pedro. And the kids in church.*
> *See you later —   Sheldeen*

I felt like calling the kid; I would've loved to hear more details, but I didn't want to be pushy. After all, I knew all about pushy tennis parents and overbearing coaches. Anyway, it sounded like the kid was doing alright. So I dropped him a postcard and figured he'd get in touch when he was ready.

We sat against the fence and Bonnie took my hand; she held it in her lap. I think she was reading my mind. It was an absolute blessing having her around, and I was thankful for that. But she deserved more than I was able to give her. I began to feel down about not having more money at my disposal. Maybe I need to spend less time giving it away on this god-awful court in the flats, I thought, and more time promoting my paying lessons up at the Rose Garden. There were some school teachers up there who once offered to pass out flyers to their classes. I should get in touch with them, I thought, I need to build that business more, especially if I end up losing the job in Marin.

Bonnie's hand felt good in mine, smooth and reassuring. "I should have gone to medical school," I said, "like I was planning. I should have forgotten about the whole tennis thing. It would have been better to have more bucks."

She looked at me with concern. "We have enough doctors," she said. "And dentists, and lawyers."

That kind of startled me. "You mean we don't need more doctors, but we need more tennis teachers?" (Hell, these days every guy with a bucket of balls and a pair of sunglasses fancied himself as a teaching pro.)

"Put it this way," she said, "we don't have enough grassroots coaches, ones who really know what they're doing and put their hearts into it. People who are willing to get into the trenches and teach the sport where it needs to be taught, where the kids are poor but the abilities are high. And yes, there are plenty of doctors, I would say there is an abundance of doctors, the medical schools see to it."

I had never really thought about it like that. I knew my father wouldn't agree; he had just about shit a brick some years ago when I told him I wasn't going to medical school, that I was just going to play tournaments for a while.

"So you're just going to piss away your life!" he shouted with a disgusted look. I remembered the conversation well, ugly as it was.

I told him I owed it to myself to give it a shot. "I know I started a little late, but I still think I have a chance," I said.

"You owe it to yourself to go to medical school!" he yelled, "you've been accepted at one of the best and now you're just going to throw it all away." A great pause came between us (a pause that was to remain for years to come.)

"You know, doctors play tennis too," he said after a while, looking more sick than angry.

"No, Dad, you don't understand, I'm going to give it a shot, I can go to medical school later, if I still want to."

"You mean, if they still want you."

"Anyway," I said, "I think I'd rather study psychology." He looked suddenly nauseous.

Neither of us said anything for some time. Then he asked meekly, "So how do you plan to make a living while you're doing these tennis shenanigans?"

"I think I can make enough prize money to get by," I assured him.

"Is that what we do with life, just get by? Is this what I raised a son for, to just get by?" He didn't look well.

"Look, Dad, if I need the money I'll teach tennis, I can always teach tennis."

"So you're going to be a tennis gigolo, my son the tennis gigolo." He flapped his arms in disgust. "Is this what I raised a son for, to be a tennis gigolo?" He stammered briefly about me pissing away my life, then he bumbled his way out of the room.

That was just about the last conversation we ever had. Even a few months later at my mother's funeral, we didn't talk. I wished Mom were still around; she'd understand what Bonnie was saying, that some things were more important than being a doctor. Things like being true to yourself, and giving it a shot, and contributing in your own personal way.

The rundown park was earthy and comforting with the smell of weeds and overgrown grass. Bonnie and I leaned back against the tennis fence, and she stroked my arm. "Sometimes just getting by is the best medicine for the soul," she said, "especially if it means putting your heart where it needs to be."

Medicine for the soul, just getting by. Yes! I thought about my mother, how great it would have been for her to meet Bonnie. Mom would have understood how just getting by was medicine for the soul.

"You're doing a lot more for these kids than you'll ever know," Bonnie said. We watched as they disappeared into the distance, a motley pack, dragging skateboards, rackets, and sweaters. I may have been doing a lot for them, and it was true, they were doing something for me, too, but it wasn't the same kind of thing Sheldeen and I did for each other. "Give it time," Bonnie said, "another kid with potential will show up one of these days."

Bonnie was great. And yet, I could already feel myself taking her for granted, worrying about things that weren't that important when I should just be thinking about her. So what if everything else wasn't perfect.

She opened her big drawing pad and showed me a sketch she did of me on the court; it was so accurate it almost looked like a snapshot — the droopy net, cracks in the blacktop, that beat-up sign on the fence, balls all over the place; and the kids, their rackets and skateboards, a basketball player nearby. She got it all.

I thought about those kids, some of them didn't even have fathers. And then I thought about my dad again, and the fact that he never said anything about the crack I put in the back window of his office.

Chapter Forty-Five

Here, Take My T-Bird

I was commuting to the club in Marin during the week, which was no bother. Actually, I rather enjoyed it, especially the bridge from Richmond, all that pavement rising into sky with the choppy bay not far below; water and sky, blues and grays spreading and mixing, lifting me in all directions. But when I got to the end of the bridge where it swept down over San Quentin prison my mood began to change. I wondered what it would take to end up down there, behind bars; would killing Dixie do it? What if I just chopped off her foot, would I still end up in San Quentin? I came off the bridge and drove indifferently along the wide sweeping curves of Sir Francis Drake Boulevard, pondering these questions, and others, like how many milliseconds I would last in prison. I wondered what getting a tattoo would feel like. Would the other inmates think I was a wimp if I had a tattoo of a tennis racket on my arm? What if I put it on my neck?

I felt as if I were entering a prison yard when I pulled into the parking lot of the club these days. I'd leave the old Dart next to the least expensive car I could find. Then I'd hurry into the pro shop and check in, hoping like hell I wouldn't run into Dixie. Then I headed out to the courts, where I did my thing slightly on edge for the rest of the day.

After work I swung by Mill Valley occasionally and visited with Hammer. But those days were few and far between now; I tried to remember the last time I saw him. It was three weeks ago, or more. Laura hadn't got back yet from the city, so Todd and I sat on the rug and talked tennis like it was the old days. Mostly we griped about things that were wrong with the game (or not wrong with the game, according to some people.)

Todd had just seen a women's collegiate tournament at Stanford, a match between the University of Texas and San Diego State. "It was pathetic," he said, "there was only one American girl out there, out of twelve girls! Only one American girl!" He told me it looked like a tour stop in Europe, not a college match in the States.

"They should limit the foreign scholarships," I said, "it's not fair, most of the foreigners are older, they've been out on the tour for a while and when they give up on that, they come over here and take the scholarships away from our kids. It's not right, especially at state supported schools. I want my tax dollar helping out American kids, not foreigners."

"They shouldn't allow it at private schools, either," Todd said, "it deprives our kids, and hurts American tennis."

"Unless you want American tennis to be made up of defectors from all over the world," I said wryly.

"I can't get into that," Hammer said with a solemn look as if he were sitting behind his desk in the brokerage firm. "I mean what's the point of taking people like Martina and Lendl and making them US citizens and then bragging about how great our American tennis players are? Hell, it was the greatness in those little countries that made those players, it had nothing to do with the United States."

We griped about other stuff too, like the people who wanted to slow the game down with bigger balls and slower courts or making the players serve from further behind the baseline.

"Hell, they let basketball players slam dunk," Todd said, "and basketball is supposed to be the art of shooting the ball into the hoop. So why should they keep tennis players from winning points with big serves?"

"It's crazy," I said, "you've got people complaining about serve-and-volleyers, and how boring it is to watch them, but then you've got other people who complain about the groundstrokers, about those boring baseline rallies."

"You know what they should do," Hammer said enthusiastically, "they should allow double-strung rackets, you know, those spaghetti string jobs Werner Fischer invented."

Actually, that was a great idea, then a guy could slow the game down with spin if he wanted. I recalled when Nastase got his butt kicked by one of those spaghetti jobs. Nastase cussed like hell, but the very next week he used one to put the screws to Guillermo Vilas and end his world record winning streak.

"Man, were those weird times," Hammer said. "Remember when Mike Fishbach beat Stan Smith? But then they outlawed the damn rackets. If they hadn't, people wouldn't be complaining guys were only hitting bullets. Look at ping pong, they're all using sponge bats now, slowing the game down with spin. So why shouldn't they allow more spin in tennis? Give a guy a choice, add some variety to the game."

It was true, legalizing the old spaghetti string job would probably do wonders for the game. They should at least allow a reasonable modification of the thing. I figured some fuddy-duddy in the ITF abolished it, some old geezer in a bow tie who thought tennis players should all wear whites and curtsy to each other after each point.

"Why don't you write a letter to Bill Simons," I said, "he's got one of the best tennis magazines in the country, and it's getting bigger all the time. Maybe he'll publish it." Hammer just shrugged, but I could tell he was thinking about it, there was that tiny smile. And then we drifted into a whole new subject — Spain.

We talked for a long while about Spain's growing middle class and the sad fact that its ballboys were becoming extinct. "But the future may not be as bleak as you think," Todd suggested. He took a moment to collect his thoughts and have a swallow of Heineken.

"Spain's new middle class won't be typical," he said, "it will be flavored with the salt of the earth, that hardworking peasant class. There's no telling, Spain will not only have more tennis players, but they might also be more athletic — you might see a ton of good Spaniards after a while, maybe even some world champions like the guys who came from the ranks of ballboys."

It felt like the old days, kicking back with Hammer at his place in Mill Valley; it certainly helped take the edge off a typically bad day at the club. That had been one of the perks that came with the job. But now Laura and Todd had gotten so busy I seldom saw them anymore. So all things considered, working on that side of the Bay was becoming more and more of a drag.

By contrast, pitching balls in Berkeley was refreshing. Up in the hills near the University, the Rose Garden was pretty and more peaceful than ever. And then there was our crummy old court down in the flatlands. That was the most gratifying, less lucrative, true, but at least I wasn't haunted by Dixie or any parents telling me what to do. The only thing that haunted me was Sheldeen's absence, but that was a bittersweet ache and soothing in its own way.

I began to look forward to church on Sundays, to seeing that group of kids in the flats and their eager faces. Even the ache of missing Sheldeen was something that strangely, I began to look forward to. And as the weeks went by, one after another, I realized that my life had become measured by Sundays.

More and more, I found myself thinking about what playing tennis was like when I was a kid. Actually, my buddies and I had been converted baseball players. And we may have started late, but at least we cashed in on what surely were the golden years of junior tournaments. Those were the days! We'd simply check the HOUSING box on the entry blanks and send them in. (Even if you lived close to the tournament site, you could get housing if your parents were working or you had a transportation problem.) Then we'd hop on the bus or the train, and we'd be gone for the week. Sacramento, Fresno, Stockton, San Jose, wherever. And what a tennis vacation that was! And all, more or less, for free!

Those summer tournaments were a world unto themselves. It was like *Lord of the Flies Does Tennis* — multitudes of boys and girls, mostly teenagers, with not a parent in sight for days. Behind the scenes, tournament officials kept things organized. During the day we'd swim and play tennis and ping pong, all day long at the club or the park, or wherever the tournament happened to be. Packs of cute girls wandering around, their golden tans and white tennis skirts. At night there'd be parties where youthful infatuations rocked with the music or just lay hidden in shy glances along the perimeter of the dance floor. Then sometimes, we'd be dropped off at the movies, a gang of semi-nerdy tennis players trying to be rowdy in the back of the theater.

Housing is what really made those junior tournaments. Typically there'd be two of us kids to a host family, sometimes more. And sometimes it would be sleeping bags, but usually it was bunk beds or twins, with the occasional lavish bedroom thrown in. Now and then our hosts would take us to a restaurant for a meal, but more often than not we'd just sit down and eat dinner and breakfast with the family. Once in the 18's, my partner and I got housed in Tiburon, an elegant little community across the Golden Gate Bridge from San Francisco. On the second night, the guy, who just happened to be the mayor of the city, handed us the keys to his T-Bird and told us to have a good time. That was the way it was back then; things flowed with calm and trust. Hell, these days there wasn't even a housing option on the entry blank!

I felt sorry for the kids now; for them the tournaments were all work and no play, with little camaraderie, their every move scrutinized by anxious parents. Then after a day of being under the tennis microscope, they'd have to spend the night in a motel room with their folks, too, or maybe if they lived close enough, they'd just be cooped up in a car with them for an hour listening to how poorly they played; or maybe they'd be hammered about what they'd have to do to win their next match. HELP! No wonder Danny, my former champion, quit. Twenty years ago would have been different, even his parents might have been different in those less worried times. Hell, the kid probably would have ended up on a college team, all expenses paid. But times were different now, and he ended up quitting the game altogether.

Of course, tennis has a lot more money in it these days; that's part of the problem. Parents see their twelve-year-old kid playing and they analyze it like a business proposition. A secret business, where everything is guarded. Sure, some parents are friendly with each other, but by and large they're like a bunch of spies and counterspies all hanging out in the same place. They're all on a secret mission. And they each have their own secret plan. After all, there are only so many slots on a high school team, only so many college scholarships out there. Only so many kids will make it on the pro tour, and there, at the top where all the money is, only one or two will get the best seats. But what a view they'll get from up there! floating on those big green wings of cash from continent to continent, week after week, while the rest of the world just goes to the office every day wishing it were the other way around.

I thought about Sheldeen. I suppose for him it didn't matter that he missed the golden years of junior tournaments. A flatlander kid like that still would've needed a guy like me to step into the picture. Those golden years would have been beyond his access; indeed, tennis itself would have been beyond his access, housing or not.

Chapter Forty-Six

The First Five Years

Bonnie had developed a thing for seagulls and small fishing boats, so this Sunday she was at the Berkeley marina sketching while I had church with the kids at the neighborhood park. We finished stroke production and had just begun short rallies when I noticed a fellow standing outside by the basketball hoop. He seemed to be taking an interest in the tennis we were doing, and then he began walking toward us. I put Mei Mei in charge and went out the gate to greet him.

He was tall and thin, slightly bowlegged, and appeared to be about seventy years old. His leathery face had deep creases in it like an old gunslinger. "The name's Chet," he said, "I'm with the USTA."

"Nice to meet you." I extended my hand. I could feel his calluses; he was obviously still playing in spite of his years.

"There's a new kid in Florida," he said, "down around where I'm from, talks about you all the time. He looks pretty good, saw him take a set off the number two guy for Florida State." I could feel my heart beating rapidly. So Sheldeen was already making a name for himself in Florida.

"Yeah," the guy said as he released my hand from his warm callused grip. "I always like to see where they come from, it's the first five years of coaching that make the player, you know. That's the way it is. The public doesn't perceive it like that, but that's the way it is. The first five years." His gray-blue eyes sparkled with energy in spite of his weathered old face.

He told me he was a national rep for the USTA and that he could get our crummy court fixed up. He looked over where the kids were batting balls around on the cracked blacktop, and he chuckled. "Here," he handed me some papers. "Fill out these forms. It's an application for a grant. We'll get you some rackets and balls too."

"Hey, this is just spare time stuff," I said. "I don't know how much more time I'm going to have, I have a club job too. I may even be getting married." (Actually, Bonnie and I hadn't discussed it much, but it seemed inevitable.)

The old guy looked disappointed.

"Don't get me wrong, I like the kids just fine. Or I wouldn't be doing it. But … It's just that there's never going to be any real money in it, no matter how nice the court gets or how many free rackets we give away. A guy gets older, he gets responsibilities, it takes more to make it all the time. Actually, I was hoping to be out on tour with Sheldeen in a few years. That's where the real action is."

"The USTA can only help you out a little," the rep acknowledged, "and you're right, this stuff is peanuts compared to what you'd be worth on the tour. But you're very good at it."

I felt as if he were gluing me to the dreary flats. A new surface would be poured over the court and when it dried I'd be cemented to it like a net post. I imagined warming up Sheldeen, being his traveling coach, seeing the world, being with the players, the real players. It all seemed so unlikely now.

The rep sensed what I was feeling. "Well, maybe the kid will send for you when he starts making money," he said.

"Yeah, if he even remembers who I am." The old gunslinger hung his head; he knew the realities.

I longed to see the sights, to be sitting in a coaches box with Bonnie, at Roland Garros, the All England Club, Flushing Meadow. I imagined walking along the shore at Melbourne with Bonnie and Sheldeen, talking to the kid about his next match, the intermittent sound of surf breaking against the rocks. I longed to see Sheldeen swing at the ball again. I could feel the airy weight of the grant application in my hand; then I looked over at our funky old court. I pictured it brand-spanking new, and I felt the cement hardening around me.

The leathery old-timer extended his hand; we shook thumbs up like a couple of dudes, callus to callus. "Okay, Preacher," he said, a glint of amusement in his eye. "Just fill out the forms and we'll see what we can do."

Chapter Forty-Seven

The Smell Of Turpentine

Since Bonnie was working part-time in San Francisco, she and I occasionally had lunch together on that side of the Bay. I suggested she meet me at the club some time. I still wanted Dixie to meet her, it was my last hope. Dixie had become so irritating! But if she liked Bonnie, she'd probably lighten up on me, I figured. So with that in mind, I arranged for Bonnie to meet me in the pro shop at noon, then we'd go to lunch in Sausalito.

But that morning I got behind with my lessons. And now it was 12:20! I ushered off the two housewives I was working with and picked up the stray fuzz nugs as quickly as I could. I wouldn't have been so anal about picking up every last ball, with Bonnie waiting and all, but Dixie and the prez often walked the grounds during the lunch hour, and they liked everything picture perfect. They would hold hands on the walkways between the courts when they thought nobody was looking.

Now suddenly, just as I finished tidying up, the two of them entered my teaching court, for some odd reason. I was anxious to get out of there, not to keep Bonnie waiting, but I leaned against my big shopping cart of balls and let them approach. I became conveniently optimistic. Maybe the three of us could walk back to the pro shop together and Dixie would have a chance to chat with Bonnie. Surely the prez had said something to Dixie about Bonnie; after all, he had certainly enjoyed petting her bandaged hand at the barbecue.

The two of them stood before me now.

"Nice day," I offered.

"You bet," the silver-haired gentleman replied cordially.

Dixie didn't beat around the bush. "I hear they let the pro at Lakeview go," she announced as if it were the most wonderful news.

I was shocked but tried not to show it.

"Anybody could see he wasn't right for the job," she said smugly. (Hell, Dunner had done wonders for that club in the few years he was there. Indeed, he had been an attribute to the entire tennis community.) My head began to ache.

The prez was gazing off toward Mount Tam in the distance. Dixie prodded him. "Come on, Miles, got to get back to work." He took her hand as they walked away, but she disengaged immediately. I stood there dazed, leaning against my shopping cart. I knew it was just a matter of time before she got rid of me and slipped her wussed-out nephew in my place.

Suddenly Dixie called back. "Oh, by the way, Barbie, your girlfriend, is waiting for you in the shop." Barbie? What do you mean, Barbie?

"What happened, love? You met Dixie? She thinks your name is Barbie," I blurted out as I entered the pro shop.

"I told her my name was Bonnie. But she kept calling me Barbie. She didn't seem very nice." Bonnie's voice was meek, trembling slightly.

We scooted out of there fast and had lunch at a touristy veranda-style restaurant in Sausalito, neither of us saying too much. Then Bonnie went back to San Francisco and I drove back to the club.

Behind the wheel now, I could feel my blood starting to boil. I knew how ugly Dixie could be and the idea that she would make Bonnie feel unwelcome really pissed me off. She had called her "Barbie," for crissake! I was ready to smack Dixie. I gunned the engine as if I were stepping on her; with my hands tight around the wheel, I shook her by the shoulders. But then as I pulled into the lot of the club I became weak with despair. I knew Dixie was too much for me to go up against. She had the club president wrapped around her vicious little finger. It was just a matter of time before she got rid of me.

My spirit was broken. I finished up my afternoon lessons and got the hell out of there. There would be no sense in even talking to the few friendly people I knew on the board. They would just go with the flow, and the flow was about to wash me under the Golden Gate Bridge. It was just a matter of time.

I thought about the cold water under the bridge as I lay next to Bonnie that night with my eyes wide open. I knew she wasn't asleep, so I mumbled something about my troubles at the club. "It doesn't seem to be working out," I said.

She propped herself up on an elbow. "Remember," she said, "it's just a job. When you're there you're just working, but when you're down at the park you're contributing." She emphasized the word *contributing*. "You're making a contribution at the Rose Garden, too. But mostly down at the park. Even the USTA recognizes that."

"If I had more freedom at the club, I'd be able to contribute there, too."

"True," she said, "but it's basically just a job, if you weren't there somebody else would be doing it." She told me contributing, really contributing, is when you build something new, something that wasn't there before.

Boy, this was some woman! And I guess I had to agree with her, but I told her the extra money from the club was handy. She reminded me that sometimes just getting by is the best medicine for the soul.

Medicine or not, I figured I'd hold onto the Marin gig for as long as possible. "After all," I said, "it's nice living up here in the hills."

"Wherever you want to live is okay with me, Stefan. As long as there's room for Syd and a little place for me to do my painting."

She told me, in fact, that she was going up to Oregon for a few days, to bring back some things from her studio so she could paint down here. Bonnie had been making do with pencil sketches ever since she came to the Bay Area, but now she was hungry to see the explosion of color, to put oils on the canvas again. "I've been away from the paints for too long," she said. "This may sound strange, but I miss the smell of turpentine." She also had arrangements to make in Portland about an upcoming show in Salt Lake. "Besides, it's Tammy's birthday," she said, "I'll be gone about a week."

I felt suddenly alone in the world with Bonnie up in Oregon, especially if I walked to the Rose Garden in the evening to see the sun go down over

San Francisco Bay. So I kind of avoided that. But then Sheldeen called from Florida, and I felt a lot better. It had been a while. He told me he had improved his clay court game a ton, and that the coaches were going to take some kids to Germany for a tournament. He was hoping to go. He also said, kind of shyly, that they were calling him *The Dean* now, as in Sheldeen.

"The Dean. Hey, that's kind of cool," I said into the phone. "When they give you a name like that, you know you're doing good."

"Well, yeah, I guess, I just hope I get to go to Germany." He was calling from a pay phone and his nickel was about up. So I told him I'd say hi to Mei Mei and Pedro and the kids in church. And then we hung up.

The Dean. Right on, dude. I figured I'd have to tell Hammer about that.

It was great to hear from the kid; I hadn't heard from him in weeks. It put everything in perspective. I could see what Florida was doing for him, and even though he was doing it without me, I tried to imagine a small part of me was there with him, on the clay, or in the shade hanging out with the other kids; wherever, maybe running on the beach, leaving footprints in the sand. I figured Sheldeen would jog near the water's edge where it was more packed. I pictured his perfectly muscled body glistening with sweat. He'd probably take his shoes off when he was done and go for a swim.

Chapter Forty-Eight

That Fancy Ditch

I hadn't done a lot of grocery shopping lately, but now that Bonnie was up in Oregon, I found myself pushing a shopping cart in a fancy Marin supermarket. I needed a few things to hold me over, so I stopped in after work.

The handle of the shiny steel cart felt familiar in my hand, and with good reason — it was identical to the one I had at the club. I felt in control of the cart as I maneuvered it in and out of the crowded aisles. But it seemed too light, not being filled to the brim with yellow tennis balls. So this is what shopping carts are really for, I mused as I tossed a loaf of sourdough and some English muffins into the basket. With expert precision, I swung around a freezer full of TV dinners and rolled into the produce section.

A familiar face caught my eye — it was the accountant I taught on Tuesdays. The happy fellow was searching for a flawless apple. "Every time I see you you're pushing a shopping cart," the accountant said with a wink.

"The cart? Oh yeah, for sure, you know how we teaching pros like shopping carts."

"I've noticed that." The accountant looked amused. He told me the tennis teaching industry had probably ripped off thousands of shopping carts across the country, and that they were worth about $100 a piece. "It may be grounds for some sort of lawsuit," he chuckled. "I can see the headlines now, *Grocerymen Sue Tennis Pros.*"

I wondered if he was serious. I thought about it a few minutes later as I stood in the long Express line waiting to pay for my groceries. A lawsuit probably wouldn't affect me, I decided. I had a shopping cart at the club alright, but I had found it trashed in an alley. It wasn't like I had stolen the cart, it was more like I rescued it. I scraped the rust off and gave its life new meaning.

I was glad Sheldeen had called. I imagined him as "The Dean" for a moment, and I laughed. He seemed to be well on his way. I was pretty sure he was going to make it, but chances were slim I'd have a hand in it at this point. I never made it to the big time; it would have been nice to be there as his coach. He had been in Florida some time now, but still, there was a part of me that felt more empty with each passing week. I hadn't even told Buckskin Charley yet, but I was pretty sure he'd approve of the move.

I hadn't seen the gang in quite a while — Evonne, Hitch, Hammer, Laura. I guess we were all going our separate ways.

I wondered how my old pal Spiegel was doing. I knew he became a big-time attorney in LA, and all, but I hadn't actually seen him in years. I remember how when we were kids we used to play ping pong in his basement, with the winner gaining the imaginary rights to the girl we had a crush on that week. He was the reason I got hooked on tennis in the first place, him and his perfect Tom Stow backhand. For hours on end, I tried to replicate that stroke on the back of my father's little office building on University Avenue. My dad would stick his head out the door now and then; in his white smock, he looked more confused than exasperated. He never did say anything about that big spidery crack I put in the window back there. I probably should have listened to him.

Maybe I'd go to New York, see how my dad was doing. It had been a long time and I wasn't even sure I had the address. I had his phone number somewhere, but that was risky; if we got into it on the phone I probably wouldn't feel like going out there.

The line in the supermarket shortened, and as I moved along with it, my mind downshifted to a more troublesome matter. Dixie. I usually got along with people, but this was different; even imagining her in diapers didn't help. She had offended Bonnie; she had called her Barbie, for crissake! I would never forgive her. Actually, I felt like strangling her, and as I thought about that a great calm came over me and I wondered if I was capable of doing such a thing. Probably not, I decided, but it was satisfying to think about it. I wondered if her tongue would stick out, or if she would just roll her eyes back and give one last twitch.

I knew she was going to get rid of me. I tried to be mature, not to let it bother me. Hell, there were plenty of clubs where I would be a hot item, I knew that, available single tennis pro and all. It's just that I wasn't looking forward to relocating again.

My few groceries looked meager at the bottom of the big shopping cart. My future looked meager too, and I thought maybe I should get out of tennis altogether, go be a school teacher or a counselor somewhere. And I could probably find something if I were willing to leave the Bay Area, or indeed, California. (I had heard jobs were even more scarce in Oregon.)

Then I remembered the Oakland factory; the lady had called just last week to remind me that the job was still available. Yes, that was it. I'd take the job, go work for somebody who could appreciate a tennis player. It would be nice to have benefits and a solid paycheck every week. And I'd be able to afford to keep my little place near the Rose Garden. (How I loved those woodsy hills!)

Yes, I would go to the dreary factory. I would do my time. Then later I could get the training to become a computer programmer, if I felt like it, or maybe I'd become a stockbroker like Hammer. I could even be a lab tech, after all, I had a pre-med background.

I thought about all the work I had done on a tennis court, all the hours I had spent pitching balls, and then picking them up. In truth, that was hard labor, just like digging a ditch. Sure you got to wear fancy clothes, but it was still work, and what was worse, you were expendable, just like Todd had said. No matter how much club members loved you at first, it was just a matter of time before they were tired of you. Anyway, you couldn't blame them for wanting to see a new face from time to time. And so you were doomed, even if the manager didn't have a thorn up the ass. The only way out was to own a piece of the club; those were the only pros who really had permanent jobs. But those opportunities were few and far between.

If I weren't teaching tennis for a living I knew I'd be playing a lot better. Anyway, as guys got older, the best players were never teaching pros, they were the guys who had other jobs, jobs that allowed them to be fresh for the court and fresh for their own games. And I'd enjoy the game a lot more if I weren't teaching it. I'd probably feel like a kid again, anxious to hit the ball, imagining the swing of the racket at various times of the day. Hell, when you made a job out of something, it was never the same after that. It didn't matter what it was — tennis, woodworking, fishing — whatever, when you relied on it for survival, the thrill disappeared fast. And I suppose that kind of took the edge off the glamor for the guys on the tour, too.

Yes, I would get into something else.

At last my groceries were rung up. I could have easily carried the big paper bag in my arm, but I put it in the shopping cart and pushed it through the wide automatic door. I liked the feel of the steel cart as it rolled along the parking lot with a familiar rattle. And I liked the bounce of my shoes and the smooth, loose feel of my warmup pants. I caught a glimpse of my sleek two-tone tennis jacket in the reflection of a car window, and suddenly I felt lucky that I didn't have to wear a suit and tie like the men I gave lessons to.

Around my wrist was a turquoise wristband about two inches wide; it looked good near the shiny steel handle of the shopping cart. Instinctively, I raised my arm and dabbed at my brow with the soft turquoise cotton. I was used to wearing such a wristband, even when I was off the court and didn't need it to absorb sweat. I wore a wristband everywhere. In fact, my arm felt naked without one. Sometimes I couldn't even sleep without one. The previous night for instance, unable to sleep without Bonnie, I had gotten up at two in the morning to put on the turquoise wristband. It had a black and silver logo, and I figured it was probably my favorite. But then I realized I had a whole drawer full of favorite wristbands; and suddenly everything became clear to me, and I laughed at myself. I knew

I was stuck. Hell, who was I kidding? I'd never be cooped up in a factory or an office building. I'd never change. I'd be pitching balls forever. I'd be digging that fancy ditch for the rest of my life.

Chapter Forty-Nine

Somewhere Out There

I missed the hell out of Bonnie; it was more than a week. She had called each night from Oregon, her happy voice dancing in my ear, wishing me pleasant dreams as I lay fidgeting on the sheets. She told me she was excited about the Salt Lake show and also about a special new painting she was working on. But she said she was going to be away even longer. Apparently Harold was sick; he had closed down his dental practice and now the hot hygienist had left him. Serves him right, I thought, and it made me mad that Bonnie was going to stick around up there trying to help out the son of a bitch.

"Bonnie! Bonnie!" Her name cried out in the far reaches of my mind like a distant wolf. How I loved that name, I always liked that name, even before I met her; I should have told her. I wished I had told her. What if I never get the chance, I thought, in the dark of night. What if something happens, what if she gets in a wreck or something? Or what if she just stays up there indefinitely trying to take care of the old fool.

As the weeks went slowly by, I kept thinking about the things Bonnie had taught me; about Einstein and religion, about the difference between contributing and just working. About how just getting by was medicine for the soul. I remembered when Hammer and I first stayed at their place on the way to Montana, how kind she was to sew up Todd's socks. How she stood there by the railroad tracks in her ponytail and her faded levis, waving at us. How elegant she looked when I first picked her up at the BART station, and how we sat together at that little coffee shop in Berkeley. And how my stomach ached when I went in there without her. It hurt now, even more, but I didn't mind.

I remembered Evonne and Hitch's party, when we danced close on the patio, and what Bonnie had said about funerals. That they're reminders. Reminders that life is short and that you're not going to get another shot at it. "You've got to live now. Really live." I could hear her conviction, the certainty in her voice. I could even feel her, the delicate touch of her fingers, her cool cheek against mine. And her scent, such a clean fresh scent, like a garden after a rain. Then I pictured her at the tournament desk when she had that band-aid on her finger, and I felt bad. I remembered my mother, how she used to show up at the dinner table with a band-aid on her finger.

Late one afternoon, the doorbell rang; its discordant plea buzzed at the stillness around me. It was the UPS guy with a package from Oregon, a large flat box, and I knew it was one of Bonnie's paintings. I sat there holding the box for some time, not anxious to open it, just happy to have it to hold.

Inside, I found an oil painting of me and the kids in action on the neighborhood court, that funky old flatland court with its cracks and thread-bare net. It was a lot like the sketch Bonnie had shown me, but it was much larger and alive with color. It reminded me of one of those old Norman Rockwell paintings you used to see on calendars. There were the kids with their happy mischievous faces, tennis rackets, bikes, skateboards; and of course, scattered all around were fuzzy yellow tennis balls. In one corner there was a big pile of them. An older boy in a red flannel shirt was shooting hoops on the nearby blacktop. I was kind of bent over one of the kids, adjusting a stroke or something. There was even that rusty old sign on the fence, barely discernable letters that said Tennis Shoes Only.

A wave of warmth rushed through my body, and my eyes became teary with appreciation for the woman. It was as if my mind were suddenly being rinsed clear. I found the grant application the USTA guy had given me, and I tossed it in the waste basket. I didn't want that old broken-down court to change for a long time. Then I remembered Dixie; to hell with her, to hell with the club, I thought, and I went straight to Marin to get my things. An hour later, I was standing in the parking lot of the club with the old Dart loaded up and ready to go home. I got everything but my shopping cart. I knew Sheldeen's dad would help me load it in his pickup truck if I wanted. But I couldn't see myself going back to the club, ever. I imagined Dixie's nephew using my shopping cart and my head began to ache. Not that I had anything against the kid.

I stood there in the parking lot with my head aching in the cold evening air. I wondered if Bonnie would ever come back. The sun was dropping. I gazed out to Mount Tamalpais in the near distance and remembered our hike at Mount Hood with the girls. I pictured Syd lapping up at the water's edge, the gurgling sound of that little stream. I thought about Sheldeen too, and wondered what he was up to.

The orange sun was sinking into the top of Mount Tamalpais. I stared at it for a while, squinting and savoring the last of its faint warmth on my leathery cheeks. Then I got in the old Dart and drove back across the Richmond-San Rafael Bridge for the last time.

My head still ached. I drove slowly, longing for the old days. Days when things were simpler. Days when I'd leave on a moment's notice and go play a tournament in Southern California, or maybe even in Mexico, where it was hot and the smell of the earth rose up through the courts. I pictured those eager Mexican ballboys, their brown smiling faces, and then remarkably, the pain in my head vanished. And my breathing slowed. I was at peace. It was the kind of peace that only a youngster could give me.

I felt as if Bonnie were on the seat beside me as I came off the bridge in the twilight and merged onto the freeway. The towns of Richmond, El Cerrito, Albany swept by on my left; on my right were the muddy edges of the big dark bay. University Avenue was coming up. I took the exit and went up the hump, above the hubbub of Spenger's Fish Grotto; and then down I went, way down, as if I were dropping into the rest of my life.

I stayed there in the flats where small houses were set back off wide roads. Large trees dwarfed some of the little homes. Up by the curb, low hedges and rickety picket fences ran alongside the cracked sidewalks. I was looking for a pad in the old neighborhood. I knew I could survive down there. I might have to tighten my belt a little, but my freelance lessons would get me by. Besides, those flatlands felt like home.

I cruised slowly through the labyrinth of old streets, making note of a couple of For Rent signs. In the coming darkness, groups of gleeful young girls played jump rope on the sidewalk, here and there. In front of one house, two girls were jumping over the same long rope; their skinny legs moved together like a crack doubles team. One had surprisingly broad shoulders, the kind of wide shoulders that could torque a really big serve and huge groundstrokes. An abandoned shopping cart lay on its side near the girls; its big steel jaws beckoned sadly.

I drove around the corner where some teenage boys were playing hoops noisily on a basket attached to a telephone pole. Paced by the airy bounce of the ball, their shrieks and hollers rang out musically in the suppertime quiet of the neighborhood. Younger brothers and sisters watched idly from porch steps. But one little guy stood by himself up at the curb, cheering and pumping his clenched fists every time a basket was scored. I slowed to a near stop trying to get a better look at him as the players held up the action for me to drive by. In vain I searched out the boy's face in the darkness.

I wondered where he lived. My eyes drifted down the dimly lit street, and then beyond where there was only a blur of dull street lamps and gray intersections. I wasn't sure where I was; I had turned left, then right, then left again. Actually, I was lost. The vastness of flatlands was all around me, stretching for miles in every direction.

The LOUD, howling horn-blast of a freighter lurched my car to a stop; in the near distance the train's headlamp was getting brighter by the second as it approached. Now I could see the long lean tracks as they came in at an angle toward my car. I cut the engine and watched.

A great sense of calm came over me as the dark shapes of boxcars rattled by. Familiar clanking sounds vibrated powerfully, shaking the old Dart for some time. And then at last there was silence as the freighter pushed its way further along the bayside flatlands. When its horn moaned meekly in the distance one last time, I realized I wasn't lost at all. I was exactly where I needed to be. And I'd come back tomorrow in the daylight. Because somewhere out here, in these endless flats, I knew a kid was waiting for me.

Author's Note

As with most books, many people lay hidden within these pages, completely unobserved by the reader. However, Bill Carroll as Carroll William, Bob Fenton as Old Bob Fentayne, Camilla Sutherland as Southerly, and Mabel Gong as Mei Mei, are more easily discovered. They appear in loose, fictionalized form.

Various individuals contributed unwittingly to the content of this manuscript. Among them are Chuck Bleckinger, Dan Bleckinger, Paul Aloojian, Wendell Pierce, Bill Leslie, Dennis Harbert, Don Fulton, Todd Wilson, Scott Borowiak, Jim McLennan, Susanne McAlister, and Larry Jones.

* * *

An especially loud call of thanks
goes out to
Dick Squires, Marian Allison, and Alan Hager
but still, it will not reach them
Hopefully, everybody else is still here

Acknowledgments

Meijing Gruberg — Editorial assistance was gleaned from a great many people, but nobody suffered that cause more honorably over the years than my wife. Sometimes her lips would turn up at the corners briefly, a twitch as if by reflex, and then I knew had written something absolutely hilarious. When she frowned, which was her norm after the twenty-second reading of the manuscript, I knew all was well and that so long as her nose didn't scrunch up there was nothing to worry about. My wife's recommendations always turned out to be best and consistent with those of whatever scholar I might on occasion trouble for a second opinion. I owe her a great deal and for a lot more than just this book.

My learned friend, Richard Markley, was an especially wise and tolerant editor. Others who made serious contributions include Luther Nichols, Mallory Stephens, Joe Gentle, Eugene Cantin, Rick Manning, Jeff McDowell, Mike Ryan, Bill Leslie, Dennis Gibson, Dave Engelberg, Peter Herb, Stacey Wallis, Teresa Apachea, Jim Dunigan, Greg Lehman, Rod Heckelman, Murray MacDonald, Jean Kracht, Patricia Vasquez, Don Jacobus, and David Fugate.

JG

* * *

www.TennisHobo.com

Guaranteed

If this book has not been manufactured in a satisfactory manner,
please contact your distributor for a replacement.

* * *

* * *

* * *

Comments Welcome

www.TennisHobo.com

TennisHobo@TennisHobo.com

* * *